Wedding as Text

Communicating Cultural Identities
Through Ritual

Wedding as Text

Communicating Cultural Identities
Through Ritual

Wendy Leeds-Hurwitz
University of Wisconsin-Parkside

2002

LAWRENCE ERLBAUM ASSOCIATES, PUBLISHERS
Mahwah, New Jersey   London

Lawrence Erlbaum Associates, Inc., Publishers
10 Industrial Avenue
Mahwah, NJ 07430

Cover design by Kathryn Houghtaling Lacey, incorporating a detail of a
ketubah designed by Richard Sigberman and shown in its entirety in Fig. 6
on page 161.

Library of Congress Cataloging-in-Publication Data

Leeds-Hurwitz, Wendy.
Wedding as text : communicating cultural identities through ritual /
    Wendy Leeds-Hurwitz
           p.   cm.
     Includes bibliographical references and index.
  ISBN 0-8058-1141-9 (cloth : alk. paper)
  ISBN 0-8058-1142-7 (pbk. : alk. paper)
  1. Marriage customs and rites—United States. 2. Interethnic marriages—
     United States. 3. Intercultural communication—Case studies.
     4. Semiotics.   I. Title.
  GT2703 .A2 L44   2002
  392.5'0973—dc21   2001059237
                                                               CIP

Books published by Lawrence Erlbaum Associates are printed on acid-free
paper, and their bindings are chosen for strength and durability.

Printed in the United States of America
10   9   8   7   6   5   4   3   2   1

"There was that soft-spoken man from New England
who had called her a 'delicate flower'
and asked whether she was Japanese.
But he thought of her as a rose
and she saw herself as a chrysanthemum."

—*Chung* (2000, p. 41)

Contents

Preface   ix

Acknowledgments   xv

Interlude 1   1

Chapter 1   Introduction   7

Interlude 2   39

Chapter 2   Community   49

Interlude 3   77

Chapter 3   Ritual   87

Interlude 4   123

Chapter 4   Identity   129

Interlude 5   161

Chapter 5   Meaning   169

Interlude 6   195

Chapter 6   Conclusion   209

Theoretical Appendix   227

Methodological Appendix   241

References   253

Author Index   281

Subject Index   289

Preface

This is the culmination of a long-term research project, larger than any I have undertaken previously, thus one more difficult to manage, and more time-consuming. As befits a large project, the research had multiple goals and its publication serves a variety of purposes. This project deliberately brings together what are generally separate areas of study in the United States (semiotics, language and social interaction, and intercultural communication) and studies interdisciplinary topics not generally the central focus of any of these (ritual, identity, and material culture), using a method (ethnography of communication) and a theory (social constructionism) that still are not those most frequently adopted by communication researchers to study a topic (weddings) that has attracted surprisingly little attention from any researchers, whether in communication or other disciplines. As a result of all of these influences, this book has as much to say about the ways we choose to conduct research, and the necessary interdisciplinarity of substantive projects, as about what we can potentially learn from this one investigation of weddings. It is my hope that even if the particulars of the study are not of paramount interest to a reader, at least some of the theoretical, methodological, or disciplinary concerns may be of value. It is for this reason that separate theoretical and methodological appendices have been included, placed at the back of the book so they are out of the way of those who are only interested in the primary data and analysis. Those primarily interested in weddings can safely ignore them, but other readers should seriously consider reading them before the body of the book, as they provide the framework for understanding what I have done and why.

First, this book is a contribution to *semiotics*. Specifically, it is a demonstration of how to use semiotics to analyze a particular ritual event. For this purpose, weddings serve admirably because they involve the combination of multiple signs and social codes, the building blocks of semiotics. In this guise, this book should be viewed as one of a pair, serving as an application of the semiotic theory presented in a previous book, *Semiotics and communication* (Leeds-Hurwitz, 1993). It is not essential to have read that book in order to understand this one, although many of the comments will no doubt make greater sense to a reader familiar with that work. One is intended as an introduction to semiotic theory, and the other a case study of actual behavior; discussions of abstract theoretical concepts and data are related but distinct endeavors. *Semiotics and communication* introduces the concepts of sign, code, and culture, progressively larger units of analysis (signs combine into codes, which then combine into cultures). However, the world is made up of more than one culture, so *Wedding as text* moves to the next level, examining what occurs when members of different cultures interact, when the signs and codes of different cultures come into contact and influence one another. Penman (2000) pointed out that "in many semiotic writings there is a rather strange neglect of people, as active, constituting beings" (p. 67). One of the tasks of this book is to attend to the complex ways real people manage their constructions of their own events.

Second, this book is a contribution to *language and social interaction*, using ethnography as a qualitative method to study actual communication behavior. As a contribution to the study of interaction, this book can serve as an extended case study matched to the more theoretical discussion presented in another prior book of mine, *Communication in everyday life* (Leeds-Hurwitz, 1989). This new discussion is most specifically a contribution to research in the *ethnography of communication*, a method originally developed as a way to combine linguistic and anthropologic concerns. My goal is to study what seems to me to be the most central issue of research into language and social interaction: how real people manage their interactions in real life. As Schegloff (1999) has pointed out, "'interaction' presents itself as the primordial site of the social—the immediate and proximate arena in which sociality is embodied and enacted" (p. 141). Studying social interaction implies, at least for me, that both verbal and nonverbal elements should be studied, although most research into this topic to date emphasizes language.[1] The ethnography of communication serves as a valuable tool when studying real interaction. It emphasizes long-term observations of a wide variety of related events, but always stresses the need to study what real people do, not when they are the focus of an experiment, but at home in their own lives. Because modern real life includes mass-communication influences, in particular popular culture, some of those have been included here as well.[2] Ethnography's strength is description of the pattern underlying interaction, not prescription of what people should do. In keeping with that, my goal is to describe, not prescribe, behavior. There are many patterns underlying various interactions across contexts; my goal is to discover what people in a particular context (those faced with designing an intercultural wedding) do that works for them, not to tell others what they should do.

One of my assumptions is that we jointly construct the social world, and that we do this through our communication with one another. Thus this book is also a contribution to *social constructionism*, and in many ways extends another prior book, *Social approaches to communication* (Leeds-Hurwitz, 1995). Social constructionism can be studied either with an eye to language and social interaction (people interacting directly with one another, in a wide variety of face-to-face contexts) or media (people interacting through a mediated form, whether telephone, television, film, computers, or any other of the wide variety of communication aids available).[3] Shepherd (1999) recently called for research investigating "communication ... as the maker of the social world" (p. 163), something I also take for granted as my primary subject. Social constructionism emphasizes the joint creation of meaning, de-emphasizing individual intent or interpretations.

The third central topic covered in this book is *intercultural communication*. My goal here again is to study what seems to me to be the heart of the field: how people of different cultural backgrounds interact together. Intercultural weddings (even intercultural marriages more generally) have rarely been the subject of choice for intercultural communication researchers, although they are certainly appropriate as a topic.[4] Specifically, my concerns here are with the various forms of cultural identity assumed by and attributed to individuals within the modern United States. This means I have to attend to differences in race, ethnicity, religion, and class within the U.S., issues also not traditionally emphasized within Intercultural research, which has tended instead to emphasize international differences and originally assumed that everyone within a specific country followed the same norms of interaction (although this is gradually changing). In 1988, Gudykunst, Ting-Toomey, and Chua pointed out the need for more qualitative research investigating intercultural behavior; more than a decade later, there is still far more quantitative research produced by intercultural researchers than qualitative. (Although the terms literally refer to whether or not the results of a research project depend on counting something, by convention qualitative research depends on long-term study of a small number of examples for its conclusions, whereas quantitative research depends on abbreviated study of a large number of examples; the former prefers depth while the latter prefers breadth.)[5] This book was not written as a direct answer to the call put out by Gudykunst et al., but perhaps it can serve as one part of the answer, as it certainly combines qualitative research methods with an intercultural topic.

Because I began with a genuine question (most briefly stated as: how is it possible to display multiple identity statements simultaneously when these are in fact contradictory?), not one to which I already knew the answer, I had to remain open to the answers I discovered.[6] Those I interviewed solved the problem for themselves, for it was their problem; I only came along afterwards and asked: "How did you do that?" To me, this is the central question we ask in communication: How is any interaction between individuals possible?[7] What are the resources we use to create meaning for ourselves and for others, and what do we do when we have different resources, different assumptions of what is appropriate, different views of the appropriate and possible outcomes of an interaction?

Although the following are not areas in which I have been actively involved organizationally, studies of *ritual, identity,* and *material culture* are all growing in popularity as interdisciplinary research topics. They have been widely studied by scholars in anthropology, sociology, and folklore, as well as by a few in communication. I hope that my research contributes in some way to these areas as well. And, despite the little attention *weddings* have attracted from researchers in any field, this book should obviously serve as a contribution to our understanding of that topic.[8]

* * *

I began studying intercultural weddings in 1991, and have been studying them intermittently ever since. This project has consumed two sabbaticals, as well as much of my research time between. I have been to weddings, talked to people who had weddings I could not attend, and read about weddings described by others. I have directed students who conducted additional interviews, providing me with tape recordings and transcripts. Some of my conversations have been casual, as when I was stranded in the Minneapolis Amtrak station during a snowstorm, only to learn that the family next to mine had just attended their daughter's intercultural wedding. Most of my conversations have been more formal, with a tape recorder in one hand and list of questions in the other. Sometimes I have spoken briefly with only one participant in a wedding; other times I have more formally interviewed multiple family members. When it proved difficult to meet in person, I have corresponded with people via e-mail, or spoken on the phone, depending on what was most convenient for them. In what follows, I have not distinguished between these types of sources, on the assumption that, taken together, they have all contributed to my understanding. In the end, I attended fewer weddings than I had initially assumed would be appropriate, and relied more heavily on interviews, because many of the most interesting weddings occurred without me, and I did not want to exclude them from the database for that reason alone.

In order to protect the privacy of those who have been gracious enough to permit me to intrude on their lives in these various ways, I have not used photographs of people, and have not provided real names. This is also the reason I have mainly described small pieces of weddings. The larger issues should be sufficiently illuminated by this method, while protecting the individuals. Intercultural marriages are sometimes the source of substantial conflict within families; until 1967 some forms (interracial) were actually illegal in this country, and they are still only a small percentage of the total. It is certainly not my intent to cause additional problems for those who have willingly shared their experiences with me.

NOTES

1. Soeffner (1997) pointed out several of the reasons for the overemphasis of language, and the corresponding lack of emphasis on study of nonverbal behaviors:

   What is certain is that we tend to overestimate language and its influence on our behavior. For one, language puts at our disposal a highly developed—and above all, well-described—potential for dealing with other human beings, with our environment, with our memories, with the collection and passing-on of "knowledge," and so forth. But another reason is that our profession [sociology] is defined both directly and indirectly by language: We are members of a reading, speaking, story-telling, and blustering profession. (p. 93)

   Soeffner addressed his comments here to researchers in sociology, but the same is true of other disciplines, including communication. Looking in the other direction, Miller (1998) asked why academics do not study nonverbal behavior, finding that most scholars "do not perceive themselves as part of a larger study of material culture" (p. 6). A few other scholars who have recently emphasized the importance of material culture for an understanding of relationships specifically and interaction more generally are Hodder (1994); Brown, Altman, and Werner (1991); Schiffer with Miller (1999).

2. Hannerz (1992) is only one who emphasized that those who study interaction also need study the role played by the media.

3. Traditionally researchers in the older area of interpersonal communication (more likely to use quantitative methods, and generally more interested in cognition than those who identify their research as within the area of language and social interaction) have had no interest in social constructionism, but this is now changing, although slowly (Baxter, 1998; Baxter & Montgomery, 1996).

4. I have found virtually no studies of intercultural weddings. In studies of intercultural marriage (i.e., Buttny, 1987; Hanassab & Tidwell, 1998; Romano, 1988; Root, 2001), details of the weddings are, by and large, ignored; in studies of weddings, intercultural weddings are again, by and large, ignored (i.e., Charsley, 1991, 1992, 1997; Frese, 1991; Ingraham, 1999; Woodruff, 1980). One exception is a book edited by scholars, but presenting personal stories prepared mainly by friends of the editors who are themselves in intercultural marriages (Grearson & Smith, 1995). And the large number of studies of wedding traditions around the world written by anthropologists tend to emphasize a single culture's traditions, ignoring any combination of traditions (i.e., Fried & Fried, 1980; Metzger & Williams, 1963). There are studies of relationships within interpersonal communication, even some recent emphasis on the study of ritual in families (Braithwaite, 1995; Braithwaite, Baxter & Harper, 1998; Breuss & Pearson, 1997; Cheal, 1988; Werner, Altman, Brown, & Ginat, 1993), but I have found nothing on intercultural weddings. It is surprising that so little attention has been given to even interracial marriages within communication; Dainton (1999) is a rare exception.

5. See Bavelas (1995) for a careful consideration of quantitative and qualitative research.

6. See Penman (2000) for further discussion of the nature and value of asking genuine questions.

7. See Luhmann (1990) for some wonderful comments on the improbability of communication.
8. Interestingly, there are better studies of weddings in other countries than in the U.S.: For Japan, see Edwards (1989); for Korea, see Kendall (1996); and for Scotland, see Charsley (1991, 1992, 1997). There are books on intercultural marriages in France (Barbara, 1989; Varro, 1988), England (Benson, 1981; Montgomery, 1989), and New Zealand (Harre, 1966) as well as recent collections covering the world (Breger & Hill, 1998a) but only two (Romano, 1988; Root, 2001) that I have located discussing any form of intercultural marriage in the U.S. Although there are many popular publications on weddings in the U.S., there are few academic studies; the best of these is Ingraham (1999).

Acknowledgments

First, I must thank Barnett Pearce. He is the one who asked what my next book was going to be when I was not yet ready to answer the question; by the time we finished talking, I had outlined two books. The first of those proved easier for me to finish than this one. So I also owe him thanks for his patience. Lawrence Erlbaum Associates gave me a contract for both books back in 1991; the first was quickly completed and published in 1993, but their patience while waiting for the second manuscript is also much appreciated.

Second, I am indebted to all of those colleagues who have listened to presentations over the last few years, as I was working out my ideas, asked good questions or made good suggestions: the Organization for the Study of Communication, Language and Gender in 2000, the National Communication Association in 1999; the International Communication Association in 1996, 1998, and 2000; the Seminar on Intercultural Communication, Multiculturalism, and Mixing held in Paris in 1994; the International Network of Personal Relationships in 1993; the Ethnography of Communication Conference in 1992; the Center for Twentieth Century Studies at the University of Wisconsin-Milwaukee in 1991.

Third, I must thank all those who talked with me about their weddings or the weddings they helped to organize, those who mentioned films that I should watch, books I should read, friends I should meet and interview. Usually, I like to list everyone who was helpful to my research by name; in this case, however, that would entail listing all of my friends, and an amazing number of people who started out strangers but often became friends, who were tolerant of my questions. Weddings are a topic that nearly everyone enjoys discussing, and I appreciate all of the help I received. I also will not list those I formally interviewed because that would break the agreement of confidentiality that we have. Of those I can mention, special thanks go to Victoria Chen, for setting up interviews in San Francisco for me in the spring of 2000.

And fourth, my students at the University of Wisconsin-Parkside over the last few years have been writing papers on various aspects of weddings, as I kept working through the issues of weddings that were interesting to me. In 1992, Sue Glanz interviewed couples as part of an independent study; in 2001 Dana Nelson watched several months of A *Wedding Story*. Students in Communication 440, Communication Codes, in Spring 1996 (Melissa Bird, Denise Bodmer, Jennifer Buchholz, Joel Buschmann, Patricia Carls, Kelly Conway, Theresa Cuff, Jody Davison, Scott Erickson, Damian Evans, Brad Gulbrandson, Elizabeth Haas, Chris Herman, Tracy Johnson, Gregory Jones, Kim Kogutkiewicz, Ashley LaMacchia, Juluia Lamb, Bryan Lyday, Mateo Mackbee, Raffi Mahdasian, Marilyn Margoni, Melissa Noto, Konnie Osborn, John Papara, Doug Pasniak, Laura Pope, Jason Pruitt, Robert Ryerson, Mary Saunders, Kevin Schmitz, Carrie Sharkozy, Marianne Sjoholm, Reginald Slaughter, Bart Smith, Suzanne St. Germain, Elena Swiden, Juan Tovar, Victoria Wateridge, Nicole Wendel, Mytyl Wilson, and Michelle Zorzy), in Spring 1999 (JoAn Agram, Michael Berry, Christopher Bradley, Justin Burke, Travis Carlson, Carmen Carrera, Matthew Carrick, Chad Columbari, Katie Dane, Kevin Dubiak, Heather Durden, Marlene Ernst, Jodie Fiene, Carlos Garner, Cori Graves, Beth Jensen, Mary Ellen Kanthack, Jessica Kiesler, Michelle Lambert, Deanna Lean, Susan Oboikowitch, Courtney Pace, Vien Ponesavanh, Bonnie Puplava, Christina Randall, Kim Reither, Autumn Ruge, Jeremy Santori, Gloria Schmitz, Kristin Smith, Kip Spittle, Joe Swikert, Quincy Trice, Steven Van der Heyden, Jeff Webster, Loreen Yates, and Hope Zinke), and in Spring 2001 (David Devey, Ryan Ellifson, Ramona Gapko, Michael Gonzalez, Nicole Goodwin, Jeff Hines, Hien Huynh, Jaime Jenjak, Amy Johnson, Shannon Johnson, Karin Jonsson, John Kovochich, Karen Malonee, Adam Miller, Dana Nelson, Eric Roche, JoAnn Tarnowski, Michael Tschanz, Nicole Turnquist, Jessica Tuttle, Jennifer Wehrli, William Wiedel, Kim Wright, and Chris Zanger) all helped me to think critically about this research and at times found appropriate weddings to attend or couples to interview. Some of these and other students also invited me to their weddings, once they knew I was specifically interested in the topic, although only some of these were intercultural, and so not all of them have been incorporated in the book. Where possible, I have credited these students for their efforts, although if they are related to the couple described (or, in very rare cases if they described their own weddings) they are not named in order to maintain confidentiality.

My colleague, Jonathan Shailor, took time from his own sabbatical to critique parts of this manuscript; Steve Murray provided helpful critical comments on the entire draft that were much appreciated, despite the fact that I did not follow all of his suggestions.

Finally, as with everything I write, my thanks to my husband, Marc, and my son, Aaron. As always, they have displayed incredible patience with my project, even when I suddenly would turn dinner with friends into an informal interview, to see what they could tell me of a wedding they had just attended, or provide information about friends I should contact for more information. Marc also read a draft and gave useful input from a nonspecialist's point of view, ensuring that what I wrote would make sense even to those who are not communication scholars.

Interlude 1

FIG. 1: Fabric used for *huppah* by Couple 1, now serving as a window shade in their bedroom (see color plate).

A traditional Jewish wedding incorporates the use of a *huppah*, a wedding canopy, held over the bride and groom by four family members or close friends. The *huppah* has many meanings; of these, the most important may be that it stands for the Jewish community as a whole, welcoming the bride and groom as a new couple into the larger group. Theoretically the fabric used for a *huppah* is a *tallis*, or prayer shawl, although in practice many are made of other materials, most often in blue and white, the colors of the Israeli flag. Now, imagine what changes when the *huppah* is made out of fabric from Kenya, bought by the bride and groom on a trip there. This fabric is mainly orange and black, patterned with a saying that translates essentially to "all that glitters is not gold."

Clearly this is a Jewish–African American wedding. In fact, both the bride and groom have fairly complicated cultural backgrounds (Couple 74).[1] The groom's mother is African American and Christian. His father is White and Quaker. The groom views himself as African American, and Quaker "sometimes." The bride's mother is Hungarian and Jewish; her father is Italian and Catholic. She views herself as primarily Jewish because she lived with her mother since the age of 10 and did not learn her father's religion. However, she is more culturally than religiously Jewish (she and her mother celebrated some of the holidays at home). In addition to the African fabric, the *huppah* is unusual in another way: The four poles used to hold it up were made from manzanita trees taken from property owned by the groom's family, thus connections to a particular family, as well as to social class, race, and religion, are all incorporated into the same symbol.[2]

The officiant in this ceremony had prior experience in performing intercultural weddings. As is often the case, she provided the basic outline for the ceremony; the bride and groom then worked with her to tailor it to their own needs. For example, they asked that she not mention God when blessing their union, because neither found it appropriate considering they are not sufficiently religious. Despite this lack of connection to organized religion, the bride wanted to include not only a *huppah*, but also breaking a glass, another standard element of Jewish weddings "as a way to mark her heritage." In this case, they both broke the glass together (actually, it was a light bulb wrapped in a cloth, the standard substitution), indicating the importance of equality in their relationship. As the pastor explained to the audience, "We cannot create a new world without bringing forward traditions that have shaped our histories. Where those traditions are beloved, but incorporate actions which exclude or demean, we must remake those traditions so that they continue to inform, but not limit, our lives."[3] Equality was also marked by the fact that the *huppah* poles were held by two of his friends and two of her cousins, and by the incorporation of relatives and friends on both sides into the ceremony. The pastor specifically referred to those holding the poles as representing the larger community, saying "their presence today signifies the support of their community." She also explicitly described the significance of the breaking of the glass, as well as the *huppah* and the poles, so those who were not accustomed to these traditions would understand them. There were no bridesmaids or groomsmen, but the bride's sister walked her down the aisle, and two of the groom's three sisters walked him down it (they wanted to include all family members and emphasize their own generation's involvement in the ceremony). His cousin was the ring bearer for her ring, and her friend was the ring bearer for his—both of these participants were adults. His third sister read an Alice Walker poem about love ("Beyond What"), and there were other readings by friends.

In addition to the standard exhortations to the bride and groom to work on their relationship to ensure the success of their marriage, at several points the pastor explicitly mentioned their differences. At one point, she suggested that this bride and groom, in addition to accepting the usual requirements of making a marriage work "have taken on the additional joys and challenges of blending cultures." At another, she pointed out that

> as a White woman and a man of color, you are saying to the world that love will not accept the boundaries which society has arranged to make itself comfortable. You proclaim that it is only love which opens our eyes to see the Other. In loving one another, you have taken on the challenge of love and commitment and chosen to stand among those who transform the world in the name of love and passion.

And at a third point, the pastor said:

It must be acknowledged that the world will press harder upon their relationship than it would upon a couple whose skins and cultures more closely resembled each other. In this they will need the support of their loving community. Those who stand with them, however, will benefit from the richness of their joint heritages. Their lives and those of their children, should they be so blessed, will be full and varied.

In another central component of the ceremony, the pastor asked "who stands with [bride's name] today?" and the bride's parents answered "We do. [Bride] is our daughter. [Groom] will be our son" Then she asked "who stands with [groom's name] today?" and the groom's parents answered "We do. [Groom] is our son. [Bride] will be our daughter." Both sets of parents were seated near the front but were not otherwise part of the ceremony. Given that so many parents have difficulty with interracial unions, public acknowledgment served as an explicit indicator that these parents openly recognize this marriage.

For clothing, the bride wore a traditional white dress with daisies on the bodice, and a headpiece in lieu of a veil. She held daisies (and other flowers, including white orchids) as a link to her grandmother, who liked them. The groom wore a suit with a *kente* cloth (a strip of fabric around his shoulders, understood to indicate African heritage), a gift from his aunt and uncle on his mother's side: "I wanted to have something that showed that I was thinking about my culture and my history as well." They exchanged matching gold wedding bands; she also wore an engagement ring.

This wedding took place in a park, with a nearby building used for the reception, featuring a light meal as it fell between lunch and dinner: turkey, salads, and stuffed cabbage made by the bride and her Hungarian grandmother. There was a white cake with fruit filling. A friend took the role of DJ, playing music, including "their song" ("Takes my Breath Away" by Tuck and Patti) as well as a *hora* (an Israeli folk dance often incorporated into Jewish, and now frequently, other, receptions). After the wedding, they honeymooned in Hawaii.

What was this couple explicitly aware of *not* incorporating? They did not have a unity candle, which would be standard as a part of a Catholic ceremony, especially Italian Catholic. They did not incorporate the "jumping the broom" ritual increasingly used by many African Americans in reference to a very old tradition followed by slaves (not permitted legal marriages, their unions were marked by jumping over a broom together, which was recognized as marking the equivalent of a marriage).[4] The groom mentioned that he now wishes they had included jumping the broom as part of the ceremony, but at the time (1993) they simply did not know enough about it.

After the wedding, the *huppah* was made into a shade for the window in their bedroom, where it serves as an index they see every day, a reminder of their wedding and the multiple identities incorporated into it. The manzanita sticks now lean against the same window. Both continue to wear their wedding rings, further indices of both the event and their marriage. Photographs of the wedding were kept as well, and serve as icons upon which they occasionally look.

This wedding illustrated a wide range of identities: African American, Jewish, Hungarian, marking links with particular family members and close friends, as well as more distant connections to slavery and Africa. There were obvious class markers (the *huppah* poles linked to owning land, a clear change from the days of slavery; the honeymoon in Hawaii). There were acknowledgments of mainstream American wedding traditions (especially in the rings, dress, flowers, cake, and honeymoon, as well as the inclusion of a song particularly meaningful to the couple). There was mention of the difficulties they could expect to face, matched to explicit public acceptance of the union by both sets of parents.

This wedding is unique yet also representative of what intercultural couples can create when they wish to design a ceremony that will publicly mark their marriage. The *huppah* made with fabric from Africa stands as the most visible symbol of how they have succeeded in combining their multiple identities into something new. It works as a *huppah* because it has the same component elements that a *huppah* always has: a piece of cloth, held up by four poles. Yet it marks this as an uncommon union, for instead of continuing the Jewish symbolism, African American and personal symbolism substitute: the cloth that the bride and groom chose on a trip they took together to Kenya, the poles made of trees from his family's land. This *huppah* differs from all other *huppot*,[5] yet remains recognizable to the Jewish guests of the wedding as fulfilling the traditional function. Simultaneously it is recognizable to African American guests as a link to Africa and a common history of slavery and to family members as a link to the land they now own. The creativity shown by the

bride and groom in inventing something to meet all their requirements speaks well for their ability to adapt traditional symbols of one
culture to their unique needs, their multiple identities. Its transformation into a window shade speaks to the importance of their marriage for their daily lives: In making it, they created a visible link from
the past to the present and future that says "we found a way to
mesh our identities once; we can and will continue to do so throughout our lives together."

NOTES

1. All couples will be identified by numbers (which signify only the order in
   which I transcribed their interviews), in order to protect their privacy.
2. An interesting parallel is reported in a wedding described on the web page
   www.theknot.com under the heading "Real weddings," so presumably it is
   an accurate description of what occurred. Claude Goetz and Sara Goldberg
   are described as a Jewish–Japanese couple (the groom's mother is Japanese, the bride's parents are Jewish). They also adapted their *huppah* to
   depict a revised identity statement.

   > Claude's parents spent many hours sawing bamboo and sewing silk
   > to create a unique Asian-inspired huppah ... Claude's mother, who is
   > Japanese, sewed the canopy from an antique *obi*, a sash worn with a
   > kimono. The silk brocade gold-and-green sash was a family heirloom,
   > once used at the wedding of a distant relative. They attached the fab-
   > ric to four bamboo poles, completing the simple Japanese look. "The
   > huppah was amazing because Claude's parents are not even Jewish,
   > yet they really got into helping us to combine our cultures and heri-
   > tages," exclaims Sara.

   Clearly, it is relatively easy to replace the traditional cloth and poles with others having new connotations for the couple, thus creating a new symbol
   with new meanings. It is especially nice that the *obi* adapted for the *huppah*
   in this example had seen prior service as one element in a family wedding.
   In this case, it is also mentioned that the couple made a second substitution, one relating to the traditional Jewish blessings over wine: "Instead of
   using wine for the traditional Hebrew blessings, the couple drank saki."
3. All quotes from the ceremony are taken from the text provided by the bride
   and groom.
4. See Cole (1993), Dundes (1996), and Sturgis (1997) for discussion of this
   tradition. I knew to ask this couple whether they had included it based on
   previous interviews, but they knew about the tradition from other sources.
5. *Huppot* is the proper plural form of *huppah* because it is not English but Hebrew. Many American Jews actually use a more casual form, *huppahs*,
   which combines the Hebrew word with the English plural marking.

1

Introduction

"Indeed, weddings are contested ground"
—Kendall (1996, pp. 225–226)

The United States includes individuals drawn from a wide variety of cultural backgrounds.[1] Most of us face diversity in school, at work, and in our neighborhoods, but there are an increasing number of individuals who choose to cross cultural boundaries in that most intimate of relationships—marriage.[2] These are not people who face cultural differences briefly when in the public realm or for a week when on vacation to an exotic location.[3] They have committed to living with difference in their own homes, for their entire lives "until death do us part" as many wedding ceremonies still state. A wedding marks the beginning of a marriage. As Mayer (1985) argued:

> The issue of the wedding and the marriage ceremony itself is frequently the first and most significant test of how a young couple will deal with the twin tugs of their love for each other and their dual heritage. Often that issue will affect all subsequent marital negotiations: questions concerning each spouse's familiarity with his and her respective traditions, emotional attachments thereto, attachments to parents, and varying degrees of embeddedness on the part of each in his or her community of origin. (pp. 191–192)

Other resolutions are less public, thus both more flexible and more negotiable.[4]

Naylor (1998) pointed out that "all cultural groups learn their cultures as *the* way to believe and behave, the *most correct* way, as the *true* way ... No culture group teaches new or aspiring members that someone else or some other cultural beliefs or practices are more correct than the ones they are being taught"

(p. 23). This teaching may make sense for each monocultural group when members stay at home but leads to cultural dissonance and even conflict when individuals from different groups attempt to cross group boundaries. In Naylor's succinct phrase, "cultures in contact produce conflict" (p. 153).[5] We cannot change this; ethnocentrism will continue to exist as long as it serves its primary purpose of strengthening the group. What we can do is to work with it. Conflicts can be resolved. Couples have small conflicts, in the context of ongoing, committed relationships, and thus have both an easier time of it and more reason to pursue a resolution than participants in many other contexts.

My title, *Wedding as Text*, provokes three obvious questions:

* Why study weddings?
* What kind of weddings will be studied?
* In what way is a wedding a text?

Each is answered in the following pages.

WHY STUDY WEDDINGS?

Weddings are one of a small number of rites of passage (events celebrating major changes in the life cycle, like birth and death) widely practiced across the United States and around the globe.[6] Of the various rites of passage, weddings are particularly enticing to study. Even if they have not experienced their own, most people who have been to multiple weddings, have seen weddings portrayed on television and in films, have read descriptions of weddings in newspapers, magazines, or books, and everyone has something to say on the topic. At least in the modern United States, this does not hold equally true for births and deaths. We generally participate in only the births and deaths of immediate family members, if even those, and these are neither acceptable topics for casual conversations nor celebrated in the popular media to the same extent as weddings.

Weddings, like all rituals, are complex events, composed of multiple parts. They incorporate a variety of codes (e.g., liturgy, music, food, clothing, and objects) and related events (in addition to the ceremony proper, participants may conduct multiple preceremony rituals, such as showers, bachelor parties, and prewedding dinners, premarital counseling or some other sort of wedding classes, and various postceremony rituals, such as receptions, opening presents, and honeymoons). Different groups place differing importance on these component rituals, any of which can be expanded to an astonishing extent. A wedding can, for example, be preceded by as many as 15 showers, though such elaboration is uncommon and noteworthy.[7]

As a major ritual, weddings are often planned months or years in advance, with even small details given consideration. Thus they serve as examples of what people are capable of doing when they take the time to think ahead and plan their behavior. Funerals are the opposite, generally needing to be scheduled with minimal notice because, as a group, Americans do not like to think about and plan them in advance. Often, family members do not even know what their loved ones would have preferred, having never been willing to ask.[8] Weddings happen by design, with accident influencing only small components, so they provide a good topic of study for researchers wanting to see what people choose to do after devoting considerable attention to organizing a public display.

Weddings are also worthy of study due to their considerable expense. In 1997, the average American couple spent over $19,000 (Ingraham, 1999). This is an average; obviously many couples spent far more, and the figure has only increased in the last few years. We grant weddings considerable social significance in spending such large sums on their design. Weddings are big business: 1% of the U.S. population gets married each year, but 14% of all sales are related to weddings (Lavin, 1992). The wedding industry earns $40 to $100 billion per year, depending on exactly what is included in the figure (Puente, 2000). A display of wealth has become such an expected requirement that many families willingly go into debt to pay for the ceremony. "'Over the years, I've seen fathers, even very wealthy fathers, tell their daughters, "I'll give you a blank check to put a down payment on a house" instead of an expensive wedding,' [wedding planner Marcy] Blum says. 'And not once has anyone taken it'" (Puente, 2000).

As happy occasions, there are few restraints on discussing weddings, the way there might be for sadder, but equally complex, occasions such as funerals. Weddings have sad aspects (i.e., for parents, a wedding may serve as the marker of children having reached maturity and leaving home), but only a few of the people I interviewed emphasized this interpretation. Like some other rituals, weddings are celebrations.[9] Like other celebrations, weddings incorporate elements of performance as well as entertainment, being both public and participatory (Manning, 1983b).

In these pages, weddings are discussed separately from marriages. Weddings are, unlike most marriages, relatively short and quite public. Marriages begin with the wedding, and last until either the death of one of the couple, their separation, or divorce. Studying how couples manage their continuing relationship is fascinating, but a topic in its own right.[10] I decided to stop my research at the boundary of the wedding ceremony, not moving on to the marriage, for a wide variety of reasons. As others have generally analyzed the relationship of marriage rather than the wedding alone, this requires some explanation. There are at least four rationales for stopping at the edges of the wedding, rather than continuing on to the marriage:

1. It provides a *tightly-bounded* event (usually lasting a few hours, but generally including a few days of related celebrations and rituals).

2. It is a *naturally-occurring* event (no researcher invented this analytic category, the participants did).[11]
3. It is a *publicly-celebrated* event (performed in front of a crowd of friends and relatives, unlike many aspects of a marriage).
4. It is a *widely-documented* event (participants generally arrange for photographs and/or videotapes to be taken, for their own use later).

Each of these factors has implications for research:

1. Because it is tightly bounded, the actual data I need to collect have some natural limits (essential because I use ethnography as my main method, a method known for the astonishing amount of data it can produce).
2. Because it is naturally occurring, the participants define what should be included in the event under study (essential given current concern with validity in fieldwork).
3. Because it is publicly celebrated, my presence as a researcher has little or no consequence for the form (essential given recent critiques of "subjective" research methods such as ethnography).
4. Because it is widely documented, participants have already determined on their own what is important to record for posterity, irrespective of my research interests (this characteristic also means that weddings occurring before my research began could be easily included in the database).

Marriages cannot be described as having these four characteristics and thus do not have the advantages as a research topic that these entail. Weddings are unique in their condensation of the choices made by a particular couple with regards to their relationship into a single event. They are particularly rich research sites due to this collapsing of much information into a brief occurrence. The decisions made for a wedding often foreshadow the decisions to be made for the marriage.

WHAT KIND OF WEDDINGS WILL BE STUDIED?

All weddings are potentially interesting to researchers, but this book primarily explores *intercultural weddings* held in the United States. Intercultural wedding is defined broadly, covering five major varieties:

* *international* (individuals from different countries),
* *interracial* (individuals of different races),
* *interethnic* (individuals of different ethnic groups),
* *interfaith* (individuals having different religions), and
* *interclass* (individuals from different social class backgrounds).[12]

Any one wedding can combine multiple types. An African American Baptist marrying a White Italian Catholic would appropriately be described as interracial, interethnic, and interfaith, simultaneously. The examples provided in this book document a wide variety of combinations, but clearly not all of those possible are represented in these pages.

A series of related terms are in use by different authors. *Intermarriage* has primarily been used to refer only to interfaith marriages; *mixed marriage* has often been used solely for interracial marriages.[13] The differences in cultural expectations (understood quite broadly) are most relevant, and I therefore use the single term *intercultural* to cover a wide spectrum of potential differences between bride and groom. Differences in cultural identity, whatever the source, imply differences in cultural resources available for creating shared meaning, so it is the issue, not the source, of difference that is central.[14] Despite the distinctions among these types of weddings, all share at least one characteristic: the need to blend divergent cultural traditions into a single coherent and meaningful ritual. As McGoldrick and Garcia-Preto (1984) pointed out, "Intermarriage requires a degree of flexibility not necessary for those who marry within their group" (p. 362). Although their research investigates interethnic marriages, the same is true of any form of intercultural marriage.

International

International weddings are between individuals who are citizens of different countries. These generally require that at least one member of the couple has traveled from their own home country to that of the other (although occasionally both members have traveled and have met in a third country) and usually entail explicit negotiations leading to a decision about which country will be chosen as home. In her summary of the literature on this topic, Cottrell (1990) found that "People who marry out [outside their own group] are, to some degree, psychologically, culturally, or socially marginal—at least they are not 'dead center'" (p. 163). This makes sense, and fits with what I have found, although studying who chooses an intercultural marriage was not a main focus of my research. As Varro (1988) suggested, in an international marriage, "an international confrontation is taking place at the microsocial level of the family" (p. 157). International confrontations are large and unwieldy, often remaining unresolved for long periods of time. Weddings are small and manageable, both requiring and permitting quick resolution. As is true of all international confrontations, understanding and patience are required for success. Participants in an international marriage where he's Japanese and she's the American daughter of Russian Jews born in Poland, speak for many international couples when they say: "Our home life has been sort of a cross-cultural lab" (Galloway, 1992, p. 3). (*Crosscultural* is a term developed by psychologists, and used by researchers in several disciplines, to refer to the comparison of cultural norms across national boundaries. It differs slightly from *intercultural*, which emphasizes the interactions between members of different cultures. Here, the more technically appropriate term would be *intercultural*.) In keeping with this comment, Barbara (1989) found "It is often the case that individuals are ahead of institutions. The barriers erected between countries and groups are not always those which separate individuals" (p. 211). This certainly held true for the international couples I talked to; as the bride of Couple 71 said on behalf of most of them: "the cross-cultural aspect was no problem." This was a U.S.–Cook Island wedding, in which the bride stressed the similarities between the individuals rather than the differences between the cultures. Presumably this has to be the emphasis if an international marriage is to succeed.

Varro (1988) found two major results of an international union: Either it will lead to great conflict, or to "a more broadminded, even sophisticated, personality, capable of integrating not only the material 'otherness' but his or her own" (p. 185). It will take substantial research on intercultural families, not just intercultural weddings, to discover how to ensure the positive outcome; neither Varro's research nor anyone else's has yet reached that conclusion. However, researchers have learned something about the circumstances leading to international marriages. Caycedo and Richardson (1995) found industrialization and urbanization increase the likelihood of the international marriages they studied (Chinese–American) because family bonds and neighborhood ties are weakened. As industrialization and urbanization increase around the world, this implies that the number of international marriages will substantially increase in the near future. This is probably true for any sort of intercultural marriage, not just international, because there is a cycle at work here. As boundaries between groups become less salient, more people are willing to cross a given boundary themselves, thus weakening it even further.[15]

Originally, this study only included weddings between Americans of various ethnic, racial, or religious groups. However, a number of interesting cases involving one international participant presented themselves, and I realized that the same essential cultural conflicts were occurring, and so they are included in this book. Clearly there are fewer examples of this type than there might be, and this is why. Cases involving two international participants that came to my attention were sufficiently different from weddings involving one American, so they have been omitted from the final study.

Interracial

Despite the significant social implications of racial differences, physical anthropologists (those who study the topic most carefully) have determined that race is not a valid biological construct.[16]

> Like other social constructs, races are real cultural entities. For many people, membership in a racial group constitutes an important part of their social identity and self-image. But social facts are not necessarily part of

> the biological landscape. In multiethnic regional populations, races are merely ethnic groups linked to vague, inconsistent, and stereotypical ideal phenotypes. (Cartmill, 1999, p. 659)

Because race has social, although not biological, significance, interracial couples and their biracial (or multiracial) children serve as a disruption of the expected norms whereby everyone fits into one particular category. In the spring of 2000 there was much public discussion over the new racial categories made available in the census form, permitting individuals to identify as members of more than one racial group for the first time.

Because they are a disruption of the expected, interracial weddings are still rare, although more frequent than they formerly were. Depending on the source cited, only 1% or 2% of weddings in the U.S. currently cross racial lines.[17] Zweigenhaft and Domhoff (1991) suggested that "national longitudinal data on intermarriage show that interethnic marriage rates have climbed over the past few decades for all groups except blacks. Black-white intermarriage rates in the United States remain among the lowest in the Western world" (p. 171). To briefly summarize the findings, it seems that people are more likely to intermarry if they have more education (because education both brings groups together and preaches tolerance), live away from their kin (so community norms cannot as readily be imposed on them), are later generation Americans (third generation being far more likely to intermarry than first generation), are older, and in a second marriage (both of which increase the pool of candidates who will be given serious consideration as potential mates).[18] Because they acknowledge that "Intermarriage is perhaps the most sensitive indicator that a minority group is being assimilated into the larger social-class system" (p. 171), this is a clear indicator of continuing separation between the races in the U.S.[19] Their study documents a program that successfully moved lower and working class blacks into the middle class by providing educational opportunity, yet even the students they studied did not generally marry outside their own group. Based on their evidence combined with that of other researchers, it becomes apparent that there are still fewer marriages across racial lines than across religious or ethnic lines in the U.S. This seems to be true of at least some other countries as well. Benson (1981) wrote of interracial unions in England that: "Contemporary popular ideology tells us that marriage is a matter of individual decision and private significance. In the context of a racially divided society, however, the decision to enter into an interracial union is, inevitably, a political act" (p. 13).

Of all intercultural marriages, interracial ones are clearly still the most controversial, as illustrated by the fact that they are the only type to have been legislated against.[20] In 1967, when *Loving v. Commonwealth of Virginia* resulted in a Supreme Court verdict deeming laws against interracial marriages unconstitutional because they violated the 14th amendment, fourteen states still had laws against Black–White intermarriage on the books (Pugh, 2001). South Carolina and Alabama were the last two states to have laws against it, despite the fact that these were clearly unenforceable after *Loving*. Astonishingly, when South Carolina began debate in 1998 about whether to remove the law from the books, legislators argued for keeping it on the grounds that the Bible forbids interracial marriages. McNamara, Tempenis, and Walton (1999) reported tracking down the chapter and verse most often quoted (II Corinthians 6:14), only to learn that it warns against being "unequally yoked with another." Checking with biblical scholars, they found this generally interpreted as referring to interfaith marriages, not interracial ones. South Carolina eventually did repeal their law in 1998, and Alabama followed in 2000, becoming the last state to do so. Even in 2000, 40% of those who voted in Alabama thought the ban on interracial marriage should be maintained (Amy & Tolkkinen, 2000). Also in 2000, an interracial couple was refused permission to hold their marriage in the church of their choice in Ohio, showing how strong feelings still are on this matter. However, the fact that the refusal made national news suggests that there are now also many people who consider such refusals to be inappropriate.[21]

Black–White intermarriage is not the only sort to have been legislated against in the U.S. in this century. Root (1997b) pointed out that in 1933, *Roldan v. Los Angeles County* established that "Filipinos were classified as Malays and quickly added to the list of persons prohibited from intermarriage with whites" (p. 84). Such laws sometimes lead to unexpected results. Leonard (1993) documented the fact that "since anti-miscegenation laws prohibited marriages across racial lines in California until 1948," and "since most California clerks saw Punjabi men in the U.S. without wives as colored or 'brown,' they could marry Mexican women, who were also described as brown" (p. 146). This led to a strong tradition of these two groups intermarrying, in what were termed *Mexican-Hindu* or *Spanish-Pakistani* marriages (p. 151).[22]

As Payne (1997) argued, "interracial marriages, because of their intimate and long-term nature, test racial boundaries and the willingness of individuals from different racial groups to accept each other in essentially long-lasting, egalitarian relationships" (p. 154). Even the Advisory Board of the President's Initiative on Race (1998) felt it necessary to comment on the matter. "In our view, rates of intermarriage are important for two reasons. They measure social interaction between persons of different races *and* they complicate the way the offspring of these marriages may identify themselves by race" (p. 54). Azoulay (1997), a biracial child herself, suggested "to be biracial—a cognitive and physical process of *being* in the world—in, and as a result of, a race conscious society, is *to be* an interruption, *to represent* a contestation, and *to undermine* the authority of classification" (p. 188). Henriques (1974) took the argument further than most by suggesting: "if the world is to solve the problem of inter-racial conflict the only sure foundation is inter-racial marriage" (p. xi) because "marriage between races is a mark of equality" (p. x). Taking essentially the same position, Benson (1981) argued that the hardest part of an interracial marriage is not the cultural accommodation required of the marriage partners, but the difficulties they face in the larger society that insists on seeing race as a central divide between individuals (describing Britain, but the point holds as well for the U.S.). As one bride put it: "Inside the quiet cocoon of our relationship, we are two people like any other, and our differences are just part of what makes being together interesting. Navigating the world outside is another story. There we are both a curiosity and an affront, something either to be stared at or rudely ignored."[23] Really, the question becomes whether we will accept "a fragmented polity" (Green, 1981, p. 189) or work to create a plural community, capable of acknowledging difference and then moving on to more important matters, such as our similarities. A hopeful sign is that, once intercultural marriages become accepted within a geographic area, they increase noticeably. The 1990 census figures document that California had 26% of all interracial marriages in the U.S. (McNamara, Tempenis, & Walton, 1999, p. 9).[24]

Interethnic

Interethnic marriages are those between members of two or more ethnic groups. *Ethnic group* is variously used to cover a large range of categories, influenced by nationality, region, religion, language, or even race.[25] It is used here to refer primarily to differences in country of origin for immigrant groups in the U.S., following Smith (1981), who viewed an ethnic group "as a social group whose members share a sense of common origins, claim a common and distinctive history and destiny, possess one or more distinctive characteristics, and feel a sense of collective uniqueness and solidarity" (p. 66).[26] As Wolf (1994) phrased it, ethnic groups are "conscious of themselves as owners of distinctive cultural traditions passed on along the lines of shared descent" (p. 1). In other words, like every type of cultural identity, ethnicity draws a line between groups of people, clearly marking who stands inside the line and who stands outside of it.

In the past, some authors have used *subcultures* as the term to describe the different ethnic groups (Thornton & Gelder, 1997), but currently, that word is not much appreciated (the *sub* having negative connotations for many). Instead, *cocultures* has recently been favored (Orbe, 1998a, 1998b), and "constituent culture groups" suggested as an alternative (Naylor, 1998), as well as "micro identities" (Tuleja, 1997, p. 3) or "microcultures" (Wulff, 1995, p. 65). In these pages, I use the older *ethnic groups* because that term was understood by most of those I interviewed, who did not always like *subcultures*, but were not yet familiar with the other terms.

Immediately following immigration, most groups have historically found the majority of marriage partners within the group; within a generation or two, intermarriage across ethnic lines increases in frequency. Despite this definition of ethnicity, implying that one is born a member of a particular ethnic group, a substantial literature now demonstrates that ethnic identity is *achieved* (something that has to be earned by each individual) rather than *ascribed* (a characteristic assumed to be inherited at birth). That is, whether or not ethnicity is relevant to a particular situation and will be brought into the interaction depends on the participants, who construct their identities moment by moment.[27] Construction of ethnic identity, like other elements of identity, relies on the use of language as well as various nonverbal forms of communication.[28] One result is the recognition that ethnicity has multiple layers. Nagel (1998) provided a vivid example of how this works in interaction: "An individual of Cuban ancestry may be a Latino vis-à-vis non-Spanish-speaking groups, a Cuban-American vis-à-vis other Spanish-speaking groups, a Marielito vis-à-vis other Cubans, and white vis-à-vis African Americans" (p. 242).

Interethnic marriages in the U.S., mostly between Whites of various ethnic backgrounds, are increasingly frequent, to the point that they are now the rule rather than the exception. "For white ethnics, the longer a group has been in the United States and the greater the percentage of its members in later generations, the lower the in-marriage ratios" (Waters, 1990, p. 104).[29] (*In-marriage* means marrying someone with the same background; *out-marriage* is then the term used to refer to marrying someone with a different background. These terms are widely used by sociologists, but not often by other scholars.) This led to some people feeling they have no particular identity other than *American*, which was the common first answer from many asked about their ethnic background for this study. Given the historical and political realities of the modern U.S., it invariably turned out that those who gave this answer were White, Protestant, and of western-European descent. These were the only people who felt their identity was not something to be questioned; everyone else "knew" they had a nameable identity. As Waters (1998) pointed out, "the ways in which ethnicity is flexible and symbolic and voluntary for white middle-class Americans are the very ways in which it is not so for non-white and Hispanic Americans" (p. 282). Similarly, di Leonardo (1998) suggested many researchers studying modern Americans "primarily conceive the self as unencumbered by dependent others, by community obligations, by institutions, by history" but she has found that ethnic groups and women are both "cumbered" in just the way these generalized "Americans" are said not to be (pp. 80–81).

Interfaith

Because weddings are sacred rituals, closely tied to religion, movement between different religious groups often causes the most explicit conflict about designing the ceremony. Crossing ethnic boundaries within related religious groups (different Protestant denominations, different strands of Judaism) paved the way for the crossing of boundaries between different religions (Mayer, 1985). One of the issues is that many religious representatives refuse to sanction interfaith marriages or officiate at such wedding ceremonies. A rabbi who will officiate at interfaith ceremonies clearly explains the difficulty: "*Halacha* [traditional Jewish law] simply does not recognize the possibility of marriage between a Jew and a non-Jew; there is no such category in Jewish law" (Kominsky, 2000).[30] The same difficulty holds for representatives of many other religions, including especially Catholicism. Essentially, the issue is that religious traditions have not kept up with the times. When it was common for people to meet and marry only those following the same religious traditions, it made perfect sense for a marriage between members of different religions to be a logical impossibility; in today's world, however, as such marriages increase in frequency, the inability of religious representatives to cope with the issue causes many difficulties for their congregants, who feel rejected by this refusal to acknowledge the chosen partner.[31] Sometimes the rejection of one family by the other, as mandated by religious guidelines, becomes unusually visible. In a Mormon–Christian wedding, the bride's family was literally barred from entering the church where the wedding ceremony was performed on the grounds that "Mormon temples can only be entered by church members in good standing, since they are considered sacred."[32]

Summarizing the results of his study of Black, Jewish, and Japanese intermarriages, Spickard (1989) said:

> It is worth noting, however, that there was more cultural conflict within Gentile-Jewish intermarriages, and more external pressure on Black-White and Japanese-non-Japanese unions. This resulted from a peculiarity of the American system of racial and ethnic relations. Americans see race as a greater barrier between people than religion, when, in terms of cultural conflict between individuals, just the opposite is true. (p. 358)

In keeping with this, some of the Black–White couples interviewed had a difficult time thinking of anything they had done in the wedding to mark racial identity, although most described considerable family resistance to the union, whereas interfaith couples often were immediately able to be quite explicit about the visible elements marking each religion in their wedding ceremonies.

Historically in the U.S., the first border crossings were made by White ethnics from different parts of Europe but of the same religion (as when Polish and Italian Catholics in the U.S. married). This has happened so frequently, in fact, that it is now not particularly noteworthy: "Indeed, ethnic origins seem so weakly related to marriages among whites that the term *intermarriage* may be increasingly a misnomer" (Alba, 1990, p. 12).[33] "Creating harmony among white ethnic groups was a gradual process, at the heart of which was an increase in interethnic marriages" (Payne, 1998, p. 155). In describing Jewish–Christian weddings, Mayer (1985) pointed out that intermarriers are generally high achievers who move in cosmopolitan and liberal social circles, and are likely to have high aspirations for personal advancement. "Consequently, they are more likely to have a broadened sense of their 'field of eligibles,' they are more likely to meet people outside their own group who are tolerant of intergroup differences, and they are less likely to be subject to the traditional controls of family and community in their mating choices" (p. 95). The same characteristics seem to hold for all interfaith couples, regardless of religious background.

Interfaith weddings carry particular emotional weight for many of the participants, not only the bride and groom. Because wedding rituals are traditionally framed as religious ceremonies, couples of different ethnic or racial backgrounds who share religious upbringings have a far easier time designing the event than those of different religions. Catholic–Lutheran combinations were actually some of the most controversial unions described to me, resulting in unhappy family members refusing to even acknowledge that the wedding had occurred given that it involved such an inappropriate choice of spouse.[34] Rabbi David Roller, who not only performs interfaith weddings, but also advertises his services on the Internet, gave this explanation: "My reason of being there for a couple is that I don't want them to have a reason to say we went to find a rabbi for the day we were getting married and we couldn't find anybody. I'll be there for them. I don't have many times I'll say no, unless they're crazy as loons."[35] In fact, he has turned necessity into a virtue, continuing with the comment: "If I was doing the same sort of wedding ceremony over and over again I'd be bored to tears. For me the unusual is more the interesting thing. I'd rather do a wedding that's different than every single one being like a cookie cutter."

Because weddings are religious rituals, interfaith ceremonies often involve the most difficult situations for the bride and groom and, although they were not the original focus of my research, they are heavily emphasized in this book. Christian–Jewish marriages have enough in common that many of the couples found it possible to design a single ceremony uniting both traditions, whereas Christian–Hindu or Buddhist or Muslim weddings had so little in common that it proved impossible for most couples to find a way to hold a single ceremony combining traditions. As a result, Christian–Jewish weddings are used as illustrations in this text far beyond their actual occurrence in the population, simply because they provided sufficient difference in traditional assumptions for negotiation to be required, yet sufficient similarity for resolution to be possible.

Interclass

American film weddings across cultural groups rarely depict ethnic or racial differences, but often show class differences (*Father of the Bride*, *Stella*, and *Betsy's Wedding* being just a few examples). Despite this, those interviewed rarely spoke of class explicitly. Ortner (1991) suggested: "It is well known that American natives almost never speak of themselves or their society in class terms. In other words, class is not a central category of cultural discourse in America, and the anthropological literature that ignores class in favor of almost any other set of social idioms—ethnicity, race, kinship—is in some ways merely reflecting this fact" (p. 169).[36] One interpretation would be that popular opinion holds it as appropriate to want to cross class boundaries, which have much to do with money (something external to the person), but far more difficult or questionable to want to cross racial or ethnic boundaries, which is popularly viewed as having far more to do with the intrinsic nature of the person. Perhaps it is also relevant that for an event where expense traditionally marks formality, as with weddings, class differences become unusually visible and therefore relatively easy to portray.[37] In any event, class trumps race (or ethnicity). As one of Benson's (1981) West Indian informants living in England put it: "The English lower middle classes are prepared to take in a lodger if he is a doctor or lawyer or something like that. It washes his colour out" (p. 96). Although not usually phrased so explicitly in the U.S., the same phenomenon holds. However, as Root (2001) pointed out, it is possible to argue that African Americans in the U.S. really face not just a class system but a *caste* system (i.e., a closed system in which out-marriage is essentially forbidden), which she feels is largely responsible for the still limited numbers of Black–White marriages.

Class differences were added to my research as a result of questions posed when I presented some of my early research at a conference in France in 1993. To Europeans, it seemed obvious that class differences would be critical, and so I then added some weddings involving differences in class between the bride's and groom's families. However, these were less significant in design of the ritual than other forms, for they were quite often deceptively easy to resolve. In nearly every case the family with more money (one of the standard components determining class) simply offered to cover the costs, and the wedding then displayed the higher class identity.

Multiple Forms of Difference

There are also weddings involving several of the types listed here. Some of these are more common than others, and some more likely to be successful. For example, there are connections between level of education (commonly considered one element of class) and intermarriage across racial, religious, or ethnic boundaries (because higher education generally implies increased participation in heterogeneous groups, as well as greater emphasis placed on acceptance of differences).[38] Intermarriages across religious or racial boundaries when both individuals have upper class standing have been said to be more likely successful than working class intermarriages because money can surmount some of the common obstacles (Spickard, 1989). The degree of attachment to ethnic identity is also relevant, as those who are least attached are often said to be most likely to intermarry (Spickard, 1989); similar comments have been made about attachment to religious identity (Khatib-Chahidi, Hill & Paton, 1998). There even are distinctions in whether men or women of particular groups are more likely to intermarry. Spickard (1989) found a strong link to mass media here: Popular culture (particularly films) of the 1930s and 1940s, the time when the *Nissei* (second generation Japanese Americans) were coming of age, showed Asian men as unpleasant (through one of two stereotypes: either Charlie Chan or kamikaze pilot) while showing the women as exotic and desirable; thus it should be no surprise that more women than men of this generation married outside the group.[39] More recently, the stereotype of Asian men has changed considerably. As they are now more likely to be viewed as future Internet millionaires, they are more likely to be accepted outside their own cultural group as potential husbands (Pan, 2000).

Crossing Cultural Boundaries

In general, weddings in the U.S. are the subject of extensive popular culture treatment—we have films, books, magazines, and web sites, all devoted to weddings. We also have wedding specialists, from the florists and caterers, accustomed to handling small pieces of the event, to wedding planners, who serve as contractors overseeing everyone else's part. These and other vehicles convey a "mainstream American" standardized version of what a wedding is "supposed" to look like. "An increasingly homogenized set of American wedding rituals has emerged which seem to influence couples and their families, no matter what their particular ethnic, class, or religious backgrounds" (Whyte, 1990, p. 90). Interestingly, this mainstream wedding has virtually no cultural identity markers, and so often has little interest for those planning an intercultural wedding, who want to create something more personal and original for themselves that will recognize the backgrounds of the major participants. "It was really interesting to me how many preconceived notions I had, like from TV and stuff … We wanted a wedding to be what we wanted and not what the industry told us, or what the people in the street did" (Couple 1).

It is only very recently that books have appeared describing ethnic traditions for couples who wish to follow them but never really learned them. Costa (1997) described Asian American traditions, especially focusing on Chinese, Japanese, and Korean. As she said: "Today, more than ever, modern couples are seeking ways to make their weddings more meaningful, more unique. As Asians marry Westerners or other Asians with different upbringings, the traditional white Victorian wedding is being transformed into a dazzling display of ethnic color and culture" (p. xii). At the same time, white wedding dresses have supplanted red in Taiwan, and mimicry of Western weddings is common in Western Pacific societies (i.e., Japan, Taiwan, the Philippines). Other popular books of this sort describes African traditions, with a similar emphasis on

Americans who have lost their ties to the past but wish to reclaim them, for example Sturgis (1997) or Cole (1993).

The edges of any single cultural system overlap with the edges of others, and it frequently has been suggested that what occurs at these points of overlap is particularly worthy of study.[40] More happens and more is noticeable at the boundaries than in the center.[41] Bourdieu (1990b) looked at critical moments in a culture to see characteristic features concentrated, for "Boundaries are where battles take place" (p. 228).[42] Intercultural weddings exemplify a social location where meanings come into conflict and serve as particularly fruitful sites of analysis, for they involve the voluntary crossing of symbolic boundaries. There is no chance all cultural boundaries will disappear, but they are likely to continue becoming more permeable—so it is important to study occasions when they are stretched thin or torn down entirely.[43]

Theoretically, to some extent all weddings are examples of at least minimal intercultural communication because all weddings effect the combination of individuals from different families (each of which has their own traditions and expectations) into a new whole, which will need to establish its own traditions.[44] In the majority of weddings, however, differences are balanced by the number of similarities between the families involved and their expectations; the weddings described here are those likely to have greater differences, whether due to differences in nationality, race, religion, ethnicity, or class, or some combination of these.[45] Thus, at intercultural weddings all of the issues available for study are magnified: the joining of families, the resolution of conflicts, the fulfilling of expectations, and the integration of the past with the present and potential future all come to the fore. As a result, intercultural weddings are a good starting point for research into how intercultural communication is handled on an individual, in fact, on a very personal level.

At present, intercultural weddings are but a small percentage of the whole, with most individuals choosing to marry people substantially like themselves. However, the modern U.S. is a plural, multiethnic society, with a wide variety of cultural groups together making up the whole. As Stephen (1994) pointed out, "American history can be read as an almost continuous accelerating process of cultural diversification" (p. 204). It is important to ask how such diversity is socially articulated and, equally, how it can be fruitfully combined. Because the major participants in intercultural weddings can be assumed to have the effective combination of multiple traditions as a goal, studying this one ritual event may throw light on other sorts of cultural conflict and their potential solutions. Participants in a wedding should epitomize high motivation. The new couple has greater incentive to overcome cultural conflicts of any sort than many others. Thus, studying the design of intercultural weddings should demonstrate what forms of creativity in combining different cultures are possible given sufficient incentive.[46] As those who absolutely cannot find any way to combine their different cultures generally do not get married at all, intercultural weddings not only display the efforts of those willing to attempt to cross cultural boundaries, they relate the story of those who have been most successful in the attempt.

Designing even a single intercultural wedding calls into being a new connection between two (or more) previously separate communities. Through the joining of two individuals representing different communities, everyone in their communities is joined, at least symbolically and at least temporarily, whether or not they would have wished for the joining. Because marriages most often produce children, and children are the way communities perpetuate themselves, intercultural marriages are particularly interesting in the way they make a statement about the joining of at least the fringe members of these communities. "Intermarriage breaks the old continuity of a system. It disrupts family patterns and connections on the one hand, but opens a system to new patterns, connections, and the possibility of creative transformations on the other" (McGoldrick & Garcia-Preto, 1984, p. 348). An intercultural union presents many problems; an intercultural wedding can serve to resolve them (if only temporarily). Recognizing the simultaneous existence of both positive and negative elements, Limón (1991) referred to the combination of cultural backgrounds as "an interesting complexity that the less observant might mistake for a dilemma" (p. 116).

A wedding across group boundaries redefines where the boundaries lie, with bride and groom serving forever after as mediators joining two previously separate groups. As reported by the child of an intercultural marriage

> I am awestruck by the fact that my ancestors—my mother's ancestors and my father's—lived on completely different continents, thousands of miles apart, spoke virtually unrelated languages, lived in radically different cultures, for thousands of years—and yet all of these ancestors, have, in a sense, come together in me. Me and my sisters. (Kinsley, 1994, p. 129)

If marriages are how communities reproduce themselves, then intermarriage between individuals of what are commonly viewed as being substantively different groups is significant in that it creates a new link between the groups forever. "America was founded … upon a vision of intermarriage" (Spickard, 1989, p. 4). "Who are we? The ones who dance between worlds" explains another child of an intercultural marriage (Malanka, 1994, p. 157).

If McReady (1983) was correct in saying that "It is a sign of our own maturity that we can examine our differences without feeling as though they must be eliminated, but rather that they contain valuable and uncommon insights as to what makes us most human" (p. xvii), then it is equally a sign of maturity if two individuals from different backgrounds can talk openly about their differences and find ways to reconcile them to everyone's satisfaction. At the same time, it is easy to understand why some participants find it so hard to celebrate differences in the context of a wedding, which has as its major function the celebration of similarity and unity (in joining a new couple together). Thus it comes as no surprise to learn that many parents of those about to embark on an intercultural marriage object, and attempt to cut short the connection (occasionally to the point of disowning the child who participates in an intercultural marriage), and others insist on their own background being given primary attention during the wedding service. Parents fear that their own traditions will be lost as the result of intermarriage, and they are often correct. Shakir (1997), studying Arab Americans in the U.S., found "many in the third and fourth generations are, for all intents and purposes, lost to the community, largely because of intermarriage in their family past; they may remember that one or more ancestor was Muslim, but they do not feel any personal connection with Islam" (p. 116). It is often the same for other groups; there is thus a legitimate fear that intermarriage is connected to a loss of identity. However, common should not be confused with inevitable. If cultural identity played a significant role in someone's life before marriage, it is likely to do so as well after marriage. (One implication: If cultural identity has no place in someone's life, it is not likely to be intermarriage that is primarily responsible.)

WHAT DOES IT MEAN TO STUDY WEDDINGS AS TEXT?

The term *text* originally meant a stretch of *talk*, actual speech uttered by real people, preserved on tape by a researcher and analyzed at leisure. But it has come to refer more generally to any stretch of *behavior* seen as a relatively coherent whole, having internal boundaries established by participants, rather than external boundaries established by the researcher.[47] Witte (1992) provided a useful definition of text as "any ordered set of signs for which or through which people in a culture construct meaning" (p. 269). Examples of signs could include words, music, images, or material elements of social life.[48] Ricoeur (1979) and Geertz (1973; 1979) provided the original proposal to use text as a metaphor applying to action rather than solely to literature. Their initial argument was quickly expanded to explicitly include all of the humanities, on the grounds that humans are text-producing animals and the humanities are those fields of study analyzing, interpreting, and evaluating various forms of human texts (Scholes, 1982). Others since have applied the concept of text directly to communicative behavior.[49]

The metaphor of textual analysis reminds us that communication is analyzable behavior, something available for study.[50] The image of a physical text further implies that we can read social interaction as we would a written text—bringing what we know to the material we analyze, bringing it to life through our understanding. Sless (1986) provided extensive discussion of the reading of texts, reminding us that "Any kind of reading is an active process out of which meaning is generated. Texts are like lumps of clay waiting for a reader to fashion them and give them a structure. If you simply watch the clay at a distance nothing happens; it remains an inert mass" (p. 121). Carey (1989) highlighted this concept of text in his explanation of the study of communication: "A cultural science of communication then, views human behavior—or, more accurately, human action—as a text. Our task is to construct a 'reading' of the text. The text itself is a sequence of symbols—speech, writing, gesture—that contain interpretations. Our task, like that of a literary critic, is to interpret the interpretations" (p. 60). Unlike literary or media texts, however, analysts of social texts cannot assume reader familiarity with the material under discussion, and so greater description becomes essential. But that does not make the object under discussion any less a text. "Lives are not transcriptions of events. They are artful and enduring symbolic constructions which demand our engagement and identification. They are to be perceived and understood as wholes. They are texts" (Oring, 1987, p. 258).

Considering a wedding as text implies that we consider it a particular type of behavior available for, and worthy of, analysis, and that we acknowledge the significance of placing that text into context before beginning analysis. A wedding, as with any other text, can be read or interpreted, with as many potential readings as there are readers for it. For this reason, photographs and videotapes of weddings are particularly useful to investigating the creation of meaning in a wedding. Many couples today in the United States not only have photographs taken, but also have a videotape prepared, either by a professional or, more casually, by a friend or relative.[51]

At the same time, reflexivity—the ability to step outside of a moment in time, and analyze one's place within it—is necessary. Documenting anything inscribes it, freezes a complex event into a single form. The metaphor of text as applied to behavior carries among its implications the idea that we take something disorganized, incomplete, even chaotic, and make it organized, complete, removing the element of chaos.[52] It is easy to forget the inherent incompleteness of the visual record provided by photographs or a videotape, incorporating as it does the perspective of only one participant (the photographer or videographer). This perspective is rarely identical to that of the main participants, the bride and groom, who almost never serve the additional roles of photographer or filmmaker, for the obvious reason of role conflict. In videotapes of weddings, it is not uncommon for guests to speak directly to the camera, greeting the bride and groom and wishing them a long and happy union, although as the filming occurred they were looking at the videographer. However, the bride and groom almost never speak directly to the camera. Given the general understanding that they are the primary audience for the videotape, speaking to themselves would be awkward rhetorically, to say the least. Occasionally the bride and groom seek to gain additional points of view, as when guests are provided cameras at the reception, and asked to add their photographs to those of the professional, so the bride and groom can see the event through their eyes (Couple 44).[53]

All text is "context sensitive," that is, every text is substantially influenced by the context within which it appears (Winner, 1986, p. 182), and so we must incorporate some contextual information in discussing any text. This means that, although the study of a single wedding drawn out of its context does not teach us much, the study of many weddings, in context, has more potential.

Organization of the Book

This book is divided into four major topics that cut across and underlie many of the major issues in this study: community, ritual, identity, and meaning. Each of these ideas is introduced at greater length in the chapters that follow. Obviously all of these concepts operate together during any one wedding ceremony; division is mainly to facilitate discussion, to introduce the major issues each entails.

Community.   A *community* is a group of people who share sufficient characteristics that they take the same things for granted.[54] The study of community includes an emphasis on the tension between the individual (one person and his or her own desires) and the group (the larger community and what it needs to continue, and therefore expects of the individuals making up the group). Historically, a community most often has been assumed to have its own geographic territory and distinct language and traditions. In the modern U.S., as with many other countries, that is no longer the case (if it ever really was), which has implications for weddings as well as for other cultural forms.

Cohen (1985) pointed out that "The most striking feature of the symbolic construction of community and its boundaries is its oppositional character. The boundaries are *relational* rather than absolute; that is, they mark the community *in relation to* other communities" (p. 58). The purpose of a boundary is to mark where one group ends and another begins. Communities are based on an act of imagination—a silent agreement that they exist even when they cannot be seen (Anderson, 1983). The symbolic edges of a community, although invisible, are nonetheless quite important. Appiah and Gates (1995) took this a step further, pointing out that "Ethnic and national identities operate in the lives of individuals by connecting them with some people, dividing them from others" (p. 3).

But are the symbolic edges truly invisible? In fact they leave many impressions of their existence on the material world. The boundary line between communities may not be a physical phenomenon, but members of different communities most often act, think, talk, and believe in different ways. If they did not, it would be incorrect to say that people are members of different communities, shared beliefs, thoughts, speech, and behavior being the defining characteristics of communities. Community is a social construct, not a physical one, yet the existence of a community is marked through physical means. Thus, this study emphasizes the ways in which nonverbal aspects of communication serve to mark the boundary lines of communities. People choose to eat particular foods, wear particular clothes, use particular objects, and these simultaneously serve necessary functions and embody our understandings of the borders of our community. Quite simply: If people share foods, clothes, and objects with others, then they are making a statement—not an oral statement made to one person and easily denied to another, but a concrete, physical statement, visible to all—about having something in common. If people do not share such items of material culture, they equally make a statement about not sharing common ground, although as meaning is here created through absence, it becomes less obvious and more readily denied. In this way, a community is a "social accomplishment" (Rothenbuhler, 2001, p. 159).

Cohen (1985) argued that "the symbolic expression of community and its boundaries increases in importance as the actual geo-social boundaries of the community are undermined, blurred or otherwise weakened" (p. 50). If this is true, then one would expect the symbolic differences between ethnic communities in the United States to be stressed quite heavily, because such communities generally share geographic space. Communities provide people with a reference for the creation of their social selves; they provide the larger context for the particular social text that they write at any given moment.

Ritual. *Rituals* are events with strong traditional elements, having great significance for participants. The study of rituals includes also study of the related concept of rite of passage. Among other attributes, a wedding marks a change in someone's life, from being a social individual to part of a new social group, a couple, and any event marking a major change in status is technically termed a rite of passage. Rituals generally display a tension between tradition (what has always been done) and creativity (a new invention). As Glassie (1995) so gracefully phrased it, "tradition is the creation of the future out of the past" (p. 395). Each couple demonstrates their ability to design a wedding, taking into consideration previous weddings held in their groups, yet a unique variant of the genre. Weddings, because of their expected grounding in particular religious traditions, also display a tension between the sacred (that which is connected to religion) and secular (that which is not). Intercultural couples have a particularly difficult time when religious leaders insist on the inclusion of different traditions that cannot be reconciled into a single ceremony or refuse even to recognize a union between a member of their own religious community and a nonmember. In such cases, one member of a couple can convert, or they may decide that they do not require that religious leader's approval of their marriage.

Rituals are symbolic acts used to confirm the existence of a community, the larger group within which they are understood to make sense. Intercultural weddings are potentially quite difficult (and even dangerous) to design because they must affirm the existence of a single community where none truly exists, in the combination of the bride's and groom's separate worlds. Yet once designed, they call that tenuous community into existence. Two formerly separate communities are joined now, if only at a single meeting point: one intercultural couple. Yet it would be wrong to suggest that all intercultural weddings are successful unions of diverse communities; clearly some are not. As with every other ritual, some are more coherent (and thus more successful at their efforts at integration), whereas others are more confusing (and thus less successful). As Myerhoff (1992) pointed out: "Human beings are the carriers of culture, and they may transmit their culture more or less successfully, in confusion and disarray or with a sense of coherence and well-being" (p. 227). Even so, simply holding an intercultural wedding, whether entirely successful or not, demonstrates the new attachment of communities.[55]

If, as Sutherland (1979) suggested, "Marriage is the way in which a group perpetuates itself; within the family unit the way of life—language, religion, morals, customs—of the group is maintained and propagated" (p. 53), then it is clear why parents and other relatives are quite likely to disapprove of intercultural weddings: They imply that a family's way of life is in jeopardy of changing. Weddings are one form of ritual, and rituals are events combining a series of traditions and symbols. Experience is located and reaffirmed through rituals and other events; as with physical locations of experience, a ritual "evokes and organizes memories, images, feelings, sentiments, meanings, and the work of imagination" (Walter, 1988, p. 2). To a large extent, the work of the family is to pass on traditions and symbols to the next generation. How can someone who does not share your traditions and symbols pass them on to the next generation? This is the quandary faced by marriage partners asked to commit to raising their children in the religion of their spouses, logically a virtual impossibility: How can one raise a child with traditions one has never followed and does not fully understand? As one Christian bride about to enter into marriage with a Jewish groom put it, "I said to him, I don't have a problem, and that's coming from my heart, I don't have a problem raising the children Jewish, with one exception, you need to become more religious. I said, I'm not going to raise the children Jewish while you don't attend Temple every week. I don't know how to raise these kids Jewish" (Couple 14). And yet parents and religious leaders ask this commitment all the time, expecting it to be fulfilled.

It would be wrong to imply that weddings (or any other ritual form) within particular groups remain stable over long periods of time. Intercultural weddings are not the only force for change in a sea of static events, they are one of many. Often, in fact, they illuminate changes already occurring in the larger society, rather than bringing them about. First, all cultural groups in the United States are aware of mainstream weddings, and even monocultural weddings within ethnic enclaves quite often display the influence of mass media and popular culture images.[56] And second, every ritual within every group undergoes change over time, if only because the physical or social materials that are available in one time period and one place often will not be available at a later time or different location.[57] As Tambiah (1985) pointed out, "no one performance of a rite, however rigidly prescribed, is exactly the same as another performance" (p. 125).

Identity.   *Identity* can be basically defined as a statement of who you are, most often here in terms of racial, ethnic, national, religious, or class background. It involves a tension between public (what occurs in front of others) and private (what occurs when there is no witness), for private statements can vacillate in a way that public ones cannot. Rituals convey identity, among other things. Monocultural weddings, as public ceremonies, incorporate the performance of one particular cultural identity. Intercultural weddings require the simultaneous performance of at least two different cultural identities, which makes them especially interesting to the observer but difficult for participants to design to everyone's satisfaction. The pull on the bride and groom in different directions, as they attempt to listen to the divergent opinions of all of their family, friends, and professional advisors, is so much expected as to form a substantial part of the popular culture describing weddings.

In designing weddings, the participants must not only make choices about language and ideology, they make choices about the physical props that will serve in their statements of identity. We not only *say* who we are, what groups we claim allegiance to through our words, we also *show* it through our actions and the material choices we make. As Jankowski (1991) suggested, communication is "one of the conditions for community" (p. 163). It is the codes participants use in communication, including rituals, that researchers must study to locate the boundaries of identity and community. Weddings, like all rituals, have a large number of material elements: candles, flowers, rings, and clothing are all chosen for the formal ceremony; food is served at the reception, where tables are decorated with flowers and candles or other centerpieces; music forms a part of either or both. Each choice makes the ideas and assumptions, thus the identities claimed by the new couple, evident to all who attend.

Meaning.   *Meaning* involves the use of signs and symbols combined into codes to convey what is important to participants, both to themselves and to others. Meaning is essentially the content of the ritual, what difference it makes. An invisible line is drawn between members of a particular community who understand the implications of a particular word, object, or action, and everyone else who does not. Weddings, like other rituals, are essentially the operas of everyday life. By making simultaneous use of a large number of social codes (language, food, clothing, objects, music, etc.) they require not only the careful organization of a balancing act, but the public performance of that act. It is no wonder that so many traditions incorporate the opportunity for a rehearsal.

Intercultural weddings generally convey meaning through the use of signs that take their meaning from their prior use in other contexts (technically termed *intertextuality*) as well as through the combination of old signs into new sets (*bricolage*). As Montgomery (1991) suggested, "An almost universal axiom in the study of interpersonal communication is that meanings are not brute facts; they are not indisputable assertions of what is and what is not represented by a particular symbolic behavior. Rather, meanings are a product of social negotiation" (p. 484). That not everyone takes the same meaning from the same behavior has significant implications for our understanding of the meanings entailed in the many choices made in the design of a wedding ritual.

We create meaning for ourselves and for others through our design of a variety of forms, including but not limited to weddings. Myerhoff (1992) explained:

> One of the most persistent but elusive ways that people make sense of themselves is to show themselves to themselves, through multiple forms: by telling themselves stories; by dramatizing claims in rituals and other collective enactments; by rendering visible actual and desired truths about themselves and the significance of their existence in imaginative and performative productions. (p. 257)

Weddings display who we are, and who we will become. They make the social transition from two separate individuals to a single social unit visible to the larger community (or communities) having the most invested in the change.

How do all of these concepts fit together? Most simply put, *we convey meaning about identity and community through the design of and participation in rituals*. Another way to say it is that we use *rituals* as a way of telling ourselves stories about our *identities* (who we are), and our *communities* (the groups within which we find ourselves), and through the process of telling the story of identity and community, we make it real, we give it *meaning*. Rituals have meaning for us because we conveniently forget that we ourselves have designed them, and so they readily take on larger implications.

And where does *communication* stand in relation to these concepts? Because it has no chapter of its own in this book, does that mean it is a minor issue? Not at all. Communication has no chapter of its own in this book because it is integral to every chapter. As Shuler (2001) suggested, "Because reality must be interpreted through communication, the truths we seek and find are the truths that we actively participate in creating" (p. 55). *Communication is the primary vehicle by which we create community, perform ritual, convey identity, and discern meaning, for it is through concrete interaction that we create these more abstract concepts*.

These, then, are the touchstones for discussion in this book. Treated separately for the sake of analysis, they are to be understood as different facets of the same phenomenon. They are illustrated by descriptions of actual weddings, throughout these chapters. Especially successful examples of integrating conflicting expectations are highlighted, presented as "Interludes" between the main chapters, to provide a clear sense of what such weddings do, with greater detail and larger context than that provided for the smaller examples scattered throughout the more theoretical chapters. All couples are identified by numbers (Couple 1, Couple 57), and individuals called by the roles they play (bride, groom, bride's mother, officiant) rather than names in order to protect their privacy, unless descriptions of their weddings identifying them have previously appeared in publications by others. The four major themes will be brought back together again in the conclusion, which presents a series of issues to be addressed and questions to be posed for future research into intercultural interactions.

NOTES

1. This is why Young (1996) said: "There is, perhaps, no more important topic in the social sciences than the study of intercultural communication. Understanding between members of different cultures was always important, but it has never been as important as it is now" (p. 1). When Wood and Gregg (1995) sorted through 8 years of discussions about the major issues in the field of communication, one of the four they chose was cultural diversity; Johnson's (1995) chapter in their collection argues that "we need to bring culture to the center of the discipline" (p. 163).
2. As Root (2001) pointed out, "As structured barriers to equality between race and gender continue to be challenged, the matrix of gender and race changes. The result will be more interracial marriage" (p. 75). See also Steinfels (1992).
3. The majority of intercultural communication studies emphasize brief interactions between virtual strangers and most intercultural communication theories focus on this sort of interaction (e.g., Wiseman, 1995). This is not inappropriate, as in fact the majority of intercultural communication encounters are of this sort, but it is equally not inappropriate to study close interpersonal relationships that are simultaneously intercultural. And, although relationships are a topic studied by many of those in interpersonal communication, it is rare for that literature to consider intercultural relationships.
4. As McGoldrick and Giordano (1996) pointed out "Typically, we tolerate differences when we are not under stress; in fact, we may find them appealing. However, when stress occurs, tolerance for differences diminishes" (p. 19). This is why their work concerns how to help intercultural couples in need of family therapy. Weddings are stressful events. The stress that puts tolerance to the test also adds drama, poignancy and power to a couple's ability to effectively manage its cultural differences under these conditions.
5. There is a large literature on cultural conflict, including Byrne and Irvin (2000), Eller (1999), Wiberg and Scherer (1999), and Wilmsen and McAllister (1996).
6. Appadurai (1997) summarized these as "The basic package of rites described by van Gennep, those having to do with birth, initiation, marriage, and death" (p. 27).

7. A student in my Communication 440 course in Spring 1996 reported attending a wedding with 15 showers. Woodruff (1980) described even greater excess: 36 parties held for the bride prior to the wedding, 150 people at a 7-course rehearsal dinner, and so forth.

8. On several occasions I have given students an exercise requiring them to design their own funeral. What surprised me most was learning that many of them had given a copy of their papers to their parents or spouses, to be used in case of need. Apparently, although they found it quite difficult to discuss the subject, once they had designed a ceremony, they did not want their preferences ignored. Presenting a completed paper to others meant their ideas were conveyed without necessitating a conversation they were not sure they really wanted to initiate.

9. There is a large literature examining celebrations, mostly within folklore and anthropology. Abrahams (1987), Browne and Marsden (1994), Gutierrez and Fabre (1995), Manning (1983a), and Santino (1994) provided good beginning points.

10. Also potentially relevant are studies investigating intercultural friendships or intercultural relationships prior to marriage; see, for example Gareis (1995) and Gaines (1997), respectively, on these topics. In addition, there are now a few studies of gay and lesbian commitment ceremonies, which are different from my emphasis here, but less so than might be imagined (Lewin, 1998, is one introduction to that literature). Gay and lesbian couples sometimes feel just as strongly about the significance of a traditional ceremony as heterosexual couples. As one member of a lesbian couple planning a commitment ceremony put it, "I'd definitely like to follow the traditional wedding as closely as we possibly could. Just because we're both women it's not fair that we wouldn't be able to do that" (Couple 110).

11. Obviously weddings are in fact cultural rather than natural, but I follow common usage by those who study interaction in considering things that are created by the people studied as natural. For example, Farnell and Graham (1998) defined naturally occurring discourse as "utterances that occur in the context of social interaction, in contrast to utterances specifically elicited by a linguist or ethnographer" (p. 411).

12. Sometimes these categories overlap in interesting ways, and occasionally other categories come into play, particularly geographic distinctions. Lipson-Walker (1991) supplied an interesting study of the connections between religious and geographic influences.

13. Also, specific terms have developed to refer to specific populations, such as *métis(se)* in France, which translates as *mixed*, traditionally used to refer to multiracial people: "Alternative translations of *métis(se)* can extend beyond 'racial' that is 'Black'/'White' discourses to encompass convergences across ethnicities, cultures, religions and nationalities" (Ifekwunigwe, 1999, p. 19); or *mestizaje* in the U.S., originally referring to mixed Indian and Spanish heritage in Mexicans, but now proposed as a broader term for any sort of cultural mixing (Aldama, 1997, p. 94).

14. See Philipsen (1989) for a detailed exploration of this point.

15. There is now a large literature considering the increasing globalization, or transnational nature of modern life; some useful sources are Appadurai (1996), Hannerz (1996), Ong (1999), and Tomas (1996). Although my research does not examine why intercultural weddings occur, these authors give us clues: as people move away from where they were born, the potential pool of spouses outside of their original group increases.

16. "To those of us classified to one extent or another by it, 'race' is both a curse and an invention, a problem and a celebration" (Penn, 1997b, p. 6). Also: "Too few people know the difference between racism (which does exist) and race (which doesn't). The reality of the former implies nothing about the latter" (Spencer, 1997, p. 130). Mukhopadhyay and Moses (1997) gave a considered overview of the nature of racial categories (see also Templeton, 1999).

17. McNamara, Tempenis, and Walton (1999) cited Census Bureau figures that demonstrate ½ of 1% of marriages were Black–White couples in 1970, but by 1995 that figure had jumped to nearly 2%. They also pointed out that in 1993, 9% of Black men who married that year married a White woman, which may be why many African Americans I interviewed thought the figure was far higher than 2%; from their perspective, nearly 1 in 10 Black male friends had married White women, not 1 in 100. Payne (1998, p. 164) cited 1994 figures showing 2.4% of all marriages in the United States are interracial.

18. See Roberts (1994) for good historical data on Black–White intermarriage in the United States; see Root (2001) for discussion of current realities. Wilson and Jacobson (1995) found that Black–White intermarriages are most likely among individuals with the following characteristics: if they are young, professional, upper middle class, college educated, and have no strong religious convictions. Kalmijn (1993) found the category of interracial marriages with the greatest current increase in numbers to be Black men with White women, and further found class to have relevance (the bride was more likely to marry up in class). For other discussions of who is likely to marry outside their own group, see Jansen (1982), Kitano et al. (1984), Kouri and Laswell (1993), Sandfur and McKinnell (1986), Tucker and Mitchell-Kernan (1990), and Wilson (1984).

19. "Intermarriage is regarded as the ultimate sign of assimilation because the children of intermarriage are no longer of one ethnic ancestry or another but a mix" (Clark, 1998, p. 143); and "marriage across ethnic and racial lines is the measure of true melting and of assimilation" (p. 153). See also Alba and Golden (1986), Gurak and Fitzpatrick (1982), Lieberson and Waters (1988), and Sung (1990) on the implications of intermarriage for assimilation.

20. Staples (1992) pointed out the impact of the history of Black–White interracial unions quite vividly: "It is a fact that the scars of nearly 400 years of the worst human bondage known are not healed, and disapproval by many black and white people of interracial love affairs is one of the wounds" (p. 970). See Kitchen (1993) for additional historical data on Black–White interracial marriages.

21. For the basics of the story, see Price (2000). A quick search on the internet turned up dozens of similar articles published in a wide range of newspapers across the country.

22. See also Leonard (1992). La Brack (1988) studied the same population, pointing out this is an example of what happens when two minority groups "share similar occupational and social status, work in the same locales" that is, they "eventually intermarry" (p. 189).

23. Taken from a description of a relationship posted on the web site "American love stories" (www.pbs.org/weblab/lovestories/stories/teamwork/story26.shtml). The groom is African American and working class; the bride is White and middle class. The influence of negative responses from others on the children of interracial cou-

ples is documented in Wagatsuma (1978), who studied the Black Japanese children resulting from liaisons between African American soldiers and Japanese women.

24. See Root (2001) for a good analysis of interracial marriage, especially for her consideration of what factors lead family members to accept the marriage; also her "ten truths about interracial marriage" (p. 167), which is an effective summary of what she learned.

25. Hechter (1986) is one who follows this broad usage of ethnicity:

> Whenever individuals or groups from different social formations come into each other's presence, they become aware of a host of differences that separate them, differences including language, demeanor, dress, music, cuisine, style of life, physiognomy, and values. Ethnicity is the social scientist's shorthand to describe this protean set of distinguishing markers. (p. 14)

Because I am discussing race, religion, and social class separately, it seems appropriate to use a narrower definition of ethnicity.

26. See Barth (1969) for the classic discussion of ethnic groups, and DeVos (1995) for the classic definition: "An ethnic group is a self-perceived inclusion of those who hold in common a set of traditions not shared by others with whom they are in conflict" (p. 18). For my purposes, Cohen's (1974) definition is more useful: "a collectivity of people who (a) share some patterns of normative behaviour and (b) form part of a larger population, interacting with people from other collectivities within the framework of a social system. The term ethnicity refers to the degree of conformity by members of the collectivity to these shared norms in the course of social interaction" (p. ix). Ellis (1999) provided one of the few considerations of ethnic groups and their influence on interaction by a communication scholar; Stephen (1992) called for study of the influence of nationality, race, ethnicity, and social class, although he only discussed studies of family life.

27. In her study of interracial friendship between young girls, Wulff (1995) discovered "To these girls, ethnic mixture was both attractive and self-evident, something they managed as cultural agents in their everyday lives" (p. 77). It is important that she found such clear sense of control, because so many researchers have traditionally assumed otherwise. Similarly, Leonard (1992) found that the children of Punjabi–Mexican marriages she documented had substantial control over their identity descriptors:

> The descendants themselves could choose among different markers of ethnic identity as they progressed through life. Being Hindu had meant one thing in early childhood, something slightly different as the second generation came of age, and something entirely different as large numbers of new immigrants challenged that identity. If the childhood years had emphasized the Mexican or Hispanic component of identity and early adulthood the Indian or Hindu component, as they matured, Punjabi-Mexicans emphasized their identity as Americans. (p. 202)

28. Staub (1989) stated this well: "As a negotiated and negotiable social identity, ethnicity is an achieved identity. Individuals and groups continually express and reaffirm a variety of social identities through social interaction" (p. 42). He demonstrated the application of this concept to the ways in which the group he studied, Yemenis in New York City, achieved their identity through the uses of food. The classic collections of readings on the construction of ethnic identity are Barth (1969), De Vos and

Romanucci-Ross (1982), Romanucci-Ross and De Vos, 1995). See Kendis (1989) for a discussion of the behavioral as well as psychological elements of ethnicity.

29. See also Bernard (1980) for similar comments, as "Intermarriage, while certainly not the only indicator of immigrant assimilation, provides an excellent means of measuring such interactions" (p. xix), and Whyte (1990) who found that over time "for reasons that are still not clear, there appears to be a real reduction in the tendency to marry within one's own ethnic origin group" (p. 103).

30. Hanassab and Tidwell (1998) found that "intermarriage was seen as a betrayal of important values" among the population they studied, Iranian Muslims and Iranian Jews who had immigrated to the United States. This same sense of intermarriage as betrayal is clearly evident in many groups.

31. The same issue arises for same-sex couples, some of whom go through quasi-weddings, sometimes even conducted by religious functionaries.

32. Taken from the web site "American love stories" (www.pbs.org/weblab/lovestories/stories/Navigating–Faith/story32815.shtml).

33. The same shift occurred in Canada, where in the 19th century intermarriage was across ethnic lines, but by the 20th it was more likely across religious lines (Richard, 1991).

34. Jewish–Christian unions are also still often controversial. When Rabbi Dena Feingold was elected President of the Wisconsin Council of Rabbis, several other members resigned because she admitted to conducting occasional interfaith weddings, although only for members of her own congregation who promised to raise the children Jewish (Grossman, 2000). The underlying concern here is the increasing frequency of Jewish–non-Jewish marriages in the U.S., standing now at about 50%. Cowan and Cowan (1987) gave a humorous peek into such unions, and the different assumptions individuals bring to them, with their story of a Christian wife married to a Jewish husband who "thought Passover and Hanukkah would decorate a life with an American core. They would be appendages to Christmas and Easter, part of a secular calendar" (p. 17). Unfortunately most discussions are more heated than humorous.

35. Interviewed April 20, 2000.

36. See Ellis (1999) for explicit discussion of class and its impact on communication; see Wray and Newitz (1997) for an unusual study of the intersection of race and class.

37. Charsley (1991) described the class differences in British weddings as being fewer than expected, although still evident. "Enthusiasm for cut, fresh flowers and a keenness to provide them in some quantity for decorating the church, if they can be afforded, is a predominantly middle-class value. It goes with a tendency to scorn the artificial blooms and feathers with which working-class weddings may be lavishly decorated" (p. 187).

38. See the substantial discussion throughout Spickard (1989).

39. In a later book, Spickard (1996) went on to show that by the 1990s Japanese Americans were intermarrying frequently, over 50% (p. 146). See also Diggs (2001) on Japanese American marriages.

40. As Yuri Lotman (1990) suggested, "the hottest spots for semioticizing processes are the boundaries of the semiosphere" (p. 136).

41. One resource in the study of cultural boundaries is Lamont and Fournier (1992). They suggested: "one of the most important challenges that we face today is understanding how we create boundaries and what the social consequences of such actions are" (p. 1).

42. Ulf Hannerz (1992) expanded on this theme, arguing for the study of "the inter-faces, the affinities, the confrontations, the interpenetrations and the flow-through, between clusters of meaning and ways of managing meaning. For those are the places and the events where, in some way and to some degree, diversity gets organized" (p. 22). And Barth (1969) pointed out: "The critical focus of investigation from this point of view becomes the ethnic *boundary* that defines the group, not the cultural stuff that it encloses" (p. 15). Saldivar (1997) also studied the border metaphor, as did Gupta and Ferguson (1997a), Conquergood (1991), Donnan and Wilson (1999), and Vila (2000).

43. To use a metaphor from linguistics, it is possible to argue that each intercultural wedding is an example of a *pidgin* (a new language created so two people who speak different languages can communicate). What follows a pidgin is a *creole* (a pidgin sufficiently developed to serve as the first language of the next generation). In other words, each couple attempts to find a way to create a new yet meaningful ceremony out of the different traditions they acknowledge but do not share; their children will take that particular combination of cultures for granted (regardless of its infrequency in the wider world), and will grow up with the combination providing their assumptions about, and expectations of, the world. Hannerz (1992) warned of danger in using metaphors in this way, since "whenever one takes an intellectual ride on a metaphor, it is essential that one knows where to get off" (p. 264). I will not push the pidgin–creole metaphor further here, although it is an interesting thought.

44. Stone (1988) suggested that families are primarily female inventions, which might explain why it is generally the bride (and her mother) who have the strongest opinions about what must occur in a wedding. Specifically, she said: "despite the convention of patrilineality, the family is essentially a female institution: the lore of family and family culture itself—stories, rituals, traditions, icons, sayings—are preserved and promulgated primarily by women" (p. 19).

45. Grearson and Smith (1995) reported that many would-be participants in their study of intercultural marriages thought their relationships were intercultural because of differences in age, geography, and profession. The same was true of those I interviewed. As I have done mostly, they discounted these as being more minor distinctions.

46. Rapport (1997) and Harris, Blue, and Griffith (1995) are among the recent books emphasizing individuality, and individual creativity, over cultural influence.

47. Schieffelin (1985; 1998) argued against the metaphor of behavior as text, on the grounds that behavior has a uniquely performative aspect that may be lost if the metaphor is followed too closely, and Geertz (1979) found text "dangerously unfocused" as a metaphor (p. 175) but then goes on to propose several advantages to the metaphor as well (p. 176). Becker and Mannheim (1995) said that "By treating social action as text, the analyst acknowledges that it has an objective quality that removes it from the grasp of individual participants ... Once an event has taken place, its meaning has escaped the grasp of the agent of the event and becomes common currency of the participants" (p. 239); see also Conquergood (1991). Collins (1996) argued that "The difficulty lies in grasping the complex reciprocal relatedness of the social and textual" (p. 203). See also Eco (1990) and Titon (1995) on the nature of world as text.

48. See Leeds-Hurwitz (1993) for an extensive discussion of signs.
49. For example, Kress (1988) provided a definition of communication as the study of social behavior as meaningful action organized in the form of texts. Real (1989) identified cultural studies as the center of the text metaphor in communication today when he said: "The positive mission of cultural studies is the interpretation of cultural phenomena, such as super media, as a text" (p. 53); see Fiske (1987) for further use of the metaphor of text with regard to media; see Shotter and Gergen (1989) for application of the metaphor to identity. This metaphor also has been applied to particular genres of communication; for example, see Hay (1989) on applying the metaphor of text to advertising. Halliday (1978) suggested linguistic texts function as potlatch, being "perhaps the most highly coded form of the gift" (pp. 139–140), arguing that they are especially valuable because giving a text away does not in any way impoverish the giver; once texts are expanded beyond language to other aspects of interaction, the same might be said of all forms of interaction and ritual: they also are gifts that also do not impoverish the giver (although for extreme forms, as with especially expensive weddings, this will no longer be true—these serve the same function as the original potlatches, with conspicuous consumption an important element of the event). Duncan and Ley (1993a) applied the metaphor of text to cultural geography, concluding that "Every landscape … is a text which may be read to reveal the force of dominant ideas and prevailing practices …" (1993b, p. 393). See Stock (1990) and Duncan (1990) for other sources on the metaphor of text as applied to the physical world. See also Branham and Pearce (1985), Solomon (1993), and Solomon Watson (1995) on the topic of text in communication, especially as related to context; see Buttny (1993), Duranti and Goodwin (1992), Hufford (1995), Hymes (1962), Katriel (1995) and Owen (1997) for further discussion of context.
50. See Leeds-Hurwitz (1989), and Gusfield (1989) for discussion.
51. Because the entire purpose of these materials is to document what happened, it proved relatively easy for me to obtain access to such materials, using them to study weddings that had already occurred. See additional comments on photographs and videotapes in the Methodological Appendix.
52. "So the very fact of transforming an event into a text raises the degree of its organization" (Lotman, 1990, p. 222).
53. As reported by Susan Oboikowich (1999) in Comm 440: Communication Codes, in Spring 1999.
54. Because there is so little explicit consideration of the concept of community within communication (Chaney, 1982, and Rothenbuhler, 2001, being exceptions), much of my discussion draws on literature from sociology and anthropology.
55. "Living in a mixed marriage can be an intimate performance of juggling identities and the ideologies associated with them, a dance sometimes threatening to perform as well as to behold" (Breger & Hill, 1998b, p. 28). Bateson (1993) pointed out the negative aspects of the juggling metaphor (that one will lose a ball) and recommends the metaphor of improvisation as more suited to multicultural communication.
56. See Stern (1987) for a wonderful photographic introduction to what can best be described as monocultural ethnic weddings.

57. This theoretical point is nicely made with regard to Zapotec materials by Royce (1982):
     The symbols of what is considered to be Zapotec are constantly being re-
     vised as Juchitecos move with the times. Dishes and bowls are still thrown to
     one's friends during the parades associated with *velas*, but now they are
     made of plastic instead of the pottery of ten years ago. The white flounce on
     the regional costume is rarely made of Swiss lace, which is almost unavail-
     able now; one sees instead permanent-pleated Dacron ruffles. The content
     of Zapotec style has changed gradually over the years, but the purpose to
     which it is put remains constant. It is manipulated by members of the
     Zapotec middle and upper classes and, in certain instances, by the Zapotec
     lower class in order to retain economic and political power within Juchitan in
     the face of opposition from outsiders (p. 177).

Interlude 2

FIG. 2:   Groom's cake showing *tunjo* figure used by Couple 84.

FIG. 3:   Close up of *tunjo* figure from Columbia.
Photo by Don Lintner, University of Wisconsin-Parkside.

*M*any American wedding receptions include not only a bride's cake (the large, white, multitiered affair referred to as the wedding cake), but a groom's cake (smaller, usually dark, often chocolate) as well. Couple 84 found this a perfect vehicle for meshing mainstream traditions with cultural identity and their own history together. As the bride reported:

> The groom's cake was special to us.... It was rich, dark chocolate, chocolate icing, and it had a Colombian symbol. It's called the *tunjo*. And it's a figurine you see in a lot of Colombian gold jewelry, it's from the indigenous tribes, and the first conversation I ever had with [groom] was about, he was wearing a lapel with, that was the *tunjo*, so we talked about it. *Tunjo* was just very Colombian, so we had that, we wanted that somewhere ... so it was on the cake.

In response to this description, the groom complained that he never got a chance to eat any of what was reputedly his cake.

The bride is from Texas, nominally Methodist but never religious, White and middle class. Her mother's grandparents came from Sweden, and her father's family came from England long ago, "but it was never anything talked about or felt was real"; instead, "we were Texas." Clearly, regional identity took priority over both ethnic and religious identity for her family, and this was reflected in several of the choices made when designing the wedding. The groom is from Colombia, born and raised Catholic; he was living in the United States when they met.

Before announcing their engagement, they took a trip to Colombia, so she could meet his family. While there, she acquired an engagement ring, though not quite in the usual American manner. She explained:

> His mother has always had a favorite jeweler who makes all of her jewelry for her, and because high-quality gold jewelry is very inexpensive in Colombia, one of the things in the way of shopping we were going to do was to have the jeweler come and visit. And when the jeweler was coming to visit, I said to [groom], "you know, in my culture, it's customary, when a couple gets engaged, that the man gives the woman an engagement ring." And he said, "really, well we don't do that in Colombia." Period. And I said to myself, "it's really important to me to have an engagement ring. I can't really

face going back and telling my friends and family we're engaged without an engagement ring," so I bought myself an emerald solitaire from my mother's, my mother-in-law's favorite jeweler, so that I could go back with an engagement ring.

The groom doesn't remember any conversation about it at the time, but considers this telling quite likely.

The original goal was to have a ceremony with two officiants, but that did not work out. They told this part of the story contrapuntally:

Groom: "The weddings I went to, I do not know of any wedding that was not part of mass. And I still don't conceive of a wedding without a mass."

Bride: "It would have excluded 95% of the guests [the Americans who could easily attend but who were Methodist]."

Groom: "And the 5% that knew how to follow it, wouldn't have understood it."

Bride: "Because it would have been in English, and all the Catholics knew Spanish."

Groom: "So it was not an option, really."

Bride: "It wasn't a sensible one."

They did try to have a Methodist minister work with the priest they had chosen, but he proved unwilling to cooperate sufficiently for a joint ceremony. In the end, they had the priest officiate but did not incorporate a mass.

After the engagement, the next event to occur was the rehearsal dinner. The bride told this part:

In Colombia as in the U.S., the groom's parents ordinarily pay for the rehearsal dinner, and ordinarily it would be in a nice restaurant. His parents were coming all the way from Colombia. This was going to be quite expensive, and we wanted to invite a lot of people to the rehearsal dinner, and we didn't think it was at all reasonable for them to foot the bill for all this. So we said, well, we'll just have a nice, informal dinner at our apartment. And we'll serve Colombian food, and that way all the Americans will get to see what Colombian food is like. And so we were going to have Sangria, and *arepas* which are like corn tortillas, only really thick, and they're very good, and a Colombian friend of ours was going to make *tamales*, which are not at all like Mexican *tamales*, except that they wrap them in banana leaves, but apart from that they're very different. She was going to make those, and, did we have *sancocho* do you know? Don't think so. So anyway, we had all this Colombian food planned. And his parents got there, his parents and his brother, and we said okay, here's the deal on the rehearsal dinner, not a thing to worry about, everything's under control. And they were sort of, "well, we could have paid for dinner at a nice restaurant." And it's not like they were really offended or angry but they were a little bit put out that their chance to contribute to this was sort of not in the picture, and also that the food we were serving was poor people food ... and one way they dealt with this is that, in Colombia, if you're throwing a party and if you're middle class, you have to have Chivas. It can't be any old alcohol, it has to be Chivas, by God, so they got a couple bottles of Chivas, and I think very little of it got drunk, because my family doesn't really drink hard liquor, so they had a refrigerator full of beer, and that went pretty quickly, but most of the Chivas was still there.

The attempt to have foods marking Colombian identity was not entirely successful because they simultaneously conveyed an inappropriate class marker. Even once the appropriate class marker, Chivas, was added by the groom's parents, the effort was still not entirely successful, both because the Americans present were not accustomed to it, preferring to drink beer, and because Chivas does not serve so clearly as a marker of class in the U.S. Expensive alcohol and food also serve as a class marker in the U.S., of course, but this particular form was not a readily available sign for the population at the wedding.

Although originally the bride had thought she would not want a long white gown, the alternatives she tried on just did not look right, so in the end her choice was fairly traditional (white fitted bodice, long skirt, lace) with a pink cummerbund but no veil. Instead the bride's mother helped her find a plain white hat, decorating it with some lace, "and then about 3 yards of wide white ribbon, so that it went down like to my knees. It went down all the way to my knees and it was like a veil, the length was there, it was like very elegant, but it wasn't a veil." The groom followed the American tradition of renting a tuxedo (black), rather than the Colombian tradition of wearing his own suit. The bridesmaids wore teal. When it came to what the parents would wear, the bride anticipated a likely cultural clash, and so was able to prevent it:

> I remember when we were giving his parents various instructions. His mother was having her dress made in Colombia. And I said to [groom] "tell her no black, no red, no white." And she said, through him, she could understand why she wouldn't wear white to a wedding, but what's wrong with black or red? And I thought, thank goodness it occurred to me to say, because I'd been to Colombia and they would come to a wedding in black or red … because it's elegant.

In the end, her mother-in-law chose a dress of teal fabric, which blended nicely with the bridesmaid's gowns.

There were flowers at the wedding. The bride held some pink and white flowers to match her gown, but mainly yellow roses "for the yellow rose of Texas. My parents wore yellow roses. My dad wore, in his lapel, a yellow rose, and my mother wore a yellow rose in her corsage." The groom's parents wore orchids "because they grow a lot of orchids in Colombia" where an orchid is the national flower. The groom wore a boutonniere with both a yellow rose and an orchid, to indicate his position between his bride and his parents. The flower girl wore pink (to match the bride's cummerbund).

The couple designed the wedding ceremony together with the priest who had a little booklet of suggestions, which they found surprisingly amenable. The vows, for example, were easy. They had expected to have to revise the language (e.g., taking out the part about how the bride would obey the groom which many modern couples revise). In fact, the bride stated, "It wasn't there to take out." They selected three readings: one from the Old Testament, one from the New Testament, and a sonnet from Shakespeare.

The majority of the wedding ceremony was conducted in English, but there were a few moments of Spanish. The priest spoke in English, the bride reported, "but he said if we wanted him to try it in Spanish he would try. And we thought, a Vietnamese priest, speaking in Spanish, maybe not." One of the readings during the service was read by the bride's brother, who surprised them:

> My brother was supposed to read one of the scripture lessons, and that was a big surprise because he got up and read it in Spanish. He speaks no Spanish at all but somebody at work had translated it for him and had run him through it. And so he got up and read it in Spanish, which none of us expected him to do, so that was nice.

The groom's brother read the other biblical passage, and it also proved a bit of a surprise:

> There was a responsive reading that his brother read, and so he read it in Spanish, and it was a response that all the Catholics knew what the responses were. And so it was kind of a funny moment, because the Catholics knew to stand up and they knew to say "blah-blah-blah." So that he'd read three lines, and they'd all say "blah-blah-blah." So this is like 10 or 12 people out of 100 stand up and respond, and the rest of them are going, what is going on here, because that was all in Spanish. It was hard to know, was it, it was partly strange because it was Spanish and partly because it was Catholic, because none of my family is Catholic.

This highlights the fact that for those who do not know how to interpret a cultural marker, it can be difficult even to identify the source of confusion. Differences in either language or religion could have been the cause here.

A variety of mainstream traditions were incorporated in the wedding and the reception. The ceremony included a unity candle, lit by the mothers of the bride and groom. At the reception there were matchboxes and napkins printed with the names of the bride and groom, and date of their wedding; the napkins were mint green, with teal lettering to match the color scheme; there were favors, probably the common Jordan almonds wrapped in net with a ribbon giving their names and the date, although they are no longer certain. There was a variant of the typical wedding cake, and a groom's cake, as already described. However, the bride did not throw her bouquet or have a garter toss, quite deliberately, as a statement about the inappropriateness of these activities in her mind (i.e., sexist ideals of marriage). There also was one unusual addition having nothing to do with cultural identity or politics: The bride's brother dressed up in a gorilla suit and picked her up "and there's a very nice picture in our wedding album of this gorilla, grabbing me ... I'm holding on to my precious hat, and dying of- laughing."

Of the various objects incorporated, the rings had greatest importance. Originally, the bride and groom chose matching gold bands for the ceremony, and the bride wore hers with the emerald engagement ring. But she is actually now on her third wedding band.

Well, the first one was very thin. And the first year that we were married, I slipped on some ice, and hung it on a chain link fence and it broke. So I had it soldered together and wore it for several years, soldered together, looking like something I'd gotten out of a crackerjack box. And then, one anniversary, when we renewed our vows in Colombia, because we were in Colombia where jewelry is inexpensive, I said, "okay, I want something more." And so he got me a wedding band and engagement ring with, both with several small emeralds. Always emeralds, because that's Colombia's thing. And so I had those for a while but the little emeralds kept falling out. And when they fell out, I'd have to take it to the jewelry store, it took a couple of weeks to get it replaced. And so I'd wear my old one, while that was happening. And then one fine day in the park with my old one I washed my hands and shook them to dry it, and (shhht) off it went, into the grass. I said "that's the end of that." I did get a metal detector and try to find it, but I knew I wasn't going to. And then, I had the ones with the emeralds, the small emeralds, and after a while I just got tired of them always falling out. So the last time we went to Colombia I got yet another one.

She now wears the third wedding band, and the second engagement ring (the emerald in the first one cracked and had to be replaced). In part, this detail is interesting for being uncommon, but it gains importance when we learn that it follows family precedent: "And I should say, this is a time-honored tradition in his family. His mother has had several wedding rings. She has one for a few years, then gets tired of it, has it melted down, made into something else.... In this one thing I think I'm like my mother- in-law."[1]

A caterer prepared the food at the reception, and it did not include anything Colombian; having Colombian food at the rehearsal dinner seemed sufficient. They served champagne, the traditional drink of special occasions like weddings, but no other alcohol, a deliberate choice because many of the guests had long drives home. The music included "The Eyes of Texas," some country western, and some polkas. "The connection to Germany is only that my uncle was stationed there for a few years during the war," but also polkas are not uncommon in Texas dance halls.

After the wedding, the bride initially kept her wedding dress in her old room in her mother's house. A few years later, much to her amazement:

> She tried to sell it, she put an ad in a newspaper and tried to sell my wedding dress.... Without telling me. And she had a friend getting married, and she had the friend come over and try it on in case it would fit her. And told me after the fact.... And it was after all of this that she said, "oh by the way, [friend's name] tried on your wedding dress and it didn't fit, and I haven't been able to sell it." And I said, "what are you doing selling my wedding dress? You didn't buy it!" "Well, what are you going to use it for?" And she sort of didn't understand that that wasn't the point. So I have my wedding dress in a box, in a plastic box. I do take it out.

Several other symbols from the wedding lasted past the end of the event. First, they saved the top layer of the wedding cake to eat on their first anniversary, and it was reported to have been delicious "because they told us exactly what to do to be sure it didn't get freezer burn." Second, they had photographs taken, and view the photo album at least once a year, in various combinations of the parents and the two children they have had since they married. There was one other connection to Colombia in terms of material culture: His parents gave them Colombian blankets as a wedding present, which are very warm and which they kept on their bed for many years.

This couple had an abbreviated honeymoon, incorporating a rather unusual point of interest:

> His parents and brother were still there, none of them speaking English, so we couldn't be gone for very long, but we did want to go somewhere, so we went to this lovely old turn of the century hotel, down on the Gulf coast ... and stayed for three days. And in the area was the South Texas Nuclear Project ... A museum defending nuclear power as clean and safe and the reason I knew about it was the whole time I was at [university] there were protests against the STNP and so I said, wouldn't it be cute to go the STNP on our honeymoon. So, not everybody goes to see a nuclear reactor on their honeymoon ... it was unique. But the nice thing about that short simple honeymoon is that we have then felt entitled to as many honeymoons to exotic locations as we can manage, so we've had lots and lots more.

They originally planned to have a second ceremony in Colombia, but that never happened. Instead they renewed their vows on their 8th anniversary, together with his parents who were celebrating their 40th anniversary, because the wedding dates were very close together.

They had a big party, with new clothes, new rings, lots of food and friends. Because a modified ceremony for a wedding when one participant is not Catholic exists in Colombia, they chose a variant of that for their renewal of vows. And they are talking about another renewal of vows on their 18th anniversary, which will be his parents' 50th anniversary. The bride anticipates choosing yet another new ring for that occasion.

This couple succeeded in combining those identities of greatest importance to them: the fact that she is from Texas (the yellow roses, the music), and he is from Colombia (the gold/emerald rings, the food at the rehearsal). They included a nod to religion (having the priest officiate), and multiple references to personal history (from the *tunjo* symbol he was wearing when they met to their choice of where to go on their honeymoon). They incorporated family and close friends into their ceremony. They even included a variety of mainstream American traditions (wedding cake, wedding gown, unity candle), although they revised these at will (the ribbons in lieu of a veil, for example, or the omission of the bouquet and garter toss).

NOTE

1. Although changing wedding rings from the one given at the wedding is symbolically odd, it is actually less uncommon than I had initially expected. Couple 99, for example, reported that the bride's original wedding ring was "a highly set solitaire diamond subject to catching on things," and so she later got a new one to match her husband's, that is, silver and gold with little diamond chips. And, for their 25th anniversary, Couple 106 chose a new band for her, melting down the old engagement ring and wedding band both. They then used the resulting gold and diamonds to make pendants for each of their daughters. Couple 91 chose platinum for their rings, but the bride's broke after the wedding, and they replaced it with the same design, but now made in gold, which is a harder metal and less fragile.

2

Community

"Community, therefore, is where one learns and continues to practice how to 'be social'. At the risk of substituting one indefinable category for another, we could say it is where one acquires 'culture.'"
—Cohen (1985, p. 15)

Every ethnography begins with the identification of the particular community studied: a group of people with similar experiences and expectations, who can most often understand each other's intentions, who generally share a language, and so forth.[1] This ethnographic study of intercultural weddings is unusual in examining the combination of different communities through the ritual of wedding ceremonies, investigating not one but the overlap between multiple communities.[2] This change in emphasis reflects the shift taking place more generally in the field of anthropology (although it has not had as much influence on the field of communication as yet). Sherry Ortner (1991) provided a good summary of the logic behind the change in focus:

> In the past there has been a strong tendency on the part of many anthropologists studying America to "ethnicize" (the domestic version of "orientalize") the various groups, classes, and even institutions (e.g., corporations) under study, to treat them as if they were in effect separate tribes.... There are indications now that the anthropology of America is shifting on this point (this study is part of that shift), and beginning to recognize the importance of studying the relationships between whatever unit one undertakes to study and the larger social and cultural universe within which it operates. (p. 186)

Similarly, Hannerz (1992) concluded: "one of the main weaknesses of writings on subcultures is that they often give scant attention to what happens at the interfaces within the larger culture" (p. 69).[3] This study describes what happens at the interfaces, not just between one group and the larger culture surrounding it but between multiple groups.[4] As Halperin (1998) pointed out: "Community is not just a place, although place is very important, but a series of day-to-day, ongoing, often invisible practices" (p. 5). It is immediately obvious when a person crosses from one geographic community to another but, in today's world, communities often share geographic space, and it is not always immediately obvious that different sets of longstanding but often invisible practices are in play when people from different communities interact. This book describes how real people handle the issues arising from the attempt to combine different communities' practices.

COMMUNITIES INVOLVED IN AN INTERCULTURAL WEDDING

There are at least three communities to be considered in any intercultural wedding occurring within the United States:

- The bride's community;
- The groom's community; and
- The dominant, mainstream culture within which their wedding occurs.

"Community" here includes at the least the family, relatives, and friends, of the bride and groom, involving any and all relevant national, ethnic, racial, religious, and class affiliations.[5] Of course, either or both of the marriage partners may come from a heterogeneous community, complicating matters noticeably.

Intercultural weddings then, most simply, entail combining the expectations of two (or more) dissimilar communities. (If both the bride and groom belong to a single community, their wedding is not intercultural but monocultural and the problem does not arise.) It was still surprisingly rare for Americans of a previous generation to move outside of their community of origin in the search for marriage partners. Of course, if they did, that increases the likelihood that their children will do so again.[6] (This makes sense because, as with any idea introduced into the home, cultural difference comes to be taken for granted by the children of those who had to struggle to get their parents to accept even small differences between themselves and their marriage partners.)

Like any ritual uniting members of different communities, an intercultural wedding erases the currently existing (although imaginary) boundary lines around the community, drawing new ones, uniting what was previously separated. The boundary lines are imaginary because they are social constructions rather than physical barriers. (No physical rope ties all the members of a single ethnic group together, although they may sometimes act as a unit.) As Cohen

(1985) suggested, "we approach community as a phenomenon of culture: as one, therefore, which is meaningfully constructed by people through their symbolic prowess and resources" (p. 38). To say that community is *constructed* is to consider it a social fact (an idea), not a physical fact (a natural formation). This suggests that we must attend to the significance of drawing a new boundary line joining members of different communities together as a new unit, as happens in an intercultural wedding. Like the old boundary line, this indicates a separation between those perceived as members of the community and those perceived as outside membership in the community. Thus there is still a boundary drawn between members and nonmembers. Where that line falls has changed, however, making all the difference in the world to the participants. As social constructions these boundary lines are simultaneously quite flexible (they exist wherever people assume they exist) and quite rigid (we grant them a symbolic reality not readily open to revision).[7]

POTENTIAL SOLUTIONS TO THE PROBLEM OF DESIGNING AN INTERCULTURAL WEDDING

Although an unlimited number of unique solutions to the issues posed by the conflicting community expectations of intercultural weddings exists, these fall into four major varieties:

1. A wedding presenting one of the possible cultures to the exclusion of the other(s), thus ignoring the problem.
2. A wedding presenting two (or more) possible cultures in different ceremonies, thus honoring both (or all) but maintaining them as separate, thus avoiding many of the difficulties.
3. A wedding presenting no one's culture, thus avoiding the issue entirely.
4. A wedding presenting a combination of two (or more) cultures in a single ceremony, thus facing the difficulties head-on and seriously attempting to resolve them.

Each of these major types are briefly described next. The majority of this book documents examples of the fourth type because they occasion the greatest cultural creativity and are therefore the most significant theoretically. All four types are possibilities, however, so it is important that all be clearly understood.

A Wedding Presenting One of the Possible Cultures to the Exclusion of the Other(s)

Having a wedding that completely follows either the bride's or groom's traditions is one of the simplest solutions, but inherently disingenuous because it denies the intercultural nature of the marriage. This variant often occurs when one member of the couple considers it quite important to have a wedding conforming to religious or cultural tradition, whereas the other does not particularly care, feels obligated to forego tradition, or willingly gives up tradition for the sake of harmony. Respecting his family's code for honoring the bride's family, one marriage between a Mexican American of Catholic faith and an Anglo American bride of Russian Orthodox faith followed her traditions almost entirely, the exceptions being a closing prayer by a Catholic priest at the ceremony and *mariachi* music at the reception (Couple 11). They divorced 5 months later. I asked the groom if he saw a connection between these two facts, in other words if he thought giving in so completely to her expectations at the wedding had carried implications for their marriage (having given in once, she might then expect him to always give in to her desires). He said he had not thought so at the time but later wondered if that had been symptomatic of their difficulties in managing personal and cultural differences. My suggestion here is not that this wedding design somehow caused a problem, but rather that it was a symptom of relational issues that were never directly addressed or unable to be resolved by this couple.[8]

Sometimes an international couple gives one culture's traditions pre-eminence during the ceremony based on where they decide to hold the ceremony. In this case it makes sense to follow the traditions of that country, to the exclusion of any other. Couple 22 involved a Japanese bride and American groom, who held their ceremony in Japan exclusively, following traditional Japanese expectations. This case incorporated an interesting elaboration: When the bride was born, her parents planted a tree in her honor. For her wedding, they had the now mature tree cut down and made into furniture for the new couple's home. Obviously having the wedding held in the country where the tree had grown facilitated this gift. In this case, because the couple had already decided to live in her home country, there was no conflict caused by having a Japanese ceremony.[9] In other cases, couples have reported considerable pressure from family members (especially extended family members, who might not be able to attend a wedding in another country) wishing to influence their decision.

Couple 71 involved an American bride (Church of God in Christ) and a Cook Island groom (Cook Island Christian Church). The bride told me "we did not combine elements of both cultures at all. We never really even thought of it, that our wedding would be an 'identity statement,' or statement about each of our cultures. We got married in my husband's village, and I just went along and did what they do there." Later she added:

> I felt that since we were marrying on his island, it was fine for me to go along with their customs. But the customs are not very different from mine. I wanted to be married in church, and so did he (as opposed to the beach or some other place). We had a reception in the Sunday School hall of the church, with plenty of food, and a white cake, but no alcohol. This is

the same thing we would have done if we had gotten married at my home church in California. I'm sure that if he had wanted to do something wildly different from what I would have wanted to do at home, I wouldn't have felt so comfortable going along with whatever he wanted. But since almost everything he suggested was the same as what I would have suggested if we had been in my home, I felt happy doing what he wanted to do.

They disagreed, however, about the choice of wedding dress. "Their custom is that the groom buys the wedding dress for the bride. He kept wanting to get one for me, but I had one that I wanted to wear. It was a white dress that I had bought on his island the year before—a totally Rorotonga-style muumuu, but an unusually beautiful one. I wanted to wear that, and I did." Both the bride and groom wore the traditional tiaras and *leis* made of fragrant white flowers (*tiare Maori*). In this case, as the bride explicitly noted, the fact that there were few substantive differences in their opinions of appropriateness made their decision easier.

An American groom marrying an Armenian bride described his participation in a traditional Armenian service (held in an Armenian church, with most of the service in Armenian, and an Armenian band at the reception) as a way for him to become accepted into the bride's family (Couple 29). By showing his willingness to participate in her traditions in lieu of insisting on his own, he successfully facilitated his integration as a new member of her family.[10] Similarly, the groom of Couple 107, an American married to a woman of Chinese descent, made a point of going to her father to ask permission to marry her in order to follow Chinese tradition. "I did go to *ask*, I didn't go to *tell* him we were getting married. I did go to say, if this is okay with you because I felt, and rightly so I found out later, if he wasn't going to say okay, it really would alienate her from her family in a way that I don't think would be healthy for anybody, so it was an interesting meeting."[11]

For other couples, the decision about what should happen was determined by whose family was more attached to their traditions. For Couple 4, it was important to the groom's family, who were Greek and quite religious, that the wedding take place in the Greek Orthodox church.[12] The bride's family (German, Irish, and French on one side, and Bohemian on the other, all of whom were Roman Catholic), not being as religious, had less impact on the wedding. It seemed obvious to this couple that the wishes of family to whom it was more important should take priority. Similarly, the choice seemed clear to Couple 88. The groom said: "Her mom really wanted it to be in a Catholic setting and I'm Lutheran. My mom wasn't really too concerned. I don't really go to church a lot."[13] Because it had more significance for one family than the other, so it seemed obvious to the couple whose wishes should prevail. In other cases, one of the parents of the new couple suddenly demanded visible adherence to a church or set of ethnic traditions that, until then, had not played a terribly significant role in the family's life. This never failed to confuse the couple, who would express astonishment at the expectation that they conform in a way their parents never had.

A Wedding Presenting Two (or More) Possible Cultures in Different Ceremonies

Holding two separate ceremonies serves as a second possible wedding design. In this way the bride and groom honor both of their traditions. However, this resolution pretends there is no contradiction between them and so can be more a temporary finesse than a permanent resolution of the matter. In some cases, an international couple will have two ceremonies, one in each country, based primarily on logistical constraints. For example, Couple 34 held one ceremony in the United States with a Protestant preacher, and another in Mexico with a Catholic priest.[14] As her extended family in Mexico was unable to get to the United States for the ceremony there, another was held when the couple went to visit her relatives. This solution has the advantage of permitting both sides of the family to present the new family member to relatives and friends. At the same time, it has the disadvantage of not bringing the two sides of the family together on a happy occasion, another traditional (and often quite significant) function of a wedding ceremony. Instead, it maintains the two families as essentially "separate but equal." Separate but equal being a difficult balance to achieve, this solution has the disadvantage that someone often ends up feeling slighted in the end.

An Italian American bride and a Chinese groom decided to please everyone by separating the events into two parts. On Saturday, they had a traditional Italian American Catholic ceremony and reception for 175 hosted by her parents. Then on Sunday, the bride "donned a traditional Chinese red and gold silk wedding dress, given to her by her in-laws, and both families participated in a Chinese wedding feast in Manhattan, hosted by the groom's parents" (Mayer, 1992a, p. 15). Speeches at the banquet Sunday were given in both Chinese and English. Family members wore red badges to indicate their relationship to the couple, a Chinese custom. The couple and the groom's parents had a private tea ceremony on Sunday, following a Chinese tradition. Although they divided the events, there was overlap of participants: About 100 family members attended the ceremonies held on both days.[15]

Other couples also choose this solution when substantial differences in religious beliefs come into play, as was the case with Couple 12, a Hindu–Christian couple (although nonpracticing in either faith), in which the bride and groom each had one Hindu parent from India and one Christian parent from the United States. In this case also the two ceremonies were held on consecutive days, with completely different clothing (a traditional white bridal gown for the American Christian ceremony; two different *saris* at different parts of the Hindu ceremony, one white and one red). There were also different participants (not only the officiants but the extended family members and friends who attended each ceremony varied substantially—all those invited to the church wedding were also invited to the Indian ceremony, although they did not all come; members of the local Indian community were invited to the latter only, adding considerably to the number of guests). Aside from the bride and groom and their immediate family members, flowers provided the only continuity between the two ceremonies. Each reception illustrated quite different selections of food and music. The traditional American white bridal gown worn for the American ceremony was actually made in India by a seamstress sent sketches and the bride's measurements, so there was some small crossing of cultural boundaries of which many of the participants were not even aware but, on the whole, the differing traditions were kept separate.

In the United States, which is largely Christian, the same issues arise whenever Christians marry Muslims, Hindus, or Buddhists, and so two ceremonies have become the standard solution, as in the cases previously described. There is more often an effort to combine rituals with one Jewish and one Christian participant, presumably because more similarities in traditions exist. Thus many of my examples throughout the remainder of this book document that particular combination.

Weddings in the United States actually involve recognition from multiple authorities: secular as well as sacred. The secular authorities normally do not object to recognizing a union between individuals following different religious guidelines, but religious leaders often do, thus forcing the couple to have either two ceremonies, or none. Couple 21, a Muslim–Baptist couple, decided two ceremonies were necessary. It was specifically noted that they took care not to serve pork at the reception of the Baptist ceremony, lest they offend some of the Muslim guests, documenting a noticeable but unusual overlap of participants.[16]

It also sometimes happens that a couple will have a first, secret civil ceremony, and a second, more formal ceremony with family present. Often this occurs when the wedding itself is for some reason controversial, and so the couple decides to make a legal commitment before convincing family members to accept its inevitability. In their book, *Love in black and white*, Gail and Mark Mathabane (1992) follow this pattern. He is South African and Black; she is American and White. Even after they had been legally married, at the point when they were willing to make a permanent commitment to one another, as Gail explained they knew "in the eyes of society, we would not be considered truly married unless there was a wedding, and I must admit, a part of me did not want to miss out on any of life's official rites of passage" (p. 137).

In other cases, the issue is not so much controversy as mere convenience. Couple 73 involved a German bride and American groom. The bride's parents already are an intercultural couple, one Protestant and the other Catholic; the bride considers herself Protestant. The groom's family is Italian Catholic on both sides. They first had a civil ceremony in the United States, at city hall, incorporating no ritual elements. About 6 months later they held a religious ceremony in the small town in Germany where the bride grew up. In this case, a few concessions were made to the groom's traditions. As a courtesy, the bride asked the Catholic priest of that town to conduct the ceremony, which he agreed to do. He performed a traditional Catholic mass (the groom took communion but the bride did not), conducting the service partially in English, to permit the groom and his family to understand the critical elements, and Protestant songs were included as well as Catholic ones, this time for the bride's family. Everything else was essentially German: the couple's clothing (the bride's outfit was described as being more like a European evening dress than traditional American "princess" wedding dress; the groom wore a suit rather than the American tuxedo); the traditional German wedding contract (signed by the bride and her sister, the groom and his brother, as well as the priest); the music at the reception (mainly a German band in *lederhosen*, but also Italian folk songs, because the bride liked that music), and the food (no traditional American wedding cake, but a German dessert table, with fruitcake, and a variety of Bavarian sweets, such as *oblaten* and *lebkuchen*). They held a party the night before the wedding, but because the bride did not appreciate the American custom of bachelor parties, they invited everyone, male and female, young and old, friends and family, and felt that all participants had a great time. In this case, the formal wedding followed primarily German expectations, because it occurred in Germany, with a few nods to the groom's language and religious traditions as a matter of courtesy. One of the bride's parents shared her new husband's religion, and so no one viewed the compromises as terribly awkward or even difficult.

Yamani (1998) documented the fact that the international couples in her research sometimes found it necessary to hold two entire weddings in two countries in order to satisfy everyone. In this case, each ceremony followed the traditions of the country within which it occurred. This solution permits everyone on both sides to be happy, because the wedding they see follows their expectations of what it should look like. It would, however, be interesting to investigate whether later solutions to cultural differences among couples who chose this solution over a single intercultural ceremony differed. Those who have two entirely separate weddings essentially duck the issue, leaving it unresolved for a later time. Clearly the couple cannot give equal time to both home countries for their entire lives, and at some point choices will have to be made.

A Wedding Presenting No One's Culture

It is possible for couples to choose to entirely avoid the issues posed by an intercultural union in several ways.

Civil Ceremony.   The first obvious solution is to ask a judge (or some other neutral, but legally accredited figure) to perform a civil ceremony, accompanied by virtually no ritual. Mayer (1985), studying Jewish–Christian weddings, found this to be the most frequent choice as did Leonard (1992), studying Hindu or Sikh–Catholic weddings. This choice has the advantage of being least likely to offend participants from either family by substituting only civil recognition of the union for the more standard combination of civil and religious recognition. So long as both sides of the family recognize the same civil law, difficulties are avoided. Although a civil ceremony usually is held in a courthouse, Couple 42, combining a Russian Jewish groom with a German American Catholic bride, held the ceremony in the judge's home.[17] Several couples formed of international students from different countries whose parents could not attend reported choosing a civil ceremony at city hall as the simplest solution. The only problem is that "legal registration is distinct from and utterly insufficient to the *social* recognition of matrimony conferred in the performance of a wedding ceremony" (Kendall, 1996, p. 9; she described the situation in Korea, but it holds as well for the United States). However, some couples deem legal recognition alone to be better than nothing, when social recognition becomes difficult or impossible to obtain.

In lieu of a judge, a couple can choose an officiant in one of several relatively neutral religions who helps the bride and groom emphasize their similarities in general terms, ignoring their (very real) differences. Algernon Black, a leader in the Ethical Culture Society, published a book in 1974 describing the weddings he conducted, many of which were intercultural. One of these joined a Zulu man raised in South Africa with a Greek Orthodox woman raised in Turkey: "Since neither was traditionally religious, it was easy to agree on a simple ceremony which would emphasize the common ground of faith in human values and human potentialities" (p. 85). This couple's clothing made a particular impression on Black. The groom was "naked except for a loincloth made of zebra hide … His head was topped by turban of zebra hide, and on his left arm was a shield of the same zebra design. In his right hand he held a spear." The bride "wore a long plum-colored gown reaching to the ground … around her throat hung a brilliant blue turquoise necklace sent especially by the Zulu people in honor of the occasion" (p. 86).

Similarly, James Ishmael Ford, a Unitarian Universalist minister, shared with me the script of a wedding service he had designed. Although his central intention was for it to serve "as a vehicle for two people to make profound promises to each other," it was simultaneously designed to avoid potentially offensive elements. He described it as "essentially your standard western Christian service, pretty much generic, anything you look at in anybody's prayer book for the last 600 years is pretty much it. Except that it's inclusive language, except there's no direct references to divinity, and except that everybody makes the same promises to each other." Even so, he reported:

What I've found in this service is that Catholics, Episcopalians, Lutherans, Methodists, Congregationalists, they all think they've just heard their own wedding ... And yet there's nothing to offend a Jew, a Buddhist, a Hindu, or a reasonable atheist.... What I believe I've achieved here is something that's not intrinsically offensive to anyone and yet has substance ... I would call this an American liturgy.[18]

For similar reasons Couple 91 chose a Unitarian minister; as the bride put it, "they marry any kind, the Unitarians." In this case, the issue was that the bride was Catholic and Mexican, whereas the groom was Protestant and American.[19]

In addition to Ethical Humanists and Unitarians, there is a large category of minor religions (in the sense of having a brief history and few adherents) permitting practitioners to receive legal authorization to conduct wedding services with only nominal preparation. These seem especially prevalent in California, where it is not uncommon to request a permit entitling one to conduct weddings through the mail, in exchange for a small fee. Due to the value placed on freedom of religion, neither state nor federal governmental authorities wish to eliminate the possibility of any religion setting their own standards for ordination or the acquisition of a license to perform weddings. Because they do not come from well-established religions having strict guidelines for membership, many of these officiants are not only happy to celebrate intercultural weddings, but see themselves as fulfilling an important need. A surprising number of those interviewed could not even identify the religious connection that permitted their officiant to conduct the ceremony, when for a prior generation that would have been the sole criterion.

Eloping.   A second possible way to avoid the issue of differing family expectations is to elope, thus making do with virtually no ceremony.[20] (Eloping generally involves the same civil ceremony as that conducted by a judge, and occasionally even involves a religious officiant, but without prior notice to family and friends it generally feels to participants like only a partial replication of the standard model wedding.) In some cases, couples choose eloping as the only possible solution to extreme conflict between their families. Couple 50 reported that the groom's parents wouldn't attend the ceremony if they married in her Lutheran church, and the bride's parents wouldn't come if they married in his Catholic church. To resolve the impasse, they finally went to city hall, with no notice, and no parents in attendance. (In this case, the couple was in fact officially later recognized as married in both churches, though that additional step is uncommon.)[21]

In describing British "register office weddings" (comparable to the brief ceremony occurring in an American courthouse or city hall when a couple elopes), Leonard (1980) pointed out that they "have the same basic structure as a proper wedding but with each item drastically reduced (e.g., the bride in a short white dress with no veil, a buffet reception at home) and some items omitted altogether; the whole being marked by less formality, less publicity and less solemnity" (p. 116). These characteristics usually hold as well for American city hall weddings, and can be explained in semiotic terms as an example of metonymy (the part standing for the whole). Deprived of the opportunity to display all of the symbols they might originally have expected, the couple opt for an abbreviated version rather than none.

Mainstream American Weddings.   Most of the weddings described here took place in the United States, where there is always an alternative to choosing no ritual, and that is to choose a neutral one. Though the various groupings of Americans do many things differently, we share a language and a common body of media products (books, magazines, newspapers, television shows, films, internet, etc.) and, as a result, we share many assumptions and expectations.[22] In particular, the United States has an extremely strong tradition of what may be termed "dominant generic mainstream American" weddings, virtually independent of any strong ethnic or racial or religious identification, sometimes called "white weddings" (referring to the predominant color displayed in material culture choices, not the race of the participants). In fact, although the symbols utilized in "white weddings" are largely White, Anglo-Saxon and Protestant (WASP) in their primary affiliation, this is somehow (surprisingly) invisible to many of the participants, WASP culture being the closest thing to a "taken-for-granted" within the larger American mix of cultures.[23] As Crane (1992) put it, "The dominant culture is always presented as *the culture*, the reference point for the society as a whole" (p. 87). Not only television, films and books, but newspaper articles and the many magazines available specifically for those planning a wedding (as Ingraham, 1999, outlined in detail) all popularize this mainstream image of the wedding.

As with other aspects of mainstream culture, mainstream weddings can be described as relying on the lowest common denominator, and thus they are often quite bland. Despite this blandness, the mainstream wedding is a difficult tradition to miss. Any wedding organized in the United States will be judged by participants in terms of the extent to which they can understand it in light of their prior experiences, and shared expectations. It will either conform to the norms, or take them into account in a variety of ways, but it is virtually impossible for couples not to have their choices judged in relation to pre-existing expectations. Even deliberately *not* doing the expected will be interpreted in relation to it. For those with little knowledge of their own traditions, a mainstream wedding provides a safe outline. This was the case for Couple 38, with a fourth generation Japanese American bride whose family had completely acculturated to mainstream American norms, so it seemed obvious to have what she termed a "regular" American wedding.[24]

Although it would be a gross oversimplification to assume a single standard for American weddings, and no two weddings are ever identical, the common baseline used by the majority of Americans when they design a wedding forms what I call a "mainstream" wedding. As such, it functions as one of many mechanisms used to create a sense of community across the entire United States.[25] As Williams (1996) suggested, "To establish its stable existence, a community must create a sense of belongingness, a commonality of purpose and aim, and identification between subjects" (p. 93). Sharing assumptions about the central elements of rituals, such as weddings, is one vehicle through which we create a sense of community across groups that have little daily contact with each other but a shared political identity as a nation.

The media are largely responsible for constructing our shared identity. In this case, that means the vast majority of film weddings follow mainstream guidelines. Hall (1977) suggested the media fill this role as a way of coping with the plurality of world views common to modern society.[26] Being widely available and generally shared, the media serve to bring common images and experiences to a wide range of audiences, and eventually their images become the taken-for-granted (Gross, 1989). When this happens, ethnic group norms become marked as noticeably different, requiring explanation, whereas the mainstream norms become both increasingly bland and expected.[27]

Where does this standard come from? The simple answer is "tradition." More specifically, certain elements of wedding rituals are repeated over time until they come to be accepted as normal and appropriate, leading to the assumption that they will continue to be present, and to surprise at their omission. Appadurai (1996) called this "habituation through repetition" (p. 67). As Anderson (1983) pointed out, any country, including the United States, is an "imagined community"—although we do not all know each other, we assume we share certain traits in common, take some of the same assumptions for granted. Although we never meet most of the other members of this "super" community, we acknowledge our similarities. The various mass media, in conveying multiple images of mainstream events but very few of any other sort, are largely responsible for making this possible.[28] Newspapers, films, popular magazines and web sites (including those specifically targeted to brides) promulgate the mainstream wedding.[29] The lists that many of the popular magazines provide to help a bride organize all of the details necessary to planning an elaborate mainstream wedding send a clear message about the expectations of what should be included.[30] In fact, nonmainstream weddings are so uncommon, they may make it into the newspapers. As is the case with many others, my local paper, *The Milwaukee Journal/Sentinel*, regularly prints photographs (usually with only captions, not accompanying articles) of weddings that violate the standard in some significant way. So that a wedding held for a baseball player at County Stadium,[31] or a wedding held for a trainer at the Milwaukee Zoo incorporating a sea lion,[32] will be held up as unusual examples worthy of publicity. The interest extends to noteworthy events held overseas, as when a fashion show in Tel Aviv in 1991 included a bridal gown with the model wearing a gas mask rather than the more traditional headpiece.[33] Occasionally an actual wedding will be incorporated into a public performance, as when two singers were married in a concert called "The Honor of your Presence" in Milwaukee in 1992. Invited guests had reserved seating, but the general public was also eligible to attend both the concert and the reception, for a price.[34]

Couple 109 was typical in describing how they were influenced by prior weddings in the planning of their own.[35] This wedding united a Catholic groom (with a mother who had been raised Lutheran, but who had converted in order to marry his Catholic father) and a Lutheran bride. In some cases there was an explicit borrowing of a discrete element, as when the bride said, "We just picked a DJ that we had heard at several weddings, we thought he would be good. And we told him that he could play a variety of music." At other points, it was more a matter of keeping track of what others did, in order to have a range of appropriate behaviors to choose from, as with church bulletins. (These now see common use as a tool explaining particular components of a wedding and their significance for guests who might otherwise miss the intent; as such, they are actually a good indicator of the increase of intercultural weddings. After all, if everyone can safely be expected to know the meaning of all elements, there is little need to provide explanations in writing.) The bride said, "I knew I was getting married, so, a lot of my friends had gotten married in the last two years, so I saved all of their bulletins from the weddings." She specifically noted having gotten the following ideas from friends' weddings: to put a thank you to everybody for coming, to include notes explaining parts of the service, having the bride and groom each write something about the people included in the wedding party, and including a poem at the end. At other points, the bride admitted having no idea of the meaning of an element, but as others had included it, she did as well. For example, as one part of their Lutheran ceremony, they lit the unity candle (originally a part of only Catholic ceremonies, but now spreading to other Christian denominations, including Lutherans). The bride admitted: "Do you want to know something? I don't even know the history behind it. I just know that's what people do. That's just something that you do when you get married." (Later the bride realized that the unity candle is incorporated in the Lutheran hymnal, which is why they and others include it.) And at still other points, they made a deliberate decision not to follow traditions they had observed at prior weddings. The groom said they chose to put out bells for people to use when demanding that they kiss at the reception, rather than leaving that function to the more typical clinking of silverware on glasses, because "we wanted something different and unique." (This was actually a bit less unique than he realized, as bells are increasingly commonly provided for this purpose.) And the bride quite deliberately created a totally new invention for the reception: she made a photo album of friends and family to serve as guest book, pointing out that: "It gave people the opportunity to sign the book wherever they felt it was of importance to their lives ... we didn't want just the traditional regular book. How often are you going to look at that? This is something we look at all the time." Every couple walks this line between following the traditions their peers incorporate and inventing something new. The trick is to incorporate enough tradition that people recognize what they are attending as a wedding, but enough new elements to successfully demonstrate your individuality.

Why does a standard exist at all? Why is it not appropriate for everyone to just create their own, totally unique, ceremony? Although everyone is unique, and each ritual different from every other example of even the same ritual, people are more comfortable if some elements repeat from variant to variant of a form. Such repetition permits us to disattend the ordinary aspects of an event and attend only to the noteworthy elements. Because there will always be fewer new distinctive elements, this cuts down drastically on the amount of information we have to process in order to understand what occurs.[36] Shotter (1989) addressed what happens when people fail to perform as they are expected to: "If we fail to perform in both an intelligible and legitimate manner, we will be sanctioned by those around us" (p. 141). Such sanctions work to prohibit even the thought of deviation. Schwartz (1992) reported that in the farm community she studied, people "share the view that the church is the proper site for a wedding ceremony, and other possibilities go unexplored. Husbands and wives are properly united only by priests and ministers" (p. 108).

Wedding specialists in particular rely heavily on the existence of a common set of expectations for weddings. As a result, these serve as a neutral choice for a couple who are having difficulty in deciding whose cultural expectations will be met, or how to successfully combine divergent practices. Because bride and groom are both likely to be familiar with the mainstream norms, they always have the option of defaulting to them. Caterer Abigail Kirsch tells couples: "Stay away from highly seasoned, unrecognizable ethnic foods ... It's best not to offend anyone" (quoted in Pollan & Levine, 1989, p. 42).[37] Typical of advice from wedding specialists, the central argument here suggests: Do not try to combine different traditions, in fact, steer clear of them entirely so as not to upset anyone. Wedding consultant Marcy Blum put it bluntly: "Not too many years ago, the concept of what was elegant meant completely sanitized of your ethnic background" (Mayer, 1992a, p. 15). To turn to wedding invitations, saleswoman Bess Harris of Cartier, asserted: "We're very firm about etiquette. An invitation with the Cartier imprint assumes perfection; that's why people come to us and they abide by what we tell them" (Seligson, 1973, p. 33). Rather than change its guidelines for each wedding depending on the unique characteristics of the bride and groom, Cartier promulgates mainstream wedding traditions to the exclusion of all others. Clearly it is to their advantage to do so; the only surprise is that so many people follow their rules.

Sometimes one or both members of a couple learn about mainstream traditions by working as, or for, wedding specialists. Both members of Couple 107 worked for a caterer prior to planning their own wedding, and report having worked approximately 50 weddings.[38] Because they had firsthand knowledge of what options had become standard, they developed a clear sense of what they did and did not want to do at their own ceremony.

How is a standard maintained? Because weddings are such a major ritual form, there are ritual experts (priests, ministers, rabbis, etc.) and secular specialists (caterers, jewelers, florists, etc.). For the ritual experts, adherence to the religious requirements implies substantial repetition across weddings. For secular specialists, on the other hand, it is simply more convenient if those organizing a wedding stick to what they have already learned to do well, rather than having to incorporate a lot of new and different elements. As Marcy Blum suggested: "Buying a wedding is putting your self-image in concrete terms.... It can be the self-image you actually have or the one you'd like to have. It's taking the ephemeral and making it real. There's nothing tougher to buy" (as quoted in Pollan & Levine, 1989, p. 40). Ideas are ephemeral, whereas wedding gowns are real, therefore participants use such concrete aspects as choice of wedding gown to convey ideas. Because this occurs, analysts can study the concrete details to discover something of the ephemeral ideas conveyed to participants.

"Conforming generally attracts no attention to the particular performance, raises no question as to what the performers mean by it. They do not usually mean anything by it; it is just what one does in getting married" (Charsley, 1991, p. 149). But, whatever decisions are made about the major elements of a wedding, the bride and groom know their performance will be judged against the background of what others have done before them. For the choice of wedding gown, for example, "resonances set up with dresses seen in the past, whether at weddings attended, or television weddings, or even royal weddings, clearly also have a part to play" (p. 70). The bride and groom make their choices in light of what others have previously chosen to do, and the friends and family who are their guests evaluate the appropriateness of their choices based on similar (and overlapping) prior knowledge. Because many of the guests will be older than the new couple, they will have a wider range of experience to bring to the judgment, and usually a well-defined (and narrow) sense of what is appropriate. Giddens (1991) called this knowledge of the past "accumulated expertise" (p. 3). But the bride and groom know what is important to them, and are usually willing to make some changes in order to see that their individual preferences are met. For this reason, even after taking expectations into account, couples may decide to deliberately go against them. In fact, the ability to change a ritual in ways that will be accepted is a marker of competence: You cannot revise traditions to make them appropriate to your individual circumstances if you do not understand them fully. Couple 1, a Jewish–Christian match married in their late thirties, reported having been to a large number of weddings prior to organizing their own, through which they developed a clear sense of what would have meaning for them. The bride stated: "We wanted a wedding to be what we wanted and not what the industry told us, or what the people up the street did … We knew what we wanted. The problem is that's not what anyone wanted to sell us." Rather than give in to arguments with the industry specialists, she continued interviewing florists, caterers, and jewelers until she found those who would do as she asked, rather than what they as experts initially considered appropriate. But not everyone has this much perseverance.

Deviating from tradition draws attention to what is omitted as well as to what is added (Bronner, 1992b).[39] Even when they do not follow the expectations of all of their guests, an intercultural couple call those expectations to mind by the choices they make. The old is not forgotten, but changed, and there is a very large difference between the two. We edit the past as we create the present in order to ensure that the meanings we convey to ourselves and others will be the ones of greatest significance to us at that time.[40]

A good example of how a couple can end up by conveying little of either of their cultures in opting for a traditional mainstream American wedding involved an Italian American Catholic bride who married a Greek American, Greek Orthodox groom (Couple 68). They were married in a Catholic church (mainstream American weddings are nearly always Christian, so this did not constitute a significant deviation from the pattern). Because the groom had wanted to hold it in his Greek Orthodox church, he refused to participate in the planning, so the bride and the groom's mother planned it together, reportedly with little conflict (attributed by the participants to the fact that the groom's mother was a professional party planner with extensive knowledge of such events, and the bride was happy to let her make the major decisions). The groom had given the bride a white rose on their first date, so white and roses served as the main color and theme; the bride described the result as just "too perfect." The church was heavily decorated with white roses, and white and teal (the second color chosen) carnations (flowers on each pew, and on the altar). The bride's gown was white, the bridesmaids' gowns were teal, matched to the teal flowers and teal ink on the wedding invitations. During the service the bride and groom handed each other's mothers a white rose, then lit candles from their mothers' candles, and then jointly lit the unity candle on the altar, where it was surrounded by white rose petals. The rings they exchanged were white gold with white diamonds. As guests entered the reception, they walked under an arbor with white roses and baby's breath, and a photographer took a picture of each guest. Every table had a centerpiece with two white roses in the middle, and the buffet table was scattered with white rose petals. The food was elaborate, including multiple types of seafood for appetizers, two pigs cooked on a spit, and more. The food was served on china with silver, and the servers all wore white gloves and had white roses in their lapels. By using the accepted standards for high formality within a mainstream wedding, this couple avoided the issue of whose background would be given favor; in the end, neither side's ethnic traditions or religions were even represented in most of the choices (although social class certainly was—and the bride had no objection to the groom's family taking charge of the decisions, as they were the ones who knew how it should be done, and were willing to pay for it to be done "right").

As with the other solutions presented so far, the cases described in this section also seem to be avoiding the issue. Although this clearly feels appropriate to many couples (at the time, if not later when they have had a chance to develop second thoughts), it only postpones some difficult decisions. Such issues as where to live, how to raise the children, or family visits at holidays, always wait just around the corner for intercultural couples. Additional research would have to be conducted to determine whether the various sorts of avoidance and postponement described thus far make the later choices easier or harder. There is some argument for each case. With more time and experience making decisions as a couple, perhaps the more difficult choices come easier; yet there is something appealing about establishing a combination of important elements to both individuals at the beginning, which happens when a truly intercultural wedding is designed and carried out.

A Wedding Presenting a Combination of Two (or More) Cultures in a Single Ceremony

The final possibility, and the most intriguing theoretically, combines aspects of more than one tradition into a single ceremony. The edges of any single cultural system overlap in a multitude of ways with the edges of others; what occurs at these points of overlap being particularly worthy of analysis. More happens, and more is noticeable, at the boundaries than in the center of communities. Weddings where the bride and groom have faced the issue of how to bring their divergent backgrounds together serve as exemplars of overlap situations, and particularly fruitful sites of analysis.

These couples do what Staub (1989) called "cultural code switching" (p. 128). Linguists term conversation that moves fluently between two or more languages "code switching"; as Eastman (1992) suggested, "codeswitching is a way people handle resources" (pp. 9–10). Staub (1989) extended this to refer to instances where the participants move between two or more sets of cultural expectations, not only two languages. He went on to point out a potential problem for second or third generation ethnics in the United States, that "they may be expected to be fully competent in traditional cultural patterns to which they have only partial access" (p. 128). A very real issue, this comes up in wedding descriptions throughout this book. For this reason good and dutiful children sometimes end up saying their wedding vows in a language they do not fully understand; for this reason they, or their new spouses, may choose to incorporate traditions they have never previously viewed, cannot explain, and do not fully comprehend. Of course, understanding the connotations of your own family's traditions, no matter how well or incompletely you can follow them, is easier than realizing the implications of those of your new spouse. As a Roman Catholic Irish Cuban bride married to a Hindu South Asian reported, "I am able to deeply offend whole assemblages of Indians with an offhand comment or look."[41] No matter the good will, offense can be given, and taken. Eastman's (1992) comments on marked and unmarked variations of language indicate how cultural codeswitching works in weddings: When codeswitching is common, it is unmarked; when it is uncommon, it stands out as marked behavior that people notice and discuss (p. 1). Similarly, introducing multiple cultures into a wedding is marked behavior at the present time; when it becomes more common practice, it will go unremarked.

This type of wedding is presently the least common, but small numbers do not change the fact that weddings where the participants choose to combine their variant traditions have great theoretical significance. These couples have chosen to do something quite difficult, therefore it deserves attention. Aside from intrinsic interest, Rosaldo (1989) pointed out that borderlands are "sites of creative cultural production" (p. 208) because, as Vila (2000) said, on the border "similarities and differences meet" (p. 21).[42] Intercultural couples are not always literally at a geographic border, but they are definitely at a social and cultural border: They stand between two cultural groups (that of the bride's family, and that of the groom's), a difficult place to be, socially. In order to learn about what happens at such points, we can study the difficulties that they face, and the solutions they develop, many of which are creative and original. Clearly we should study the conditions of cultural creativity wherever it occurs.

A wedding between a Greek Orthodox groom, and an Irish, French, German, Bohemian Catholic bride, exemplifies how couples can design an event with an eye toward making all of their guests comfortable (Couple 4).[43] They were married in a Greek Orthodox church, because his family was quite religious while hers was not, so that was an easy choice for them. However, the Greek Orthodox ceremony requires that the best man be Greek Orthodox in order to fully participate in the religious aspects of the ceremony, and the groom's best friend, otherwise the obvious choice for best man, was not. In the end, they had two best men. The groom's godfather was labeled his *koumbaro*, the Greek equivalent of best man; he performed all the essential parts of the religious service. The groom's best friend was labeled his "American best man" playing no role in the religious ceremony, although he made the toast at the reception, and bought the first round of drinks at the bachelor party, typical American expectations of the individual filling this role. Both were listed in the program with their separate titles.

The bride wore a long train on her wedding gown because it appealed to the groom's sense of family tradition:

And I wanted a long train. It had to have a long train. Because my mom's wedding gown, there's a picture, every time I'm in awe when I look at it. And there's one wedding picture where my mom's train, you know, they've been married about 40 years. So they got married in the '50s and very classic. My mom had a very long train. And I just wanted, when it's on the stairs and the back of the bride is facing everybody. That's what people are watching, so I just wanted a long train because it looks beautiful in the back.

For this couple, food choices were particularly meaningful. The reception was held in a restaurant in Greektown, with a menu the groom's father had selected. At the reception, a series of compromises were reached, so that no one would be uncomfortable. As the groom said: "For the Greek side, they're used to the Greek salads and the Americans aren't used to that. So what we did we had the oil and vinegar in separate bottles so they could make their own, but the salad itself was a garden salad with … feta cheese that you could pick off if you wanted to." The soup was also carefully planned:

Bride: "In fact, cream of chicken and rice soup is a Greek thing."
Groom: "It's a *lemon* chicken and rice soup."
Bride: "Right. But we had the chicken and rice soup with the lemons on the table."
Groom: "So what we did was we had cream of chicken soup made but we made sure that all the tables had lemons cut so the Greeks could just squeeze the lemon in."

The main dish was prime rib, chosen because the groom's father was a butcher. The groom reported: "Ours was 16 ounces without the bone … I personally picked out all the meat. Personally hand-delivered it to the banquet hall … and I also took them hamburgers [for the children] … and for them I didn't want to waste the prime rib. So we had cheeseburgers and french fries made for them."

At the reception, they did include the American tradition of tossing the garter as a nod to mainstream tradition. As the groom said: "Gotta have the garter. Now that's nothing Greek, I mean, that's just the wedding." It is an interesting side note that in another Greek–American wedding incorporating the garter toss, the Greek bride reported that some of her relatives were quite shocked by this part of the ritual, as they had never seen it before and considered it completely inappropriate (Couple 35).[44]

After the reception, the couple was driven off in an undecorated limousine, this time as a marker of social class. The groom said:

I worked my way through school, being a chauffeur. I used to drive all the aristocrats on the North Shore [of Illinois]. At the cheesy weddings that I'd have to do, they'd want me to decorate the cars. But the wealthiest, the most classy weddings, they wouldn't, the cars were black and it was, it just looked so nice. It was just a clean, uncluttered wedding. And [bride] wanted a very formal wedding, and I agreed with her.

So, although this couple had a few nods to mainstream or class expectations, they spent the greatest energy on finding ways to incorporating recognizable Greek markers while making it easy for the non-Greek participants to either accept or reject them.

The majority of this book documents examples of this fourth type of wedding design, incorporating two or more different cultural traditions into a single ritual performance. The mainstream norms for a wedding, however, can never be ignored. Each person attending a wedding matches it against all prior weddings experienced, whether in person, or through media. Because the majority of those are likely to be mainstream weddings, understanding what these involve is essential. And so references to mainstream traditions recur in the remainder of the book, although they are not the primary topic.

It is my argument that three of the four possibilities (choosing one culture over the others; presenting a ceremony meeting each culture's expectations, but at alternative times; or choosing to act in accordance with neither family's expectations, but to find some relatively neutral alternative) all resolve cultural conflicts, but at the cost of ignoring the potential provided by the occasion for creating something new and wonderful. Because some brave souls do opt for the fourth possibility, figuring out a way to design a ceremony that appropriately combines elements of what each family expects, we can, and should, study those weddings in order to learn what works. In this case, the researcher's task is not to not tell people how to conduct their lives, but rather to follow behind them, asking what choices they have made, and how they have carried these out in practice. Many researchers have lofty goals of understanding communication, to teach others how to better communicate. My goal here is much more modest: I want to locate some of those who have already figured out what works, and ask them what they did, to learn from their creativity. Intercultural couples are the most highly motivated people one can imagine, they have determined to live on a daily basis with major differences in assumptions about appropriate and expected behavior. Therefore, it is in their own best interests to figure out a potential solution, and they work hard at it. We could do much worse than to learn from them.

METAPHORS DESCRIBING INTERCULTURAL COMMUNICATION

One way to describe the wedding design choices is through the metaphor that describes the event most appropriately. The earliest metaphor used in the study of interactions between different cultural groups in the United States was the *melting pot*.[45] In this image, each group lost its uniqueness quickly, but all contributed something to the flavor of the whole. Although recently it has been proposed that this metaphor has negative implications, originally it was positively valued: Analysts assumed the only way members of different groups could interact without difficulty was to all give up their original cultural identities, all ending up part of the same larger group. The melting pot depended on intermarriage as the standard way to combine originally separate "ingredients," or members of different groups (Spickard, 1989). Margaret Mead (1982) clearly stated the contradictions implied by this metaphor: "So we have the uniquely American dilemma: the ethic of cultural pluralism, of ethnic separatism, pitted against the ethic of ethnic assimilation, the doctrine of the melting pot which states that the kind of product desired from the melting process may change through time, but the goal is always production of a standard product" (p. 185).[46] This book is about how particular people have walked the tightrope brought about by exactly this contradiction: how to acknowledge, even celebrate, distinctions between groups while simultaneously bringing members of different groups together through interaction. In terms of wedding rituals, the mainstream wedding reflects the melting pot metaphor best: A new whole is created with none of the original elements clearly recognizable as distinct.

Once scholars developed widespread dissatisfaction with the melting pot metaphor, they introduced additional metaphors to explain the process they saw occurring. The *salad bowl*, one of the first of this second generation of metaphors, assumes that each ethnic group retains all of its unique characteristics, even when physically located next to groups with differences. An alternative variation is the *mosaic*. This has the advantage of assuming smaller, unevenly sized and shaped pieces, seeming to be a whole when you gain enough distance. Again, however, this metaphor permits no blending, implying that each piece remains homogeneous, even after contact with others.[47] Both the salad bowl and the mosaic apply appropriately to weddings in which there is some attempt to incorporate diverse cultural elements into a single ceremony. An example of a wedding appropriately described by the mosaic metaphor combined a Puerto Rican, Catholic groom with a Korean American Methodist bride. This couple incorporated a Puerto Rican band playing folk songs into their reception, followed by a traditional Korean bowing ceremony asking for their parents' blessings, wearing traditional Korean wedding clothes (Brady, 2000, September). Each element indicating ethnic or religious identity appeared as a unique piece, apparently not modified by the presence of other, different identity statements.

There are several variants of the mosaic metaphor: the *quilt* (Allan & Turner, 1997), the *coat of many colors* (Eoyang, 1995), the *rainbow* (Martínez, 1998), the *kaleidoscope* (Waldron, 1992), none of which really permit blending of the constituent elements, but rather place them next to one another. And so researchers needed still another metaphor, one falling between the melting pot (where no original elements are maintained unchanged) and the mosaic (where no group significantly influences others).

The *tapestry* metaphor attempts this compromise.[48] A tapestry can be described as a piece of fabric created by joining differently colored threads, which together combine to create a picture more complex than any of them could display alone. This conveys the image of meshing different traditions into a single whole, and so manages the conflict between maintaining differences while establishing similarities better than the other metaphors. It also suggests viewing the completed tapestry as a new and unique creation, of far greater value than its constituent threads would suggest. The tapestry metaphor explicitly intends to refer positively to cultural pluralism (the state of multiple ethnic groups co-existing peacefully, aware of differences, but not fighting as a result of them). Essentially it moves from the standard "either/or" situation to a new "both/and." That is, a mosaic is made up of distinctly separate pieces; if you are one piece, you cannot simultaneously be another. A tapestry, although made up of individual threads, only shows the intended image when all those threads are viewed together, as a new kind of whole.[49]

The image of weaving together different lives makes particular sense to intercultural couples, and some of the original language written for their wedding ceremonies uses the same image. Couple 85 had two ceremonies, one for the groom's Jewish side, and another for the bride's Hindu side. Their wedding invitation invokes the tapestry metaphor:

> We invite you to join us in celebration of our commitment to each other. Help us create joy and gladness, mirth and exultation, pleasure and delight, harmony and companionship with your presence at our commitment ceremonies. Come laugh, dine and dance as we gather and weave together the threads of our lives, our friends and families, into a living tapestry. The happiness that we share we would like to share with you.

Of these metaphors, although none is perfect, and more suggestions will no doubt be offered in the future, I find the tapestry the most accurate and thus the most useful image to keep in mind for how different cultures can simultaneously maintain their own traditions, yet also successfully blend into a larger society. It also has the advantage of subtly referencing the metaphor of social life as "fabric" frequently used by many who study interaction (more common perhaps in sociology than communication, but a significant visual image nonetheless).[50] Those weddings highlighted in the Interludes of this book best illustrate the tapestry metaphor for they seriously attempt to interweave elements of two or more cultures into a new, single whole.

NOTES

1. Compare Cohen's (1985) quote, as cited at the beginning of this chapter, with the discussion in Leeds-Hurwitz (1989, pp. 62–65) about the relationship between culture and communication. One helpful summary of the types of definitions of culture which have been used by various scholars of intercultural communication is Philipsen (1987) who divides them into three categories: culture as code, as conversation, as community (see Hall, 1997, for further discussion of these definitions). In this book I try to integrate all three faces of culture because it seems to me all must work together. Hall also emphasized the significance of the creative element in culture, as I do here, when he reminded us that, whatever else it is: "Culture is an ongoing creation of the everyday activities of interconnected people" (p. 14).

2. This emphasis on the study of a community that is not to be located in a single place is hardly unique to this project, of course. Blu (1996) pointed out that "Rarely do 'a' people, 'a' culture, and 'a' society inhabit 'a' place anymore, if they ever did" (p. 220), and it is possible that all assumptions of monocultural groups were overgeneralizations. See also Hymes (1996), Lavie and Swedenberg (1996), Marcus (1998), and Matthews (2000) for related suggestions that the traditional connection between a culture and a geographic location was no more than an inaccurate assumption. But the implications of this understanding are not yet clear, as Gupta and Ferguson (1997b) pointed out: "At the level of anthropological theory, then, the turn away from the ideas of whole, separate 'cultures' would appear to be fairly well established. Yet what such a shift might mean for ethnographic practice, we suggest, is still very much in the process of being worked out" (p. 3). They go on to conclude that this shift does not imply giving up "anthropology's traditional attention to the close observation of particular lives in particular places" (p. 25). My own answer to the issue is to study interaction at the borders of cultural groups, as in this investigation of intercultural weddings.

3. Ohnuki-Tierney (1993) spoke for most anthropologists when she said: "We now recognize diversity and complexity within any social group ... We have indeed wrongly represented a people in a single voice. Every social group is pluralistic, with every individual having multiple cross-cutting social identities arising from but not determined by class, gender, age, ethnicity, and other factors" (p. x).

4. Orbe (1998b) argued for the significance of the former, but others argue for the equal significance of the latter. As Denzin (1997) pointed out: "American ethnography is deeply embedded in American and world culture. As that culture has gone postmodern and multinational, so too has ethnography. The ethnographic project has changed because the world that ethnography confronts has changed" (p. xii).

5. In Putnam and Stohl's (1990) terms, I am studying *bona fide* groups. As they defined them, bona fide groups have "stable yet permeable boundaries" and "interdependence with immediate context" (p. 256).

6. Not only was this true in my own research, but it has been previously documented by Bernard (1980), and Varro (1988).

7. Myerhoff (1992) pointed out that rituals are expressive, communicative acts. Merely by having an intercultural wedding, the parties involved make a statement

about a shift in community boundaries. But, as she also pointed out, "Rites of passage certainly do not *cause* social integration; rather they may be expected to reflect
and enhance it." (p. 227). Communication, including ritual events, is a "condition"
for the creation of community (Jankowski, 1991). And "the performance of community reinforces its own social base" (Noyes, 1995). See also Shepherd and
Rothenbuhler's (2001) excellent collection of essays on the construction of community in a wide variety of contexts.

8. This same groom later described his second wedding as again meeting traditions of
the bride, a middle class, Anglo American of Methodist faith (this time also including new traditions created by the couple). He did not remember his comment to me
several years earlier regarding an unequal wedding design as potentially symptomatic of a problematic relationship, although he did agree that it was something he
could well have said. He also explained that the importance of including his family's cultural traditions in the second wedding was diminished because nearly all of
his family was unable to attend.

9. As reported by Brad Gulbrandson in Comm 440: Communication Codes, in Spring
1996.

10. As reported by Raffi Mahdasian in Comm 440: Communication Codes in Spring
1996.

11. Interviewed by Eric Roche for Comm 440: Communication Codes, in Spring 2001.

12. Interviewed by Sue Glanz for Comm 499: Independent Study, in Spring 1992.

13. Interviewed by Ryan Ellifson for Comm 440: Communication Codes, in Spring 2001.

14. As reported by Bob Ryerson in Comm 440: Communication Codes, in Spring 1996.

15. Another example is a Jewish–Hindu marriage where separate weddings were performed on separate days, documented in Brady (2000, April). This is a regular Sunday
column documenting interesting weddings (most often, this means celebrity, upper
class, or both) by a photograph and a brief description. Having read this column
faithfully for years, this example is one of the few where an intercultural couple was
chosen as the focus. Given that, it seems highly marked that the cultural differences
between the bride and groom are not mentioned at all. This can be compared to the
description of an intracultural couple, where both the bride and the groom are Native
American (Brady, 2000, July), with extensive description of each one's background
supplied. As Gaines (1997) pointed out, "if we are ever to transcend ethnicity, we
much acknowledge ethnicity in the first place" (p. 134). Pretending that cultural differences are invisible is not especially likely to resolve them.

16. As reported by Damian Evans in Comm 440: Communication Codes, in Spring
1996.

17. As reported by Melissa Noto in Comm 440: Communication Codes, in Spring 1996.

18. Originally interviewed June 9, 1994, with additional clarifications provided in June
of 2001.

19. Interviewed by Nicole Goodwin for Comm 440: Communication Codes, in Spring
2001.

20. That eloping was chosen in order to resolve conflicts due to intercultural marriages
was documented as early as Golden (1954). Although he is discussing interracial
unions, the solution is just as effective with other forms.

21. As reported by Mary Ellen Kanthack in Comm 440: Communication Codes, in
Spring 1999.

22. See Moffatt (1992) for discussion of "American" culture. Anderson (1983) not only pointed out that our sense of community is in important ways imagined, he also pointed out the role of the media in creating a common sense of community.

23. Gedmintas (1989) expanded beyond the traditional view of WASPs as being the mainstream Americans, referring to "invisible ethnics": the third or fourth generation of those who are White, and of European descent. He studied Lithuanian Americans, discovering that members of this group broadened their definition of group membership to include others closely associated; they now all belong to a larger, more unified ethnic group of Eastern Europeans. They share some aspects of culture, such as common foods, which can serve as markers of unity.

24. As reported by Bart Smith in Comm 440: Communication Codes, in Spring 1996.

25. It is this sense of a shared expectation that permits novelists to assume that readers will understand when someone violates the norms. For example, Carson McCullers (1946) described a young girl who chooses a completely inappropriate outfit for her brother's wedding. If readers did not share an assumption of appropriate clothing for guests at a wedding, they would not understand the point being made. Later in the story, the character concludes "It was so unlike what she had expected ... there was, from first to last, the sense of something terribly gone wrong" (p. 138). This phrase perfectly describes the feelings of any participant in a wedding who is surprised by what occurs; most often it is not described as a pleasant surprise, a learning of another potential way to do things, but a sense of something gone terribly wrong. See Bruner (1994) and Brown (1994) for descriptions of intercultural marriages in literature.

26. Fiske and Hartley (1978) referred to "the culture's felt need for a common centre [sic]" (p. 86); see also Fiske (1987). Handler (1988) argued the opposite position, that there is in fact no "American center" but rather "a host of culturally constituted social domains" (p. 2).

27. Crane (1992) expanded on these ideas, proposing the theoretical concept of amplification: "once a subject enters the cultural arena via one of its subchannels, it is very likely to be taken up by many other channels, because these channels are linked by interorganizational and individual social networks. As more channels disseminate a particular subject matter, the more impact that subject has in terms of the number of people aware of it, either passively or actively" (p. 22).

28. Kendall (1996) pointed out that, for Korea, "any meaningful discussion of weddings must be cognizant of the mythologies generated by women's magazines and television soap operas" (p. 22). The same is true for the United States, of course. As Ingraham (1998) pointed out, "The contemporary white wedding under transnational capitalism is, in effect, a mass-marketed, homogeneous, assembly-line production with little resemblance to the utopian vision many participants hold" (p. 74).

29. Some advertisements for products unrelated to weddings assume familiarity with mainstream weddings in order to make sense to their audience. For example, Häagen-Dazs uses an ad with a bride choosing to eat their brand of ice cream rather than be on time to her own wedding, with the tag line "they can start without you" (published in the New York Times Magazine on 5/21/00, on p. 41), and NextMonet encourages their audience to purchase unique pieces of art by showing an image of dozens of couples dressed almost identically, getting married simultaneously, with the tag line "fight sameness" (published in the New York Times Magazine on 4/30/00,

on p. 20). Notice that these ads were published at the height of the wedding sea-son, when wedding imagery could be assumed to be in the minds of the readers.

30. Browning (1992) pointed out the significance of lists as a form of communication.

31. *The Milwaukee Journal*, April 2, 1991, photo on p. C2 documents a wedding where the groom was a baseball player (minor league) who said his vows at home plate before playing a game; he wore his uniform, the bride wore a traditional gown, veil, and held a bouquet of flowers. See also the related example published in *The Milwaukee Journal*, June 27, 1990, photo on p. D2 where the setting was again the Milwaukee County Stadium. The men in the wedding party wore Brewer shorts and tuxedo jackets; the bridesmaids wore blue and yellow tea-length dresses; the bride wore the traditional white gown and held a small bouquet (the groom had a flower in his buttonhole). The food was that usually served at tailgate parties: beans, brats and burgers, supplemented by a wedding cake. There was a 4-minute ceremony per-formed by a judge, then everyone ate at the tailgate, then they all entered County Stadium together to watch the game.

32. *The Milwaukee Journal*, October 6, 1991, photo on p. A2 describes a bride who is a trainer at the Milwaukee Zoo having her reception at the zoo, complete with a sea lion in attendance.

33. *The Milwaukee Journal*, February 12, 1991, photo on p. A2 shows a bride at a fashion show in Tel Aviv wearing a traditional white gown with a matching gas mask and headpiece (note the timing: the Gulf war was going on).

34. The Milwaukee Skyline Women's Barbershop Chorus had a performance February 15, 1992, which culminated in a wedding of one of the members to a member of the Milwaukee Skyline Chorus. The performance was described as outlining their ro-mance and courtship through songs, and included three other groups: Milwaukee Transfer, All That Jazz, and the Greendale Men's Barbershop Chorus-Midwest Vocal Express. Everyone was asked to dress in black and silver. The wedding was per-formed by a minister on stage, at Vogel Hall of the Performing Arts Center. Seating for general public was priced at $14 for the concert, with an additional $4 for the re-ception. The musical *Tina 'n Tony's Wedding* provides an example even further re-moved from reality, as it involves the audience in the wedding being staged as if they were legitimate guests. At the version I attended (performed in June 2000, in Milwaukee), it was sometimes difficult to be certain which characters were actors and which guests.

35. Interviewed by Jessica Tuttle for Comm 440: Communication Codes, in Spring 2001.

36. See Leeds-Hurwitz (1989) for further discussion of this theoretical point.

37. Although, only a decade later, Gabaccio (1998) suggested: "What unites American eaters culturally is how we eat, not what we eat. As eaters, all Americans mingle the culinary traditions of many regions and cultures within ourselves. We are multi-eth-nic eaters" (pp. 225–226). One implication is that restrictions on types of foods to be served at wedding receptions may shortly be lifted.

38. Interviewed by Eric Roche for Comm 440: Communication Codes, Spring 2001.

39. "Creativity and tradition are intertwined, and represent the complex processes of humans expressing themselves to others in ways that carry value and meaning" (Bronner, 1992a, p. 3).

40. Van der Vliet (1991) provided an interesting example of what happens when there is a split between the couple on what to retain and what to change, specifically when

husbands want to retain some (not all) aspects of traditional marriages (sexual freedom, mainly), but when the wives want to have modern marriages (greater equality in all matters). See also Wilson (1978) for an interesting discussion of which ritual forms persist and which either change or are dropped.

41. Taken from the web site "American love stories" (www.pbs.org/weblab/lovestories/stories/Extended_Family/story32786.shtml).

42. See also Gupta and Ferguson (1997a) and Wilson and Donnan (1998).

43. Interviewed by Sue Glanz for Comm 499: Independent Study, in Spring 1992.

44. As reported by Mary Saunders in Comm 440: Communication Codes, in Spring 1996.

45. Interestingly, although researchers in the United States have largely rejected the melting pot as a metaphor, it is still used elsewhere, as documented in an article about Australia (Arndt, 2000); equally interesting, it is used by this author in exactly the same way it was formerly used in the US: this is an article about how intermarriage in Australia is creating a melting pot.

46. Or, as Appadurai (1996) put it: "The central problem of today's global interactions is the tension between cultural homogenization and cultural heterogenization" (p. 32). See also Louw (1998).

47. See Hannerz (1991, p. 107; 1992, p. 73) and Tuleja (1997, p. 3) for further discussion of the mosaic metaphor.

48. Deegan (1998) used the tapestry metaphor in her book, specifically tying the concept of tapestry to rituals: "Rituals create a community stage for cultural experience, symbols, and values. They can generate, change, destroy, and maintain meaning, and in the U.S.A. they can engage in these processes simultaneously and rapidly. The patterns emerging from this complex, dynamic fabric of life create a tapestry with recognizable and meaningful images and symbols" (p. 3).

49. The poem by Patricia Jobling quoted in McNamee and Gergen (1998, p. 29) clearly shows how tapestry works as a metaphor.

50. One variant of this appears in Rieff (1964): "The social order does swiftly clothe the actors born into it in the self-understandings they are, thereafter, reluctant to shed even for the rare privilege of a glimpse of themselves in their nothingness" (p. xiii).

Interlude 3

FIG. 4:   Cover of wedding invitation used by Couple 75.
Photo by Don Lintner, University of Wisconsin-Parkside.

*I*n the United States, and now in some other parts of the world as well, the bride traditionally wears white. In China, the bride traditionally wears red. In the United States, white has connotations of purity and innocence, whereas red implies the context of a bordello rather than a wedding (Frese, 1991). In China, red connotes happiness and good luck, whereas white carries connotations of death because it is what you wear to a funeral (Costa, 1997). Even in the U.S., women who are marrying for the second time often do not wear white, feeling that it inappropriately represents them at that stage. Instead, they usually chose some variant of off-white, referencing wedding white without quite claiming the innocence and purity it represents.

The bride of Couple 75, born and raised in France, wore a red dress to her second wedding. "I was forty when I got married, and I thought getting married in virginal white, at forty and with two children, is a little bit ridiculous."[1] Although not from China, she is a Sinologist (one who studies China), had lived there for several years prior to her marriage, and met her husband there. He too is not Chinese, but was born and raised in Mexico (although now living in the United States) to a family of Eastern European Jews who immigrated there several generations back. "The reason why it's red is because red is the traditional wedding color in China, and so, as a Sinologist, and I like, also because it's a symbol of life and happiness."

The bride is well aware of the traditional associations of red in the U.S., although she did not grow up here, because some of the same connotations hold for France.

> Of course in the Christian symbology, red is really the color for prostitution … completely inappropriate for a wedding or for a funeral. And I got a few sneers, I have to say, for wearing red at my wedding.… And my mother was surprised that I wore red. She was a bit shocked, she was a bit shocked. And my sister explained to her it's a traditional color for Chinese weddings.

Despite the responses it incurred (many admiring comments were made as well as the negative reactions mentioned), the bride said: "It felt completely appropriate. And red suits me better than white, as well." In fact, red solved her problem: She really did not want to wear the traditional white.

What of the groom's reaction? "We did this traditionally, he had never seen the dress, he didn't know at all what I was wearing ... because in a traditional French wedding the man mustn't look at the dress.... He was surprised ... but he liked it." Having also worked in China, he immediately understood the connotations of the color there, and so was not as surprised by it as some others.

Several aspects of the dress in addition to color had particular meaning for the bride. It was made of fabric given to her as a wedding gift by a friend in Australia. Designed as a sheath with spaghetti straps, it was sewn by another friend as her wedding gift, but there is more to that story:

> It's very nice because the woman who made my dress actually "stole" my last boyfriend ... so it was to make herself be forgiven she made my wedding dress.... I was more angry with him than with her, I have to admit ... It took me a while to forgive her, but yes, I forgave her before, and several years later she made my dress for the wedding.

The bride's first husband was English, and they lived in Australia for many years, so both of these friends were from Australia. There was an additional connection to both France and Australia in the clothing. A silk sheath not being particularly warm, it was a problem that the wedding was scheduled for December, and so the bride needed something to cover the dress. "Originally I wanted a big boa, because that's very Parisian, but the boa would not have covered my arms, so this was the closest thing to a boa." After some searching she found a jacket made of feathers as a boa would be, but these feathers were red to match the dress. "It was funny because I got it from this shop ... that's on the Haight, and they got all the costumes for *Priscilla, Queen of the Desert*, you know that Australian movie? So there was another Australian loop, in my jacket." And the choice of feathers? "That was something that came from being French. It has nothing to do with weddings, just the Parisian touch." So the same outfit linked the bride to the three countries of importance to her prior to her arrival in the United States: China, France, and Australia.

There were additional connections to family and friends in the wedding. Her sister gave her away, a friend of the groom served as witness for him, and a friend of hers from Australia was her witness. Both of the bride's children traveled from Australia for the wedding, but were given no specific role to play. Her son's girlfriend had asked if she could be the ring bearer, so she was. Being Chinese, she wore traditional Chinese clothing, in gold. The groom's family attended, although the bride's parents did not. "And that's an interesting thing for you because the reason they didn't come is miscommunication."

The miscommunication involved a series of issues:

- **The choice of officiant:** A close friend,

    "he did seminary studies ... but then when it came to being ordained he didn't want it ... But because he had been trained as a minister, we knew he could do a ritual. And he's American, African American in fact, and we're not. So we wanted him to marry us. And then we would have gone to the city to do the legal paper and he could do the ritual part, the ceremony. But he got so excited about it he actually got ordained, you know in this thing where you send in a 25¢ stamp (laughs) ... It's recognized and he actually is a Reverend and he is legally entitled to marry us. He did this for us, he actually got ordained for us."

- **Location:** The wedding was held in a restaurant.

    "I told them [her parents] that we were going to get married in a restaurant, so they assumed it was just going to be a party with some friends, and for them to come all the way from France, the language problem, and all this, to do what they thought was going to be a party with some friends with [the officiant] doing a bit of a speech, was not truly worth the while."

- **Timing:** The wedding was held at night. In France a wedding would have been scheduled during the day.

- **Details:** "It's also the way I told her [bride's mother], because I didn't give her very many details, because I took the details for granted."

After the wedding was over, the bride's parents realized what they had missed.

Then when they saw the photos, and they saw we had spent money on it ... they were surprised, and they said, oh, they didn't realize, and if they had known they would have come, but it's the way I told them what was going to happen, they didn't realize it was going to be a wedding, they just thought it was going to be a party, so they didn't come.

When asked if her mother forgave her for not making it clear she should have come, "Well, it is more did I forgive her for not coming. She felt pretty bad, very bad about it, when she realized."

The groom's father and stepmother attended, but there was also a small misunderstanding. They were concerned about the age difference and the fact that the couple did not plan to have children, and also worried that this was a marriage of convenience so the bride could get an American passport (which was not accurate, and which they realized quickly).

> His parents came, but without a present.... My parents sent us a big gift. Because they took the marriage seriously, they just didn't think we were going to do anything for the wedding. You know, I'm ten years older than [groom]. And I think his parents didn't take the marriage seriously. As opposed to my parents who took the marriage seriously but not the wedding, his parents came to the wedding but did not really approve of the marriage.

The different responses in terms of presence and presents showed the bride and groom just where the misunderstandings with their parents lay, and what they had to explain to each.

In terms of religion, the ceremony was "basic U.S. Christian ... with God taken out of it ... the religion was taken out because he's Jewish [the groom] but he's not religious." Asked about the possibility of adding in some of the traditional elements of a Jewish wedding, the bride responded: "If he'd had a Jewish wedding, he would have had a traditional Jewish wedding" but they felt that "it would take the meaning out of ritual" to use some elements but not others. "In his mind you cannot take the bits that suit you out of a ritual because a ritual is socially meaningful, you know? So if you're not Jewish and you're not having a Jewish wedding, you don't have these little bits of Jewish stuff in it. Then it becomes cutesy, it loses the power." As to having an entirely Jewish ceremony:

> "Well, that was out of the question because I'm not Jewish and I would not convert and he would not expect me to convert, especially just to marry ... at some stage we thought we might get a rabbi who might be happy to perform ... a wedding between a Jew and a non-Jew. We thought about it, but then because of [their friend the officiant], we chose [him]."

The bride had a few final thoughts on this matter, which she shared: "I don't know if I would want to marry into his tradition. You know what I mean? We had to find something in-between which belonged to neither of us.... Our solution to the ritual was to strip it, really to its bare essentials." Part of this stripping of the ritual was that they had previously attended weddings that were

> like a smorgasbord, a smorgasbord of ritual, right? ... And in part it seemed ridiculous to us because we both come from traditional societies where we have traditions. So it seemed, and that's why we have nothing of Jewish ritual in there, it was also a reaction against this sort of stuff where, oh, "I like that, I take it," but actually you haven't been raised with it, so it has no meaning to it.... But it's a bit of a California new age thing that you think that ritual becomes more powerful if you have more of it. The more symbolism you have, it's more symbols actually.... It's just the whole idea of quantity versus quality.[2]

As a result, they designed a short and simple ceremony, including primarily an exchange of vows and of rings.

> Because we were from two different cultures, two different religions, and also an odd wedding, because he's ten years younger than me, so we never intended to have children, so there were a couple of things that were important to me: rings, and that he would not see the dress. And that came really from the French, what I thought of the French tradition, that you don't see the dress. And apart from that we had to find a middle ground. And we couldn't think of a better middle ground than something that is American. And you don't find more American than someone from the south [their officiant was from the south] with an American wedding.

The officiant worked with them on writing the vows. "[The officiant] had the traditional vows, and he asked us if we liked them, and what we didn't like we took out. Actually [groom] was kind of fussy because he really did not want any religious influence."

The rings were made by a jeweler friend in Mexico. She had first made the bride's engagement ring, with turquoise and aquamarine, and then later made them identical gold bands. "We wear exactly the same kind of ring." One step yet remains: "And it should have each of, the other one's name engraved in it, but we haven't got around to doing it yet. But we intend to do it one day. So I will have his name in my ring, and he will have my name in his."

In addition to the vows and rings, the ceremony included speeches by several close friends and the officiant, some of which were quite pointed and funny, and greatly appreciated by the bride and groom. The restaurant supplied flowers (red, white, and yellow), and candles on the table with the food. The bride did not hold flowers, and the candles had no ritual purpose. "We told them what we wanted, flowers, and the color scheme, so you see the red, there's a lot of red in there [in the photo of the flowers set out on the buffet table]." After the vows and exchange of rings, the bride and groom cut the cake; a fairly traditional design, it was white and multilayered, with a bride and groom on top.

> And the bride should have been red.... They apologized, that's the first thing when we came in, they apologized and they said they hadn't had time, and they thought of painting it, and they thought that with the heat it might go into the cake, and they didn't dare to mess up the cake.... It bothered me a little bit, but that's all. Because they were very kind about it.

After the wedding ceremony, there was a reception in the same room, including food and dancing. There were two kinds of music: a *bolero* trio for the link to Mexico, the groom's choice for the traditional romantic songs. "That was the one thing he wanted from his culture, which was the Mexican culture, not the Jewish culture." They did not know anyone in the *bolero* group, just got a recommendation for a good group. They also incorporated a rock band, because one of the members was a friend. The ceremony began at 9 p.m., and so the food consisted mainly of appetizers rather than a full dinner (and, of course, the cake). Also, although nothing during the ceremony was explicitly linked to Judaism, there was a brief connection during the reception. "The Jewish people at the wedding gave us a Jewish toast, right, called *mazel tov*, they did it the Jewish way, and that was nice because they acknowledged it [the wedding] in Jewish terms."

Just as the dress had connections to particular individuals with a past link to the bride or groom, so did the photographs. The photographer was a close friend of theirs, one of those who spoke during the ceremony, who put together an album of the event as a gift. He constructed a specially designed cover, filled with red feathers as a link to the bride's outfit. (The feathers did not come from her jacket, although the bride has not worn it since the wedding.)

The wedding invitations also held special meaning: "now they're interesting because he [the groom] organized that and they were Mexican." Although his sister was living in Mexico when they got married and was not able to attend the wedding due to a last minute problem with her flight, she participated by locating the artist. The groom worked with him at long distance, explaining that he wanted very modern Mexican art as the cover to the invitation, which is exactly what they got.

In this wedding, there were limited references to any religion, but extensive connections to the countries of importance to the bride and groom's life and work: France and Australia for the bride, Mexico for the groom, China for both. Also, they highlighted ties to close friends. Compared to mainstream American weddings, "it was more individualized. And it came out in terms of the intimacy of it, like someone made my dress, the friend married us, all the people around were friends." In fact, about 100 friends and relatives came from Mexico, France, and Australia, as well as various parts of the United States, to witness their marriage. Many of the essential components were contributed by friends: the officiant who designed the ceremony and performed it, the photographer who documented the event and prepared a photo album, one friend bought the fabric for the bride's dress and another sewed it, a friend designed both the engagement ring and matching wedding bands, another friend brought his band to play at the reception. There were limited bows to mainstream American wedding expectations: the relatively traditional cake (although if the restaurant had managed to paint the figurine bride's dress red as had been arranged, it would have appeared far less conventional to the guests), and the flowers (especially the fact that they were carefully matched to the bride's dress, regardless of the unconventional color). This couple was unusually aware of the design of rituals, planning their own with great care. Unlike the friends whose wedding they had attended, they did not view all symbols as powerful, the more the better, but deliberately stripped the ritual down to the key elements having the greatest meaning for them.

NOTES

1. This is a sentiment repeated by others. The bride of Couple 111 wore a cream colored, knee length suit "because I was an old lady with three kids." In this case, "old" meant in her thirties, and previously married (interviewed by Kim Wright for Comm 440, in Spring 2001).

2. Deborah Root (1997) described herself and her friends in the 1970s California as guilty of much the same sort of thing: "We so blithely appropriated bits and pieces of what appeared to us to be floating cultural exotica" (p. 226). However, she expresses surprise that others are continuing the behavior in the 1990s. I would agree: presumably we understand a bit more about cultures and ritual today than 20 years ago, and should realize that "borrowing" bits and pieces of others' traditions is not generally either respectful or appropriate. See Ziff and Rao (1997) for an interesting discussion of cultural appropriations.

3

Ritual

"Since ritual is a good form for conveying a message
as if it were unquestionable, it is often used to communicate
those very things which are most in doubt."
—Moore & Myerhoff (1977, p. 24)

Communities use rituals as one way to convey information to members, marking occasions of some significance. Myerhoff (1992) provided a typical definition: "Ritual is an act or actions intentionally conducted by a group of people employing one or more symbols in a repetitive, formal, precise, highly stylized fashion" (p. 129).[1] A symbol is a type of sign; the definition of a sign is something that stands for something else.[2] A symbol is that type of sign where the relationship between the visible aspect (the something present in the interaction) and the implicit aspect (the something else, generally not present) is arbitrary. For example, when the color white is assumed to stand for virginity or innocence, it is being used as a symbol because no literal connection exists between the abstract concept of innocence and the visible color white. This is made especially clear by the fact that different cultures associate different attributes with different colors. That is, a white wedding dress in the United States makes use of the symbolic meaning of the color white, and therefore is understood by the majority of the participants (whether explicitly or not) as implying something about the bride's virginity, or at least her relative innocence. In China white is associated with death and funerals, and so red, the color of happiness, is deemed a far more appropriate choice for a bride's wedding dress. A French bride wearing red because she has previously been married, has two children, and does not wish to wear the white of innocence, but who conducts research in China where red is the color of happiness (Couple 75, as described in Interlude 3), requires a fairly sophisticated audience to follow along and correctly interpret the implications of her use of color symbolism. This is the value of symbols: permitting complex ideas to be communicated relatively quickly, and with a minimum of explicit explanation for those who share an understanding of the symbol. The fact that members of a community share this understanding reinforces their sense of belonging. When some members of the audience cannot correctly interpret the symbolism used, it emphasizes their lack of co-membership in one or more relevant communities.

One way in which we understand meaning is to think in terms of a hierarchy organized according to the size of unit under analysis. A symbol can be grouped together with other symbols (and other types of signs, which do not always have to be arbitrary) and understood as part of a larger whole; the larger whole is then termed a social code. That is, all symbols relying on clothing as their vehicle to convey meaning are part of the same large set or social code. In addition to clothing, other examples of social codes examined in this book are food, objects and, to a lesser extent, language and music. Just as there are other types of signs than symbols, there are other types of codes than social. For example, logical or mathematical codes also have their place, but as that place is not normally in ritual, they play no role in the discussion here.[3]

Just as symbols combine into social codes, social codes also combine to form a larger unit, a culture. All cultures have the ability to make use of the same types of social codes (i.e., every culture makes use of food, clothing, objects, language, and music). What changes are the specific symbols used by each culture to convey meaning within each social code. That is, people do not eat the same foods the world over, and when they do, they do not cook the foods in the same way. One implication is that people who are raised within one culture will find every other culture to be a bit disorienting, at the very least. (This feeling of disorientation is technically termed *culture shock*.) If you are used to eating rice as the basis of every meal, it will be seem odd when someone from another culture expects to eat potatoes as the basis of every meal. If you think brides are supposed to wear white, when one chooses to wear red it will require some explanation before you understand that she does not mean by her choice of red what you would have meant by the choice of red in that same situation. Because symbols are arbitrary, they are different in each culture.[4] That is why they are an especially fruitful topic to study for those interested in understanding intercultural interactions, and why symbols often stand at the center of cultural misunderstandings.

Rituals are a vehicle used to combine selected symbols into meaningful patterns (Firth, 1973).[5] That is, a ritual combines individual symbols, often drawn from different social codes, into a coherent whole, as a way to convey multiple, complex messages. "Rituals reveal values at their deepest level ... men [sic] express in ritual what moves them most, and since the form of expression is conventionalized and obligatory, it is the values of the group that are revealed"

(Wilson, 1954, p. 241).[6] Inventing rituals to mark occasions of significance seems to be a uniquely human attribute: just as no animal society has been found that invents rituals, no human society has been found that does not (Fried & Fried, 1980).

THE PURPOSES OF RITUAL

Rituals are primarily about continuity, so they are largely predictable, at least for anyone familiar with the form displayed.[7] That is, anyone familiar with a culture who has previously attended a specific type of ritual can reasonably assume that later versions of the same ritual will be similar. If the bride has worn a white wedding gown in the last five weddings a participant has attended, it is not unreasonable to assume the bride in wedding number six will be likely to do so as well, and for surprise and confusion to result if she chooses any other color instead.

In Driver's (1998) phrase, the "social gifts of ritual" are order, community, and transformation (p. 132). Of these, the role played by ritual in creating a sense of community and a sense of order is usually emphasized, for rituals provide predictability and structure to members of a group. As such, they are "some of the plastic stays (the days of whalebone being long gone, of course) in society's corset" as Soeffner (1997, p. 73) so vividly phrased it.[8] Rituals provide a way of reaffirming social bonds within a group (Turner, 1969; van Gennep, 1960), as well as a vehicle for the "transmission of family culture across generations" (Troll, 1988, p. 628). Those who share your rituals are part of your community, and those who do not understand the meaning behind what occurs are not. If a family chooses to provide lemon for the chicken soup, everyone else who responds the way you do (say, squeezing the lemon juice into the soup) together make up the group of people who share assumptions, and in this case also the ethnic identity of being Greek American, with you (Couple 4).

Sometimes the felt need to adhere to custom is clearly marked by the way in which people describe their decisions. For example, the bride of Couple 95 said: "we had the cake top for the first year—*you* save that and eat it on your first anniversary (emphasis added)." Notice the pronoun *you*: What it indicates here is an understanding that "this is just what people do," and clear intent to follow the same guideline. (The bride of Couple 103 put even more explicitly: "We just took the top of the wedding cake for our first year anniversary *like most brides do*" (emphasis added). The bride of Couple 95 said at another point: "[the wedding was] very formal, because I used red roses for my bouquet ... back then that was the tradition, *if you were a bride it was roses*" (emphasis added). And because it was the tradition with which she was familiar, carrying some other color, or other type of flower was not even seriously considered. A surprising number of the brides in thus study followed the rhyme requiring that they wear "something old, something new, something borrowed, and something blue." A few even followed the final line, "and a sixpence in her shoe," although this was invariably changed to a penny for convenience, and often carried, not put in the shoe at all. Those who followed this tradition invariably assumed everyone else did also.

Sometimes the desire to follow traditions is made more difficult by the fact that some couples design and plan their own weddings before having been to very many, and they express concern that they might not have done it "right" as a result. The bride of Couple 99 married at 21, and expressed comfort with some of the basic elements. For example, she knew "the norm was the photographer took pictures, so that was your only way to look back at the day and so it was significant." But at other times she clearly indicated less comfort with their prior knowledge in some areas, such as dancing: "We hadn't been to very many weddings to know really what was the norm, if there was a norm." They did not incorporate dancing in the reception, mainly because the groom didn't dance, and were concerned that "this may have been a disappointment to our guests."

Rituals both mark and create the boundary dividing each group from others. Every time another bride wears white, you are reassured about the appropriateness of that choice. If a bride chooses to wear red, she must not be a member of your community. And all brides who chose to wear red are in some way part of the same community. When the bride of Couple 107 wore a red velvet dress, it indicated an affiliation, although distant, to China: Her parents had grown up in Hong Kong, although she herself was raised in England. And the groom's red velvet cravat made to match indicated his role as the link between his bride and American assumptions of appropriate wedding attire: "I was coming from a little bit more of my own, sort of United States with the tuxedo, but also had the red."[9]

Yet despite the lack of attention paid to it in many prior studies of ritual, what Driver terms the third gift of ritual, transformation, is at least as important as the first two. Rituals often serve as vehicles for the presentation and recognition of change.[10] As Santino (1994) concisely stated, "Rituals change things" (p. 11). This would seem to contradict the frequent emphasis on rituals as repetitive and traditional.[11] Perhaps it is most accurate to say that rituals primarily display continuity and structure, and secondarily are about change; they are, in any case, complex enough to convey more than one idea to participants. (If a symbol can convey multiple meanings, surely a ritual made up of many symbols can do so even more effectively.) Baumann (1999) suggested: "Culture maketh man, but it is men, women, and youths who make culture. If they ceased to make it and remake it, culture would cease to be; and all making of culture, no matter how conservative, is also a remaking" (p. 25). Rituals are one of the ways a community communicates ideas to its members; rituals must be flexible enough to incorporate new understandings achieved and new ideas developed by those members.

Eco (1990) proposed that "every work aesthetically 'well done' is endowed with two characteristics: It must achieve a dialectic between order and novelty, in other words, between scheme and innovation" (p. 91). Thus anyone designing an instance of any ritual faces the challenge of how to mesh continuity and change in appropriate ways: enough continuity that the audience recognizes what is occurring as a valid example of a particular type of ritual; enough creativity that the audience will recognize the appropriate adaptation of an old form to new and changing circumstances.[12] The same bride who wore red considered it completely appropriate to match the flowers to her dress (matching colors across social codes being a marker of formality quite common in weddings). Thus did her wedding demonstrate a balance of old and new elements. This couple did think it important to have a wedding, after all, only revising the form a bit to suit their unique circumstances.

My emphasis on the creative aspects of a ritual, rather than on treating rituals primarily as stable events, is unusual, but deliberate. I agree with Willis (1990) that "we are all cultural producers in some way and of some kind in our everyday lives" (p. 128). To me, rituals are interesting specifically for the ways they combine maintenance of traditional elements with changes over time. And, despite frequent instances of rhetoric to the contrary, all rituals do change over time, shifting to reflect the current needs of the participants.[13] "Cultural change means people coming to act differently and to regard the new ways as normal and even proper" (Charsley, 1992, p. 128), so culture "must be understood as it unfolds, develops, changes, erases itself, and rewrites itself" (MacCannell & MacCannell, 1982, p. 11).[14] That is why so many examples in this book illustrate real examples of how people revise old symbols to convey current meanings, while maintaining many aspects of the basic wedding ritual as their framework. Social actors "never simply enact culture but reinterpret and reappropriate it in their own ways" (Gupta & Ferguson, 1997b, p. 5). Rituals gain their power from their role as a visible link connecting the present with past traditions. If they vary too significantly from the expected, it becomes evident that they are not repetitions of past events but new social constructions, and they lose some of their power. But if they do not change over time, reflecting changes in the circumstances of their practitioners, they become obsolete and meaningless, and will be abandoned. Rituals require considerable time, effort, and resources: Why would anyone bother unless they were seen as valuable?

Rituals transform the participants, creating a community of separate individuals, and supplying a single identity for that community (Martin, 1996). Simply by being present at the same event, individuals come to see themselves as having something in common. Rituals integrate the performers with the audience members; they thus come to be called "collusive dramas" (Myerhoff, 1992, p. 167). To be successful, rituals generally require both performers and audience; either one alone is insufficient. One implication is that merely by being present at an intercultural wedding, participants grant their recognition of the new couple as a viable social unit. This is why some parents or relatives who are exceedingly unhappy about the proposed union refuse even to attend the ceremony, and why their absence is so notably marked and hurts the participants so much.

Couple 106, married in 1952, faced considerable opposition to their wedding because she was Roman Catholic (although her father had been raised Baptist, he converted in order to marry) and Irish American, when he was Missouri Synod Lutheran and German American. Knowing the considerable objections to their marriage, the bride hid the fact that she was sewing her wedding dress by choosing a blue fabric. "I wore blue … because I didn't want my mother to know I was making a wedding dress." Although his family was supportive, hers was not. Although she did not wear her engagement ring at home in order to hide her engagement, a colleague of her father's saw her at her fiancé's church, and so the secret was out. Her priest threatened excommunication: "I couldn't go to Catholic church and take communion or the sacraments any more because I had done what I had done. I was excommunicated from the church." As a result, "I had no one to stand up for me. My dad didn't come … I didn't walk down the aisle because I didn't have anybody to walk down with me." Although the bride's family normally is heavily involved in the planning, in this case "[groom's] family took over the whole wedding. We had a wedding reception in the basement and the backyard of their house. It wasn't until [daughter] was born and we named her after my grandmother and my mother that she came to the house … something like six years later." It is unusual for a family to wait 6 years before reconciling (although it is extremely common that the birth of a child serves as the catalyst for reconciliation), but this was hardly the only case where there was significant opposition, or where absence at the ceremony served as a marker of rejection of a child's choice of spouse.[15] Luckily, in this case at least, after the reconciliation with her mother the bride reported that "my husband wound up to be one of her [the bride's mother's] best friends."

The problems between Catholics and Lutherans continued for quite some time. The last wedding described occurred in 1952, but in 1970, the bride of Couple 103 found almost as much resistance from both her minister and her family. This time it was the Lutherans who objected, and the Catholics who accommodated the union. The bride said of her minister: "he was of the old school, very traditional. He wouldn't do it and I've never set foot in that church again … I was confirmed in that church, I had graduated from that grade school, it was a slap in the face." No religious traditions were incorporated into the ceremony because "we were both very hurt because I couldn't get married in the church." And she wore "off color white, ivory … I didn't feel I could wear white, I didn't really want to, because I was marrying outside of my religion. It still did bother me."

In other cases, distance prevents even accepting family and friends from attending. Couple 93 united an American groom with a Costa Rican bride.[16] Because the marriage was in Costa Rica, only his mother and stepfather were able to attend. But he was in the Peace Corps, and said "Peace Corps is kind of like my extended family so those people were there." Here, the presence of his surrogate family adequately compensated for the absence of the majority of his biological family.

Continuing with stories of the significance of attending weddings as a visible demonstration of support, in her study of Gypsies in the United States, Silverman (1991) reported: "Gypsies think nothing of traveling 600 miles by car in one day to attend a Gypsy wedding and then traveling home the next day" (p. 115). Many of those I interviewed also emphasized the critical importance of the statement made by attending (or refusing to attend) a wedding. When parents or relatives strenuously objected to a union, they occasionally made their objections visible by refusing to attend the ceremony. On the other hand, when even distant cousins or friends wished to make a statement of solidarity, they went to great effort to attend the ceremony, to make their support visible. As Toelken (1991) suggested, it sometimes seems necessary to participants to make a visible and public statement of identity especially in situations of great stress and conflict.[17] And "because identity touches the core of the self, it is also likely to be bound by powerful affect" (Epstein, 1978, p. 101), so emotions, as well as traditions, become relevant.

WHAT TYPE OF RITUAL ARE WEDDINGS?

The most important rituals are *rites de passage* (rites of passage), those marking the major life stages through which most members of a society pass: birth, puberty, marriage, death.[18] In the United States, there are no standardized rituals for birth; there is surprisingly little agreement about the point at which children become adults; and we try very hard to pretend we won't die, rarely planning funerals ahead of time.[19] But we make a big fuss about planning weddings, and for only this one event we do have a lot of traditions shared by a large proportion of the population. We spend more money on weddings than any other ritual (in fact, usually more money than on anything else except the purchase of a home), even in this day when half of all marriages end in divorce. Clearly these facts indicate the great importance weddings have for us. As with any ritual, "the ceremony marks marriages as an institution worthy of communal celebration and communal oversight" (Modell, 1985, p. 86). Because it is important, we celebrate; in celebrating, we increase the event's significance.

WEDDING RITUALS AS SOCIAL CONSTRUCTIONS

There is an unstated distinction assumed whenever the concept of social construction is brought up, and it is the difference between physical reality and social reality. Physical reality is, by and large, a given in our world. Most of us do not now and never will actually create parts of the natural world: mountains, trees, animals, plants (despite the potential of cloning). We do, however, create social meanings for these and other parts of the physical world (think of rainbows, a natural phenomenon given social meaning by the people who view them). As well as adding social meaning to the physical world, people do actually create the social world. This means we invent texts of various sorts (including rituals), also inventing significance for these and other social productions (which may have physical form: houses, clothing, tools, musical instruments, or not: songs, stories, jokes). So, we first invent a candle as a way to produce light, and then attach religious and ethnic connotations to the use of a particular set of actions relating to a candle during a wedding ceremony (as with a unity candle, most often seen in Italian Catholic weddings).

Intercultural weddings have one aspect that many other rituals and even other social constructions do not. As Moore and Myerhoff (1977) noticed:

> Underlying all rituals is an ultimate danger, lurking beneath the smallest and largest of them, the more banal and the most ambitious—the possibility that we will encounter ourselves making up our conceptions of the world, society, our very selves. We may slip into that fatal perspective of recognizing culture as our construct, arbitrary, conventional, invented by mortals. (p. 22)

If every wedding you attend incorporates the same symbols, it is possible to forget that ritual is a human construction, designed by people like yourself, and grant it substantial religious significance. However, when people do something you have never seen before, that highlights the fact that all weddings are socially constructed. This danger is most likely to occur with an intercultural wedding, because it is more obviously a social construction than a monocultural wedding. Although group boundaries are fictional (being social inventions and invisible), moving even a fictional boundary to incorporate members of two different groups, as happens during an intercultural wedding, effectively marks the joining of the two groups. For example, when a *huppah* has all the essential parts (cloth, 4 poles), and is used in the traditional manner (held over the bride, groom, and officiant), then those who expect to see a *huppah* will accept it as one, despite the fact that the cloth may be from Kenya, and the poles may be manzanita trees (Couple 74, as described in Interlude 1). When the family on the other side of the room recognizes only the African cloth and manzanita trees, they understand something entirely different (a statement of connection to Africa and the land). This subset of the audience may not have previously seen a *huppah*, and probably will not understand the symbolic connotations of one (representing the incorporation of a new couple into the existing Jewish community). Instead they may simply assume the canopy as a way to visually mark the bride, groom, and officiant as separate from the remainder of the participants.

The audience of peers and family judges a new couple based on the extent to which they are able to construct a new ritual without the fact of construction being too obviously apparent and intrusive, for "A ritual fails when it is seen through, not properly attended, or experienced as arbitrary invention. Then people may be indifferent enough not to hide their lack of conviction; their failure or refusal to appear to suspend disbelief is apparent and the ritual is not even efficacious as a communication" (Myerhoff, 1992, p. 183). During a ritual such as a wedding the participants must jointly construct a whole, making use of symbols to convey ideas, and then pretend not to notice their own role as designers. A successful intercultural wedding most often will be just as deliberately constructed as an unsuccessful one, though calling less attention to the constructed nature of the event.

Yet it is oddly possible for the reverse to be true as well. As with ethnic festivals celebrating traditional rituals in front of nongroup members, where the new audience requires that the event be framed and explicitly introduced so the newcomers will understand and appreciate what occurs (Abrahams, 1981), in some cases it seems that deliberately calling attention to the parts of an intercultural wedding that not everyone will understand makes for a more successful event. For example, in a wedding conducted by a Catholic priest between a bride who was White and Catholic and a groom who was African American and Baptist, the priest "was extremely careful as he spoke, trying to explain things as he went along. He really was very, very good, because knowing that [groom's] family was not of Catholic background, that he was trying to explain things" (Couple 9).[20] The participants appreciated his efforts to be inclusive, to ensure that everyone participating would understand the significance of the major parts of the ritual, even those parts new to them.

Intercultural weddings are more visibly social constructions than mainstream weddings in their attempt to combine the traditions of multiple communities, thus they are more difficult to construct well, and more dangerous if they are not. If a ritual is too visibly a construct of the designers, it is deemed a failure by many of the participants. This is the difficulty faced by couples designing intercultural wedding ceremonies: They must combine contradictory parts into a seamless whole, and they will be censured if the seams show too clearly. And yet if they do not let the seams show (as when explanations of particular elements are made for nonmembers of the community using them, so they will understand what is occurring), half their audience will be confused. And confusion is as inappropriate during a ritual as visibility, for those who do not understand the symbols cannot appreciate them. "Ritual may do much more than mirror existing social arrangements and existing modes of thought. It can act to reorganize them or even help to create them" (Moore & Myerhoff, 1977, p. 5). Intercultural weddings deliberately highlight the connections between two or more groups, providing a statement that ritual is not being tossed out, merely revised to accommodate current reality. By definition, intercultural weddings are more reflexive than mainstream weddings because they require that participants more actively decide what elements to include, rather than taking for granted that what others have done in the past will be appropriate for them.[21] (Being reflexive means to step outside of interaction temporarily, in order to notice the role played by oneself as well as others. For intercultural weddings, the point is that the bride and groom must be conscious of the differences in the assumptions of their guests, so that they do not inadvertently omit a symbol that will insult one side, or include a symbol that will insult the other.)

Even if self-consciously "created rituals" (Duntley, 1993, p. 7), such as intercultural weddings, show the seams a bit more than most, that does not make them any less important; in fact, it probably makes them more so. Peacock (1990) suggested "A performance is not necessarily more meaningful than other events in one's life, but it is more deliberately so; a performance is, among other things, a deliberate effort to represent, to say something about something" (p. 208). A wedding is nothing if not a carefully planned, deliberate performance. And sometimes changes in social life require changes in the expected wedding rituals (Reed-Danahay, 1996).

While presenting a paper on intercultural weddings at a conference in Paris several years ago, the European participants expressed astonishment that Americans have so much freedom to design their own weddings.[22] All of those from Europe, and also the several from Israel and Morocco, said that they would simply be told what to do by the religious leader, and they would have to do it, with virtually no choice possible. They considered it peculiarly American that we both have so much freedom and do not recognize the uniqueness of our position.

Assuming that intercultural weddings are rituals specifically designed to convey particular meanings brings up the question: How do we learn to create a ritual? The answer: As we learn everything else in culture, by participating in similar prior events, by our exposure to similar events through mass-media products, through direct teaching from our parents and elders, through the guidance of friends, relatives, and ritual specialists (Rosenthal & Marshall, 1988). Children wander through adult activities and are simultaneously "exposed to conversations, value judgments, and commentaries which set up for them a context for evaluation of others and reinforces whatever expectations are articulated" (Vélez-Ibáñez, 1993, p. 129). What they learn can be described as an extension of the linguistic concept of "communicative competence" (Duranti, 1988; Hymes, 1971): they learn to appropriately display their knowledge of the past through a unique revision of it in the present.[23] Myerhoff (1982) pointed out: "now we know rituals are not God-given but socially constructed, we are free to construct our own rituals" (Walter, 1994, p. 180). Turner (1987) took this further, arguing that "Religion, like art, *lives* in so far as it is performed, that is, in so far as its rituals are 'going concerns'" (p. 48). Intercultural weddings are certainly alive in this sense, for they respond to the immediate context, and the unique characteristics of the major participants, in ways mainstream weddings generally do not. That lack of flexibility to handle immediate circumstances is their strength, but it is also their weakness (strength, because mainstream weddings reassure guests that the old patterns are being continued; weakness, because they cannot appropriately take into account the needs of individual couples).

Wedding rituals are the first indication of how an intercultural couple proposes to combine their traditions, and "planning the wedding ceremony ... can serve as the emblem of how well the couple are able to deal with their disparate religious traditions" (Schneider, 1989, p. 134). Schneider was speaking here of interfaith weddings only, but the notion can be generalized to any sort of intercultural union. Obviously it is possible for a couple to reach different accommodations at different points in their relationship, but never again will the accommodation they reach be made evident in so public a statement. That is one reason why it is given so much emphasis, and treated so seriously by the participants. If it were easy to reach an accommodation, to reconcile clearly divergent requirements, public demonstration of that ability would not hold so much significance for the participants. As ritual is "the public face of private experience" (Gerholm, 1988, p. 195), we study rituals to understand otherwise private aspects of social life.

Because rituals are closely tied to particular communities, all of the rituals within a specific community have similarities (Cartry, 1992). This is one of the major difficulties in creating an intercultural wedding that successfully integrates elements of multiple traditions: no matter what occurs, it won't "properly" resemble other rituals within any one community represented at the wedding, so everyone will be startled and potentially disappointed at the result, no matter what their explicit intentions or their intended support of the marriage. It just won't "feel right" to the participants because it won't fit cleanly into the progression of prior rituals (including especially prior weddings) they have experienced. A ritual event is expected to be one of a continuous series (one person's birth, coming of age, wedding, funeral; all the weddings in a single extended family, all the weddings held in a single church, etc.). Intercultural weddings stand out as disjunctive, different from the rest, noteworthy, marked. "We engage in rituals in order to transmit collective messages to ourselves" (Leach, 1976, p. 45). Intercultural weddings raise questions that monocultural weddings do not. What kind of message are we sending ourselves if not all participants can understand or even recognize some of the symbols used? Who is the intended audience, if some of those present do not understand the message? Thus, despite an explicit rhetoric of uniting divergent audiences, if an intercultural wedding is not quite carefully designed, it will serve instead only to mark (and thereby intensify) the division between the multiple groups attending.

Bouissac (1990) took this point even further in his explanation of the various ways in which sacred performances are made profane. Briefly, he said we profane the sacred when we do any of the following things:

1. A particular object assigned to a certain place or position is moved to and placed in an inappropriate place or position.
2. An object that should be manipulated in a certain manner (or simply be seen) by a particular person or class of persons, or is manipulated in this manner (or is seen) by an unqualified person, or is manipulated in an inappropriate manner.
3. A patterned behavior that should be performed in the presence of an object or person is performed in the presence of an inappropriate object or person.
4. A patterned behavior that is prescribed in a specific context is performed in another context or is not performed in the prescribed context.
5. A word or text to which a prescribed interpretation is attached, is interpreted in another manner or, still worse,
6. The consequences of this new interpretation are actually implemented. (p. 196)

Reviewing this list, it becomes obvious that intercultural weddings inadvertently involve making the sacred elements of each of the expected performances profane. No wonder the participants' parents and religious leaders so often object! The solution occurs when, as with other elements of ritual, the notions of what constitutes sacred and profane change over time.

In keeping with this, Unitarian Minister James Ishmael Ford told me "I'm very pleased to claim that my weddings are usually tearful events ... people know that something profound is happening."[24] In other words, a ritual has not served its purpose if the participants leave emotionally untouched. And, obviously, knowing that something profound has happened is only possible when participants from different groups either share sufficient background understandings or are explicitly brought into the circle of the initiated. Rituals are most successful when everyone becomes involved. An American of Sephardi (Middle Eastern) Jewish heritage, Robin Schaer, echoed this comment on the significance of active involvement for her and her husband:

> "I think it's important to adapt and reinterpret traditions rather than forget about them altogether," offers Robin. "It was really meaningful for Adam and me to learn as much as we could about the wedding ceremony. We didn't want to do *anything* just because we *had* to. We wanted to feel a part of what we were doing and understand it. There was not a single element of our wedding that Adam and I didn't put ourselves into. The wedding is an epic moment. I think the more you learn, understand, and incorporate your own personality into the wedding, the more powerful it will feel for you and your guests."[25]

Occasionally the effort to incorporate family traditions that the bride and groom themselves have not previously followed leads to the bride or groom uttering statements during the wedding ceremony in a language they themselves do not understand. This happened when part of a service was in Hindu, with particular sections that the bride or groom were required to repeat after the officiant, for Couple 12. In this case, both the bride and groom have one parent from India, and one from the United States. The central participants were willing to say "I am Indian" in a language neither of them understood, and the audience members, many of whom did understand the language, were willing to accept that statement, knowing that the speakers intended to declare symbolic membership in their family group despite their lack of literal understanding. Similarly, Couple 26 involved an Indonesian bride with Dutch background, and an American groom who married in Holland. In this case, the groom understood very little of the ceremony conducted in Dutch, but considered it of no consequence—only his commitment to the marriage was of concern, and that transcended the language issue.[26] Other times, a similar concern with what really matters leads to the opposite result in terms of language choice, as when the Christian groom of Couple 1, marrying a Jewish bride, said: "I didn't want to make my vows—binding commitments—in a language I didn't understand. It was important to me that my vows be fully heartfelt, and I felt they couldn't be if I had to understand them through an interpreter. Also, it was important to me that they not say anything that I didn't believe."

Couple 72 involved a Tunisian Jewish bride marrying an American Jewish groom in Israel, in a ceremony conducted in Hebrew (a language that the groom knew only slightly at the time). As a result, the groom reported: "As for the ceremony, I barely understood it and made a 'funny/cute' mistake under the *chupa*[27] I repeated the rabbi's request to someone to bring the cup (to break) because I had been told to repeat everything he said to me." In fact, he added: "It is fair to say that most of the time I had only a very faint idea about the significance of the rituals." This despite the fact that the bride's father had asked the Ashkenazi rabbi of the town, instead of the Sephardi one, to conduct the service, as a courtesy to the American guests (the distinction concerns what part of the world one's ancestors come from; the bride's family was Sephardi, but the groom's family was Ashkenazi). Ironically, it was not only the groom who did not understand everything that occurred; the bride was born and raised in Israel, so she did not know much more of the Tunisian traditions incorporated into the ceremony than the groom and his family. Despite this, "she felt that it showed them [her parents] honor to allow them to plan everything." In these examples, the emotion attached to the event was sufficient that it transcended even basic comprehension of the language used, or real understanding of the various components of the ritual.

Other couples report deliberately changing the ceremony so that everyone will be able to understand all the parts. In a Jewish–Christian wedding, the Christian groom decided not to wear a *kipah* (skullcap), the usual sign of respect that a Jewish man would wear on any sacred occasion, because he did not want his family to see it as an indication that he was converting, because, in fact, he was not (Couple 5).[28] As with other symbols, this one is complex, conveying different meanings to different participants: For Jews, the *kipah* connotes respect for God, and so any male participating in a religious service is permitted or even expected to wear one; for Christians, it connotes being Jewish, because only Jews wear *kipot*. However, the groom of Couple 1, another Jewish–Christian marriage, the one who considered it inappropriate to say his wedding vows in Hebrew, a language he did not know, said "I would have worn a *yarmulke* [synonym for *kipah*] as a sign of respect, had I been asked."

Sometimes a couple will choose to include particular elements of a wedding because they feel that their relatives would mind if they were omitted. Several brides with Polish background reported incorporating, as one described it, "that dumb Polish thing with the woman putting on the apron" (Couple 3).[29] Although these brides felt awkward donning an apron at the reception for the sole purpose of having guests stuff the pockets with money, they did not want to omit an element of a wedding which had been incorporated into the weddings of their siblings, or parents, and that these family members would miss were it absent.

Other times, the couple include elements for the meaning they have for themselves. Several people described the significance of the father of the bride giving her away to the groom. For example, the bride of Couple 92 described this as "one of those things that I think every bride dreams of, having her father give her away. I think it's really cool. And I was fortunate enough to have him do it twice." The bride of Couple 95 also stressed the emotional power of that same moment: "I remember my father taking my arm and connecting it with [groom's] arm. My father did not give me a hug, but it meant a lot to me that he took [groom's] arm and adjoined it with mine."

The same point in the ceremony can be slightly tweaked, depending on circumstances, to take on additional meanings the individuals wish to convey. Couple 89 were separated by 22 years, and the groom had been married six times previously. The father of the bride modified the moment of passing his daughter to her new husband as follows:

Minister: "Who gives [bride] to [groom] to be married?"
Bride's mother: "Her mother and father who've loved her for the last 25 years."
Bride's father: "I'm giving her hand in marriage but I'll never give her away."
[Smile from daughter and several guests.]
[Noticeable pause and startled look from the minister before he continues.]
Minister: "Thank you."

Perhaps this father's hesitation was justified, for this marriage did end in divorce.

In a multicultural society, rituals must speak to multiple participants, and change to accommodate new audiences. Baumann (1992) argued that "instead of assuming that rituals celebrate the perpetuation of social values and self-knowledge, I suggest that they may equally speak to aspirations towards cultural change" (p. 99).[30] Intercultural weddings fit nicely here: combining multiple strands into a new whole, they exemplify the changes occurring in the larger society. As Hughes-Freeland and Crain (1998) put it, today "ritual is most usefully and relevantly theorised as a contested space for social action and identity politics—an arena for resistance, negotiation and affirmation" (p. 2). Rather than display a rhetoric of continuity within a single community, modern rituals can serve as a "challenge to cultural homogeneity" (p. 8). Certainly intercultural weddings do such service.

Weddings symbolize, among other things, the historical connections of the major participants: "The sense of history is celebrated in collective ritual. Ritual acts are also expressions of commitment, be it to a religion, to a nation of loyal citizens, or to an ethnic group. Such acts are a collective experience that teaches those who participate who they are" (De Vos & Romanucci-Ross, 1982b, p. 365).[31] The major participants are granted a public opportunity to demonstrate what they have learned of telling stories about themselves, even while being constrained by prior stories told by others (Rosenwald & Ochberg, 1992). "The tales we tell each other (and ourselves) about who we are and might yet become are individual variations on the narrative templates our culture deems intelligible" (Ochberg, 1992, p. 214).[32] Extremes are remarked upon: Weddings held on a beach instead of in a church, red wedding gowns in lieu of white, black bridesmaids' dresses instead of the expected pastels, children of the bride and groom who participate in the ceremony; all these are sufficiently unusual that they are remarked upon by guests.

RITUALS AS PERFORMANCE

Ritual always involves a performance; it is not a ritual if you simply read a description out loud. A wedding requires what Austin (1999) called "performative" utterances; that is, speaking specific words serves as an action, in that the words cause a change in status. "When I say, before the registrar or altar, 'I do,' I am not reporting on a marriage; I am indulging in it" (p. 64). In other words, uttering the ritual phrase "I do" actually performs an activity turning two individuals into one publicly acknowledged couple. (This is the traditional explanation for why Jews do not have rehearsals prior to their wedding ceremonies, although Christians do: Uttering the words, even if framed as a rehearsal, is understood to be so powerful an act that the bride and groom would be married from that point on, making the scheduled wedding ceremony moot.) As Hymes (1981) put it, "performance is a mode of existence and realization that is partly *constitutive* of what the tradition is" (p. 86). It is through performance that people make such intangibles as identities visible.[33] In other words, any ritual is a performance when it does something, changes something.

A ritual not only marks tradition, but serves to maintain it. Tradition, being abstract, does not really have concrete existence. Rituals, being made up of visible symbols with concrete existence, are one of the primary ways in which tradition finds life. Further, if Bauman (1986) is correct, "Every performance will have a unique and emergent aspect, depending on the distinctive circumstances at play within it" (p. 4). That means that it really is not unusual to notice the changes occurring in intercultural weddings; what is unusual is when guests at mainstream weddings find the smaller changes there to be unremarkable. No wedding perfectly replicates any past wedding, but most of the time only intercultural weddings are seen as sufficiently new and different to warrant extended commentary from guests.[34]

It is often stated that rituals convey meaning through symbols; although this is certainly true, Schieffelin (1985) warned that it is only the beginning. "Symbols are effective less because they communicate meaning (although this is also important) than because, through performance, meanings are formulated in a social rather than cognitive space, and the participants are engaged with the symbols in the interactional creation of a performance reality, rather than being merely informed by them as knowers" (p. 707). In Schieffelin's formulation, an idea can have meaning in a cognitive space (within one person's mind), or in a social space (among a collection of individuals, a group of some sort). He is most interested, as I am, in what happens between people, rather than in what happens within one person's mind only. It is the use of symbols in performance that makes them meaningful; active participation in a performance gives it significance, not the mere fact that a ritual presents specific messages in a specific form. It is "by socially constructing a situation in which the participants experience symbolic meanings" (p. 709) that rituals gain their rhetorical force. The experience (and the attendant emotions) stand at the forefront, not the logical sense of what is presented. For example, Americans recognize a groom's cake as a standard element of a wedding. Colombians recognize the *tunjo* symbol as an indicator of Colombian identity. A groom's cake with a *tunjo* on it combines the expectations of both groups, each of which is free to ignore the significance of what has meaning to the other (Couple 84 as described in Interlude 2). Combining these symbols shows members of both groups that their expectations are being met, perhaps in a slightly different way than expected, but still met.

One element of ritual as performance is the attention to the element of time. Particular events are expected to happen in a specific order. One has showers before the wedding, and a honeymoon after. But, as with other events, there are discrepancies in assumption between different cultural groups. As a result, elements may hold different positions in the sequence for different groups. For example, most couples give gifts (to the wedding party) at the rehearsal dinner (sometimes with the expectation that gifts will be incorporated into the wedding, as when bridesmaids are given jewelry they then wear during the ceremony), but some now give gifts at the reception following the wedding. Couple 105, who had *padrinos* (mentors), made a point of honoring them publicly at the reception by naming the aspect of the wedding each had sponsored, but also giving gift certificates, and a photograph of themselves in a nice frame. One possible explanation for this is that some of their relatives were unfamiliar with this standard Hispanic tradition, and they had some resistance initially from people who considered it odd to be asked to "sponsor" some part of the wedding (mainstream American tradition assuming that the bride's parents will cover the majority of the costs, with a few specific elements covered by the groom's parents—usually the rehearsal dinner—but apportioning none of the cost to more distant relatives or friends).

Another critical element of any ritual performance is the use of space. Space and time sometimes combine in interesting ways. Couple 95 described how their placement of the wedding photograph album changed over time:

> Back then when we were first married, you set them [photos] out on the coffee table and so when guests came over they would just look at them … for the first fifteen years of our marriage, I always had it setting in the living room out on a bookshelf or out in the open on a coffee table or something so if people wanted to see they could … now up in my closet on a shelf.

This movement of the photo album over time was repeated in the stories of many other couples. When the wedding is recent, photographs representing it are placed where they will be immediately publicly accessible, and they are shown often to friends. (One bride, of couple 108, specifically mentioned how, in one way, it was sad that virtually everyone who was invited to her wedding actually came, as that limited the number of people who would want to see the photographs of the event; but one groom, of Couple 90, specifically mentioned that they had shown the videotape and photographs to those who were there, so obviously some disparity exists between groups about who should be shown photographs and on what occasions.) As the years go by, the photo album is generally moved first out of immediate sight, but close enough that it is still accessible for anyone who asks (and many couples reported looking through the album themselves on their anniversaries, or later with their children). Eventually, in a very long marriage, the wedding album becomes less significant, being put away in a box, a closet, the attic, only to be pulled out if requested. (But virtually all couples indicated they knew where photographs of their weddings could be found if they were again wanted.) In these cases, the length of the marriage seems to be what makes the photographs of the wedding less significant. The wedding stands as only the opening marker for the marriage, which itself comes to represent the relationship, rather than the photographs of the first moment of that formal relationship. Diamont (1985) suggested:

> Most people want the standard pictures of the principals: bride, groom, their families and attendants—and for good reason. These photos take their place in a gallery of family portraits, and even the corniest poses—like cutting the wedding cake—assume historical proportions when placed next to a nearly identical shot of your parents doing precisely the same thing thirty-five years ago. (p. 128)

Other elements of the wedding were frequently preserved so they, too, could be made available to friends and family members as support for discussion of the wedding, and as a memory jog. Most couples displayed at least one photograph of themselves, and a surprising number had particular elements of their ceremony preserved in various ways (the dress was often professionally dry-cleaned and put in a box that had never been opened, residing now in some closet; it was not uncommon for someone to have laminated the wedding invitation or preserved it in a frame or mounted it on a piece of wood, as a wedding gift; cake toppers were generally kept, and often put out for display; sometimes multiple indices for the wedding were stored together, in a shadow box or on a knick-knack shelf).

CHANGING THE FORM OF RITUAL

The possibility of creating intercultural rituals prompts an interesting question: How much change can the central narrative bear? Sometimes the changes mandated by circumstances are too much for some of the participants, even the bride or groom. A bride from Panama who was Roman Catholic and a groom from Kuwait who was Muslim, were married by a Justice of the Peace, because they could see no other possible solution to their differing religious and cultural expectations. Afterwards, the bride was not entirely satisfied because it had been so different from her prior experience of weddings (Couple 2).[35] Legally, she was married, but as a result of her own prior expectations, she didn't feel sufficiently, fully married. In contrast to this, couples who follow traditions they have seen incorporated into prior weddings have an easier time of it. The bride in a monocultural Lithuanian American wedding said: "'My favorite part of the wedding was dancing the *Rezginele* with our friends.... It really made me feel married. I had done it for so many friends' wedding, and now it was my turn.'"[36]

One of the most significant changes in the wedding ritual involves the incorporation of children into the ceremony. As it is becoming more common for couples to have children prior to their marriage, whether with each other or not, in a prior marriage or not, such children are today often given a role in the wedding ceremony.[37] Girls are flower girls; boys are ring bearers if they are quite small, or ushers if they are older. Couple 44 included the groom's son as mini-groom and ring bearer. Later, at their reception, the first dance between the bride and groom was followed by a second between the bride and the groom's son, and a third, where the bride, groom, and groom's son all danced together.[38] In another wedding, the bride from Venezuela and the groom from the United States had a 3-year-old daughter at the time they married, who served as their flower girl (Couple 59).[39] This same couple celebrated their wedding outdoors, with the bridesmaids in black, sexy dresses they could wear again on other occasions. The bride chose to wear a white gown and veil; though she recognized it was generally accepted as a sign of virginity, she decided it could alternatively stand for being a virgin at getting married. She also wore sunglasses (it was an outside, summer wedding and they were practical) and the bouquets she and the bridesmaids held were made up of red flowers. The couple reported that these details shocked many of the guests. In these cases, prior commitments are brought into the wedding ritual in a substantial way. Children need to be assured that they are important to their parents, and that the new marriage will not diminish their role. By including the children, the bride and groom make public statements about their past history as individuals and prior commitments still having significance for them.

RITUALS AS COMPLEX EVENTS

Rituals are complex events, with many elements distributed across multiple codes, sometimes incorporating multiple events staged at different sites on different days. At the least, wedding rituals include language, clothing, objects, and usually food, music and dance as well. Different couples have slightly different ideas about the essential component events of a wedding, based on their past experience at the weddings of others. In addition to the central ceremony, the various components can include everything from an engagement party to the honeymoon. In fact, it is now possible to tie the parts together more closely than before. Some couples invite a small number of guests to an exotic location for the wedding, and then stay together through what would have been the honeymoon; traditionally called "destination" weddings, these have now been named "wedding-moons" (Bulcroft, Smiens, & Bulcroft, 1999, p. 166).

Because not all elements of even the central wedding ceremony can be attended to equally, some gain more attention; these become *key symbols*. Key symbols are those granted greater significance than other symbols, those more frequently present, more obviously visible, most often found in a typical form.[40] Key symbols are important to study, although certainly not the only elements worthy of attention. Each social code is represented by at least one key symbol in a ritual. Ortner (1973) examined key symbols in detail, suggesting the following characteristics:

1. Informants tell us X is important;
2. Informants seem positively or negatively aroused by X, but not indifferent;

3. X comes up in many contexts;
4. There is greater cultural elaboration surrounding X than other symbols; and
5. There is greater cultural restrictions surrounding X than other symbols.[41]

Following these criteria, at least four key symbols are present at mainstream American weddings. For the social code of language, the key symbol is the set of vows exchanged by bride and groom. For the social code of clothing, the key symbol is the bridal gown (logically, what the groom wears should be granted equal significance, but this clearly is not the case in practice).[42] For the social code of objects, it is the wedding rings.[43] For the social code of food, it is the wedding cake, present not at the formal wedding ceremony but at the reception that generally follows (when there are multiple cakes, it is the bride's white cake that counts, not the groom's dark cake).[44] For all four key symbols, the standards of acceptable variants are quite narrow. Typical vows are mutual and fairly brief (unlike the various material culture key symbols, the vows need to be approved by the officiant ahead of time, and often the exact words are dictated by religious affiliation). Several officiants told me they would not marry a couple unwilling to say their marriage would last "until death do us part" or some variant thereof in their vows (the logic is that if a couple does not even make the attempt to make their marriage last forever, they are certainly not likely to succeed.)[45] The standard for the bridal gown is that it be white (understood to symbolize purity, innocence, virginity), long (symbolizing modesty and formality), use elements of fashion no longer deemed appropriate in any other context (a link to the past), and be of fabric such as silk and/or decorated with lace and pearls (symbolizing expense). The standard for the wedding rings is that they be gold bands (symbolizing expense and durability), of the same or related design for bride and groom (symbolizing unity), and it is often commented that they are unending circles (representing that the marriage is to be unending). The standard for the wedding cake is a multilayered, white cake decorated with white frosting and either sugar or real flowers, often with a miniature bride and groom (although sometimes with alternatives such as doves or bells) on the top layer. The cake is generally said to symbolize abundance, that there should always be enough food for the new couple to eat. Because these parts of the wedding are so central, one of my students termed them the result of "grand planning" in mainstream weddings.[46]

Three of these key symbols for weddings are aspects of material culture, what Charsley (1992) called "materialized customary action" (p. 129). Material elements of the wedding ritual receive emphasis in these pages over the verbal elements because ritual objects appear to be far less flexible than ritual language. Words can be changed for multiple participants (as when vows are uttered in one language and then immediately repeated in another), but it is characteristic of material symbols that they are more often singular. There is generally one wedding cake, one wedding dress, and there used to be one wedding ring, for the bride alone, although now there are usually two matching rings. Of course there are exceptions to this, but they are always interesting and often quite revealing. A second reason to emphasize material elements of weddings is that objects endure long after words have been uttered and forgotten, so they are particularly powerful symbols for the participants, and especially easy to study.[47] The use of material objects in rituals is one way we hold on to the event:

> Ritual acts and utterances may be experienced as ephemeral, even though their effects endure. Ritual objects, in contrast, provide a sustained physical presence, a constant, tangible reminder of the rituals of which they have formed and will again form a part. They serve not only as a reminder but also as a stimulus, focus, affirmation, guide, and resource for ritual activity. They are activated by ritual acts and utterances, at the same time that they possess a power of their own. (Kirshenblatt-Gimblett, 1982, p. 145)[48]

As has been pointed out by Hoskins (1998, p. 198), objects can provide "an alternate form of biography." This is why so many important symbols from the wedding ceremony later find their way into the central participants' home: Most couples continue to wear the rings they exchanged; most brides keep their wedding gowns; wedding cake toppers are often kept with other small objects of value on public view; photograph albums and videotapes are routinely viewed, either by the bride and groom or by family members together, as part of a discussion of family history, and many people have their wedding portraits hanging on their walls, for guests to view.[49] "The things we make, appropriate and use are a manifestation of social forms while also shaping them" (Dant, 1999, p. 12). Therefore the same objects serve to teach our children family history occurring before they arrived, and simultaneously to shape their expectations for designing a comparable ritual they marry in turn.[50] Whether during the ceremony or after it is long over, material elements, being more concrete than language, play significant roles and should not be ignored.

As the bride of Couple 99 pointed out, in addition to key symbols, there is a common set of central elements to be expected in any mainstream wedding. She described hers as having been the "standard American wedding: Church service, exchanging rings ... the standard ceremony was the bride walks to the bridegroom ... and the changing of the hands from the father to the bridegroom and the pastor saying a few words, saying the wedding vows, which at that time were standard ones ... then we marched back down the aisle and left. It took about 20 minutes."

Each cultural group develops its own material culture elements of a wedding. The *huppah* is so much a central part of the Jewish wedding ceremony that artists often use it to symbolize a wedding. This is shown in a sculpture by Susan Fullenbaum incorporating only three elements: the groom in black, the bride in white, and a *huppah*.[51] Despite this, technically neither the *huppah* nor the rabbi is essential to the performance of a Jewish wedding: The exchange of something of value and saying the vows are the only essential components. As Rabbi Aryeh Alpern said:

> I tell couples that I prefer working with co-officiants ... because the essence of the Christian wedding is the vows, the essence of a Jewish wedding is the rings. So the vows are done first, then I do the rings, and I look up and say, well, now that you're officially married in two traditions, you certainly have our permission to kiss twice. I thought it was corny the first time I said it, but it brought the house down.[52]

Because material culture elements remain as indices after the wedding ceremony ends, particular ways of handling them develop. Because stepping on the glass is so frequently a part of Jewish wedding ceremonies, whole businesses have grown up around the effort to preserve the shards of glass that result. The Complete Jewish Wedding web page advertises:

> Rather than disposing of the broken glass at the end of your wedding ceremony, create a family heirloom you will cherish for years to come. Break one of our colorful handblown glasses at your wedding and save the shards. Your shards will then be integrated into one of the following items: Mezuzah, Star of David sculpture, Candlesticks, Kiddush cup, Menorah.[53]

Notice their assumption that anyone who follows the religious rituals to the point of including breaking a glass in their wedding ceremony will later follow at least one of the other religious rituals implied by this list (saying the Sabbath prayers at home, which would require the use of candlesticks and a *kiddush* cup; placing a *mezuzah* on the door to bless the home; celebrating Hanukkah, requiring a *menorah*, etc.).

Occasionally a new symbol is developed. Something called a "family medallion," a piece of jewelry devised 12 years ago by Roger Coleman, a chaplain in Kansas City, is now available for couples who need to incorporate children into their ceremony.

> The medallions, which cost up to $125, have three interlocking circles meant to symbolize the new family's love. They're often presented along with the wedding bands as part of the formal ceremony. "The medallions are one small way of reinforcing families and making children feel included," says Coleman.... Whether they're any more effective, long term, than any other sort of wedding jewelry remains to be seen, but children seem to like them. Some couples who have used the medallions at their betrothals report that their kids don't want to take them off. (Kirn & Cole, 2000, p. 54)

Although I have not interviewed anyone who made use of a medallion, one showed up on the television show, A *Wedding Story*. In this case, the bride already had a 10-year-old daughter, who was incorporated into the ceremony by the groom putting the medallion over her head, and stating: "In the placing of this family medallion we pledge to you, J'Aysha, our continuing love, even as we surround you with our arms of support."[54] If enough people choose to incorporate these medallions in their weddings, they may eventually become a key symbol, accompanying or even replacing the older symbol, wedding rings.

Sometimes an entire wedding is planned around the choice of a single key symbol of great importance to the couple. Loeding (1992) described a wedding in which the bride wanted to wear her mother's 1940s dress (which was too small, and had to be resewn) as one way of "preserving a piece of personal history" (p. 14). The remainder of the wedding was designed using a 1940s theme, with flowers, veil and jewelry chosen to match the dress; the bridesmaids rented outfits to match the bridal gown's design. Other elements were also matched: they had big band music at the reception, rented a 1940s car for the day, and invited guests to wear 1940s fashions.

Whether or not it is the central symbol of a wedding, the bridal gown is a focus of substantial attention for nearly all. It is not only the United States where wedding clothes are granted great importance. Johnson (1998) documented a case study in the Philippines where the bride wore a U.S.-style white wedding dress to both the ceremony and the reception (the accepted standard being to wear traditional Filipino clothes to the ceremony, and an American white dress only to the reception).

At first I had thought that I had stumbled upon my first example of cultural innovation, since I knew, both from the previous wedding I had attended and from previous pictures of weddings I had seen, that it was usually men who wore Western style clothing for their weddings. I was slightly disappointed, therefore, when the groom's mother (actually his mother's sister) who, because the bride's family objected to the wedding, had taken charge of the marriage arrangements, told me somewhat apologetically that they had rented the wedding dress at a discount from a gay-transvestite beautician friend (who also did the make-up/hair-do for the bride). Apparently they had not been able to afford to buy the cloth and pay to have a traditional outfit made for the bride. Moreover, I soon discovered that the dress had become the subject of widespread gossip in the community; some people expressed the opinion that it was scandalous and disgraceful for a Muslim woman to have worn a "Christian" wedding dress for Islamic wedding rites.

Whatever the reason for the choice in the first place, the groom's mother suggested that it was better to wear a Western-style wedding dress than risk the humiliation of either having to ask the bride's parents to provide a suitable outfit, or borrowing a suitable outfit from friends. As it was, she told me, she and her husband had borrowed so much money from friends they were "unable to hold their shame." (pp. 220–221)

Similarly, among the San Blas Kuna of Guatemala, the groom's family provides the bride with a complete set of clothes, and it is generally accepted that their choice publicly indicates the treatment she will receive from her new husband and his family.

> Along with their immediate use value for the day's events, the clothes are seen as a reflection of how well the woman will be treated in her new role as wife. If the wedding *traje* [traditional Kuna clothing] is exceptionally fine, her parents are relieved to think that their daughter will be well taken care of. Even less expensive outfits can signal the future well-being of a bride if a family of modest means takes care to buy the best they can afford. However, clothing that is inferior or below the standard that the family is able to afford does not bode well for the marriage. For example, a *huipil* [traditional blouse] with relatively few designs or one done with long loopy brocade stitches and poor-quality thread is regarded as a public announcement of bad things to come. And it is embarrassing for the bride's family to realize that all who attend the wedding will see from the clothing the potentially unhappy situation that the young woman is enduring. (Hendrickson, 1995, p. 121)

To return to the United States, a wedding gown is so thoroughly associated with weddings that it functions effectively as a metonym (a part understood to represent the whole): An image of the gown alone is sufficient to convey the information that a wedding is occurring or has occurred. Many 1940s or 1950s films close with a scene of bride and groom, dressed appropriately, and no more need be said: the viewers know they married and "lived happily ever after" as the fairy tale ending puts it. Leonard (1980) described the problem of renting or buying a used wedding gown. Men may rent their suits, and in the United States nearly always do, but "the bride is to be 'pure' and 'unsullied' in a way not applicable to the groom" (p. 132) and so should have a never previously worn gown. This is not entirely logical, as the groom of Couple 88 pointed out in the following conversation.[55]

Groom: "Don't you normally rent wedding dresses?"
Bride: "No, we are buying mine, we are buying my wedding dress."
Groom: "You rent a tux?"
Bride: "Yeah, you rent a tux."
Groom: "You never rent a wedding dress?"
Bride: "You can, you can do that."

Clothing designers often end their shows with an elaborate new style of wedding dress, often one that no actual bride would seriously consider wearing. Their designs show up in bridal magazines and even newspapers (the *New York Times Magazine* frequently includes photographs of unlikely wedding gowns by famous designers), but rarely at actual weddings.[56] Diamont (1985) pointed out that "wedding clothes are the most important ritual garments most of us will ever own" (p. 67), which may well account for some of the elaboration of this particular symbol.[57] But it is not only the bride and groom who dress up for a wedding; guests must also. Bridgwood (1995) found in her study of Turkish Cypriot weddings held in England that, "Weddings offer an excellent forum for display and conspicuous consumption, and people usually take care to look their best" (p. 39). It is no different in the United States: Describing a farming community, Schwartz (1992) noticed "People take advantage of weddings as opportunities to wear their finest, most stylish outfits" (p. 108).

In their study of group marriage, Constantine and Constantine (1974) found that the ring seemed to be the minimal representation of marriage that everyone accepted: in a group marriage, bridal gowns were deemed superfluous, but everyone wanted a ring (p. 91). Diamant (1985) provided some of the historical explanation for the inclusion of the ring in wedding ceremonies.

> In Jewish law a verbal declaration of marriage is not legally binding in and of itself. There must be also an act of *kinyan*—a formal, physical acquisition. Without the groom's giving and the bride's acceptance of some object of nominal value—something *shaveh p'rutah*, literally, "worth a penny"—there is no marriage. Since the seventh century a ring has been the traditional and preferred object of exchange. (p. 69)

Although originally a Jewish tradition, this is now an integral part of Christian ceremonies as well.

Even a single change in a key symbol is understood to convey information. A Catholic bride of German heritage who was White, married a Baptist groom who was African American (Couple 9).[58] For their wedding cake they made a deliberate decision to have a chocolate–vanilla marble cake; as the bride said "That was significant!" They described this as one way to explicitly display the combination of their backgrounds, in the face of considerable family objections to the marriage.

Sometimes, when a bride and groom want to change a key symbol, other participants are so upset, they give up. One couple had eaten ice cream sundaes on their first date, and wanted to substitute ice cream sundaes for the cake at the reception. But the bride's aunt talked her out of it: She said a cake would be expected by their guests, and so they must have it (Couple 30).[59] This shows the power and significance of key symbols: If they are not displayed, the entire ritual performance can be significantly weakened. Other symbols in the wedding can more readily be changed, without the same prediction of dire consequences. For example, in a wedding between a Malaysian and Muslim bride, and a groom who was raised Christian in the United States, but who converted to Islam, the groom wanted to kiss the bride (the marker that the couple is now formally wed in mainstream American weddings), but that would be inappropriate in a Muslim ceremony. The compromise reached was that he kissed her forehead (Couple 36).[60]

Whether a wedding is mainstream or intercultural, it still needs to meet a significant requirement of all rituals, to be clearly distinguishable from everyday life. As Handelman (1990) phrased it, public ritual entails "a comparative formalization of space, time, and behavior that distinguishes these from the living of mundane life" (p. 11). This is one answer to the underlying question about why people make such a fuss over weddings: We want to mark a particular change in status as important, and the way to do so is to have an elaborate ritual marking the change. Given Handelman's emphasis on the formalization required by ritual, it should be no surprise that formality in American mainstream weddings is highly elaborated, as described earlier. Wedding gowns are among the most elaborate examples of clothing anyone ever wears; wedding cakes are about the most elaborate examples of food people actually eat, and among the most time-consuming to create. Just as wedding gowns and wedding cakes are among the most expensive examples of clothing and food, engagement and wedding rings are frequently the most expensive jewelry (or even the *only* expensive jewelry) most people ever purchase. But it works both ways: These key symbols have become hyper-elaborated because they are such significant elements of a major ritual.

Because the bride and groom are not expected to know how to design an appropriate ceremony by themselves, without guidance, weddings have developed their own secular specialists to serve as expert advice givers. Designers, caterers, jewelers, florists, printers are all available to share their knowledge of past weddings. The fact that these experts primarily encourage the couple to follow mainstream norms rather than displaying their own unique cultural identities says something about the strength of the normalization (melting pot) process within culture.[61] One example is when a Mexican American–Anglo couple wanted Mexican food at their reception, to mesh with other Mexican elements during the ceremony, and the Mexican music at the reception, but the caterer refused (Couple 64).[62] In other examples, caterers have introduced ethnic foods common to their geographic region having no connection to the ethnicity of the bride and groom (as with Couple 66, who ended up with Mexican and German foods deliberately, as a reflection of their own identities, but also with some Italian foods because that was what else the caterer knew how to prepare).[63] In fact, mainstream American wedding rituals have become so elaborate that an entirely new category of expert, the wedding planner, has evolved to manage interactions with all the others, someone to guide the bride and groom through the maze of potential choices. The services of a wedding planner cost money but organizers justify the cost on the grounds that whoever is paying for the wedding (most often the bride's family, but this can vary) will save money with each of the individual specialists. In fact, what they most often do save is face, their primary task being to ensure that the resulting wedding offends the minimum number of people. And for that purpose, a mainstream wedding is ideal.

One topic for which a decision must be made concerns establishing the boundaries of the wedding. Because different groups name different beginning and ending points, this becomes an issue. One extreme would have it that only the formal wedding ceremony itself should be viewed as relevant. The other extreme includes everything that occurs from the moment of deciding to marry through to writing the last thank you for gifts, or even the couple viewing the videotape of the wedding every year, on their anniversary, with the children (Couple 47 mentioned this).[64] Couples who go to city hall for a civil ceremony before a judge, usually describe few other events attached to the wedding. I am quite sympathetic with the largest possible boundaries, because in real ways all surrounding events are, to some extent, a part of the wedding.[65] Often there is room for considerable creativity in the events surrounding the wedding, and fewer difficulties in introducing new elements at these points.[66]

When multiple traditions are incorporated into a single ritual, even with the best intentions, sometimes the result is not a complete success. In Couple 76, both the bride and groom are Jewish, but he grew up in the United States, she in Israel. Both families are ethnically Russian—two parents are themselves immigrants, one is first generation, and one is second generation, but both sets of parents are well acculturated into their respective countries. In this case, the problems arose not from a clash of cultures between Americans and Israelis, but between Russians who had acculturated and those who had not. When the bride first came to the U.S., she stayed with her mother's first cousin and her family, who stood *in loco parentis*. They define themselves as culturally Russian, although they have been in the U.S. for decades.

This couple actually had two weddings, and two receptions, spread out across three dates. They married first in the U.S., in a brief civil ceremony, with only one friend in attendance ("we just kind of walked in and did it"). Then the bride's parents organized a large (religious) wedding celebration for 200 people in Israel, complete with a reception afterwards, which the groom's parents and sister attended. Of this, the bride said: "we didn't try to incorporate a lot of American things, except perhaps for one big thing: We really looked for a rabbi that speaks English. Because it was really important to us that his parents were going to understand." They chose a rabbi who was an American living in Israel, so he would be fluent in both languages (although in fact he spoke almost all Hebrew during the ceremony, translating only one major speech into English). All the usual traditions were followed, as the bride explained: "We did it very traditionally, because in Israel you have to do it traditionally." The groom had experienced the weddings of some Jewish friends in the U.S., and elaborated on this point: "I think that American weddings are very influenced by the society here. I think that I've noticed a lot of the people I know are using a lot of sort of Christian traditions, like recessional and the best man and the bridesmaids.... They take American traditions which are also based on Christian traditions." Clearly he is correct: American Jewish weddings often combine mainstream Christian elements (elaborate bridal parties, bridesmaids, groomsmen, flower girls, a ring bearer, and a rehearsal, being the most common of these) with traditional Jewish elements.

The third event was a reception held by the groom's parents in the U.S., which the bride's parents attended. Although the two weddings and the first reception had been remarkably uncontroversial, difficulties arose when trying to design the reception to be held in the U.S. Although the groom's parents were paying for it, the bride wanted to ensure that the Russian relatives who had first taken care of her in the U.S. would be happy with the arrangements. She now thinks this was perhaps a mistake, and that she inappropriately gave their views too much weight in the decision making. As she said: "I guess I was doing too much talking with my relatives and trying to see what they would feel comfortable with and what would accommodate them and I didn't think of ourselves." After the fact, it was easy for the bride and groom to see how the problem developed. But at the time, the two weddings and first reception having gone so well, they did not expect trouble.

The type and amount of both food and drink served at this second reception were critical matters. The bride and groom told me that food was very important to the Russian relatives. (Although everyone involved had Russian heritage, in conversation with me, they divided the major players into three distinct groups: the Americans—his family, the Israelis—her family, and the Russians—her mother's cousins.) Here is the bride speaking:

> So what happened is that they told me something like that: In Russian parties you start eating, and the kind of appetizers is a bunch of salads on the table ... could be cold cuts ... plates of meat ... and food ... and it looked like an entire meal but that's only the appetizer. And for some reason, the amount of these appetizers is really important for them, and it's more important for them the amount of the appetizers than actually the main dish. The main dish could be pretty simple. And also, another thing is there's supposed to be vodka on the table, and there's supposed to be this meat, and a lot amount of food, and the dessert, there's supposed to be a lot of desserts, there's supposed to be a lot of food. So we got this really fancy catering [sic], and we asked him to make us, and he's trying, and he bringing us this soup, borscht, as an appetizer, and he describes it to us very elegantly, like this is a Russian borscht. And then we come back and borscht is kind of considered like peasant soup.

So, first there is an evaluation of the particular *type* of food to be served. The caterer considered borscht (red beet soup) to be a gourmet food, appropriate for a fancy dinner; the Russians considered borscht to be peasant food, a class marker, and thus clearly inappropriate. Also, the Russians wanted platters of cold cuts to be the appetizer, but, as the groom reported, his Americanized father said "you're not putting cold cuts on my beautiful table." Second, there is an evaluation of the *amount* of food to be served. For the Russians there should be large amounts of food, far more than anyone could eat; for the Americans, it was the quality of food that counted, not the quantity. As the groom explained:

> My family are very interested in presentation, quality. They like to go to restaurants and have waiters be really sweet to them. And they like good service, and they like to feel special, and they're very American. Now, her family cares very much about the amount of food on the table. Irrespective of the quality, oftentimes, but there better be—her aunt, we'll go to her house, and there will be enough food on the table for 50 people to eat for a week, and she'll say there was nothing to eat. Inevitably, no matter how stuffed, no matter how many people was there, no matter how much food was left over, there was nothing to eat. So we were very worried, we were very worried that her family here would be insulted by my family's way of doing things.

Third, there is an evaluation related to *the type and quantity of drink*. Traditionally these Russian relatives expect to drink a lot of vodka at a celebration. Concerned about the price of buying the anticipated ten or more shots of vodka for each guest, the bride and groom arranged instead to have a bottle of vodka on each table, which is what the Russian relatives had told them would be considered appropriate. As the bride said:

> From the beginning, the biggest issue you have is Russians drink a lot of vodka ... we were very concerned that we would have bottles of vodka on the table. Now you can only do that in maybe five of the places in this city. You can't put bottles ... And that shaped everything. As we think back, that changed everything because we had to have it at a place that would allow us to do that.

In the end, the Russians did not only speak of their disapproval, but showed their disapproval of the quantity and type of food served by not drinking the vodka which had been so carefully supplied. The groom reported: "So in the end, the interesting thing, we had nine bottles of vodka left. Nobody drank a drop of vodka.... They were upset. They were sitting there with bottles of vodka in the middle of the table and they didn't even open them." In the bride's interpretation of this action:

> I think what happened is that this whole thing created this like, them against us, Americans against Russians. So they finally thought, you know what, this is an American event and we'll do the favor and we'll come in, but we're not going to behave as us. We're just going to behave as if, like, we came to an American event, like as if we're strangers. So they didn't open the vodka. Not opening the vodka, not drinking the vodka, symbolized for me like they were not celebrating.

And the groom continued:

> That's right, because when they're going to celebrate, they're going to
> drink. And the thing that upset my father is that we had so many fights with
> him. The whole reason we were there was the vodka, and they didn't even
> open it. He, to this day, is upset.... He was just thinking, we tried, and they
> didn't care that we tried. And they thought, they didn't care enough. The
> funny thing is that this wasn't even her parents. Her parents were trying to
> stay out of it.

The bride continued with an interpretation of her parents' attitude: "I think that
my parents were embarrassed by my relatives and their behavior. I think my parents thought, they're American, and they're going to do it their way, and we're
not going to interfere, because this is their thing and they're paying for it, and
we're not going to say anything."

In sum, the first wedding was noncontroversial, because virtually no one was
present to pass judgment on it. The second wedding and first reception, held in
Israel, were noncontroversial because virtually everyone present was
monocultural (Israeli), and the bride's parents simply organized it in ways the Israeli guests expected. The second reception, held in the U.S., was controversial
because the bride tried to combine the expectations of the groom's family (the
Americans) with those of her mother's cousin's family (the Russians). Her own
parents (the Israelis) were irrelevant here because they expected the party in the
U.S. to be designed according to American standards. By trying to accommodate
both the American and the Russian expectations, when these were directly contradictory, the result was a confusing event that did not fully meet anyone's expectations. The Russian relatives, being unhappy with the decisions made,
showed their negative evaluation of the performance by refusing to even drink
the vodka, and thus refusing to celebrate. And their negative reaction ruined
much of the fun for the bride and groom. As the groom concluded: "That's what's
so sad about looking back at it. We each loved the wedding so much, and we look
back at the reception and we think, ugh." This example shows the power of ritual:
The bride and groom should have been happy that they had their formal wedding
ceremony, and not one but two receptions, but the difficulties caused by trying to
unite the food and drink expectations of the different populations present was
central to their experience of the event and prominent in their memories of it.
This is how ritual gains import: By making ephemeral ideas and emotions concrete through choices about such elements as food and drink.

NOTES

1. Rothenbuhler (1998) gave a more current, but not significantly different definition:
   "Ritual is the voluntary performance of appropriate patterned behavior to symboli-

cally effect or participate in the serious life" (p. 27). Grimes (1990, p. 14) presented a far longer list of the qualities of ritual:

> performed, embodied, enacted, gestural (not merely thought or said); formalized, elevated, stylized, differentiated (not ordinary, unadorned, or undifferentiated); repetitive, redundant, rhythmic (not singular or once for all); collective, institutionalized, consensual (not personal or private); patterned, invariant, standardized, stereotyped, ordered, rehearsed (not improvised, idiosyncratic, or spontaneous); traditional, archaic, primordial (not invented or recent); valued highly or ultimately, deeply felt, sentiment-laden, meaningful, serious (not trivial or shallow); condensed, multilayered (not obvious; requiring interpretation); symbolic, referential (not merely technological or primarily means-end oriented perfected, idealized, pure, ideal (not conflictual or subject to criticism and failure); dramatic, ludic [i.e., playlike] (not primarily discursive or explanatory, not without special framing or boundaries); paradigmatic (not ineffectual in modeling either other rites or non-ritualized action); mystical, transcendent, religious, cosmic (not secular or merely empirical); adaptive, functional (not obsessional, neurotic, dysfunctional); and conscious, deliberate (not unconscious or preconscious).

As it is not clear to me that this longer list is substantially more useful for my purposes than the shorter, older definition provided by Myerhoff, I will stay with that one.

2. The expanded version of the explanation that follows about symbols, other signs, codes, and cultures, can be found in Leeds-Hurwitz (1993). Here I intend only to provide the briefest explanation, so those who have not yet read that book will not lose the main thread of the argument.

3. Again, for more extensive discussion of these issues, see Leeds-Hurwitz (1993).

4. Leach (1968) pointed out: "All of us in our private daily lives manipulate the symbols of an intricate behavioral code, and we readily decode the behavioral messages of our associates; this we take for granted" (p. 524). This is why intercultural weddings are a problem: We expect to be able to understand the symbol systems, because we can within our own culture, but we cannot interpret symbols accurately when they are based in a culture new to us. That moment of surprise at an unexpected lack of understanding is the issue.

5. As Tambiah (1985) put it, ritual is "a culturally constructed system of symbolic communication. It is constituted of patterned and ordered sequences of words and acts, often expressed in multiple media, whose content and arrangement are characterized by varying degrees of formality (conventionality), stereotypy (rigidity), condensation (fusion) and redundancy (repetition)" (p. 128).

6. See also Schudson (1989):

> This is how ritual transmits culture: the viewer is also actor, the audience is participant, and the distinction between the producer and consumer of culture is blurred if it exists at all. Culture is simultaneously attended to, institutionalized, and resolved in action. Thus, the bride and groom in the marriage ceremony repeat the wedding vows after the presiding officer, surrounded by witnesses, encircled by other symbols of the wedding. The repetition of the vows becomes, in the often shaking voices of the couple, a palpable act of marriage, a commitment in itself, not just a statement about a commit-

ment. The ritual as an act, the saying of vows as a "speech act," is performative, at once a cultural and social experience. (p. 173)

7. See Mac an Ghaill (1999) for a current discussion of continuities and discontinuities in culture. See Pearce and Littlejohn (1997) on the importance of making a new place to stand, in response to divisiveness and different assumptions.

8. There is a clear tie to Chapter 2 and the concept of community here. As Kertzer (1988) put it: "Through participation of such rituals, people's dependence on their social group is continually brought to their mind. Just as importantly, it is through these rites that the boundaries of the social group, the group of people to whom the individual feels allegiance, are defined" (p. 62).

9. Interviewed by Eric Roche for Comm 440: Communication Codes, in Spring 2001.

10. As Rothenbuhler (1998) pointed out, "among the devices for order, it is one of the most gentle and most available to rational reform when it is needed" (p. xiii). See also Soeffner (1997), who said rituals are "a small part of the total of symbolic forms in which we bed our social order" (p. xii).

11. See Boyer (1990) for a thoughtful discussion of the attributes of tradition.

12. "What is critical here is the *active* relation to ritual. Instead of having rites performed on us, we do them to and for ourselves, and immediately we are involved in a form of self-creation that is potentially community-building" (Myerhoff, 1982, p. 130).

13. Leach (1989) argued the newly accepted position that "A changeless cultural system would be a complete anomaly" (p. 45). A culture is made up of individuals, and "Change is the sum of individual choices.... We must recognize the essential fact that the social system at any one time is the momentary end product of such a process" (Goldschmidt, 1990, p. 230).

14. "The understanding of change over time is therefore not something extra, a desirable bonus to add to synchronic study; it is essential if the nature of human culture is not to be grossly misunderstood" (Charsley, 1992, p. 5). See also Handler and Linnekin (1989) on the essential nature of tradition as incorporating change.

15. This family provides an interesting example of the extension from interfaith unions in a former generation to interracial unions in this generation. This bride reported that her brother (who was adamantly set against her marriage to a Lutheran) had a daughter who has now married a man who is Hispanic. "She's happy as a clam with this guy but my brother never acknowledged him." Perhaps for her niece also, a child will serve as the catalyst for reintegration of the nuclear family into the extended family.

16. Interviewed by Jaime Jenjak for Comm 440: Communication Codes, in Spring 2001.

17. Although Toelken was discussing Native Americans, I think the point can easily be generalized to any group that feels isolated and under attack.

18. Van Gennep (1960) looked for the essential structure common to all rites of passage, and found a typical division into three parts: the part before a major change in status occurs, the change itself, and the part after. The first part is essentially a time of building up to something, and the latter is a cooling off time, before leaving the old for the new. Turner (1969, 1974) refined Van Gennep's work with his extensive study of "liminality," which he defined as "the state of being in between successive participations in social milieux dominated by social structural considerations ... [it is] betwixt and between the categories of ordinary social life" (1974, p. 53; there is also a nice introduction to the topic in Davies, 1994). In simpler terms, liminality is

the stage in a ritual when a participant has lost whatever original status or identity was held, but not yet gained the new one. Although a standard focus of ritual studies, liminality does not seem to be the central issue in American weddings, whether intercultural or mainstream.

19. For a good study on birth as a ritual in the U.S., see Davis-Floyd (1992). Unlike birth, puberty, or weddings, death rituals are suddenly a major topic being studied by sociologists; for an introduction see Clark (1993), Moller (1996), and Walter (1994). An odd combination of marriage rituals with funeral rituals in a single study is available in Grimes (1995). Even the architects are studying rites of passage, as exemplified in Harris (1999), a surprising effort to apply the metaphor of life cycles to buildings.

20. Interviewed by Sue Glanz for Comm 499: Independent Study, in Spring 1992.

21. See Babcock (1980) for further discussion of the concept of reflexivity, and the ways rituals are reflexive; see Hobsbawm and Ranger (1983) for the concept of "invented tradition"; see Wagner (1981) for further discussion of the concept of invention as a cultural attribute.

22. My paper from that conference is Leeds-Hurwitz (1994). I am indebted to the participants at that conference for their thoughtful responses and ideas when I was near the beginning of this research.

23. See Wiseman and Koester (1993) for applications of the concept of communicative competence to intercultural contexts.

24. Interviewed June 9, 1994.

25. Quoted on www.theknot.com, under "Real weddings."

26. As reported by Kim Kogutkiewicz in Comm 440: Communication Codes, in Spring 1996.

27. "Chupa" and "huppah" refer to the same thing—they are just different transliterations into English of the same Hebrew word. Although I use the more standard "huppah" elsewhere, I am quoting here from an e-mail received from the groom, and so spell the word the way he did.

28. Interviewed by Sue Glanz for Comm 499: Independent Study, in Spring 1992.

29. Interviewed by Sue Glanz for Comm 499: Independent Study, in Spring 1992.

30. Baumann's own study of how Punjabi celebrations of Christmas are designed (using diaries written by the teenagers who wish to combine popular culture models with their own family traditions) is completely different from my study of intercultural weddings, yet some of the lessons learned about meshing cultures, and the importance of popular sources to the meshing of sacred and secular elements, are quite similar.

31. See also Connerton (1989).

32. See a similar point by Myerhoff (1992):

> Rituals provide continuity of two distinct but related kinds, the individual's sense of unity as a person (individual-biographical continuity) and the sense of being 'One People' on the part of the whole group (collective-historical continuity). Despite great changes and disruptions, the individual must be convinced of his/her continuity; thus, must be able to re-experience parts of the past in the present, and of course, the most changed and essential segments of this retrieval come from the remote past, the events of childhood. (p. 151)

33. Or, as Schieffelin (1996) said, "the articulation of ritual structure within social reality, insofar as it is actually *enacted*, is unavoidably a performative process" (p. 82). See also Bauman and Briggs (1990), Charland (1987), Kapchan (1995), MacAloon (1984) and Schieffelin (1985) on the performative aspects of ritual; see Strine (1998) on the importance of attending to performance for communication scholars.

34. Abu-Lughod (1991) reported:

> Within the first week of my arrival in the Bedouin community in Egypt where I was to spend years, the young girls in my household outlined for me the exact sequence of events every bride went through in a Bedouin wedding. Over the years, I attended many weddings, all of which followed this outline, yet each of which was distinct. For each bride and groom, not to mention their families, the wedding would mark a moment of major life transformation, not just of status but of associations, daily life, experience, and the future. Each wedding was different in the kinds of families being brought together, the network of relations created and the goods exchanged, spent, and displayed. (p. 156)

So even when all the traditions are followed in a society strongly governed by tradition, no two performances of a wedding are identical.

35. Interviewed by Sue Glanz for Comm 499, Independent Study, in Spring 1992.

36. Taken from an interview provided on the web page www.theknot.com, under "Real weddings."

37. A second marriage led to the oddest role I have ever played in a wedding: Our son was the best friend of the bride's son, and each of the four prior children (both the bride and groom had been previously married, and each had two children) was allowed to invite one friend, with accompanying parents (because the children were in middle school). None of the four resulting sets of parents was part of the social circle of the bride or the groom, which led to a frequent question about who we were. Imagine yourself explaining: "We're the parents of the bride's son's best friend," and getting the response, "Oh, we're the parents of the groom's daughter's best friend." Convoluted relationships indeed.

38. As reported by Susan Oboikowich in Comm 440: Communication Codes in Spring 1996.

39. As reported by Marlene Ernst in Comm 440: Communication Codes, in Spring 1999.

40. See Leeds-Hurwitz (1993) for further discussion of key symbols.

41. In fact, Ortner extends the concept of key symbol to include rituals, so weddings in their entirety could accurately be described as an American key symbol.

42. "At the cultural level a girl—almost always so termed—becomes an embodiment of an important symbolic idea, the bride, when she is appropriately dressed and on her wedding day. In this sense the outfit is essential to the bride. Securing the outfit is a fundamental requirement, and its main component, the wedding dress, becomes very special ... A wedding dress is not therefore simply a dress in which a woman is married; it is a dress uniquely associated with her as a bride on that occasion, a dress which is a key part of the way in which she embodies the idea of a bride" (Charsley, 1991, p. 66). See also Miler (1993) and Simeti (1991).

43. Sometimes the connection between the ring and what it stands for is fairly literal, as with Couple 91. As the bride said, the design was "the moon and the stars be-

cause what's what we promised, the moon and the stars." (Her engagement ring was in the shape of a star, and her wedding band was a crescent moon, with an opening for the star to fit into.)

44. Apparently, in Scotland it is the wedding cake that is the most significant of these: "A wedding cake to be cut is, even ahead of a wedding dress for the bride, perhaps the most generally known and essential requirement for celebrating a marriage" (Charsley, 1991, p. 54).

45. An interesting exception was Couple 107, who deliberately went the other direction. The groom reports: "we made a commitment for a one year renewable contract, you might say … the idea was that on our anniversary each year we would get together and see if we wanted to go further … so part of the commitment was to re-negotiate the commitment as we went" (interviewed by Eric Roche for Comm 440: Communication Codes, in Spring 2001).

46. Georgette Sampson, a student in Comm 440: Communication Codes, in Fall 1991. These comments on rings, cakes and dresses are summaries drawn from multiple interviews conducted either by me or my students with wedding specialists.

47. Dorson (1982) provided the basic logic of studying the role of material culture in celebrations. For a summary of the study of material culture, emphasizing its symbolic importance in human life, see Leeds-Hurwitz (1993).

48. Her emphasis is hardly unique; see also Leach (1984): "Spoken language is ephemeral. The details of an utterance have vanished, even as an impression on the memory, almost as soon as it is uttered" (p. 357).

49. As with other elements, each of these is open to differentiation. For example, although Christians often display a wedding portrait in the relatively public space of a living room, Jews more often display only the *ketubah* (wedding contract), and that most often in the private space of the couple's bedroom.

50. I have had female students (never male) who have already planned out their entire weddings (from color scheme to food selection, from their dress to the location), even before they are engaged. This, of course, causes enormous conflicts if their fiancés do not appreciate the same symbols, as is generally the case in intercultural marriages.

51. Viewed on the Artistic Jewish Promotions web page, at ajp.com.

52. Interviewed April 21, 2000.

53. Quoted from the web page ketubahs.com/other.htm.

54. A *Wedding Story*, segment broadcast January 3, 2001.

55. Interviewed by Ryan Ellifson for Comm 440: Communication Codes, in Spring 2001.

56. Benatar (1990) documented some of the worst extremes, also Vaughen (1991).

57. Rubenstein (1993) perfectly described the emphasis given to choice of wedding gown by many women when he says: "It may look like just an elaborate party dress on the hanger, but what a woman wears on her wedding day has to not only embody a mother's hope, a father's fantasy, a husband's desire and precisely the way a woman would like to be seen on this all-eyes-are-upon-her-day, but most important, it must be absolutely scene-stealingly smashing" (p. 47).

58. Interviewed by Sue Glanz for Comm 499: Independent Study, in Spring 1992.

59. As reported by Marilyn Margoni in Comm 440: Communication Codes, in Spring 1996.

60. As reported by Marianne Sjoholm in Comm 440: Communication Codes, in Spring 1996.

61. The extreme case of letting ritual experts take over is an unplanned wedding held in Las Vegas, which offers "the facsimile of proper ritual, to children who do not know how else to find it" (Didion, 1967, as quoted in Rubinstein, 1990, p. 111).

62. As reported by Steve Van der Heyden in Comm 440: Communication Codes, in Spring 1999.

63. As reported by Joan Agam in Comm 440: Communication Codes, in Spring 1999.

64. As reported by Kevin Dubiak in Comm 440: Communication Codes, in Spring 1999.

65. At the same time, books have limitations, and so I focus my energy here on the ceremony and reception.

66. At a bachelorette party, the bride's friends gave her a white baseball cap with a veil attached for her to wear all night (Couple 27). The groom in this couple was also inventive: During the rehearsal dinner, he gave the bride an emerald ring when they practiced exchanging rings, much to her surprise, simply because she had wanted one, and he thought that would be a novel way to give it to her. (As reported by Ashley LaMacchia in Comm 440: Communication Codes, in Spring 1996.)

Interlude 4

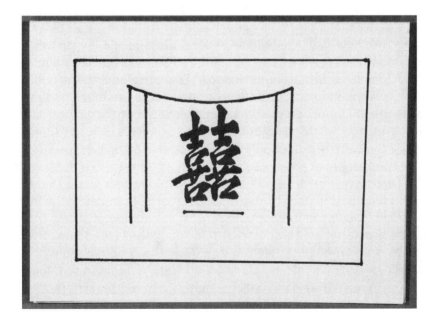

FIG. 5:   Cover of wedding invitation used by Couple 77.
Photo by Don Lintner, University of Wisconsin-Parkside.

*W*eddings are large and complicated ceremonies. It is un-usual, but not at all inaccurate to say that the invitation marks the beginning of the event, and the photo album marks the ending. Everything that comes between can thus be treated as part of a single elaborated ritual (the parties, the wedding ceremony, the reception, etc.).

In their Jewish–Chinese wedding, Couple 77 anticipated the fact that the invitation would tell their guests something about their identities and how they were going to handle the differ-ences in their backgrounds. "Our wedding invitation, actually I designed it, and my husband did the calligraphy ... in red on ivory ... and the symbol is of the two, the double happiness un-der the *huppah* ... I must say, it is beautiful." This couple took one of the major symbols of each of their traditions, combining them in a new way: The *huppah*, a central image of a Jewish wed-ding, stands over the Chinese character *shuang-hsi*, or "double happiness," a central symbol used in Chinese weddings. In addi-tion to appearing on the cover, both symbols are explained in-side the invitation, so guests unfamiliar with either tradition will understand the meaning of both. The text reads: "Our children have chosen the red 'double happiness' character, because it is a symbol of joy at a Chinese wedding. It is framed by a Huppah, or canopy, where they will be married by Jewish law." These words are written from the parents' point of view, because the in-vitation follows the mainstream American tradition of having the bride's parents invite guests to their daughter's wedding. The bride is an American Jew from New York; the groom is from the People's Republic of China and an atheist. In addition to differ-ences in religion and nationality, there is also a class difference: Her family has money, whereas his does not.

They talked of having one wedding in the United States, and an-other in China, each following their own traditions, but there were visa concerns, and so in the end they only had one ceremony, in the United States. For the wedding in China, she would have worn a red *cheung sam*, and they would have followed Chinese traditions. Because at the time they assumed there would be a second wed-ding, there was no discussion of what she should wear in the U.S.: it was obvious to both of them. She wore the traditional mainstream American outfit: a long white gown with a veil, and she held white flowers. In addition, she followed the mainstream tradition of wearing something old (her grandmother's necklace, heart shaped with small diamonds), something new (her bridal gown), something borrowed (earrings from her aunt), and something blue (although she could not remember what it was, she was certain she had followed the rhyme through to the end). In addition to these items, she also wore something unique, as a symbol meant only for the groom: because she was not wearing a red dress on this occasion, "I wore red underwear."

The officiant was a Reform rabbi, not the bride's family's rabbi, but one willing to perform an interfaith marriage. Because none of the central players was a member of his congregation, the wedding ceremony was held at the restaurant where the reception was planned. The rabbi provided the *huppah* (blue with a gold Star of David in the center, a fairly common design), and also the basic format of the ceremony. The groom was "was willing to do everything but would not wear a *kipah* [skullcap]." Despite the lack of prior connection, the bride felt that the rabbi "was really lovely, I still remember some of the things he said, I was very moved by his sermon." The ceremony can be described as a fairly standard traditional Jewish wedding—in addition to the rabbi's sermon, the groom stepped on the glass, the bride and groom gave each other wine, they exchanged vows and rings (matching plain gold bands), and all the appropriate prayers were said.

The wedding party included seven bridesmaids and a matron of honor, but no groomsmen. "Because he came from China, and my network of friends was all women, so I only had bridesmaids, there were no ushers. So my brother was the best man, and members of the wedding party held the *huppah*." Other guests included friends of the bride and groom, her extended family, and his parents. (Because the groom's family did not have enough money to pay the airfare to the United States, the bride's family paid their way.) "They were basically coming to our thing.... They were totally our guests, in terms of you know, we brought them over, we bought their clothes. And so they were total guests at the wedding, they were not participants in planning or creating it.... This was totally my family's thing, my parents' thing."

A major moment of cultural miscommunication occurred during the ceremony, although it was not evident until the photographs arrived. "There's one funny picture where he [the rabbi] says, 'okay, you may kiss the bride,' and right in the margin, where you see there's the *huppah* and his parents are standing right outside it, they're like this [makes a shocked face, open mouth] to see us kissing in public, this gesture of hysteria." Because she could not see the shocked reaction as it occurred (the bride and groom face the rabbi as he conducts the ceremony), no one explained the cultural appropriateness of kissing at that point in the ceremony to the groom's parents.

No traditional Chinese elements were incorporated into the wedding because:

> There was very little momentum for honoring the Chinese side of it. And I think we always thought that we were going to do another wedding in China, which never did materialize.... He really didn't want anything to do with his Chinese-ness. I honored the Chinese-ness much more than he did ... I used Chinese as the language of our home, I raised our daughter bilingually, but very limited, in the domain of raising a kid.

Although the bride was not fluent in Chinese, she had taken a course in it, and also had learned many conversational phrases while spending 6 weeks with his parents when they came to the U.S. for the wedding.

Despite the lack of explicitly Chinese elements, the bride did make an interesting nod to China:

> To do the bridesmaids' dresses, I just bought tons of Chinese-look-ing fabric, and I just gave them several yards and said, make any dress you want, about mid-calf, and short-sleeve. You'll see the bridesmaids' pictures. So they're all in this pink silk. And my maid of honor was in a different color pink silk. And they chose their de-sign. I just wanted them to have a dress that they could keep. None of my girlfriends have a lot of money, so I didn't want to do things the traditional way, so I just gave them the fabric, and said do what you want.

Although hardly a traditional color for Chinese weddings, pink nicely blends the Chinese red with the American white (as well as being one of the pastel colors commonly used for bridesmaids' dresses in the United States). Despite the differences in dress design, using the same fabric clearly marked the bridesmaids as a set, all holding iden-tical bouquets of pink and white flowers. The mother of the bride and mother of the groom both wore light blue. This was not deliberately coordinated, but rather was based on finding an outfit fairly quickly for the groom's mother that would both fit and be comfortable, and it just happened to be close in color to what the bride's mother had already purchased. Regardless of the lack of deliberate choice, it must certainly have looked carefully planned to the guests.

Since the reception was held at a French restaurant, that dictated the food choices; as a result, there was no effort to incorporate Chinese foods. There was music and dancing, including the traditional Jewish lifting of the bride and groom on chairs. The bride specifically remembers that the four people who lifted her were not well matched, and there is a photograph documenting her screaming as the chair tips and she nearly falls out.

At the reception various toasts were made; included in these "I had a cousin who made a toast in Chinese for the in-laws." This same cousin was seated with the in-laws, as a courtesy, so they would have someone to talk to who knew their language while the groom was occupied as host. Other mainstream elements were incorporated. The cake was traditional: white, multitiered, with flowers for decoration. "You also have to keep in mind that this took place on Long Island, and I lived [elsewhere], so this was for my parents. So this was a parents' wedding." The bride's mother chose the cake, as well as being responsible for the majority of the planning. The cake was cut with the usual fanfare, and the new couple fed pieces to one another. The bride threw her bouquet into the crowd, and the photographs document the fact that a young girl caught it. When asked about that (because generally only those of marriageable age make the attempt), the bride responded "What did we know of what we were doing?" Finally, the couple's car was decorated with balloons and, in shaving cream, the words "Just married."

Their wedding photo album is red leather with gold trim. I asked: "Deliberately?" (red and gold being colors traditionally associated with Chinese weddings). The answer: "Yes." The album includes formal photographs of the bride and groom, as well as some informal photographs, those in the wedding party, and various combinations of friends and family members.

In summarizing the event, the bride now says: "It was really a wonderful wedding. It wasn't a great marriage after 12 years [the

point at which they divorced], but it was a wonderful wedding."[1]
We talked about the fact that the wedding invitation was a critical
element: "The invitation is where you're telling the world, you
know, that's how you're framing this world event…. The invitation
is almost like a speech act. It's announcing a new entity, a new
creation in the world." The invitation and the photo album, both
similarly influenced by Chinese symbolism, were perfect book-
ends for this event. In addition to marking connections to China,
there were clear references to Judaism (most of the central elements of the ceremony), as well as to mainstream American traditions (the cake, the flowers, the decorated car) in this wedding.
The class difference was handled as it most often is; the family
with money simply paid for the entire event, including participation by the essential members of the other family. In exchange,
they got to design the event, choose the locale, and choreograph
the critical components. Of all these parts, for me, the *huppah*
over Chinese calligraphy on the invitation stands as a unique
symbol of how this bride and groom united their divergent identities at one point in time, even if the marriage did not last.

NOTE

1. Although it was not one of the intents of this research to document whether
   intercultural couples are more or less likely to divorce, I have been asked on
   multiple occasions about the frequency of divorce among this population. It
   is my impression that divorce is *less* likely among intercultural couples,
   since of necessity they work out most of their different assumptions explicitly, and prior to the marriage rather than during it (and only a small number
   of those I interviewed who had been married for some years had divorced).
   It fascinates me that the people who have asked this question have generally assumed that there would be a *higher* rate of divorce, on the assumption that considerable cultural differences would be impossible to work out.
   However, because many of the couples documented in this book were just
   marrying as I observed their weddings and interviewed them, a definite answer would have to wait some years.

4

Identity

"Cultural identities come from somewhere, have histories. But, like
everything which is historical, they undergo constant transformation."
—Hall (1990, p. 225)

In any wedding, but especially visible in intercultural weddings, *the ritual serves
as a vehicle for the performance of identity* (among other functions).[1] It has already
been explained how weddings are rituals, and performances. New here is the
question of exactly what is performed; my answer is identity. Intercultural weddings are especially valuable as sites of identity statements, for any one culture
increases in visibility when contrasted with a second. Lukes (1975) told us that
"a community is reminded of its identity as represented by and told in a master
narrative" (p. 70). A *master narrative* is an underlying theme used repeatedly by
members of a group, and it is certainly possible to suggest that weddings serve
as one such master narrative in modern American culture. In other words, each
group tells itself a story about itself, and that story serves to reinforce identity.
Combining these ideas, weddings can appropriately be described as *performance
narratives*, because each bride and groom is given an opportunity to create, and
then display (perform) in public, their own story (narrative) of identity: Who they
have come from, who they are now, and who they wish to be in the future. Like
other types of stories people tell, weddings not only say what the tellers wish to
be true, the telling itself actually makes the statements true, for it is through the
display of identity that it becomes real (Rosenwald & Ochberg, 1992). For this
reason rituals have been termed "dramas of persuasion" (Myerhoff, 1992, p.
156); what they persuade us of is the identity of the performers. Fortes (1983)
expanded on this theory:

Displaying self through performance makes an idea concrete. How does one know one is a Jew, or anything? One can only know it, obviously, by *showing* it is some way; to sit back in your armchair and know gets you nowhere; it is meaningless. So if you want to know who you are, you have got to show it, and anthropologists know that one way of showing it is by performing a ritual or ceremony. (pp. 394–395)

Thus the families of bride and groom want their own cultures shown because they want to see a public commitment to continue them.[2] As Grimes (1995) put it, "a wedding rite is a ceremonial realignment, not just an invention, of ties that bind a couple.... In a wedding, two people ceremonially make relatives of each other" (p. 99). But, in fact, they do more than just make relatives of each other: in becoming relatives, they inherit one another's relatives as well, bringing into being a new, larger family, with themselves at the nexus. As Root (2001) put it: "The most significant product of families is future generations" (p. 78). Children of an intercultural couple are even more closely tied to both sets of grandparents by blood rather than marriage, which may be why even parents who refuse to accept an intercultural son- or daughter-in-law often reconcile once there are grandchildren.

Not all weddings are equally revealing. This book emphasizes intercultural weddings for a reason: The conveyance of identity in the presence of others equally concerned to simultaneously convey different identities is especially difficult and, therefore, worthy of extended investigation. It is through the design of particular combinations of cultural identities in a wedding ritual that the new couple not only displays their intentions (the performance aspect) but makes them true (the constitutive element).[3] This harks back to the concept of social construction: We construct (constitute, or make real) our identities, making them visibly manifest, both for ourselves and so that we may share them with others. This is one part of what Goffman (1959) named "identity management," referring to the element of deliberate control evident in identity displays.[4] We make choices about what to present in a ritual such as a wedding, thus we can be seen managing the presentation of our identities, our selves. We know who we are, but when others with different identities are present, we are more likely to mark our identities visibly.

Just as researchers once assumed definite boundaries between communities, and studied each one at a time, so they originally assumed each person has a single primary identity, granted at birth, and unchanging until death. This outdated theory has now been replaced by a more flexible view of identity, that it is not something beyond our control, but something we use and manage, deliberately more often than not.[5] And it is something that can change over time, as our allegiances change. In her discussion of California's Punjabi Mexican families, Leonard (1992) made this clear by following the same individuals through a paper trail of legal documents: "A boy born as Francisco, whose father corrected his birth certificate to Gurdev, witnessed his brother's wedding as Frank"

(p. 197). Thus the mother's Mexican heritage first shows in the name chosen for the birth certificate, the father's Punjabi heritage shows up in his correction to that document, and the child's integration into mainstream American culture shows up in the name he lists for himself, as an adult.

Myerhoff (1992) argued that people make sense of their lives for themselves and others through the creation of multiple symbolic forms, with stories and rituals foremost among these. A wedding ritual provides a vehicle for the participants to make explicit statements concerning who they are. Culture, as a social fact, normally remains invisible, but is amenable to being put on display at those times people wish to publicly establish their identity. A wide variety of communication forms (including but not limited to rituals) are used to create and affirm cultural identity.[6] The study of identity is thus central to the study of communication, for, as Coover and Murphy (2000) argued:

> The essence of communication is the formation and expression of an identity.... Identities are formulated and maintained over time through interactions both mediated and unmediated, direct and indirect, interpersonal and intercultural. Communication, then, is integral to the ongoing negotiation of self, a process during which individuals are defined by others as they, in turn, define and redefine themselves. (p. 125)

Following these scholars, it is assumed in these pages that the study of communication and identity complement each other, and should be analyzed simultaneously.[7] That is, we convey identity, among other matters, through communication. As Edwards (1998) put it, "Social categorizations are interaction's business, its matters in hand, not its causal effects or conditions" (p. 33).[8] Thus we study examples of real people interacting in real situations to learn how identities are claimed and made.

A culture is, among other things, a very large context; within that context, each of us has an identity, a role to play.[9] More accurately, each of us has multiple identities, multiple roles to play, only some of which become relevant at any particular moment of interaction.[10] Once we understand that "identity is available for use: something that people do which is embedded in some other social activity, and not something they 'are'" (Widdicombe, 1998, p. 191), it becomes apparent that participants have the ability to construct identities for public display in a wedding, as they do at other times, for other events.[11] Because weddings figure as such major rituals in our lives (marked by the expense, the elaboration of the design, the number of witnesses, etc.), they are particularly significant statements. If we are not willing to acknowledge who we are here, when will we? Varro (1988) suggested "An international confrontation is taking place at the microsocial level of the family, in which each nation and culture vie with the other to acquire one more citizen, one more native speaker. Each parent tries to win the child over by imprinting elements of identity, language, culture, and way of life" (p. 187). It is far easier to study one single wedding at a time than larger cultural confrontations, and doing so has the potential of teaching us something that we can later transfer to understanding larger contexts.

There is always some tension caused by the fact that people can make choices, yet social groups must have certain choices made if they are to continue.[12] (To give the most obvious example, any individual may choose to have children or not, but if everyone decides to have no children, the group effectively terminates.) This is why so many researchers have investigated the topic of the relationship between the individual and society, and see it as such a central issue. On the one hand, as Hutter (1985) pointed out, "people are not born into social vacuums; the society they live in always exists prior to their arrival" (p. 130). On the other hand, "the social world is made up of individuals who speak and act in meaningful ways; these individuals create the social world which gives them their identity and being, and their creations can only be understood through a process of interpretation" (Moore, 1990, p. 111). The problem is always how to mesh what the individual wants with what the larger social group needs. This is why Myerhoff (1992) was able to say: "Thus rites of passage both announce our separateness and individuality and at the same time remind us most vividly that existence apart from the group is impossible" (p. 222). Weddings, as with other rites of passage, may explicitly acknowledge this tension, and intercultural weddings are especially likely to do so. Each bride and groom makes statements about membership in and allegiance to those groups of greatest importance to them, while simultaneously making claims to unique individual identities. The only surprising thing is how readily we permit such apparent contradictions to stand. Of course everyone is both an individual and a member of a variety of groups; we see it as so obvious that the paradoxical nature of the claim remains in the background. In this chapter, three major topics are addressed: vehicles for conveying identity, influences on identity, and types of identity.

VEHICLES FOR CONVEYING IDENTITY

Cultural identity is particularly easy to demonstrate via material culture (Stern, 1987). The Balch Institute for Ethnic Studies once persuaded B*ride* magazine to sponsor an exhibit on ethnic identity as displayed in weddings because "ethnicity is the very essence of what weddings are all about" (Lalli, 1987, p. 2), despite the fact that this and other popular magazines on the topic hardly acknowledge race or ethnicity in their pages (Ingraham, 1999). Mayer (1985) pointed out that ethnic identity specifically connects to the consumption of traditional foods, but rather than just serving what prior generations ate, the current, acculturated generation often expects "to blend the taste of the immigrant with the style of the successful American" (p. 29). This can be easy to do, or it can be difficult. In a Jewish–Christian wedding, the Jewish groom's father offered to pay the difference in cost, if the bride's parents (who were paying for the food at the reception) would agree to *kosher* catering, so some of his relatives would be able to attend (those who keep *kosher* follow a particular biblical passage requiring the separation of meat and milk). The bride's family readily accepted because they "thought it only a matter of etiquette that all guests partake of the food equally" (p. 190). If only all differences of opinion were so easy to resolve by appeals to etiquette! But, as Kendis (1989) demonstrated, sometimes there is a specific assumption within one group that the norms of the other are clearly inappropriate. In her example, "hors d'oeuvres, cake and punch receptions are seen as a Caucasian practice and looked down upon" by Japanese Americans, who expect not only a full meal, but the inclusion of a wide range of people not included in mainstream American weddings, such as "parents' business friends, family physician, and old school friends" (pp. 113–114). When cultural expectations clash so directly, a reasonable compromise can be difficult to shape.

Throughout this book, material culture examples are given priority, for a variety of reasons already described. However, one danger in using material culture to represent identity is that it can lead to what Kobayashi (1993) termed "red boots multiculturalism" (p. 206). She is referring to the tradition of having ethnic festivals, complete with folk dancing in costumes (Eastern-European folk dancers often wear red boots, presumably the origin of her phrase), and ethnic foods. These fairly superficial forms of sharing, what Gans (1979) called "symbolic ethnicity,"[13] often result in highlighting differences between groups at a surface level rather than resulting in any substantial sharing at a deeper level of meaning (Abrahams, 1981). Knowing what types of food others eat for dinner, or what types of dances they include in a performance, does not necessarily lead to any substantive understanding of either real similarities or real differences, but only to the most superficial show of that understanding. Some intercultural weddings fall into this trap, but the most successful ones (as highlighted in the Interludes of this book) find ways to combine meaningful symbols for multiple groups into something new conveying not only some of the old meanings, but an original synthesis as well.

INFLUENCES ON IDENTITY STATEMENTS

Weddings take into account at least three sets of influences. First, the voices of tradition: Parents, extended family members, and friends who have attended previous weddings and know what is appropriate behavior all tell the bride and groom. Their message is: "That's just how it's done!" expecting that every new wedding will, in all significant ways, mirror past weddings. This is where ethnic, racial, national, and family identities predominate. Second, images from popular culture convey mainstream assumptions. Having seen weddings portrayed in films, magazines, newspapers, it can be difficult for participants to not follow the expected norms. The message in these forms is: "Do what everyone else does!" This is where mainstream American influences fit. Third, there are wedding specialists with the job of planning weddings, who expect to be believed when they say "We know how to do it!" There are two major categories of specialists. The first category, ritual specialists (priests, ministers, rabbis, etc.), feel their expertise and advice are the most critical, as they represent religious tradition, and the majority of weddings are still religious ceremonies. The second category is made up of secular event specialists with expertise in designing aspects of weddings: the photographers, caterers, florists, dressmakers, and jewelers; they all have to be involved, because they provide essential services to the bride and groom, and all tell clients how to do it "right." For these sorts of specialists, doing it right implies holding a mainstream wedding, because that is the norm they see most often, and take for granted. Their focus is not on incorporating different signs creatively, but rather indicating formality and cost by increasing the amount of particular signs (and so it is possible to attend weddings where uncounted thousands of dollars have been spent on displaying out-of-season flowers, simply as an indicator of the great expense to which the family has gone). Given the different expectations from these groups, it is not surprising that most couples have difficulty making some of the central decisions; rather, it is actually surprising that more couples don't elope in order to avoid designing a ceremony. Clearly the fact that so many public ceremonies take place despite the various stresses indicates their significance for the participants.

A wedding connects current individuals to past traditions within a given family, although that is only one of its roles. In describing her own as yet unplanned wedding, one of my students reported "An object that would be present is my great-grandmother's pearl necklace. She left it in her will saying that she'd like each granddaughter to wear it at her wedding. This connotes her spiritual presence at our wedding" (Couple 48). This is a very literal linking of the bride with her forbears, an effective way to remind at least family members of their connection to the past. It is echoed in several of the stories reproduced in the Interludes, which include multiple indicators of connection between past and present family members.

Alfred Schutz (1967) provided a useful separation of people into four categories, depending on the extent to which we share time and space with others:

1. *Consociates* (people with whom we share time and space, and interact with directly);
2. *Contemporaries* (people whom we are aware of as living at the same time, although we never meet in person);
3. *Predecessors* (we cannot influence them, but may be influenced by them); and
4. *Successors* (can orient our actions toward them in anticipation).

Each of these categories of people may play a role in the design of a wedding. We most often do what our consociates and our contemporaries do and expect of us; we sometimes take into consideration what our predecessors did and would have expected of us, but it is harder for us to take into account what our successors will do.

For many couples, the wedding serves as a clear reminder of connections not only with the past, but also with the future. Many couples save the top layer of their wedding cake to eat on their first anniversary. One couple could not comply with this mainstream American tradition because the bride was in labor on their first anniversary, so they changed the way the event played out: They ate the remaining cake on their new baby's first birthday, thus incorporating him into the celebration (Couple 62).[14] Or, in another example of multiple links across generations, the jade necklace used in the wedding of Couple 13 was first used by the groom's mother, and is now being saved for the wedding of a potential daughter sometime in the distant future.

TYPES OF IDENTITIES RELEVANT TO WEDDINGS

Cultural identity is displayed through details of behavior. Through their decisions about how to design a wedding, the bride and groom may identify at different points in the ritual as individuals with specific histories, as members of particular families, ethnic groups, religions, races, social classes, geographic regions, or citizens of particular countries. Edwards (1989) pointed out that "parents are typically more concerned about how a wedding will reflect on the family as a whole; the couple usually want to make a more individual statement" (pp. 95–96). He wrote this of couples in Japan but, in my experience, the generalization applies to most couples.[15] Parents and others of their generation wish to see themselves reflected in the choices made by their children, for only thus are they assured that they have successfully passed on their traditions.[16] But to the children often in early adulthood, demonstration of their own preferences, and accommodation to each other's desires, may be more important.

In designing a wedding ceremony, it must be decided whose identity the ritual will present: that of the bride and groom, their parents, or their guests (and, more often, which several of their various identities will be incorporated). Different couples come up with different answers. Some make compromises in the wedding ceremony to please their parents, because the wedding is really for them, but note that they planned the honeymoon only to please themselves (Couple 40).[17] Other couples take the opposite position, as was the case for a White and Puerto Rican–African American couple, where there was considerable controversy caused by this marriage, to the point where they decided that their focus had to be on making themselves happy, rather than worrying about anyone else

(Couple 52). Given the negative response to the fact of the marriage by several family members, this couple felt they were not left any other choice.[18]

Although I had originally intended to investigate only those aspects of cultural identity traditionally of greatest concern to intercultural communication (those being ethnicity, race, and nationality), it became clear as my data accumulated that almost all of the couples equated the various pulls on them, not weighting these elements above others (including individual characteristics, family concerns, geographic location, even membership in voluntary associations). Therefore I had to expand the questions asked, as well as what I considered relevant in their descriptions of what made their weddings unique, and which elements portrayed particular aspects of their identities. I later added a concern for gender identity, mainly in terms of what topics brides versus grooms were willing and able to discuss. Although my primary concern is with how people resolve the tensions between their different identities in any one area at a single time (that is, how two different ethnic identities might be displayed simultaneously, for example), there are some things I have learned relevant to each of these topics, and so some brief discussion of each follows.

Individual Characteristics

When there are extreme differences in race or ethnicity or religion to manage, individual concerns seem of lesser consequence, but when there are fewer of these large areas to cope with, individual characteristics come to the fore. Nearly every couple integrated some unique element into their wedding, and explained its presence as the result of a desire to link their wedding to significant experiences prior to the event. These served especially as a way to differentiate between multiple, otherwise mainstream, weddings within a single community.

For example, Couple 98, made up of a groom who describes himself as atheist, and a bride who was raised Catholic, ended up with a Methodist minister because she was someone they knew and were comfortable with. The bride explicitly said "I don't think it was really mainstream because I think we made it what we wanted it to be." And she was correct: They included several elements clearly not commonly seen in mainstream weddings. For one thing, they incorporated a Wiccan element, which is a bit of a long story. The bride explains:

> The unity candle wasn't just the normal unity candle. The unity candle was also a candle spell that is commonly used by Wiccan people. And what they do is they carve into the sides of candles things that they wish for…. And I did it the day of the wedding and, to tell the truth, I forgot to tell [groom] the day of the wedding…. There are four things written on the candle that I wanted to have for [groom] and I in our marriage. And the first is understanding—they really aren't in any order, since it is a

four-sided candle. The other is love. The other one is passion. And the last one is unity.

Just as they modified the standard expectations for a unity candle, they modified the cake topper as well.

> Neither of us wanted a cake topper that was frouffy … I was adamantly opposed to a Precious Moments frouffy kind of thing. But then we had been to a wedding where they had Princess Leia and Han Solo on top of the cake. And it kind of gave us an idea, well, we could do something like that too. And as we were thinking of people, Marge and Homer popped up and that's who we ended up going with. [Groom] made our cake topper. We couldn't go out and find a Marge and Homer cake topper so … we bought the toy figures and they actually sell the cake topper kits so people make their own.

They did toss the garter during the reception, but modified that tradition as well. "I think that it tends to be more of a striptease than anything else. I mean people tend to make it out to be more sexual than it should be … so [groom] didn't take it off, but we did throw a garter that I had made." Thus did they maintain the critical element (symbolically marking the next man to marry) without maintaining the striptease element that so many women are beginning to find inappropriate and seek to eliminate. So this couple modified three of the central symbols of the wedding to ensure a better fit with their own understandings of themselves as individuals. They also modified several of the surrounding events: They held a joint, potluck picnic instead of the traditional shower, and had a joint party in lieu of the more traditional bachelor party. This couple felt quite strongly about the importance of various parts of the wedding ritual, but they needed to modify the standard model ceremony so that it would better reflect who they are.

Couple 100 reported a different modification of the lighting of the unity candle, one that was important to them.[19] They asked their parents to light the unity candle with them, as it seemed to them the critical element was the joining of two families, rather than two individuals. Couple 92 requested rocks: Everyone in the family selected heart shaped rocks for their rock garden to symbolize the love and support of the bride's large family for the new couple. One sister brought a stained glass heart as her gift. And, as further evidence of family support, they were married by the bride's brother who was a train conductor, in his official uniform.

Couple 110, a lesbian couple planning a commitment ceremony, went to choose a cake a week after they decided to hold this event, and had great fun tasting the different types of cakes. Coping with the traditional cake topper of a bride and a groom, however, proved a bit more difficult.

Bride 1: "How do you get away from the bride and the groom?"

Bride 2: "We want a bride and a bride."
Bride 1: "And the best was, they look like us. We got them so that they look like us, long red hair and short black hair."

So, in addition to the fact that they are modifying the traditional heterosexual couple represented by the figures on the cake, they felt it important to also show their individual characteristics, even to hair color and length. (Of course, the real story here may be that bakeries now makes such options available.) This same couple wanted to follow as many of the heterosexual traditions of the wedding as could be modified to fit their situation: They wanted a big shower, the only difference would be that it would be, said bride 2, "a big, joint one" because "It's traditional. We still want to follow the traditions that everybody else follows." They even want to follow the tradition of the bride keeping her dress a secret until the day of the ceremony; again, the difference will be that they will both keep their dresses secret from each other.

Bride 1: "We've got our dresses picked out but neither one of us has seen our dresses."
Bride 2: "We want it to be a surprise."
Bride 1: "We don't want to see each other until the ceremony."

Part of what I found interesting about this is that many couples do not even follow this tradition any more, yet it seemed an obvious element to them.

Sometimes a particular activity has sufficient importance to either the bride or groom that they want to include a reference to it. The groom of Couple 20 wanted to serve venison steak at the reception to represent the importance of deer hunting in his life. His bride agreed, but added chicken as a second option, out of concern that some guests might not be familiar with venison.[20] Other times the desire is to mark the particular way in which the couple met, or one of their early experiences together. Couple 58 decided that, since they had met at Chuckie Cheese, they wanted the character to attend the reception. The company was so flattered by the request that they reportedly did not even charge for the service.[21]

There are dozens of other possible descriptions of minor changes made to the mainstream wedding, but presumably the point is made: nearly every couple does one or more things that are unique to mark the wedding as their own.

Family

In the simplest instances of family tradition, the bride and groom do something that one or the other was accustomed to doing at home, with immediate family members. For example, Couple 100 served steak because the groom said "when I was younger, we always ate steak on really special occasions."[22] For him, this marked the wedding as a continuation of traditions within his family. Other times, the couple replicates an element from the wedding of one set of parents or the other. Couple 95 chose bridesmaids' outfits based on the colors the bride's mother had chosen for her wedding: "I had all the pastel colors. I recall them all. They were chiffon with big, floppy hats. Green, yellow, pink, blue, lavender.... Back when my mother got married they did a lot of the rainbow colors and I decided to do the same thing ... the groomsmen all wore ruffled tuxedo shirts to match the dresses." In a sequence of American mainstream weddings, the same bridal gown was used by five brides in the same family (Knoerle, 2000). Couple 106 followed an extended family tradition with regard to the cake; this couple married in 1952, so this is not a standard tradition today, but back then "they baked a coin in the cake and the person who found the coin was the next one being married ... it was like a 2½-dollar gold piece ... it's smaller than a dime ... everyone in [groom's] family got a 2½-dollar gold piece on the date of their birth ... we have it in a drawer." Here, the gold coins served to mark various rites of passage for family members, from birth to marriage.

Couple 99 chose to repeat an element across multiple related families: The groom's brother was best man, and made a particular toast at the reception, which the couple later had engraved on glasses as a gift at the best man's son's wedding. Couple 97 followed a tradition across siblings rather than across generations: Each child in the bride's family married in a different month in consecutive order (June, July, August, September, October). Sometimes the couple pays homage to family members who are deceased. Couple 109 put a basket of flowers at the front of the church to represent all those in the family who had passed away prior to that day. As the bride said: "the basket of flowers, which to us was very, very important, because we know in our hearts all those people that had gone on before us would be there that day."[23] This was not the only couple who took comfort from the flowers and what they represented, although most other couples referred to a figurative, rather than such a literal, inclusion of the deceased.

Sometimes family traditions developed out of membership in voluntary associations. Couples reported a series of behaviors associated with fraternities (e.g., putting on a skit, or the bride's father and his fraternity brothers singing a song to the groom). These had greatest meaning to the members of the association, for obvious reasons. These are only a few of the examples of how couples maintain a wide variety of family-related traditions. From their comments, marking membership in a family served as important identity markers in exactly the same way that marking membership in an ethnic group served.

Geographic Location

Sometimes it is not only membership in a specific family with its own traditions that requires marking, but membership in a particular geographic region. Couple 107 demonstrated this by following the tradition of the place they lived and having a potluck for the reception, instead of a catered meal.[24] They added a unique element, by asking that guests bring their "best dish" instead of gifts. This was a bit awkward since the bride's father and brother had to travel from England to the United States, but even that was worked out; they brought the basic ingredients and then added fresh fish caught locally. Couple 78 had met in Hawaii, and so it was important to the bride that a friend from Hawaii brought flower leis (*hakulei*) for the bride and groom to wear at the ceremony.

Sometimes the identity displayed is not limited to a single city or state, but implies connection to an entire geographic region.[25] Lipson-Walker (1991) made the point that there were so few Jews in the south at one point that a regional loyalty was deliberately developed. No one community had enough Jews to stand alone, despite the fact that regional loyalty was directly in contrast to the more usual southern pattern of affiliation with a single small town. Her study of Jewish weddings in the south just after World War II suggests that the tradition of expanding the wedding weekend to a week's worth of events was viewed as the display of proper southern hospitality (unlike the north, where there is often only a wedding and reception). This makes particular sense when the extended family and friends of the bride and groom must come from far enough away that a short weekend of events does not seem worth the trip.[26] This tradition is still followed by many Jews now, regardless of where they live, if family members are scattered and only come together for major celebrations, such as weddings.

Occasionally it was not the place that required notice as much as the typical occupation of those living in that place. Couple 95 was married in 1974, and the bride described the substantial attention paid to the food served at the reception. "People judged a lot of the wedding on the food. They were very judgmental back then. It was important to have a good meal." She went on to explain that it was important because the majority of the guests were farmers who worked hard, so they expected provision of a solid meal, not just appetizers.

The bride's comment in Interlude 2, that "we were Texas," exemplifies the feeling of many couples, that some element of regional identity was significant enough to require public display and confirmation at the wedding, either in addition to, or in place of, the more traditional ethnicity, race, and nationality markers. These were not terribly frequent in my data, but when they did occur, the couple felt quite strongly about their importance.

Gender Identity

In popular culture, brides are portrayed as knowing a great deal about weddings and having great interest in even minor details, whereas grooms are portrayed as having no major say in what occurs. As it turns out, this is fairly accurate, but there are a few exceptions, which are worthy of note. First, let me document some of the ways in which weddings demonstrate how gender is socially constructed. In some interviews, grooms explicitly stated that they were not expected to know the details of weddings, neither the planning of their own nor their parents'. As the groom of couple 98 said, "being the guy I'm allowed to forget these things [speaking of minor details] and not be killed for it." Later, in response to a question about whether there was a similarity between his wedding and his parents' wedding, he said "we're guys. We don't generally ask those questions." One specific topic mentioned by multiple couples was the common tradition (at least in the Midwest) of freezing the top of the wedding cake to eat on the first anniversary. Generally, the brides knew of this custom and considered it quite reasonable, and even romantic; but the grooms, whether they had heard of it previously or not, considered it bizarre and unlikely. For example, here Couple 88 discusses the topic:[27]

Bride:	"We're also going to do that cake tradition where you keep the top of the cake and you freeze it for a year and you eat it on your anniversary."
Groom:	"Yeah, it sounds quite incongruous to me."
Bride:	"It is *not* appetizing."
Groom:	"She wants to save the cake and freeze it and we're supposed to eat it a year later."
Bride:	"Everybody in my family's done it."
Groom:	"It sounds disgusting."
Bride:	"My parents ended up doing it."
Groom:	I'll call you [interviewer] over and let's try it. It sounds gross to me."
Bride:	"I've heard it is not good, but I've never tried it."
Groom:	"I've never heard of it."
Bride:	"It's just a tradition."

For the bride, the fact that this was tradition ended the discussion. It was just one of those things "everybody" does as part of a wedding, and so they too would do it.[28]

Another frequent topic showing the construction of differences by gender was clothing. As already documented, grooms tended to find it odd that the bride's dress should be purchased new (and at great expense), whereas their tuxes could be rented. But most of them at least knew this was the expectation in American mainstream culture. There were a lot of other details related to clothing that grooms did not know at all, but that brides tended to have learned. Couple 109 revealed significantly different knowledge in terms of the relevant tradition regarding what the mothers of the bride and groom chose to wear.[29]

Bride:	"They didn't wear traditional mothers' outfits, they did wear dresses."

Groom: "What is a traditional mother's outfit?"
Bride: "As in suit style dresses."
Groom: "Oh, I didn't know that."

This is a nice demonstration of what Ray Birdwhistell used to refer to as the unequal storage of knowledge within a population.[30]

There are, however, specific areas of the wedding that fall quite explicitly in the groom's domain. Most of the grooms reported that, although the bride and her mother (and, often, his as well) planned the majority of the wedding ceremony, he was either in charge of or made significant contributions to the design of the reception (often helping to decide what food to serve, and usually choosing the DJ or band). Clearly the work was not quite so literally divided: Grooms generally had something to say about what they and their groomsmen wore, and usually could describe what the bride and bridesmaids wore; they also usually knew whether there were flowers and who held them, although they were far less likely to know color or flower names than brides. Brides generally had the most to say about the wedding cake, and decorations at the reception. Grooms were specifically interested in the moment of serving each other cake, far more consistently than I had initially realized. For example, the groom of Couple 100 reported specifically being told by his father "at his wedding he [his dad] said that he got my mom really bad. Everyone was laughing. He told me I better not let him down. So I nailed her."[31] Brides specifically mentioned worrying about whether their new husbands would smash cake in their faces; something they uniformly dreaded, yet often expected (as the bride of Couple 111 put it: "I just kept thinking at the last minute, is he going to smash this into my face, but he didn't").

There were some consistent exceptions to this division of labor, and they are revealing. When American men marry foreign brides, they display clear knowledge of American traditions, presumably because they are now the only one who can contribute such information. Couple 91 matched an American groom to a Mexican bride (and perhaps it is also significant that he is older than she).[32] Because he is Protestant and she is Catholic, they married in a Unitarian church. During their interview, he consistently made comments referring to whether elements of their wedding were typically American or not. For example, he called the meal at the reception "the typical catered thing;" described gifts as "pretty much your standard," described the whole event as "not super formal, but dressy," and he organized a bachelorette party for her. He described himself as "the groom, the ring bearer, the usher," indicating he knew these three roles are usually filled by different people in American wedding parties.

Similarly, the groom of Couple 93, an American marrying a Costa Rican bride, made multiple comments on the differences between their wedding in Costa Rica and American mainstream weddings.[33] In response to a question about clothing, he said: "It's not at all like here [in the United States, where they now

live and were being interviewed] where the ushers will all wear the same suits."
The bride elaborated on what would be typical in Costa Rica:

> Down there you can't ask the people, unless I want to pay for everybody's dress—you can't ask somebody to wear a color, you know, go and buy a dress, it's not the custom that you get out the money and buy it, why would you? To people that's considered wasting money. Just wear it again. And that was my feeling, why, I mean, I'm not going to do that, you know, just have them look nice and that's it. They don't match.

The wedding was held in the church in the center of her small town. As the groom put it, "it is hard to explain, it was a *town* event," so everyone in the town viewed themselves as having been invited, whether or not they received an actual printed invitation. When asked about any modifications to the standard Catholic mass, the groom pointed out that "they're not real big on that." When asked about foods, the bride explained that they had "typical stuff": *arroz con pollo* [rice with chicken and vegetables], hearts of palm, refried beans, tortillas, pastry, beef and pork dishes. The groom clarified by comparing the food in Costa Rica with that in the United States: The "fundamental foods down there are rice and beans, just like we have meat and potatoes." He did insist on including one element of the mainstream American wedding, the garter toss, but to do so he first had to locate a garter. In the process, he had quite an adventure: "I remember going into San Jose [the capital and largest city in Costa Rica] and it was hard to find one, you know, and I actually got in the middle of a riot and got tear gassed. While I was looking all over, it's not that common. So I was looking for it in San Jose, and these farmers were having a march and they put out the tear gas."

In much the same way that American grooms took the lead in explaining the differences between mainstream weddings and theirs to foreign born wives, when the ceremony took place in the groom's church, he often took the lead in explaining the central elements because then a bride of a different religion could not always be expected to know what was typical or significant. When Couple 101, a German American Lutheran bride and a Polish American Catholic groom, were interviewed, he took the lead in describing the wedding, even up to including the colors of the bridesmaids dresses and the food choices at the reception dinner. As he said, it was "pretty traditional ... walking down the aisle, sermon, and the wedding service, and the tradition of walking out." They had a band because that was traditional in his family, but they also included elements from hers: "Later in the evening we had something that was kind of traditional in [bride's] family, it was the mock wedding, where a bunch of guys dress up as a wedding party and do a mock shotgun type wedding. It's just a big comedy thing. It's a lot of fun to watch."

The same held when there was a difference of ethnicity: In that case any traditions that fell under the groom's ethnic identity were up to him to identify and explain. For example, the groom of Couple 90 (an Italian American marrying a German and Irish American) knew that they had been given "lots of money, a lot of envelopes" as gifts, and that this was "pretty typical of an Italian wedding."[34]

So, it appears that, although it is generally expected that brides will have more context-specific knowledge of weddings and the minor details of their planning than grooms, at least when the groom has to represent American tradition to a foreign born bride, or represent his religion's expectations to a bride from another religion, or his ethnic group's expectations to a bride from another ethnic group, the groom turns out to be able to describe a surprising number of elements in considerable detail. When pressed, as when only the groom was available for an interview, he often was able to compare his wedding to others and describe even colors in detail, although these descriptions were marked by noticeable hesitations in vocabulary choice. For example, the groom of Couple 90 said "We really didn't throw the thingamajig you wear around her leg, we didn't do that." The same groom came up with a color term for his groomsmen's clothing immediately (they wore "a funky gray and white patterned vest"), but stuttered considerably when asked about the bridesmaids' clothing ("the girls wore kinda like a bluish, a light bluish dress, no, it was actually more silver, because it matched, like a silverish blue because it somewhat matched what the groomsmen were wearing").

Racial Identity

As pointed out in Chapter 1, although interracial unions are the most controversial in the United States today, if the bride and groom share one religion, they have the option of not doing anything to mark their racial differences. In fact, it seems that when the differences are quite visible in terms of physical characteristics, and thus already publicly available to the guests, there is less felt need to mark the differences in other ways. Even so, there are a few elements that are often incorporated in very recent weddings to indicate some connection with Africa, and thus an identity of being African American: jumping the broom is the most frequent of these, whether in a monocultural or intercultural wedding. Couple 108, for example, united an African American Baptist groom and a White, Irish and German American Catholic bride, in a second marriage for both. The groom explained this particular tradition:

> The jump the broom part, which a lot of people don't understand, was a bonding of two people together in marriage, you know, forever, and that was our commitment, together forever.... Jumping the broom was part of that whole slave trade situation but it was also a way that slaves, that they can get married, set up house. It was the only way legally, in their minds, that they could do it.

FIG. 6: *Ketubah* designed for Couple 80 by Richard Sigberman, with calligraphy by Robin Hall. Photo by Richard Sigberman.

FIG. 1: Fabric used for *huppah* by Couple 1, now serving as a window shade in their bedroom.

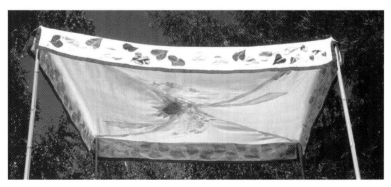

FIG. 7: *Huppah* used by Couple 13.
Photo by George Waters.

The bride continued the explanation:

> We had researched it … some of the publications said the broom repre-
> sented housekeeping. It represented a lot of different things to a lot of dif-
> ferent people. And what it represented to us when we talked about it was
> the commitment. Marriage in all times was commitment, but in those
> times, the only way they signified commitment was the jumping of the
> broom because it wasn't legal. And so we decided to incorporate that in
> our marriage.

The couple had tried to find a good description of the meaning of the jumping of
the broom to hand out at the wedding for those guests unfamiliar with it, but never
found anything appropriate, and so they finally decided that the action by itself
was symbolic to them and at least some of the guests, and that would suffice.

Their reception included some traditional southern African American foods,
although the event was held in a small town in the upper Midwest with no African American residents. This led to some interesting interactions, as related
here by the bride.

> It was funny because the guy that roasted the pig and the cow for us, many
> of our friends who happen to be Black and the relatives on his [groom's]
> side, were telling the pig roaster how they wanted the ears of the pig and
> the skin and various other items that many White people don't eat. And he
> thought they were joking until it almost got vicious at one point over the
> ears and the tail.

Bride's   "And that pig was gone, there was nothing left of that, it was
daughter: gone."

Music and dancing at the reception posed another challenge.

Groom: "That's the good part, music and dance. Since we were bringing
             relatives and friends, we brought our own disc jockey with us,
             you know, with our own music. You know, rhythm and blues was
             a big thing in me and my wife's relationship, so we decided to
             bring our music and we had a good time."

Bride: "I think we had a wide variety of people, not only in terms of dif-
             ferent ethnic groups but of different ages, from older people to
             younger people, and they were really pretty good about it be-
             cause the majority of our music would be typical of a Black radio
             station. We didn't have rock and roll, we didn't have country and
             western … I think people really handled the music really well be-
             cause it was kind of one sided."

Groom: "That was a big invasion of a large number of Blacks in a small town."

There were 150 guests, and the groom explained the significance of so many of his friends and relatives attending, although it was an extremely long drive from where most of them lived to the site chosen for the event: "I believe deeply on my side of the family it was a form of them accepting [bride] into the family, why they made that drive up to [names place], to welcome [bride] into my immediate family."

As was the often the case, this couple reported no luck in finding an interracial cake topper, despite searching for months. Finally the bride saw a miniature statue of two bears cuddling, one light brown and the other almost black in color, which is what they used on the cake. In another Black–White interracial wedding, that of Couple 19, the bride made her own cake topper out of two Barbie dolls, one Black and one White.[35] The two dolls were originally both female, so she cut the hair of the Black doll, and sewed a tuxedo for it, to better represent the African American groom. She was satisfied, because race was the preeminent factor in her consideration, but her fiancé said "it just wasn't right": The doll still seemed feminine to him. Here, either race or gender could be appropriately represented, but apparently not both simultaneously.[36] And in still another ceremony, an African American bride marrying a Swiss groom chose to use a crystal cake topper, thus avoiding the display of skin color altogether.[37]

Sometimes, couples opt for a single clear visual statement about differences in background. One White–African American couple decided to have a vanilla wedding cake (of the traditional, multitier variety) served with chocolate ice cream, as a deliberate reference to their crossing of racial lines (Couple 45). It is not surprising that their choice of music at their reception combined what they felt White and African American guests would expect.[38]

Couple 111 was also an interracial union, this one between a Chippewa (Ojibway) groom and a White bride, both of whom were Catholic, but they had a more difficult time designing a single ceremony that met their needs, in part because of geographic concerns.[39] This was also a second marriage for both (as discussed in Chapter 1, second marriages are more often interracial because there is a smaller pool of eligible spouses, and so people extend their search beyond those originally considered). Because they were living near the bride's family, but half the country away from the groom's, they essentially had two wedding ceremonies and two receptions. They knew his family would not be able to attend a wedding near her family home, and "never considered doing it out there [his family home]." First, they were married legally at the courthouse, with a reception at the bride's sister's house, including most of the bride's family, and friends of the bride and groom. This was the brief, standard wedding with a judge, who read "whatever he normally reads." At the reception, which included a formal wedding cake, the bride's brother-in-law gave a particularly apt toast for the circumstance: "May the marriage be as long as the ceremony was short." Although the first wedding and reception took about 6 months of planning, the second set were considerably more casual. As the bride reports: "We were going to the reservation and spend a week there and thought we'd show up at church one day and talk to him [the priest] and see if he'd do this and that's exactly how it happened—no planning whatsoever for that ceremony." They drove directly from the first wedding location to the second, although they got caught by a blizzard, and had to spend a night on the road. When they got to the reservation, they went to see the priest. Not expecting an immediate answer, they were dressed casually, in jeans. The bride tells the story: "We just went to talk to him and he was, like, willing to bless the union, right now, right here. He didn't care what we were wearing." He fetched a small pottery basin filled with water. "We had to wash our hands … because we both had been married before, and you wash away any past loves or evils … we washed our hands in the same water and then he read the vows … then we just kissed and we thanked him and we left." They had investigated being married by a Catholic priest in her home town, but it would have been very difficult to arrange (because they had both been married previously, and because they would have had to attend classes that they had a hard time fitting into their schedule; they at that point had 3 children each from prior marriages). But it was important to her that their marriage be properly sanctified: "In our eyes, a Catholic priest blessed our marriage. We are married in the eyes of God." For this reason, they celebrate their anniversary on the date of their second wedding ceremony, not the first. After the second wedding, there was a second reception: "That night his cousin had squirrel and they had fry bread … we had a little celebration there." But most important was the visit the next few days with his grandmother, who had helped raise him.

> I always felt like I was being taken to his grandmother on approval.… We'd already been married by the priest, we'd already been married by the judge, but we still had to go see grandma. And grandma talked to me a lot and got to know me a little bit and made us something to eat … when the whole thing was over, she said to [groom] "now you take care of her, you make sure that you treat her children as your own" and that was like her stamp of approval.

Then they drove back to the reservation, through another blizzard, and shortly after, on to the groom's mother's place (although it was the grandmother's blessing that counted as most significant, not hers), and eventually back to where they would live. As the bride described that trip, "It wasn't exactly your Hawaiian vacation or Caribbean cruise for a honeymoon."

Ethnic Identity

Ethnic identity is the most frequent type marked in weddings, as interethnic weddings are now quite common in the United States. As a result, ethnic markers are described often in these pages. A fairly typical example in terms of their ability to identify particular elements as ethnic markers is Couple 102, with an Italian American bride and a Polish and German American groom, both of whom are Catholic. In discussing the food served at the reception, the bride said: "we had a sweet table and it had all these Italian cookies … and we had the traditional *cannoli*." The groom noted "and if you had a Polish wedding you'd have had *pierogies* and those type of things but we didn't have anything Polish." When asked why not, the explanation was that the bride's family was in charge of providing the food, so they provided what they were accustomed to seeing served at receptions. Two other elements of the reception were specifically marked as Italian American. First, they followed the Italian tradition of having the new couple walk into reception, greet everyone and give the men a shot of brandy and women anisette, also the men got cigars and women got Jordan almonds. "We just did it because it was part of my heritage and we wanted to incorporate that into the wedding, that and the Italian cookies and pastries." And second, they had a special dance between the bride and groom where "all the adults threw change, coins, on the dance floor as we were dancing and what that means in the Italian heritage is good luck and wealth to the bride and groom. But we don't collect the money then, all the children that were there … were able to take up the money and then keep it." The groom had asked about including two Polish traditions, but the bride was uncomfortable with both, so neither was incorporated. The first is alternately called the broom dance or the dollar dance, where men give the bride a dollar to dance with her, as a way to build up the immediate cash reserve available for the newlyweds, on the assumption that they will need to purchase a lot of items in the process of beginning a new home together. The second was having the Mazur Polish dancers perform at the reception. This was a dance troupe from a voluntary association to which the groom's family belonged, and they usually performed while the band took a break. The groom explained that "they had traditional costumes of Poland on and the dances were in celebration of the wedding." The bride objected because "I felt that it was a reception and not a variety show." In the end, instead of his ethnic identity, his membership in a particular fraternity was represented. His fraternity brothers sang songs and everyone raised mugs and drank, and performed a skit with one pretending to be the groom in ball and chain and apron (this wedding took place in 1975). When asked about his response to not having many of the traditional elements he expected included in the wedding, the groom said: "you get over that while the planning process goes on … we didn't get caught up in 'oh, I didn't get my way' type of thing … we didn't have time to think of things that we didn't have, things just kept on moving." This essentially represents the attitude of most of those who take on intercultural marriages: if they start arguing about the small things, they know the marriage will never work, so they just don't let it become an issue. (Those who do, presumably do not end up married.)

In a very different event, Couple 94 combined a Vietnamese American bride with a Chinese American groom (this is monoracial because they are both

Asian, but interethnic because they come from different ethnic groups within Asia).[40] However, because they both grew up in the United States, there were also considerable American mainstream influences on their choices (although fewer than in weddings where only one person is Asian). Aside from the fact that this was an extremely large wedding (500 guests), as would be common for Asian couples (who generally invite everyone they know professionally as well as personally), one of the most visible markers of Asian identity was the number of dresses worn by the bride during the event. As the bride tells it:

> I changed about four times during the banquet.... We started out with the wedding gown ... it was like a princess fairy tale type wedding gown, I've always wanted something like that since I was a little girl. It was tight at the top, short sleeves, off the shoulders, very poufy from the waist down, very long, very beautiful.... The next dress I wore was a red Chinese traditional dress ... that was around when dinner started.... It is just very typical, very high up the neck, short sleeved, and red, very tight, goes all the way down to above the ankle and has two slits on the side, so I wore that for dinner. And after that we cut the cake for dessert and that's when I changed to another dress, it was American, gold, light gold gown, spaghetti straps, long and just flowing. And after that we had a dance and that's when I changed to another dress. It was a red dress, American dress.

A typical American would wear one gown for the entire event, but wearing multiple outfits is typical for most Asians (originally a Chinese tradition, this is now followed by most Asian Americans, so the bride did not feel she was conforming to her husband's traditions rather than her own in this). An interesting detail here is that, although three of the four dresses were American gowns in *design*, they followed the Chinese *function* of marking both social class (four dresses obviously being more expensive than one) and formality.

This wedding demonstrated several other elements of Chinese, Vietnamese, and American influences. Between the private ceremonies with parents and the public reception, limousines took the bridal party to a nearby lake for photographs, then the bride and groom used a horse and carriage for the trip to the reception (both elements are mainstream American social class markers because they add to the expense of the event). The bride specifically mentioned the latter as the most satisfying part of the day because the carriage took a route through much of Chinatown, where she had been working only the week before (after the wedding, she moved out of state with her new husband). The reception was held at a Chinese restaurant, with seven to nine main dishes, including several meats, duck, shrimp, lobster, and more. It also included a specific expensive liquor (XO) used by Chinese Americans as a social class marker. Upon entering, guests signed in on a long, red, silk cloth (a traditional Chinese custom now followed by many Asian Americans). The lucky color red was reiterated in the tablecloths. During the meal, guests took chopsticks and hit them against plates or glasses to indicate when the bride and groom should stand up and kiss. An important point here is that traditionally Asians don't show a lot of emotion in public. As the bride said at one point: "I do find it hard to show any kind of emotion in front of my parents, to him. It still is awkward." Also at the reception, there were markers of not only Chinese and American identities, but Vietnamese, for the Master of Ceremonies alternately used all three languages to introduce guests and songs. There were two bands, one of which was American, singing in English for the younger crowd, and the other which was Chinese, using traditional instruments for the older crowd. This combination led to some interesting moments: The couple entered the reception to a song played in English, but were introduced in Chinese, for example.

One particularly interesting point in this wedding is that, although it was very important to the couple that they perform the traditional Chinese rituals to publicly mark their marriage, they never obtained an official marriage license from any legal body, so in American law they are not yet married. In the morning, the bride and her family and friends waited at her parents' home for the groom and his friends to arrive, they shared food, took pictures, and honored her family members and ancestors, and were given gifts (mainly money in red envelopes for good luck, and jewelry). Then the bride, groom, and their friends went to his family and repeated the experience to indicate that each was accepted by the other's family. The bride reported:

> The strongest traditional part that I remember was the bowing three times ... basically, you go in order from your ancestors, to grandparents, to parents, then your aunts and uncles, your siblings that are older than you are.... We had to basically serve them tea, while you kneel in front of them. They take a small sip and give it back and in return they give you a gift ... either money or jewelry.... They put it on you, too, so that at the end of the day I had bracelets going up to my elbows, and I had chains all over my neck.

However, asked about the marriage certificate, she said:

> We didn't do the legal paper marriage thing that every couple does. We didn't get a chance to do it and basically it wasn't that important to us. And we've been married close to three years ... we still haven't went to city hall and go through all that paper stuff. So legally we're not married. But that's not important to us. As long as we both know that we're married, to us we're married ... family, friends, everyone knows that we're married.

Similarly, they do not now wear their wedding rings, as most Americans do, as a daily visible symbol of the marriage: "We just know that we're together and everyone else knows that we're together and it is fine with us."

International Identity

International weddings typically follow the standards of the country where the wedding occurs, but there are times when multiple traditions are accommodated. A German–American couple held two ceremonies, the first in Germany and the second in the United States (Couple 56), the first ceremony was small and informal, in keeping with German expectations, whereas the second was much more elaborate and formal. At their second ceremony, the couple chose a cake that was half Black Forest cherry to represent the German heritage, and half butter cream, a more typical American choice.[41]

Couple 86 matched a Spanish Catholic groom to an American Jewish bride; because he came from a region of Spain noted for its embroidery, the couple asked the groom's mother to embroider a panel using that specific technique. She included a very small reproduction of the Spanish flag as her signature. The bride's aunt then turned the embroidery into the centerpiece of a *huppah* for use at their wedding ceremony in the United States. (There is actually a longer story here, concerning the fact that the bride's extended family had a *huppah* unavailable to them, due to a family agreement that it was not to be used for interfaith weddings.)[42] This couple had a civil ceremony in Spain, and then a more elaborate ceremony in the United States a year later. Invitations for the U.S. wedding were in both Spanish and in English. That wedding was conducted by a Humanist rabbi who followed most American Jewish traditions chosen by the couple (the seven blessings, stepping on the glass, exchange of vows and rings) with a few additions.

* The blessings over the wine were said by one of the bride's grandfathers, using a cup from the other.
* The Spanish tradition of *arras* (gold coins) was included in revised egalitarian form: The bride and groom exchanged these coins, thus accepting fiscal responsibility for one another, though the more usual procedure has the groom unilaterally accepting fiscal responsibility for the bride.
* Since standard American Jewish practice is to have the bride and groom enter each accompanied by their parents, the bride's grandmother and grandaunt accompanied the groom in lieu of his parents who were unable to attend and remained in Spain.
* His parents wrote a letter, which was translated into English and read aloud as part of the ceremony.
* They incorporated Sephardic Spanish music into the ceremony and the reception, thus meshing her Jewish background (because those who wrote the music were Jews) and his Spanish background (because the words were in Spanish, and the music comes from Spain).

As the bride put it, "Any time we could, we threw in anything Spanish or Jewish." Although the groom had worn a *kipah* while attending other Jewish ceremonies with the bride's family, he was not comfortable wearing one for his own wedding. He explained: "It was different because I was the center of attention. I wanted to represent myself as I am." One thing was the same at both weddings: the inclusion of *padrinos*, the godparents of the wedding. Traditionally, in Spain, the *padrinos* consist of the bride's father and the groom's mother. For the Spanish civil ceremony, the father of the bride's Spanish host family served in that role, along with the groom's mother, since the bride's parents were not present; in the U.S., an aunt and uncle of the bride served. Whereas the Spanish wedding followed Spanish traditions only during the civil ceremony as well as after (there was a reception at a restaurant, with typical Spanish foods, and then a more spontaneous party at the groom's parents' home), the U.S. wedding and reception combined mainstream American traditions (white formal bridal gown, bridal bouquet of calla lilies, bridesmaids also holding calla lilies, young cousins serving as flower girls and ring bearers, a multilayer white wedding cake); Spanish national and regional traditions (the groom's mother's embroidery, the Spanish flag, *arras*, the inclusion of *padrinos*), and American Jewish traditions (the largely Jewish ceremony, the *huppah*, at the reception everyone danced the *hora*, and the bride and groom were raised on chairs).

Religious Identity

Many of the couples interviewed for this project emphasized the importance of religion in their lives, and therefore at their weddings as well. The bride of Couple 109 spoke for many when she pointed out the significance of being married in her church: "My family has always been very religious, so to me it was very important just to be there."[43] The bride of Couple 98 elaborated on the religious significance when she said: "You're making a commitment to someone for the rest of your life and what you say has to be true, otherwise it doesn't mean much." Because weddings most often occur within a religious context, and confer the religious leader's approval of the new couple, religion plays a large part in most of the weddings described in this book. As Couple 109 continued:

Bride: "We tried not to get wrapped up in the glamour of the wedding, not to forget what the purpose of the day is, joining two people in marriage, a lifelong commitment. And it's not about being the most beautiful person. It's not about having the perfect shoes."

Groom: "It's not about having the fanciest wedding, and trying to do what other people did."

Bride: "We wanted it to be a day where God united us in one and a day that the people who meant the most to us could help us celebrate ... It was a wonderful day that we can cherish for the rest of our lives."

Because so many of the weddings documented here are interfaith, conflict with religious leaders unwilling to approve a marriage to someone outside the religion plays a large part in the stories told about these weddings.

Sometimes religious affiliation leads to following a long line of prior weddings in activities that are not at all the mainstream. In a wedding celebrating the union of a Serbian Orthodox groom with a Catholic bride (Couple 7), enormous significance was placed on doing things the way the groom's family had always done them, and the tie this demonstrated for him with his predecessors.[44] The ceremony was primarily in Serbian, a language the bride did not understand, and the bride and groom wore Eastern Orthodox crowns. When these were put on, the bride turned to the groom and began laughing at how he looked. She later said she had suddenly thought of the old Imperial margarine commercial, where, after an actress tastes the margarine, a crown appears on her head. Clearly the connotations of the crown were quite different for each of the major participants. (Connotations are connections with something outside the present event.) The groom took it for granted that they would wear crowns because that was how couples always got married in his family. But only the groom and his friends understood this connection. For the bride's friends, as for her and her family, the message about tradition and affiliation with predecessors was invisible. The bride reported that her friends thought the ceremony was "medieval" and she had to agree. For this couple, the decision to be married in his church, in the traditional manner, was easy because the groom's family was not present: His parents had died and his brother was not able to come to the United States for the ceremony. The bride agreed to the crown (and all the other Serbian Orthodox requirements) because she understood the importance of tradition for him. But that was not quite the same as understanding the significance of every symbol herself, a fact revealed in her inappropriate moment of laughter.

At the same time, not all major decisions for this wedding were related to Serbian Orthodox traditions. For example, the bride carried three long-stemmed calla lilies because the florist recommended them as an appropriate match to the bridal gown. Also, the bride's mother suggested placing red roses in the seats the groom's parents would have occupied. There was no announcement of what this meant because they assumed everyone would be able to figure it out.[45]

Other times, especially when the bride and groom now follow a religion different from the one their parents follow, they may decide not to include some traditions that other family members considered standard. Couple 111 matched an American, Protestant groom to a Mexican, Catholic bride, married in a Unitarian church.[46] Because they did not have a Catholic ceremony, they omitted the giving of the coins (*arras*), and the Mexican Catholic substitute for the unity candle, giving flowers to the Virgin Mary.

Couple 105 united a groom who is Puerto Rican, White, and Panamanian, but who was raised in an African American community, born Catholic, with a bride who is Puerto Rican and Panamanian, also Catholic. Currently they are both heavily involved in a nondenominational Christian church, which had considerable influence on their choices at their wedding. The bride's mother wanted them to include several Hispanic Catholic traditions: the *lasso* (where a rosary is wound around a couple after they say their vows, symbolizing their new unity), and the *arras* (where *padrinos*—sponsors— walk down the aisle with coins, "pretty much promising that you'll never be without" in the bride's words). As the bride continued, "I stressed how I felt, that I didn't understand it, the true meaning, or I didn't understand the purpose of that if it's not dealing with God or anything" and so they omitted these elements. Their inclusion of the one, *padrinos*, was confusing enough to those unfamiliar with the tradition, because it requires that others than the couple's parents take on responsibility for portions of the event (e.g., one purchased the wedding cake). Because of their involvement with their new church, at the reception they deliberately omitted particular types of music, especially songs that included swear words, and alcohol. They reported that some of their guests did not attend as a result of these decisions. However, one mainstream American tradition that they did include caused the bride some anxiety:

> I was kind of nervous, when [groom] was taking the garter off, it gets kind of nervous, especially after you get saved, showing, having someone see you do something, you know, go underneath your dress and pull out the garter, it's kind of embarrassing, to some extent. But it was fun after a while, it was fun. I guess I started to realize that I am married, I'm allowed to do those kind of things, people don't have to look at me funny. So it was fun after I started getting used to it.

It is interesting that they even included the garter toss, given the deliberate exclusion of other elements based on religious considerations. Perhaps they might not have if they had fully discussed the implications ahead of time.

Occasionally one member of a couple will go out of his or her way to learn about the culture of the other, with sometimes surprising results. The Christian bride of Couple 14 decided to learn about Judaism so she would know what to do, only to discover, much to her chagrin, that she had managed to learn even more than her husband and his parents knew. As she told me: "I took out almost every book from the library that I could. I knew nothing about Judaism. Actually, by the time we got engaged, I was angry, because I felt I knew more about Judaism than [groom] did … and more than his parents did." Those who are born into a particular religion may feel little need to research its history, but those who were not must do so if they are to understand it.

Social Class Identity

In most mainstream American weddings, formality is indicated through matching of colors (of the bride's flowers to those the bridesmaids carry, of the bridesmaids dresses to the groomsmen's vests, etc.). In one complex example, roses were chosen as the theme, and so roses appeared everywhere: The bride's bouquet consisted of cream and pale pink roses, the bridesmaids carried blue and cream roses, baskets on the aisle held cream and pale pink roses, tables at the reception each had a candelabra decorated with a cream rose, and the butter on each table was carved into the shape of a rose (Couple 43). Whatever the degree of elaboration, the attention to detail marks the occasion as important, worthy of far greater attention than mere everyday events. Extreme matching across codes generally costs more, as in this example; this not only indicates the significance of the event for the participants, but serves as a social class marker.

Other times, it is not only money but the extravagant use of time that indicates social class. Couple 96 united a German, French, and Polish American bride who was Wisconsin Synod Lutheran, with a German and Italian American groom who was a nonpracticing Methodist.[47] The groom described the wedding as "Clampetts meet the Clintons" due to the disparity in social class. In illustration, he said that although some of his side of the family wore formal wear, some of the bride's side showed up in jeans and Harley shirts. The bride clashed with the groom's family over location (she wanted it in her father-in-law's university cafeteria, which often served students as a reception hall for weddings); surprisingly, although his parents were paying for much of the event, she won on this point. The time element became relevant when the photographer took the bride and groom to multiple locations in order to obtain perfect photographs, regardless of the fact that 225 guests were being kept waiting several hours for their dinner as a result of her desire to capture the perfect image.

MULTIPLE IDENTITY STATEMENTS

Clearly these examples show that many intercultural couples are faced with having to make multiple identity statements in multiple dimensions simultaneously rather than just in one (i.e., a single couple can have an interracial, interethnic, interfaith marriage, which is far more complex than when a couple only has to cope with one of these types of variation). In a study of wedding ceremonies in Kenya, Karp (1987) demonstrated how "the potential for complexity inherent in performance allows the performers and their audience to 'speak' with more than one voice at the same time. The different voices may contradict one another. If the result is confusion, such is the essence of social life" (p. 142). It is surprising how rarely confusion is the result, although that would seem the obvious implication. Participants frequently manage ritual performance with more competence than might be expected. Sometimes the bride and groom find especially graceful ways to combine visual statements of their cultural identities. One couple wanted to incorporate his African heritage and her African Seminole heritage: "So she wore Seminole jewelry with her American-style bridal dress, and he commissioned a jeweler to make traditional Kenyan necklaces which he and his attendants wore with their tuxedos. After the wedding, [the groom] presented the necklaces to his attendants" (Mayer, 1992a, p. 14). Another couple combined Puerto Rican with Puerto Rican–Chinese heritage through a combination of material items. First, the bride and groom greeted each of the 167 guests individually "presenting them with *copias*, a Puerto Rican custom. These tiny favors were made of feathers tied with ribbons printed with the couple's name and wedding date." Second, "guests also received small ceramic figurines representing the bride and groom, another Puerto Rican tradition" (Mayer, 1992b, p. 12). Their reception combined Chinese food with Latin American music.

Couple 67 joined a groom who is Greek, Mexican, German American and Catholic to a bride who is Mexican American and Catholic, incorporating several Mexican expectations, but with a twist. The service was held in her family's Catholic church (and was to have been conducted by the priest who had known her for many years, but he was moved, and so the new priest conducted the ceremony). They followed the Mexican traditions of having a *lasso* (her best friend's mother obtained a special one for them in Mexico) and *arras* (gold coins). The ceremony was both in English and Spanish, to such a large audience (nearly 500 people) that the groom had to be told by the priest that it was time to enter (the priest first looked into the visiting room and nodded to the groom, then when that did not result in his entry, the priest waved his hand for the groom to come)—he reported hesitating both because of the crowd and nerves. The bride and groom exited the church first, as is traditional, and were greeted by a large *mariachi* band, who not only played at that point, but then at the reception for several hours serenading the bride, groom, and their guests. At the reception they also had a DJ (for line dancing, as well as country, rap, and hip hop music), as well as continuing the Mexican theme through the traditional *salsa* and *meringue*. But because the groom and bride had been quite involved in a Latino fraternity and sorority respectively, they also had stepping. This was originally an African American tradition in the south, now carried on by many African American fraternities, who have taught it to other fraternities, including Latino ones.[48] Although I was surprised at this convoluted path, the groom took it for granted as obvious. The groom told me how he had 15 fraternity brothers present, all stepping together, when he missed a step and turned his ankle. His new bride's cousin taped it up with some basketball tape that happened to be in his car, and he insisted on continuing the dancing for the remaining few hours. "I'm not getting married again, so there was no way I was sitting down." Unfortunately, it later turned out that he had a bad fracture, and walked on crutches for 3 weeks as a result of the accident. The link to his fraternity and her sorority was also made visible through the choice of those colors (purple and shocking pink for hers, royal purple and white for his) as their wedding colors. The bridesmaids wore purple, and the flower girls were in shocking pink. Her mother wore cream; his mother wanted initially to wear white but could not find anything she liked, so ended up in pink. In addition to bringing in individual history through the colors and dancing, they revised the tradition of giving flowers to the Virgin de [of] Guadeloupe, and put up photographs of his grandmother and hers (his grandmother had died 2 years earlier, hers only 2 weeks prior to the wedding), and laid flowers in front of the photographs, which served as indicators that they were present in spirit. In this case, then, not only ethnicity was marked, but also membership in voluntary associations, as well as immediate family history.

NOTES

1. Identity is a "hot topic" just now. Within communication specifically, see Antaki and Widdicombe (1998a), Hecht (1993), Jackson (1999), Mokros (1996), Tanno and González (1998) as beginning points. References from other disciplines that are especially relevant are Gergen (1991) and Gumperz (1982). Seeing identity as a construction leads to such comments as "*Filipino American* is a state of mind rather than of legality or geography" (Root, 1997a, p. xiv).

2. DeVos and Romanucci-Ross (1982b) described the logic behind insisting that cultural identity be displayed publicly: "To be without a sense of continuity is to be faced with one's own death. Extinction of a group occurs when, as a California Indian once remarked to anthropologist Alfred Kroeber, 'the cup of custom is broken and we can no longer drink of life'" (p. 364).

3. See Briggs (1988) on many of the issues related to performance. See Myerhoff (1992) for such insightful comments as this: "Performance is not merely a vehicle for being seen. Self-definition is attained through it, and this is tantamount to being what one claims to be" (p. 235). See Sigman (1995) for elaboration on the concept of the "consequentiality" of communication, that is, the difference communication makes in our lives.

4. See Cupach and Imahori (1993) for an example of how to apply Goffman's ideas to intercultural communication.

5. "Identity is something that is *used* in talk; something that is part and parcel of the routines of everyday life, brought off in the fine detail of everyday interaction" (Antaki & Widdicombe, 1998b, p. 1).

6. Carbaugh (1990) put this well when he discussed "situations in which different culture patterns are communicated simultaneously, situating social relations differently, thus interweaving cultural identities and their distinctive patterns of action and meaning into one performance" (p. 152). He was describing the goal of papers in one section of his reader, but the same goal applies to this study as well.

7. See Jackson and Garner (1998) for a discussion of the concepts of culture, ethnicity, and race.

8. "In the field of communication, there is increasing attention paid to the fact that identities, such as cultures, no longer can be conceptualized as self-contained, fixed, and stable but are, rather, constituted and reproduced within the process of communication and everyday interactions" (Hegde, 1998, p. 37).

9. Leeds-Hurwitz (1989) devoted a chapter to the concept of context; see also Owen (1997).

10. See Feldman (1979) for a particularly helpful discussion of how we manage multiple identities (by turning them into what he called "nested identities"); see Nagel (1998) for discussion of a similar concept, "layers of ethnic identity"; and see Spivak (1990) for a warning: "One needs to be vigilant against simple notions of identity which overlap neatly with language or location" (p. 38). Scales-Trent (1995) figured out a way to turn the often negative position of having two identities (where an individual is fully accepted by neither group) to a more positive image: "I think that if you turn the word 'marginal' over, you find the word 'bilingual'—and at the same time you emphasize inclusion and richness rather than exclusion and isolation" (p. 114).

11. As Kim (1996) pointed out, researchers tend to exaggerate both the exclusivity and the permanence of cultural identities.

12. See Mead (1962) for the classic study of self and society; Wick (1998) is a current examination of essentially the same issues.

13. As Gans (1979) explained, "ethnics have always had an ethnic identity, but in the past it was largely taken for granted, since it was anchored in groups and roles, and was rarely a matter of choice" (p. 8). Symbolic ethnicity refers to claiming an ethnic identity when one has a choice not to. See also Roosens (1989) for discussion.

14. As reported by Michelle Lambert in Comm 440: Communication Codes, Spring 1999.

15. A suggestion supported by the fact that other authors make similar comments about other populations; Leonard (1980, p. 35) is one such.

16. "One of the creative processes of marriage is the particular combination of cultural behaviors put together by each new couple out of those they bring from their separate heritages" (Troll, 1988, p. 628). Although to a small extent this is an issue for all couples, it is more problematic for intercultural couples.

17. As reported by Nicole Wendel in Comm 440: Communication Codes, in Spring 1996.

18. As reported by Mike Berry in Comm 440: Communication Codes, in Spring 1999.

19. Interviewed by Michael Tschanz for Comm 440: Communication Codes, in Spring 2001.

20. As reported by Scott Erickson in Comm 440: Communication Codes, in Spring 1996.

21. As reported by Deanna Lean in Comm 440: Communication Codes, in Spring 1999.

22. Interviewed by Michael Tschanz for Comm 440: Communication Codes, in Spring 2001.

23. Interviewed by Jessica Tuttle for Comm 440: Communication Codes, in Spring 2001.

24. Interviewed by Eric Roche for Comm 440: Communication Codes, in Spring 2001.

25. See Allen and Schlereth (1990) for discussion of the significance of regional identities in the United States.

26. Diamont (1985) had another take on the expansion of a wedding over time, that it blurs the boundary between sacred and secular concerns:

    In Hasidism there is a willingness to ignore the boundaries between everyday life and holiness. Thus your wedding begins when you first announce your decision to marry and includes every aspect of planning and preparing for the big day. Even arguments about who gets invited and what gets served for dinner are part of the festivities. Nor is your wedding over until the last thank-you note is written, the last photograph is pasted in the scrapbook, and the last bill is paid. If you are reading this book as a bride or groom, these words are part of your wedding. (p. 16)

27. Interviewed by Ryan Ellifson for Comm 440: Communication Codes, in Spring 2001.
28. The same issue arose for Couple 98. The groom reported that the cake top is in the bride's parents' freezer:

> waiting for our one year anniversary. It should taste like everything else in the freezer by everybody else's accounts. That's the thing that you learn from having other friends get married first. [Two friends] just had their one year anniversary about a half a year ago now, and they said that over the course of the year the cake tends to absorb the flavors of everything else in the freezer. So it's actually something that I'm not terribly looking forward to.

29. Interviewed by Jessica Tuttle for Comm 440: Communication Codes, in Spring 2001.
30. Although I have never found this comment in his writing, it shows up repeatedly in notes from courses I took with Birdwhistell in the 1970s at the University of Pennsylvania.
31. Interviewed by Michael Tschanz for Comm 440: Communication Codes, in Spring 2001.
32. Interviewed by Nicole Goodwin for Comm 440: Communication Codes, in Spring 2001.
33. Interviewed by Jaime Jenjak for Comm 440: Communication Codes, in Spring 2001.
34. Interviewed by David Devey for Comm 440: Communication Codes, in Spring 2001.
35. As reported by Kelly Conway in Comm 440: Communication Codes, in Spring 1996.
36. The problem of locating interracial cake toppers has been sufficient that there are now several internet companies making a point of advertising that they will create cake toppers specifically for the individuals concerned, matching not only such details as hair length and skin color (www.jahdae.com) but also whether the groom is wearing a kilt or uniform (www.plaidpalette.com). One company (Blind Heart) explains on their web page how they got into the business:

> Blind Heart consists of a husband and wife partnership based in New Castle, Delaware. After planning our own wedding, we were inspired by the difficulty we experienced in finding an interracial caketop. Our own research concluded that most stores (whether online or not) did not have interracial caketops readily available. We also noticed the lack of caketops and accessories representing the various ethnicities and their traditions. We decided to provide a central place for people to obtain these items. A place where people can feel secure that the product they select will not only be of quality, but also an elegant reflection of who they are. (www.blindheart.com)

It is interesting to review what other wedding accessories Blind Heart offers for sale and which groups they sell to: For African Americans they have wedding brooms, wedding broom magnet favors, and an embroidered garter with a cowrie shell. For Asian Americans they have a white satin heart-shaped guest book for the reception, featuring red embroidery that says "love, health, happiness" in Chinese characters. They also have objects for Hispanic, Irish, or Jewish weddings, but no other groups; presumably this is an indicator of the current demand.

37. As shown on A *Wedding Story*, segment broadcast January 3, 2001.
38. As reported by Kristin Smith in Comm 440: Communication Codes, in Spring 1999.
39. Interviewed by Kim Wright for Comm 440: Communication Codes, in Spring 2001.

40. Interviewed by Hien Huynh for Comm 440: Communication Codes, in Spring 2001.
41. As reported by Travis Carlson in Comm 440: Communication Codes, in Spring 1996.
42. This illustrates the power of symbols: Although it may seem a small matter to those outside the debate, for those involved, it was a major problem requiring considerable diplomatic skills on the part of several in the family.
43. Interviewed by Jessica Tuttle for Comm 440: Communication Codes, in Spring 2001.
44. Interviewed by Sue Glanz for Comm 499: Independent Study, in Spring 1992.
45. Leonard (1980) pointed out the overlap of flowers as one particular symbol across very different rituals.

> Flowers thus make explicit the over-lap between the life-cycle rituals of marriage and death, seen also in the very act of going to church ("only for weddings and funerals"), the cars hired (though the drivers—in their words—wear "different ties and expressions"), the hymns sung, and the meetings with distant kin. Flowers emphasize that "In the midst of life we are in death," and give a sense of family continuity through remembrance of the departed and echoes of the past christenings, marriages and funerals. (p. 210)

In the many weddings where a deceased parent of the bride or groom was represented by a flower, this connection is even more vivid.
46. Interviewed by Kim Wright for Comm 440: Communication Codes, in Spring 2001.
47. Interviewed by Karin Jonsson for Comm 440: Communication Codes, in Spring 2001.
48. Perhaps one of the reasons it worked is that music is already so well-accepted as a vehicle to cross cultural boundaries. As Frith (1996) put it: "Music is thus the cultural form best able both to cross borders—sounds carry across fences and walls and oceans, across classes, races and nations—and to define places; in clubs, scenes, and raves, listening on headphones, radio and in the concert hall, we are only where the music takes us" (p. 125).

Interlude 5

FIG. 6: *Ketubah* designed for Couple 80 by Richard Sigberman,
with calligraphy by Robin Hall. Photo by Richard Sigberman
(see color plate).

*O*ne of the elements of a traditional Jewish wedding is a *ketubah*, or marriage contract. The words of the contract are usually written in Hebrew in the center of the page, often with artwork decorating the edges. These come in varying levels of elaboration, from printed versions (with just the names, the date, and signatures by the rabbi and witnesses added in during a brief private ceremony immediately prior to the wedding proper) to unique original art created for a specific couple. Not all Jewish weddings include a *ketubah*, but when they do, it is generally read out loud during the wedding ceremony so the guests hear and witness the bride and groom's agreement. It is extremely rare for an interfaith couple to incorporate a *ketubah*, but it does happen, and when it does, the result can be fascinating.

Working with Richard Sigberman, an artist used to creating unique visual representations of his clients' backgrounds in the form of *ketubot*, a Chinese–Jewish couple designed a very special *ketubah* for their wedding (Couple 80). The groom is Chinese (his father from China, and his mother ethnic Chinese from Malaysia) and an atheist (although his mother is Buddhist, his parents were not very religious); he was born in Malaysia, raised in Canada, and now lives in the United States. The bride's mother is Swedish, raised Lutheran, but converted to Judaism when she married the bride's father, who is Jewish and partly a second-generation Romanian American. The bride identifies as Jewish, although she looks Swedish, and reports being questioned frequently about whether she's "really" Jewish; she was born and raised in the United States. Sigberman incorporated all of these elements and more into their *ketubah*.

The largest and most central image at the top of the page is the Hebrew letter *chai* drawn in gold, intertwined with the Chinese character *shuang-hsi*, or double happiness, drawn in red. Artists often incorporate the *chai* into *ketobot* as a visual marker of good luck specifically, and a symbol of Judaism more generally. The Chinese *shuang-hsi* essentially serves the same purpose: specifically a wish for happiness used in multiple forms at weddings, it serves more generally as a marker of Chinese identity. Combining these two characters was a deliberate choice. The couple reported that, during a conversation about the design of the *ketubah* with the artist, they were shown examples of prior artwork.

> **Groom:** "There were Chinese–Jewish weddings before, and Richard showed us the *chai* and the double happiness, side by side. We discussed this and we said, well, if it's going to be marriage, and since a marriage is a union, then, why—"
>
> **Bride:** "Shouldn't they be together?"
>
> **Groom:** "Why don't they be together? And arrange it such that neither one predominates. Unfortunately, the color is bad [in the photograph we're viewing] but if you look at the actual *ketubah* now, it does actually look like it's melding, and overlapping one another."

Thus it was the use by other couples in prior examples of *ketubot* that led them to consider even incorporating the *chai* and the *shuang-hsi*; seeing them side by side, they realized they wanted their characters united, as they would be in marriage.

Richard Sigberman described the process he follows with prospective clients:

> When the couple comes over I show them a lot of past pieces. And I just let them look at it, and absorb. Then, at the end of the session, if they seem interested, I give them a couple of printed forms. One concentrates more on the text and the technicalities involved with that, and the other is more about the graphic and art end of the deal. And we set an appointment for a week or two later, at which point they've given it some thought and filled in the two forms. Then I pull out a big piece of paper and I look at everything they've listed, I review it with them, talk it over, and sometimes prioritize a little, and I start sketching. It depends on the shape they choose for the design, that is, what's prioritized may depend on the shape. Like this one [indicates a photograph] it seems pretty obvious to me that the most important scene should be at the top because it kind of comes to a point there. And this shape has been borrowed from some 17th and 18th century *ketubot*, which are my favorites.

It was this 17th century shape which this particular couple had chosen. Sigberman emphasized the role of the couple in influencing the design he draws: "Well, I can't do anything that they don't approve of or like. I don't do anything that's just my own musing, and idea. I feel very strongly about who this is for, and it's not for me."

The bride and groom walked me through the remainder of the symbols in their *ketubah*, which included references to an astonishing number of elements in their lives. As the groom explained, "It's our family coat of arms." (Although not the original intent of the wedding contract, which initially served only as a legal document, this is an accurate assessment of what they have created.) Sigberman echoed this sentiment, "It's way more than just part of the wedding. It goes beyond that. It should be something they'll be looking at for the rest of their lives."

Among other things, this *ketubah* incorporates:

+ The Chinese symbols for each of their names (because her name does not exist in Chinese, his father used a computer program to devise a transliteration of her name into Chinese characters);

+ A tiger, representing the Year of the Tiger (the year the groom was born) and an ox, for the Year of the Ox (when the bride was born);

+ A red ribbon running throughout other elements (the groom explained the Chinese tradition this way: "Upon your birth, the Emperor of Heaven links you to someone. This celestial being selects your name along with your future spouse's name from a cosmic registry. A red ribbon is tied to the two names. Thus the Chinese refer to a marriage 'tying the red ribbon'");

+ Irises (the bride's favorite flower);

+ Trillium (the provincial flower for Ontario, where the groom was raised);

+ A clamshell (to represent the regiment in the Canadian Forces to which the groom belonged, which used a clamshell as a cap badge);

+ A specific type of curlicue (taken from a doodle that the bride makes);

+ Lions from the Golden Gate Park (these guard the Asian Arts Museum there and are used in the *ketubah* to represent the park where the bride and groom met);

+ The acronym "WOMAD" (for World of Music and Dance, the organization, founded by Peter Gabriel, that sponsored the concert where they met);

- A *menorah* (symbol of Judaism and Israel);
- A Romanian embroidery design (taken from a blouse the bride was wearing when they met with the artist, to represent her Romanian heritage);
- The Chinese symbol of longevity (for luck and to balance the Romanian design);
- A helix pattern representing DNA (actually incorporating the major and minor grooves of real DNA—requested by the groom, to represent his particular scientific training); and
- A Viking ship (to represent the bride's mother's Scandinavian heritage).

Calligrapher Robin Hall added the words on the *ketubah* after the design was completed. They were in English because it was an interfaith marriage and were the words that the groom wrote for the occasion (the traditional text generally states that the bride and groom intend to follow the laws of Moses, clearly inappropriate for an interfaith union). Instead they wrote something the groom described as "vaguely ecumenical." Among other phrases, this text has them promising to build a home "founded upon the varied yet common brick of their lives" (an explicit reference to their multiple and various cultural backgrounds); "A haven shall be made to welcome, comfort, and calm the wandering fate-linked souls of present and future generations" (in reference to the red thread tying couples chosen by the gods together); and "In their complete house, they shall together touch the canopy of their huppah-roof and marvel at the sly laughter of heaven" (this sly laughter refers to the fact that they did not just meet during a concert in a park, they actually met when standing in line at the port-a-potties, which they consider to be a good joke; as the groom explained: "Well, I wanted to get away from the image of a serious, omnipotent being in heaven with a severe white beard. Instead I wanted to convey someone with a sense of humor. If you think about it, it is funny how we met."). The *ketubah* was read during the ceremony, and the fact that it incorporated Chinese elements was explicitly mentioned.

In addition to this amazing document, this wedding also incorporated a number of other references to the varied backgrounds of the participants. The invitations caused a minor problem:

They were printed listing both sets of parents' names (a common Jewish tradition in the United States), but the groom's parents were listed as "Mr. and Mrs." His mother wanted them to read "Dr. and Mrs." but the invitations had already been printed by the time she knew what they were to say. (This issue was resolved in fairly straightforward fashion: The groom paid the costs of reprinting enough to send to guests on his side of the family because they were the ones his mother would care most about.) Unlike the *ketubah*, the invitations were printed, not handmade. They were printed in blue ink (the bride did not like the traditional black), and featured a gazebo on the cover (because they actually were married inside a gazebo). The bride wanted the invitations to be recognizable but a little different and really did not want to include "those wedding bells and the doves and the silver writing, oh please." Choosing a gazebo also substituted for the traditional *huppah* in a Jewish ceremony, a symbol that they did not incorporate.

The cantor from the bride's parents' congregation performed the wedding (the rabbi, as is the case with most, would not perform an interfaith ceremony). The couple was required to take a course in the basics of Judaism before even she would officiate. The service was essentially a Reform Jewish ceremony, including some Hebrew (despite the fact that the groom and his family did not understand it). The groom did step on the glass (represented, as usual, by a light bulb), and they said the blessings over the wine. There was an additional link to the Romanian side of the family incorporated here: They placed a cloth embroidered by the bride's father's grandmother under the wineglasses.

Other elements of the wedding incorporated both mainstream conventions and specific references to their own cultural backgrounds. The bride did wear a typical white wedding dress with a small train, and she also had a veil. But in place of the more common pearls, the photographs show her wearing a beautiful jade necklace. "My mother-in-law gave me that jade necklace. And she got it from her mother, so now I'm the third generation to get it."

Despite the fact that she wanted to be married in the standard American white dress, the bride also tried to tie in Chinese tradition.

> I went to several vintage clothing stores to find a Chinese robe. I did not want to wear a *cheung sam* [typical Chinese dress] be-

cause I wouldn't look good in it. I did find a beautiful midnight blue robe that was over one hundred years old. So then, that was my way of interpreting Chinese tradition.

The bride changed into the robe at the reception (wearing it over "a simple white shirt and elegant slacks"), just before cutting the cake. When I asked the groom about his parents' reaction to it, the bride found out for the first time that her choice had not been quite perfect: They initially thought it was black (because it was such a dark blue), and traditional Chinese would never wear black to a wedding, so they were quite startled.[1] But he assured her that they appreciated the thought.

The bride's ring was her grandmother's engagement ring (on her mother's side, so it was Swedish), inherited when still in college. Because she does not like diamond rings (for "the whole political thing in South Africa"), she decided this would be her wedding ring. So she asked a cousin in Sweden to find a good jeweler, and they found a ring that was a close match for the groom. They had them engraved each with the other's name and the date of the wedding. The bride's parents have their rings similarly engraved.

The bride did not want to choose specific colors for the wedding, but the mother of the flower girl needed to know what to buy her to wear, so they finally decided on red and gold (the traditional Chinese colors used in weddings), as well as blue and gold (for the Swedish connection) as accent colors. Ribbons in all three colors were used in the table decorations by the florist (a close personal friend who gave her services as a wedding present). She also managed to find them oranges with leaves. (Tangerines, or oranges, represent prosperity and wealth to the Chinese, a symbol they wanted to include in some way.) The wedding cake table was decorated with oranges and red and gold ribbons, in addition to flowers. The cake followed Swedish tradition: a sponge cake filled with vanilla cream and fresh strawberries and covered with whipped cream.

The favors were another connection to China. The bride and her mother selected sandalwood fans for the women, and the men received pens. All the favors had red and gold ribbons attached, imprinted with the couple's names and the date of the wedding. (Because the wedding occurred in August, the fans were also functional, helping guests stay cool.)

The best man and Master of Ceremonies at the reception was the groom's brother, who made toasts in English, Chinese, and Hebrew. The bride and groom toasted each table (a Chinese tradition). Then there followed a Swedish tradition: teasing the bride and groom publicly. The son of the florist called the groom, among other insults, a "dark Swede." The bride was said to want to teach them all a Hungarian folk dance (instead of a Romanian one—a family joke, as the bride has a reputation for wanting to get cultural attributions straight). The more mainstream elements of tossing the bridal bouquet and the garter were omitted, testifying to their lack of significance for the main participants. In terms of music, the new couple told the DJ to play a little bit of everything. They wanted a Bob Marley song ("No Woman, No Cry") as their first dance but the DJ lost the tape, so he played their second choice, ("Pitié"), a song from Zaire by Tabu Ley Rocherleau, with a message of fidelity (representing the fact that they both like world music, and their initial meeting at a WOMAD concert). Later during the reception, the DJ played a song with the chorus "Romania, Romania, Romania" reinterpreted as "Seattle, Seattle, Seattle" (where the bride was born).

When the bride's parents got married in New York, her mother did not invite any of her Swedish-American relatives because it was a Conservative Jewish ceremony, and she had converted prior to the marriage: "I wanted the day to be nice, so I didn't invite them because I knew they were uncomfortable about my becoming Jewish." By the time their daughter got married, the family had not only learned how to handle an interfaith wedding, but an interethnic, international and interracial one as well.

NOTE

1. Costa (1997) described a similar mishap due to insufficient knowledge of the culture by someone trying to do what was appropriate. Traditional Chinese invitations are printed on red paper with gold ink; one couple sent out invitations printed in red ink on white paper, only to be told by a relative that red ink is inappropriate because it looks like blood (p. 33). Unfortunately, this implies that the invitation used by Couple 77 described in Interlude 4 may also have seemed inappropriate to anyone familiar with Chinese traditions.

5

Meaning

"Yet, we are left with the problem of meaning: How do words and gestures come to have meaning for people? How is it that we reach common understanding or often fail in our attempts to understand?"
—Gergen (1994, p. 253)

The combination of community, identity, and ritual determine meaning. That is, by understanding the various communities involved, the design of their rituals, and the relevant identities of the participants, we can begin to understand the meanings that events, and the symbols they incorporate, have for participants. This works because, as Peacock (1986) reminded, us: "Culture is shared meaning. To comprehend meaning, one must see the world as others see it, to comprehend experience in terms of the others' frames of reference" (p. 99).[1] Members learn meanings slowly, over all the years they spend in a community, gradually increasing their understanding. Nonmembers (including analysts) need to focus deliberately on meaning, playing a fast game of catch-up, if they are not willing to spend a lifetime with each community, letting meanings gradually accumulate. Essentially the process of understanding begins by focusing on one particular behavior at a time, and placing it into context. "Rituals are inherently ambiguous in their function and meaning. They speak with many voices" (Muir, 1997, p. 5). Thus they lend themselves to multiple interpretations. Meaning is a shared cultural production: It does not lie in the event waiting for us to discover it, and is not produced by a single individual, rather it is the result of combined numerous interpretations of the event by multiple participants, and so "it is constantly changing with our every act of participation" (Penman, 2000, p. 71). Fiske (1987) in his study of television culture emphasized that "Meanings are determined socially: that is, they are constructed out of the conjuncture of the text with the socially situated reader" (p. 80). Although here he was speaking of television, the point is no less true for rituals: The meanings of any ritual are determined socially, in the interpretation of the ritual performance by participants. It is this interpretation that the late-coming analyst must work hard to discover, through a combination of observation and explicit questioning of participants about their understanding of what has occurred.

In a mainstream, or monocultural, wedding, everyone knows what to expect, and how to interpret what they observe, for "the quintessential referent of community is that its members make, or believe they make, a similar sense of things either generally or with respect to specific and significant interests, and, further, that they think that that sense may differ from one made elsewhere" (Cohen, 1985, p. 16).[2] Choosing a mainstream wedding design ensures that the vast majority of participants will understand what occurs and will hold that understanding in common. In fact, even brief and incomplete references are understood by members of the same community, for people "whose biographies significantly overlap" can share minimalist narratives and gain meaning from them (Rosaldo, 1986, p. 98). In Wolf's (1990) terms, this illustrates who has power, because

> Power is implicated in meaning through its role in upholding one version of significance as true, fruitful, or beautiful, against other possibilities that may threaten truth, fruitfulness, or beauty. All cultures, however conceived, carve out significance and try to stabilize it against possible alternatives. In human affairs, things might be different, and often are.... Hence, symbolic work is never done, achieves no final solution. The cultural assertion that the world is shaped this way and not in some other has to be repeated and enacted, lest it be questioned and denied. (p. 593)

In an intercultural wedding, unlike a monocultural wedding, the question of who has power remains open to negotiation. The different communities represented have different expectations based on different past experiences and, as a result, may interpret what occurs differently. Each side will try to maintain power by influencing what elements are incorporated, to the exclusion of others. This fact is responsible for much of the tension felt by a couple in designing their ceremony. There are often parts where the wishes of each family are mutually exclusive, and successful negotiation at those points can be quite difficult, despite the best of intentions. Participants in rituals convey meanings primarily through the use of symbols, and it is traditionally assumed that symbols hold the same meanings for all members of a single community, or at least the same range of meanings. Yet, as Cohen (1985) reminded us, "Symbols are effective because they are imprecise" (p. 21). This is nowhere more obvious than in an intercultural encounter, where any single symbol may be interpreted in multiple ways by different participants. It is the goal of this chapter to consider how symbols are imprecise and how this permits them to work effectively in intercultural weddings. Five related concepts of particular value in understanding how intercultural weddings produce meanings will be presented below: polysemy, intertextuality, *bricolage*, redundancy, and ambiguity.[3]

POLYSEMY

Briefly, polysemy (also sometimes termed *multivocality*) refers to the fact that every symbol is inherently capable of conveying multiple meanings simultaneously. This critical ability serves as one way of addressing the central problem of intercultural weddings: how to simultaneously meet the needs for identity displays by two (or more) different cultural communities. When a single symbol can be displayed once, but is understood to convey different meanings to different groups of participants, it becomes a particularly valuable tool in the hands of the designers of intercultural events.

For example, polysemy permitted Couple 82 a graceful way to solve the problem of when to schedule the wedding. The bride was raised Catholic, although she was nonpracticing at the time of their wedding and became Buddhist afterwards; the groom was raised Jewish, minimally practicing Reform Judaism at the time, although he later became Orthodox. They were married by a Justice of the Peace because, as the bride said: "our different religious backgrounds made that seem like the most sensible path." As they were students at the time, they wanted a simple wedding, but one that reflected what was important to them. The bride explained:

> We had the wedding at the home of a couple who rented out their dining room and yard for weddings. We were married in their beautiful garden. That meant a lot to both of us, because we have always shared a love for the outdoors, and wanted to avoid an impersonal "wedding hall" atmosphere. We also had a delicious sit-down dinner, something that was important to me. And we had a small group of musicians play Renaissance and other acoustic music. This was also very important to both of us because of our shared love of good music.

Although they agreed on holding the wedding outdoors in a natural setting and the type of music for the reception because these were shared interests, there was some negotiation over when to hold the wedding. Because Catholics traditionally schedule a wedding for Saturday when it is not to include a mass, the bride felt that Saturday was the most appropriate day to be married. As she learned in the course of planning the wedding, however, Jews cannot hold a wedding on Saturday, because it is the Sabbath (weddings, or other moveable rituals, cannot be scheduled across previously existing holidays, including Sabbath). To resolve this, the bride continues:

we were married just after sunset on a Saturday in March. That way, we preserved the Catholic tradition of a Saturday wedding (I had officially left the
Catholic Church by that time, but was still operating within the culture
back then) as well as the Jewish proscription on weddings during *Shabbos*
[Yiddish for sabbath].

This elegant solution to the problem worked because the Jewish and the
Christian calendars count days differently: the former sunset to sunset, and the
latter midnight to midnight. Therefore, by Catholics, Saturday evening was still
Saturday, but by Jews, Sabbath ends at sunset, so a wedding scheduled after
sunset on Sabbath no longer conflicts with an existing holiday, and so is permis-
sible. A single moment in time balanced delicately between two different meanings, and everyone was happy with the resolution.

Historically, research in communication began with the assumption that
each symbol had a single meaning, which was either accurately or inaccu-
rately conveyed.[4] Although theoretically this idea has been proven false, it
still recurs, so it must be quite attractive to researchers (certainly it simplifies
the research). More recently, there has been a move toward what are termed
dialectic models, emphasizing two extreme points having tension between
them, recognizing that most interaction falls somewhere on the line between
the two (thus leading to more or less emphasis of each extreme in each interaction).[5] Despite the appeal of either of these models, intercultural situations
such as the weddings studied here make it abundantly clear that multiple (not
one, and not even two, but more) meanings are rampant in many social situations; there is simply no other way to understand what occurs. Often it is not a
case of having to choose between two things but learning how to have both
present simultaneously.

Members of each community represented at an intercultural wedding view
their own understandings of the symbols utilized as quite obvious. And why
shouldn't they? They, and all of their friends and relatives, have the same interpretation, therefore they assume that everyone present will also share the same
interpretation. This assumption is implicit rather than explicit (it seems so obvious to participants that they do not even question their assumption). However,
Fernandez and Herzfeld (1998) reminded us that "obviousness is itself culturally contingent" (p. 91). In other words, even when each group thinks it knows
the obvious meaning, every group may have a different meaning in mind. An interesting corollary is that when no one questions the meaning conveyed, the
discrepancy between assumptions may not even be discovered.

Couple 85 ran into this problem. As a Hindu bride and Jewish groom, they
planned two major ceremonies, incorporating a variety of contingent events,
with many guests participating in both ceremonies. The bride explained the
moment that became problematic because of multiple interpretations of a single symbol:

> In the Hindu ceremony, there is a moment when the groom has been welcomed by the bride's parents (feet washed, fed a sweet, etc.). The bride is escorted in by bride's mother's brother (since my mom is an only child, an old family friend). When she comes in the space where she sits is divided from the groom's with a white cloth. The plain one my parents had brought was too big for the space that resembles a *chuppah*. So the priest/doctor used the one he had brought which had a huge swastik on it (which is reversed from a swastika and means good luck in Hinduism). [Groom's mother] went white. [Groom] asked priest to explain the significance of the symbol who did, saying that it had been appropriated by the nazis. [Groom's mother] was very upset with the situation.

In this case, a last minute difficulty led to an unplanned substitution, so the bride and groom were unable to prepare the groom's family ahead of time with an explanation of what would occur and what meanings it should be understood to convey. Although weddings be organized months in advance, surprises can still occur; at these points differences in interpretation are most likely to be discovered and to cause misunderstandings.

Mainstream weddings are the result of a single, powerful voice stating its assumptions about what is "normal and expected" behavior in the United States. The specialists who advise couples about how to design their weddings find it easiest to take this single voice for granted; clearly it is simpler for them if all weddings look basically alike. However, Fiske (1987) pointed out that

> A single voice, or monoglossia, is one that attempts to exert control from the center and to minimize the disruptive and vitalizing differences between groups. Heteroglossia not only results from a diversity of voices emanating from a diversity of social positions, it also helps to maintain this diversity and its resistance to the homogenization of social control. (p. 89)

Using his terms, a mainstream wedding shows the influence of a single voice, or *monoglossia*, whereas an intercultural wedding demonstrates multiple voices, or *heteroglossia*. In a later work, Fiske (1989) went on to argue that "Television's heteroglossia reproduces social heterogeneity" (p. 73). This is equally true in other contexts. That is to say, social heterogeneity (multiple cultural groups sharing the same physical space) results in heteroglossia (multiple voices speaking at the same time). Given the current multicultural situation in the United States, it becomes clear why those participating in intercultural weddings consider it natural to represent multiple cultures in their rituals. Heteroglossia within rituals such as weddings thus accurately reflects the current political reality.[6]

As a result, intercultural weddings can be said to function as a palimpsest, with layer upon layer of different versions of the same event piled one on top of the next. (*Palimpsest* is the term for a manuscript that has had its initial lettering erased to make room for later writings. As a metaphor, it refers to something with multiple layers of meaning, all simultaneously evident to the educated reader, participant, observer, or analyst.) This metaphor permits recognition of how multiple meanings may be conveyed by the same behavior. Multiple meanings can be the result of cultural differences, and the consequent differences in community definitions, but they can also be caused by other sorts of differences. As Connerton (1989) explained:

> Concerning social memory in particular, we may note that images of the past commonly legitimate a present social order. It is an implicit rule that participants in any social order must presuppose a shared memory. To the extent that their memories of a society's past diverge, to that extent its members can share neither experiences nor assumptions. The effect is seen perhaps most obviously when communication across generations is impeded by different sets of memories. Across generations, different sets of memories, frequently in the shape of implicit background narratives, will encounter each other; so that, although physically present to one another in a particular setting, the different generations may remain mentally and emotionally insulated, the memories of one generation locked irretrievably, as it were, in the brains and bodies of that generation. (p. 3)

As always, shared experience leads to shared understanding but when different generations share fewer experiences than they assume, they discover that their interpretations also diverge. Another metaphor that has been used is "a collage of possibilities" (Stimpson, 1988, p. 90).[7] Either of these images, the palimpsest or the collage, is helpful so long as it reminds participants and analysts alike not to assume each symbol present in the wedding ritual has merely a single, uniformly shared interpretation. Knowing that multiple meanings are a possibility increases the likelihood that people will look for, and therefore find, them. People who do not even know to look for something, of course, are unlikely to find it. This implies that those who learn to cope adequately with intercultural differences in one context have a better chance of coping with them in others.

Although most meanings relevant during a wedding are related to culture, this conception of meaning as a palimpsest or collage implies that there is ample room for individual and family meanings to be added to the event. For example, in many weddings the cake topper is preserved, as a memento, and occasionally passed between family members. The usual direction of passing is from older generations to younger (as from parent to child, or older sibling to younger). But in a world where many people enter more than one marriage, a parent may celebrate a second marriage after a child has celebrated a first marriage. Thus, one bride reported originally saving her wedding topper as a memento, but later loaning it to her mother to use in a second wedding (Couple 6).[8] Presumably, immediate family and close friends recognized the link to the daughter's earlier wedding, and that was enough for the new bride. Everyone does not need to understand every meaning of any one symbol utilized in a ritual for it to be of value, but those who do not understanding meanings shared by others clearly are marked as nonmembers.

Couple 99 had a related story, but this one involved the distinction between the cake topper chosen and the one actually used. The bride told the story: "I have the cake topper which is actually not the original cake topper. Because the cake topper I picked out were the bride and groom. And instead when the cake came it had bells on it and so I made them give me the right cake topper. But actually in these pictures it has the bells on it." It is important to note that she accepted the wrong cake and topper for practical purposes (given the timing, she really had no choice), but now has an index to the event that was not there (directly contradicting the usual meaning of an index as a physical link to the original event), and so could be not incorporated into the photos. Essentially she has used memory (and the second cake topper) to correct reality, which was not in keeping with her explicitly stated choice. She refused to permit the bakery's error to influence her preference; she wanted a particular cake and topper, and so now remembers the event as having incorporated what she chose, not what the bakery supplied.

In a wedding between a Mexican American groom and an American Catholic bride, nearly all of the choices fit the mainstream American expectations, but one element was intercultural and polysemic. The groom's mother gave the bride a pearl necklace from Mexico that had been given to her when she was married (Couple 32). This had great meaning to the bride, as a marker of acceptance into the groom's family, and to the groom's family as a connection to prior tradition. The lack of visible cultural markers for the other participants was irrelevant, so long as the immediate families recognized the connection.[9] This is how polysemy works: It permits additional meanings to be displayed, for those who know how to correctly interpret them, essentially ignoring those who do not share in the knowledge necessary for interpretation.

INTERTEXTUALITY

Julia Kristeva (1980) is generally credited with introducing the concept of intertextuality, which points out that any given text relies on prior texts for its meaning.[10] Prior texts can be actual events (this wedding is like a previous wedding), or popular culture texts (this wedding has some similarity to one in a film, television show, or book).[11] Each individual text is enriched and given part of its meaning through prior experience with different, but related, exemplars. "New meanings are established with reference to old meanings and grow out of them and must be made, in some degree, congruent with them; and exchange, whenever and wherever it occurs, must be articulated with the existing system of meanings" (Schneider, 1976, p. 205). This is how traditions develop. Intertextuality thus reminds us to attend to "the general discursive space that makes a text intelligible" (Culler, 1981, p. 101). *Discursive* space here can be understood to refer to the public nature of ritual, rather than emphasizing one individual's interpretation standing alone, which would be *cognitive* space. If we share little or no past experiences with the central participants of a ritual, we are unlikely to have an easy time understanding what occurs, and the meanings others draw from the event remain unavailable to us.

Clearly, because any one participant in a wedding can reasonably be expected to have had different prior experiences, understandings of the ritual presented will always differ across participants (including guests) at least in some small ways (Schieffelin, 1985). However, as one of the attributes of a community, members are expected to share a large number of prior experiences (e.g., cousins who have attended each others' weddings, or friends who have all seen the same films). "At the broadest level, whenever we speak or write, and whether or not we do so in direct response to another speaker or writer, our discourse occurs in the context of previous (or alternative) utterances or texts and is in dialogue with them, whether explicitly or implicitly" (Mannheim & Tedlock, 1995, p. 15). In other words, once participants recognize the genre being presented, they will know something of the range of possibilities to expect. As McDowell (1981) said of another type of event, each performance is "a unique dramatization of the possibilities of the genre" (p. 73). This is as true of weddings as it is of other performance genres.

In describing what happens when someone uses a proverb, or reframes a traditional story, Briggs (1988) said: "Her words break the hold of the here and now, drawing the group through the window of the community's past. The words are no longer hers alone, for they have taken the shape of a quotation" (p. 1). This is the power of tradition: taking us out of the present moment, and into the past, it shows us not only similarities between the two, but also differences. With this in mind, we can say that each wedding is a new way of "interpreting the past" (p. 358). Bourdieu (1990b) described this phenomenon as "a present past that tends to perpetuate itself into the future by reactivation in similarly structured practices" (p. 54). And Bauman (1992) suggested essentially the same idea when he argued that people in the present "endow particular cultural forms with value and authority" as a way to make meaningful connections with their own past (p. 128).

Witte (1992) pointed out that the words *text*, *context*, and *intertext* share a Latin root, *texere*, "which refers to weaving, interweaving, or plaiting and braiding without regard to the specific material on which the operation is or can be performed" (p. 264). One implication is that we may consider the concept of intertextuality as an expansion on the metaphor of culture as a tapestry. Intertextuality thus becomes one method by which organizers of an event weave together disparate experiences into a coherent whole having meaning for them, and hopefully related meanings for others present. Other scholars have used related terms to describe the same phenomenon.[12] The exact choice of term is not critical; intertextuality is probably the most commonly understood and widely used and thus it serves best here. The concept is important, not the name we call it. Intertextuality teaches us that if we are to understand how participants interpret what occurs in a single wedding, we must know something of the past history of their attendance at prior weddings, stories told in their families of past weddings, and something of the media and literary representations of weddings with which they are familiar.

A formerly Irish Catholic bride carried yellow roses in her Lutheran wedding, which her family understood, but the groom's Lutheran family did not (Couple 15). Here my student described the wedding that was for her parents:

> My parents became annoyed with each other because of their different opinions on the wedding ceremony. Eventually, my mom decided to convert to Lutheranism.... The wedding ceremony then was entirely Lutheran, with absolutely no Catholic parts in it. My mom carried yellow roses as a sign of her Catholic upbringing. To herself and her parents this made a large difference. Since my dad's family didn't understand the connotation of the sign, they had no idea what the yellow roses were (Couple 15).

Although the bride's family appreciated the visible link to their religion, the groom's family could not take offense at what they did not recognize. To them, yellow was simply one of the acceptable colors for flowers in a wedding, and thus unremarkable. The secondary meaning, of a link to Catholicism, was unavailable to them as non-Catholics.

The significance of a wedding can be reiterated through the repetition of particular elements at later times. Sequences of weddings within families carry a particularly heavy burden of intertextuality, as it can be assumed that the majority of the guests will have attended all the weddings in the sequence, and so can be relied on to notice similarities and differences between them. For example, in *Fiddler on the Roof*, the explicit concern of the film with the issue of tradition results in a sequence of weddings moving from one uncommon only in the choice of groom (the issue is whether the father of the bride gets to choose her husband or whether she does), to a second arranged without the parents' permission (but eventually given the parental blessing) and held away from home, to a third not only arranged without permission and despite explicit statements forbidding the union, but held secretly with no family member in attendance. Here we see traditional expectations gradually violated more and more completely. The father of these brides serves as a symbol of the individual caught between tradition and innovation, whose daughters progressively move further and further away from his expectations.

The display at a wedding can be fine-tuned to demonstrate such subtle factors as the extent to which a family approves of the choice of spouse, especially when different cultural identities are involved, and it is important that this can be conveyed subtly, so that only some of the participants understand the message. Goode (1989) reported:

> In a study of a community of Italian-Americans decisions about what to serve at three daughters' weddings were strongly influenced by the nature of the match and what the family wanted to communicate through food choice. In a match involving a non-Italian groom from outside the community the menu was unusual in that it consisted entirely of homemade traditional Italian dishes. In a match involving an Italian-American groom from outside the community an expensive American catered dinner was served that included only one specific traditional item made collaboratively by the close female relatives and friends of the bride's family. However, a match with a local member of the close-knit enclave led to a dinner with no Italian items.
>
> In the first wedding a need to demonstrate a strong ethnic tradition to the outsider was satisfied. The second wedding format communicated both family status through the quality of the menu and a solid and appropriate support group through the collaborative baking. For the last wedding there was less need to convey either ethnicity or status. (p. 191)

In a separate report based on the same data, Theophano (1991) concluded that the mother "used common understandings of the meanings of foods and the structure of events to underscore and amplify the community's knowledge of these events and her feelings about them" (p. 52). But those understandings were common only for the family members present at the weddings of all three daughters, not to the grooms' extended families present at only one each.

Something very similar, but this time using clothing in addition to food to display subtle meanings to only some participants, happened in a wedding between a Zapotec (Native American) groom and a non-Zapotec bride, as documented by Royce (1982). Because there were non-Zapotecs present, "it was important to impress the outsiders with the antiquity of Zapotec tradition … and with the affluence and modernity of the Zapotec themselves" thus they followed both old and well-to-do modern traditions.

> Like the music, the food and drink provided at the party represented both the old Zapotec tradition and the well-to-do modern family—turtle eggs, *gueta bingui* (chopped shrimp coated in cornmeal), deep-friend hot peppers, and whole small crabs washed down with cold beer, on the one hand; and chicken and ham sandwiches, peanuts, and vegetable salad, accompanied by brandy and highballs, on the other. (p. 163)

In terms of clothing, "the bride wore a Western-style wedding gown for the church ceremony, as do Zapotec brides, and then changed into the Zapotec festive costume for the celebration that followed. The women guests were requested to wear Zapotec dress, and they all did, although such clothing is rarely worn to

Zapotec weddings. The women frequently wear modern pants suits or cocktail dresses" (pp. 162–163). The explicit display of one's ethnic identity has little significance when everyone else already knows who you are, but gains new importance in front of outsiders to the group. Taken together, these two examples make it clear that messages can be intended either for insiders or outsiders to a group.

We call it intertextuality when the wedding cake topper is a Precious Moments figure that the couple now displays in their home (Couple 44), for at least some of those present at the wedding can be assumed to recognize it.[13] And it is intertextuality when wedding photos are given as Christmas gifts to family members (Couple 46). Here a tie across celebrations made perfect sense to the participants—wedding photos are expensive, but people want them as reminders of the event, and so giving them as gifts was deemed appropriate. In this case, there was an earlier additional elaboration related to the photos: Some family members gave hand-decorated (empty) photo albums as their gifts to the bride and groom.[14] Even for the bride and groom, photographs have an important role, for, as one bride put it, "It was a really beautiful day and it went really fast so we just like to relive it in pictures" (Couple 102). This same couple reported looking at their photograph album on their anniversary (as do many other couples), but they have one other element of intertextuality as well that is more uncommon. As the groom explained: "We have a couple champagne glasses that say bride and groom that every year on our anniversary we pull out, and if we go somewhere special bring them along to serve as our glass for the evening." The glasses are indices, literal parts of their wedding they can incorporate into their anniversary celebration. Even if others do not recognize them (although they may, given the explicit labeling), they do, which is sufficient.

On other occasions, and for other people, photographs serve to bring the past into the wedding, rather than carry the wedding into the future. Couple 111 (a White bride with a Chippewa groom) was given a very special wedding gift by a cousin of the groom: a photograph of him with his father, grandfather, and great-grandfather. Although none of these prior generations were present at his wedding, their inclusion through the photograph was highly valued, especially as the groom did not previously have any photographs of himself as a child or his family.[15]

Intertextuality worked in two different directions when a White–African American wedding included the ritual of jumping the broom (Couple 60).[16] First, it looked backwards, in recognition of a time when slaves were not permitted church weddings, but developed their own tradition of jumping over a broom to mark a new union. And second, it reached forward, for this couple saved the broom, and the black and white ribbons tied on it by guests, to represent good luck, in a shadow box, now in the new couple's home.[17] Whether moving forward or backward in time, intertextuality provides additional layers of meaning for participants through the linking of multiple events. For those who understand the linkage (all those who were present and remember the relevant events) intertextuality can be quite powerful. And because it involves connotation (a second layer of meaning), rather than denotation (a first obvious meaning), those who were not present usually often have no idea they have just missed something important.

BRICOLAGE

Levi-Strauss (1966) popularized the concept of *bricolage*, generally understood as the bringing together of previously used signs into new (and unexpected) combinations.[18] As with intertextuality, other terms have been used by other researchers to mean essentially the same thing; for example, Crane (1992) discussed "cultural recycling" (p. 10), which may be a more vivid image for Americans unfamiliar with the connotations of the French word *bricolage*.[19] Whatever the term, the concept helps in understanding how people design complex rituals such as weddings. Constructing each one anew would be an impossible task. But taking bits and pieces from previous events, other weddings as well as other rituals, to make this new whole simplifies the task of construction considerably.

Each couple has the opportunity to pick and choose from among the range of possible elements, creating a new, individually designed wedding, to stand as one synthesis out of many possibilities. Each wedding thus stands as a contribution by a couple to the ongoing pattern of "wedding" existing in their culture at a particular point in time. As such, a wedding provides one of the few opportunities every member of a culture has to make an original creative contribution to the group. Few of us are artists, or writers, contributing concrete products (from paintings to poems) to our culture, but most of us participate in the design of at least one wedding. It is a place to demonstrate our knowledge of our culture, and our skill at *bricolage*. It is our answer to all the weddings we have attended and all the wedding scenes we have viewed in films or on television, the descriptions in fiction or newspaper articles; it is our contribution to a dialogue continuing over generations and across continents.

It is *bricolage* when a Chinese–American couple combine multiple symbols of their differing identities in new and unusual ways throughout the rituals related to the wedding (Couple 23). In this case, the American groom's father welcomed the Chinese bride's father at the rehearsal dinner with a toast and a Wisconsin cheese hat, described as a "symbol of our state's culture" as a way to welcome him into the family. After the rehearsal dinner, it was the bride's family's turn: In a formal tea ceremony, the bride wore traditional Chinese wedding attire passed down from her great-grandmother and was given family jewels from her relatives. A letter from the groom's mother, who had died, was read, welcoming the bride and expressing the wish that her pearls be given to the bride. The groom gave her his own gift, a gold and diamond necklace. The wedding was an outdoor ceremony, performed by the interdenominational minister of the groom's church. Just before the exchange of vows, the bride's grand-mother wished the couple luck in four Chinese proverbs, with the groom's fa-ther providing the English translations. Clearly, this couple was successful in their efforts to make "both of them feel welcomed into each other's family" through making a new whole by incorporating elements of what was important to each family.[20] Just as Wisconsin weddings do not normally include cheesehead hats, more often found at sporting events, Chinese weddings do not normally integrate the tea ceremony into the rehearsal dinner (in fact, they do not have one). To understand this unique event it works best to consider the way existing elements from other contexts were here joined together into a new and quite unique whole.

It is *bricolage* when a couple used to having clambakes in a variety of contexts, chooses to have a clambake for their wedding reception: "The private party *cum* clambake is becoming increasingly popular: Burney and Julie had a clambake as their wedding reception, and although some of the elders wonder whether this is quite proper, a trend has been set and others have followed" (Neustadt, 1988, p. 102).[21] And it is *bricolage* when an Irish, Italian, Catholic groom marries an "American" Lutheran bride, bringing in elements of several religions and ethnic groups (Couple 63). The wedding ceremony was performed in her Lutheran church, but his Catholic priest participated, giving his blessing. She had a main-stream engagement ring and wedding band, but his was an Irish *claddagh* ring. The rehearsal dinner was all homemade Italian foods (the groom's mother, who was the Italian part of the family, used to be a professional caterer although in other examples traditionally ethnic foods are most often made by an elderly rel-ative, standing in the role of tradition bearer). And the reception, which served mainstream foods chosen by the bride, incorporated Irish songs.[22]

Sometimes *bricolage* involves using elements in a wedding having special meaning for one or both members of the new couple, but little if any obvious meaning for others present. Couple 83 stood on a rug the groom purchased on a trip to Jerusalem 6 months before they were married. He bought it new, and so they were the first to stand on it. They have not used it since but display it on a wall, and are now keeping it for the weddings of the children they hope to have, if those future children so choose. Their officiant also tied their hands together with a ribbon, following an Eastern Orthodox tradition; because they were both raised Baptist, it is unlikely any of their friends or family recognized the tradi-tion, which was not explained (they incorporated it to represent a period of the groom's life when he was Eastern Orthodox, and so it had meaning to them, al-though probably not to others. Their officiant was a Unitarian Universalist min-ister, so the tradition was also not one he usually followed.)

In some cases *bricolage* involves borrowing symbols from a wide variety of traditions, and combining them in a new way. Heron Freed Toor, who performs many intercultural weddings by virtue of authorization from the Universal Life

Church, told me: "I've been trying to make old symbols more meaningful."[23] Later in our conversation, she said : "I do help couples construct something that is going to be meaningful to them and those around them. My job is helping them see other possibilities." In concrete terms, this involves adapting key symbols from a variety of traditions, maintaining part of the meaning but none of the religious or ethnic identifications, and adapting them to a new ceremony. For example, she makes use of a *huppah* even in ceremonies when no one is Jewish on the grounds that Abraham was the forefather not only of Judaism, but also Christianity and Islam. In such cases, she usually calls it a *canopy* rather than a *huppah* (the majority of the guests unlikely to know that term), and describes its use as being based on the tradition that Abraham had doors on all four sides of his tent. Or she integrates the breaking of the glass into non-Jewish ceremonies for the paradox it represents of strength and fragility, explaining the glass symbolizes "love which is as fragile as it is strong." Guests can have extreme reactions to the services she designs and conducts. Sometimes she will be told "you never mentioned God once" (although she explains that the couple makes that choice, she merely honors their wishes). Other times she'll hear the more positive evaluation: "I wish I'd have heard those words when I got married." As the bride of Couple 75 makes clear (in Interlude 3), this sort of mix and match method of designing a ritual does not equally please everyone. To many people, a ritual loses power when it is broken into parts and only some are maintained while others are eliminated. The critical factor seems to be the extent to which one grew up in a strong, vibrant tradition, in which the various symbols work in concert (and so pulling one or more symbols out of that whole fabric seems destructive). Whereas to someone who has few symbols of great consequence, even borrowing some from other people's traditions can add significance. This issue of who is willing to view individual symbols as separable from the whole cloth of a complex ritual is an important one, worthy of far greater investigation than it has been granted here, where my only intent is to identify the issue as having importance. Clearly, for some couples, *bricolage* works well, while for others it seems tacky and inappropriate. My intent is not to pass judgment but rather to document what couples have chosen to do in the design of their wedding ceremonies. Whether *bricolage* works for them is the critical factor, not whether it seems appropriate to me or any other outsiders.

REDUNDANCY

Few researchers utilize this term, but I find it particularly helpful in the attempt to understand a complex ritual event incorporating multiple social codes related to each other in specific ways. It is one way to understand the secular specialists' insistence on understanding weddings as having various levels of formality (usually described as high formal, formal, semi-formal, and informal), as reflected in the vast majority of popular publications on mainstream weddings.

For example, conventional wedding planners suggest that the bridal gown should be chosen first, and then the other parts of the wedding should be designed to match, in terms of level of formality (Ottesen, 1994).[24] If the bride chooses a long white dress of antique silk, with pearl buttons down the back, with a long veil, that has implications for other clothing choices (the groom then usually wears a tuxedo). At the same time, these clothing choices have implications for the food choices (a formal reception with substantial amounts of food for everyone) and object choices (use of candles, extensive use of flowers, etc.).[25] On the other hand, a choice of running clothes (white spandex shorts and a white lace tank top) for the bride leads to a choice not of a tuxedo for the groom but black shorts and black tank top, with a black bow tie. To match her running clothes, this bride chose a bouquet of a few white flowers, rather than the full bridal bouquet, which would have seemed inappropriate (*Milwaukee Journal*, 1992, p. A2).[26]

In the 1991 version of the film *Father of the Bride*, the bride's father at first fights to keep costs down and will not agree to the more expensive choice of seafood for the reception meal that the wedding coordinator has recommended. But when the bride's parents open some of the gifts that have arrived early, and see how expensive the gifts are, he changes his mind. "We have great friends, you know that? I mean these aren't run of the mill salad bowls, these are primo gifts. As a matter of fact I am so happy we have decided to serve the very chic but expensive seafood that our very posh friends will want." Thus, the quality of the gifts given to the new couple will match the quality of the dinner given to the guests, and this is put forth as a good thing. Such matching occurs in real life, not only in films. Montgomery (1989) documented one of the Vanderbilt weddings held in 1895; after pointing out that "the wedding ceremony was one of showy splendor" she went on to note that "millions of dollars in gifts were lavished upon the couple" (p. 168).

Monaco (1981) termed some of the codes utilized by filmmakers "culturally derived codes," that is, they exist outside of and prior to film (he named the way people eat as a specific example). It is his suggestion that filmmakers simply reproduce these culturally derived codes, relying on the prior experience of the audience to supply the meaning. What is intriguing about this is that communication researchers are not using the knowledge filmmakers take for granted as the resource it so obviously might be. What do filmmakers have participants eat at weddings, for example, which will be "not noteworthy," that is, which will not be distracting to the viewer? What do extras in a wedding scene wear so as not to attract attention? The answers to these sorts of questions (whether they are right or wrong) can tell us a great deal about stated assumptions of what constitutes ordinary behavior.

A sense of fairness often seems to guide the trade-offs made between the different constituencies in the wedding. Thus when a decision has to be made between conflicting cultural expectations, trading a decision in one category for the opposite decision in another often can serve as the compromise. For example, a Chinese bride and Jewish groom chose for their rehearsal dinner a multicourse Chinese banquet held in Chinatown; for their post-wedding brunch they served a traditional Jewish breakfast of bagels, cream cheese, and lox; and then split the wedding buffet between their traditional foods, including *blintzes* and potato pancakes (both traditional foods of Eastern European Jews), as well as a series of Chinese foods: *lo mein* noodles (representing long life) and chicken (representing wealth) and fortune cookies.[27]

Occasionally couples try to have it all. At what is described as a Texas–Italian wedding:

> waiters passed silver trays of San Pellegrino water, Lone Star beer and Champagne. There were buffet tables holding Italian food, and ones offering Tex-Mex. On one floor, a rock band played; on another, there was square dancing. "I'm from Texas," Mrs. Menischeschi says. "And my husband is of Italian heritage. We wanted to have something for both of us." (Wells, 1990, p. 59)

A Spanish bride and Chinese American groom also tried to have it all, whether in terms of clothing (she wore her Spanish grandmother's lace mantilla as a shawl at the reception; he wore a Chinese-inspired jacquard floral tie); readings (his sister and brother-in-law read a piece by Octavio Paz, while her sister read a Chinese poem from the 12th century); objects (they included the Spanish tradition of *arras*, exchanging 13 gold-plated dimes her parents used at their wedding symbolizing the sharing of all of life's riches during the ceremony; just after, they held a private Chinese tea ceremony, with the couple offering tea to both sets of parents); or food (including *chorizo*, grilled portobella on *polenta* cakes, as well as fried wantons and seared tuna on *daikon* wafers, and the traditional Chinese roast pig).[28] These examples are the result of trying to please everyone simultaneously, of not making choices, but including all the possibilities side by side. They exemplify the mosaic metaphor: different traditions incorporated into a single event, but not influencing one another When feasible, this may be a good solution to intercultural weddings, but much of the time choices must be made.

The careful matching of choices across codes indicates high formality. A simple example matches a bride who wears white and carries orange flowers to a wedding cake with white frosting and orange flowers (Couple 31).[29] A more elaborate example was provided by Couple 97, where the extensive continuation of the color green through multiple elements of the event conveyed formality through unusual redundancy. There were green satin dresses for bridesmaids and flower girl, with matching hats, and they carried green silk flowers; the bride carried white flowers with a few green ones; the groom and groomsmen wore green carnation boutonnieres; the bride's mother wore a green corsage; and there were matching green tissue paper bells hung from the rearview mirror of each car in wedding party as they journeyed from the church to the reception. Because such matching requires extra time as well as money, it serves as one marker of formality.

Formality can also be marked by extreme elaboration of a single sign, far beyond what would normally be expected. In a New York wedding joining two wealthy families, the *huppah* "was made of heavy velvet and trimmed on top with swags, tassels, and a two-foot crown of flowers. It was as ornate as a jewel box and as big as a studio apartment" (Brady, 1980, March, p. 46). This is a far cry from the ritual requirement of a simple *tallis*, or prayer shawl, so it conveys more than the expected ritual purpose.

It is redundancy when a Filipino American bride wears a red dress chosen by her mother as a link to the Philippines (where, as in other parts of Asia, red connotes good luck), and her maid of honor wears the same color, with icing on the cake to match (Couple 17). In this case, the African American groom found it a bit odd, but understood it was important to her, and so he did not object. It is also redundancy when the color purple runs throughout an Episcopalian–Catholic wedding (Couple 58): The bridesmaids' dresses and nail polish matched the flowers on the cake, all the same shade of purple.[30] And again when a canoe becomes the predominant theme in a wedding for outdoor enthusiasts (Couple 112). The groom's parents gave a canoe as their primary wedding gift, and a cousin's daughter crafted handmade oars as her gift. After the wedding ceremony, held outdoors near the river, the couple got into the canoe for a private time together prior to the reception. The common photograph of the bride and groom kissing at the end of the standard ceremony was converted into one of them perilously standing up in the canoe to meet in the middle for a kiss. That they did not capsize, ruining their wedding clothes, was a great relief to their families and guests watching from shore. Although they had a standard white multilayer cake at the reception, a special one was at the brunch held for family the next day, decorated with a small canoe on top. And a second gift from the groom's parents was a shadow box filled with miniature versions of everything important in their lives (for the bride, ice skates and camping gear; for the groom, a small replica of their new canoe). It is the redundancy of this symbol that grants it meaning; having one canoe would be unusual, but it is the combination of these four separate versions (the literal canoe, the photograph of the kiss in the canoe, the canoe on the cake and then in the shadow box) that grants additional significance through repetition.[31]

It is redundancy that permits guests to determine what to wear to a wedding when they receive the invitation, provided they share enough norms with the bride and groom to recognize the subtle signs incorporated into the invitation. High formality is indicated by the use of multiple envelopes, handwritten addresses, ivory paper, old English fonts, and the use of archaic language. Informality is indicated by the use of more color, more casual wording, and printed addresses. The way in which decisions made at the printers end up influencing decisions about clothing is termed here redundancy; the wedding planners desire to ensure that the various elements of a wedding mesh gracefully, and shared traditions and expectations make this possible.

And it is redundancy when repeated Italian traditions are used in multiple parts of a wedding between a bride born in England of Italian parents and a groom who could only identify as "American" (Couple 18). In this case she said "He knew how much it meant to me to have Italian traditions, and he had absolutely no objection toward this." As both were Catholic, the wedding ceremony itself was a formal, Catholic variant of the mainstream wedding. But it was in the events surrounding the wedding that her desire to follow Italian traditions became more evident. Three showers (one organized by her family members, one by his family, and one by their friends) each had different participants and different levels of formality. The weekend before the wedding her family did a "throwing money on the bed," an Italian tradition with which his family was not familiar, and so they did not participate. At the reception there were both Italian and American foods. The Italian band played a special Italian song to which the bride and her mother danced together, highlighting the fact that her father had died a few months prior to the wedding. What is "redundant" is the fact that the Italian background of the bride was repeatedly emphasized, in multiple codes, especially food, music, and dance, as well as in peripheral rituals surrounding the wedding. Redundancy thus works by reinforcing a single message repeated through multiple symbols.

AMBIGUITY

Ambiguity results from symbols having multiple meanings (polysemy), appearing in new combinations (*bricolage*), being understood primarily through references to past events (intertextuality), or in connection with another symbol in another code (redundancy).[32] As a result of ambiguity, some participants will understand what occurs in the same way as the bride and groom, whereas others will be left in the dark.[33] Ambiguity can lead in two directions: It can be positive because it may be better to be left in the dark by what you don't understand than to be made angry or unhappy by what you do; or, it can be negative because people may bring connotations to their interpretations that make sense to them, but that never crossed the minds of those designing the ritual.

One example of a negative result of ambiguity took place when a Christian bride and Jewish groom were planning their wedding (Couple 14). One issue to be resolved was where to hold the service; one potential solution was a Unitarian church (for reasons already discussed in previous chapters Unitarian churches and ministers are often the most neutral choices). The bride reported:

> When [groom's mother] walked in, she grabbed her heart, started hyperventilating. I thought she was going to fall over. [Groom's father] had to catch her. She said: "Absolutely not." ... As soon as we sat down in the place, and she looked around, she said: "There are crosses everywhere. There's crosses in the stained glass." Later, when she had recovered, the groom said: "mom, come on, be fair about this." And his father said: "this is a beautiful place." He said: "are you two okay with this?" And we said "yes." And he said "then we'll be fine with it." And she sat in complete silence. And finally I said: "I can tell that you're very, very upset here." And she said "how could I not be? you took me into someplace that is a Catholic church with crosses everywhere."

In this case, because the groom's mother was unfamiliar with Unitarian beliefs, she did not know that they do not put crosses in the building and would never have included a design in the stained glass that resembled a cross, to them. But to her, as a Jew who was already having some difficulty with her son marrying a Christian, the fit between the design and a cross was too close for comfort. Finally the bride told the groom "I know now we can't have it there. Your father said it was okay, and your mother said definitely not. I cannot do that." A related problem arose over the name of the building. The groom's mother was willing for the invitations to say "Unitarian Society" or "Temple" but not "Church." However, the actual name of the building was "Unitarian Church" and the couple had concerns that misrepresenting it might confuse some of the guests. Eventually, the couple ended up moving the location to a hotel, an even more neutral spot, to resolve the issue.

A more positive result of ambiguity is provided in the film Betsy's Wedding. The issue at hand concerns which religious elements will be included in the wedding ceremony. The bride and groom want to include some things that will be from the bride's mother's culture (Jewish), the bride's father's culture (Catholic), and the groom's culture (Scottish, they think, although no one is sure, which fact causes its own problems). The immediate decision concerns the traditional Jewish custom of the groom stepping on a glass.

Officiant: "Well, what about stepping on the glass. You gonna do that?"
Jake: "What does that represent exactly?"
Officiant: "Over the years, different things. Mainly, I think it is supposed to signify the destruction of the Temple."
Betsy: "Um, that sounds pretty religious."
Officiant: "How about this: Some people say it represents the breaking of the hymen."
Betsy: "I don't think so."
Officiant: "All right, I think, think I've got one you'll like. Stepping on the glass is breaking with the past and moving on to the future. You no longer belong to your parents' house, you have your own."

Jake: "That's good."
Betsy: "Yeah, I like that."
Officiant: "Good. We'll say it's breaking with the past, and your grandpa Morris will know it's the destruction of the Temple."
Betsy: [shaking her head] "Great."

Matters are left at that. Later, during the service:

Officiant: "And now you can step on the glass, which signifies the destruction of the T—"
[the bride, Betsy, makes a face and he changes it]
Officiant: "of times gone by"
[the bride smiles]
Officiant: "of turning to the future. You belong not to your parents now but to each other. Not to their families now but to your own. The future, with God's help, is yours."

This is a perfect example how ambiguity works to resolve conflicts between past and present expectations in an intercultural wedding. A single tradition is agreed on (breaking a glass), but it is an old tradition, having accumulated many meanings over the years. (Incidentally, these multiple meanings are not made up for this scene by this character; these and several others are all commonly recognized by modern American Jews). And so, with the understanding that there is at least one meaning the bride and groom can appreciate, they decide to incorporate the tradition into the wedding, with all parties explicitly acknowledging that at least some of the guests will assume it is intended to mean what they have previously thought it means. That is, after all, the beauty of symbols having multiple meanings; each person can see what meaning they wish to see, without destroying the meanings others see. This implies the possibility of sharing the form (the same words are spoken) without necessarily sharing the meaning (each participant will assume their own understanding of the words as the one that makes sense), although most probably assume they share interpretations. Because they make this assumption, it does not even occur to them to confirm its accuracy.

Ambiguity can occur in multiple ways, some more successful than others. In a Jewish–Christian wedding (Couple 69), the key symbol was the *huppah* (also sometimes transliterated as *chuppah*, as in the following extract, written by the bride in an e-mail to me). The bride is Jewish (Reform), and the groom is Christian (specifically, United Church of Canada). The ceremony was performed by a Justice of the Peace; however, a rabbi, who was an old friend of the family, agreed to perform just a priestly benediction as part of the ceremony (not usually part of a Jewish wedding ceremony, it was borrowed from other ritual events, as something the Jewish guests would recognize as marking the rabbi's blessing of the union). The bride explained:

Anyway, he offered to do the priestly benediction … and the night before the ceremony he met [groom] for the first time, and it was very nice, and the next day at the ceremony, at the end, he came up to do his blessing, and [groom] and I were under the *chuppah*, and he told us to get out from under it. I mean, he said, "move out from underneath," not loudly or anything, but the implication was, "he's not Jewish, I'm blessing you, and I won't bless a non-Jewish person under the *chuppah*." I don't think [groom] understood what was going on, but I was mortified. I couldn't believe it. Again, if he'd told us the night before that he didn't want us under the *chuppah*, I would have said either "Fine, don't bless us," or "Fine, we'll move," but this last-minute SURPRISE! business, well, it was just pretty awful. It really hurt, again, because I think, I wondered if he thought, well, I wondered what he was thinking (or maybe I'm projecting, maybe I wondered what I was thinking)—if he was thinking, "I disapprove, stupid [bride], marrying out of the faith." I guess that's it; there was such disapproval there (I'm just articulating it for the first time). It really hurt. I'll never forget it. I'll always feel as if he disapproves of me, as if I let him down by not doing what my father expected of me, that is, marrying a Jew. But I married someone I love deeply, someone I love and care for and respect and like and admire and want to be with and learn from, and it just so happens that he wasn't born Jewish, but he has all the qualities that I value in a human being. He has more of those qualities than any other man I ever met or was interested in, Jewish or non. And he supports my Judaism, which is more than a lot of Jewish men I know would do for their wives, my ex-brother-in-law among them.

Anyway, back to the *chuppah*, the four *chuppah* bearers went one way and [groom] and I went back the other (i.e., the four moved away from [rabbi] and [groom] and I toward him), and he blessed us, and some people I don't think even noticed what was happening, but [friend] and her sister, my cousin, were absolutely furious, and there was some talk among them of writing him a letter, but I don't know if they ever did it, and I hope they didn't. I mean, he was my dad's closest friend. My dad loved him, and he loved my dad, and I have really fond memories of good childhood times spent with [name], and I can't begrudge him his beliefs. Those are his beliefs. That they happened to impinge on my wedding—well, I think it was a lack of communication on everyone's part. I never told him how I felt. I didn't know how to say it. I'm not into those kinds of confrontations. What would I have said?

Initially, the rabbi agreed to perform the priestly blessing for the new couple, presumably thus approving of the marriage, and welcoming the new couple on behalf of the wider community. It therefore did not occur to the bride that he might not permit the blessing to be given under a *huppah*, symbol of community. Thus the major players found themselves in front of an audience before they discovered their initial misunderstanding about whether use of the *huppah* would even be appropriate for this particular couple. Because the rabbi was not performing the entire marriage service but only performing a single small part of it, the *huppah* was already in use when he entered the stage. Presumably he had several choices at that point:

1. He could accept the situation entirely, give his blessing under the *huppah* and not make a fuss; this would go against his beliefs about the symbolism of the *huppah* as an indicator of the Jewish community—the groom was not Jewish, and therefore logically could not be included as a member of that community.
2. He could reject the situation entirely, by refusing to come forward and give the benediction at all; this would cause a big fuss and a lot of comment and seem ungracious.
3. He could modify the situation he found by removing the logical contradiction (non-Jewish groom standing under the symbol of Judaism); this would cause a minimum of fuss and reaction.

Obviously the rabbi chose the third alternative and did, in fact, receive a minimum of explicit reaction from others present. The ceremony proceeded after only a brief moment of confusion.

The bride saw a discrepancy between words and actions. She understood that the rabbi was refusing to accept her new husband into the larger community, at the same moment that he formally uttered the words of blessing over the marriage. Because the symbol of the *huppah* was not salient to the groom, it conveyed no information to him, and likewise none to his extended family present at the wedding. Because the bride and her family recognized the symbol and its connotations, it was understood as a terrible rejection and caused considerable controversy. Using a ritual element intended to bless the union of two individuals, the rabbi instead drew a clear line between two communities, making a statement to the bride about the appropriateness of her choice of husband; because he was not Jewish, he lacked enough knowledge of the traditions to even realize he had been publicly rejected as a suitable spouse.

Many participants at weddings have only been to weddings of people like themselves and so take for granted the presentation of an identity statement they will recognize as part of the ceremony. When they either design or attend a wedding where there are significantly different assumptions, necessarily the case in intercultural weddings, they may be startled to learn that others do not share the same expectations and traditions. In an important way, it doesn't count as a "proper" wedding if few of the details match what you've experienced previously. This is, of course, true for all rituals—their power comes from repetition. Thus the combining of individuals from different groups having different traditions could easily result in the weakening of the experience because it no longer "feels right."

One solution to this problem is to explicitly confront the issues, whereas the other is to avoid direct confrontation at all costs. It is possible to take the concerns of the guests at the wedding into account, as when a tradition that makes sense to one side is explicitly explained to the other. In a wedding between a White bride and an African American groom, in which the African American tradition of jumping over the broom was included in the ceremony, guests were given a written explanation of what that meant before it occurred, lest half those present be confused (Couple 60).[34] This is not at all an unusual solution, as some sort of either written or oral explanation of a marked behavior is quite common at intercultural weddings, often serving to bring the uninitiated into the circle of those who understand what is happening.

Yet the opposite solution of deliberately ignoring the differences and hoping no one will notice what they do not understand also works surprisingly often. In extreme examples of difference, as when an American Christian marries a Hindu from India, it is not uncommon for the American to simply follow instructions, with virtually no explanation and no understanding of the words uttered or the significance of the actions performed. Amazingly, to me at least, few of the participants in this sort of event seem bothered by what they can not understand. This takes the principle of one party being oblivious to the meaning of what they do to an extreme.

CONCLUSION

These five concepts (polysemy, intertextuality, *bricolage*, redundancy, and ambiguity) can appear in many contexts; weddings are simply one easy place to observe how they work. Together they illustrate the complexity of social interaction, and the special complexity of intercultural interaction. It is difficult enough to ever convey meaning from one individual to another; how much more difficult the task becomes when there are major cultural differences to be accommodated. These tools are among the ways people have found to manage multiple meanings.

NOTES

1. Also see discussion of this same idea in Hannerz (1996). Emphasis on the concept of meaning is hardly unique to this book, for, as Zarefsky (1995) pointed out: "The core concept or fundamental subject matter of the [Communication] discipline is meaning" and "The most basic question of the discipline is: How do people generate and evoke meaning through interactions in which they relate to, influence, and are influenced by, others?" (p. 111).
2. See Baxter (1987) for discussion of symbols of relationship identity.
3. See Leeds-Hurwitz (1993) for further elaboration of these concepts.
4. This is the assumption underlying Shannon and Weaver's (1949) model of communication.

5. See, for example, Baxter and Montgomery (1996) and Rawlins (1992).

6. "Semiotics undoes the white myth of the *isolate*, which has spilled over from our ethnopolitics into the discipline of cultural sciences as the (false) idea that we can study and understand groups, texts, and/or genres in and of themselves without reference to their *relations* to other groups, texts, and genres" (MacCannell & MacCannell 1982, p. 8).

7. See also her comment that "a complex society, like the United States in the late twentieth century, will resound with a number of voices, with diversity and variety, with dialogues and polylogues" (Stimpson, 1988, p. xv).

8. Interviewed by Sue Glanz for Comm 499: Independent Study, in Spring 1992.

9. As reported by Laura Pope in Comm 440: Communication Codes, Spring 1996.

10. One of the implications of the concept of intertextuality is that, as Scheub (1998) wrote in his discussion of stories:

> There is therefore no canonical interpretation of story, just as there is no ur-version of a tale. This is not a weakness but a strength. Story is routinely re-cast in contemporary frames, but the traditions of that story can never be shaken, are never lost. Most critical, and most difficult of assessment, is pa-limpsest—never wholly lost, always partly visible—the experiences of the storyteller, of the members of the audience, experiences primarily emo-tional. (p. 276)

11. In terms of understanding a single choice, such as that of wedding gown, "Reso-nances set up with dresses seen in the past, whether at weddings attended, or tele-vision weddings, or even royal weddings, clearly also have a part to play" (Charsley, 1991, p. 70).

12. For example: "social deixis" (Levinson, 1983); "sequential contexts" (Schegloff, 1988); "contextualization" (Gumperz, 1992); "cumulative" phenomena (Hannerz, 1992); or "sedimented layers" (Hardt & Brennen, 1993).

13. As reported by Susan Oboikowich in Comm 440: Communication Codes, Spring 1999.

14. As reported by Kim Reiher in Comm 440: Communication Codes, in Spring 1999.

15. Interviewed by Kim Wright for Comm 440: Communication Codes, in Spring 2001.

16. See Cole (1993), Dundes (1996), and Sturgis (1997) for discussion of this tradition, as well as the mention in Interlude 1 of why that couple did not include the tradition in their ceremony.

17. As reported by Courtney Pace in Comm 440: Communication Codes, in Spring 1999.

18. See also Hebdige (1979, pp. 102–106).

19. As Rushdie (1991) pointed out, "a bit of this and a bit of that is *how newness enters the world*" (p. 394, his emphasis). Becker (1984) presented a Javanese term for essen-tially the same concept, *jarwa dhosok*, defined as "pushing old language into the present" (p. 135).

20. As reported by Liz Haas in Comm 440: Communication Codes, in Spring 1996.

21. Stern and Cicala (1991) suggested: "Symbols of ethnicity are not merely static products of ethnic culture but are solutions to problematic situations that charac-terize, project, and parody everyday life" (p. xiii).

22. As reported by Jeff Webster in Comm 440: Communication Codes, in Spring 1999.

23. Interviewed April 26, 2000.

24. For a helpful discussion of how one choice (in any context, not just weddings) af-fects future possibilities, see Ervin-Tripp (1972).

25. These summary comments are based on interviews with secular specialists and on reading numerous popular texts intended mainly for the brides, since they do most of the planning, such as *Bride* magazine.
26. When asked to predict the food served at the reception for this couple (not described in the newspaper), my students have proposed that it likely consisted of salads (given that the bride and groom are runners, and presumably health-conscious) with no alcohol (again, based on the apparent concern for health).
27. This is the wedding of Melissa Lam and Steve Bourne, taken from www.theknot.com, under "Real weddings."
28. This wedding, between Raquel Antonia Vidal and Paul Tze-Pui Chan, is also from "Real weddings" on www.theknot.com.
29. As reported by Konnie Osborn in Comm 440: Communication Codes, in Spring 1996.
30. As reported by Deanna Lean in Comm 440: Communication Codes, in Spring 1999.
31. This couple is actually Canadian rather than American, but served as such a perfect example of redundancy that I could not resist including them.
32. The study of ambiguity can lead to the study of "boundary object," a concept used in the sociology of science (Star & Griesemer, 1989). Henderson (1991) defined it thus: "A boundary object allows members of different groups to read different meanings particular to their needs from the same material" (p. 450). In the original conception, the goal was to study how representatives of different social worlds (administrators, amateur natural collectors, and scientists in Star and Griesemer's research) can share common representation. They discovered some objects were "both plastic enough to adapt to local needs and the constraints of the several parties employing them, yet robust enough to maintain a common identity across sites" (Star & Griesemer, 1989, p. 393). When the material symbol remains unchanged, it seems likely that this is an appropriate metaphor; however, in those cases where a symbol is revised to accommodate multiple cultural traditions, it goes beyond the original conception of a boundary object.
33. Sillars (1989) emphasized the importance of ambiguity in understanding personal relationships; Blau (1991) and Levine (1995) emphasized the role of ambiguity in larger social phenomena; Eisenberg (1984) analyzed ambiguity as a potential communication strategy within organizations. Kertzer (1988) and Lewis (1980) studied ambiguity as an attribute of symbols; Scheffler (1996) viewed ambiguity from the viewpoint of philosophy.
34. As reported by Courtney Pace in Comm 440: Communication Codes, in Spring 1999.

Interlude 6

FIG. 7: *Huppah* used by Couple 13.
Photo by George Waters (see color plate).

*T*he bride of Couple 13 described herself as Presbyterian, and "American mutt." Quizzed about what this includes, she came up with German and Danish components, but she was sure there were other ethnicities included as well, they just had not been highlighted in her upbringing. The groom is of Eastern European descent and Jewish (raised Conservative but now Reform). The bride wanted to have an outdoor wedding; everything else was negotiable. The groom's sister, a cantor (a clergy person trained in singing the Jewish service), provided resource material to the bride to let her know what a traditional Jewish wedding included (also suggesting songs to incorporate). One of the documents included description of a *huppah*, the wedding canopy. When the bride's mother, a weaver and fiber artist, read about it, she thought "I can help with that part." Although it surprised me that she would be comfortable creating one of the major symbols of the "other" religion, it made perfect sense to her and to the couple; she was a fabric artist, and this was an essential object she had the skills to create.

She decided to use appliqué, on white silk organza, thinking that it only needed to last for one day (a decision she now regrets because the bride and groom have kept the *huppah*, finally now beginning to show signs of wear). She designed a pattern of intertwined ivy leaves, in different shades of green, choosing fabrics from three generations of her family (a dress from her mother, a dress she wore when pregnant, and a dress worn by her daughter, the bride). She asked for materials from the groom's family but they had no comparable items representing multiple generations (a result of the Jewish diaspora: Those who leave their homes on short notice do little packing). So, instead, she took an old pair of blue jeans from the groom, and cut out four hearts, using them to reinforce the corners, where the holes for the support poles would be cut. For the central design, she chose the sun, the moon, a rainbow, and stars. As the officiant told the guests:

> [Bride] and [groom] have chosen to be married under the wedding canopy which [bride's mother] made. In Jewish tradition it represents the tent of Abraham, who is said to have had doors on all four sides of his tent, so that guests would always know they were welcomed. The pole bearers [names] represent the community of

people we all are, who are helping [groom] and [bride] as they establish their home.

In the making of the canopy [bride's mother] wanted to create a visual echo from the words of a traditional Jewish wedding blessing: The voice of love and the voice of gladness. The canopy celebrates the love and promise which unite [groom] and [bride] in marriage—may it be blessed under the heavens of the sun, moon, and stars; be open to change which the wind brings; be sustained by hope, which the rainbow promises; and be lively and loving, as vigorous, verdant, and intertwining as the growing green ivy![1]

(Notice how this officiant has smoothed over the issue faced by Couple 69 described earlier: He changed the boundaries of the community represented by the *huppah* from only the Jews present to all those present as witnesses to the ceremony.)

In addition to the elements aforementioned, each corner has a reprint (essentially a Xerox onto fabric) of one of Chagall's wedding couples because it was appropriate to the occasion, because he is a well-known Jewish artist, and because the bride loves his work. Finally, there is a border of blue ribbon around the edge of the whole, chosen to represent Israel (blue and white being the colors of the Israeli flag). The ribbon was purchased for the occasion, but all of the fabrics used in the appliqué were taken from the store of scrap fabrics of the bride's family, and so each one had a connection to a particular item of clothing once worn by a family member.

An object having traditional meaning for the groom's family, yet designed and created by the bride's family, this *huppah* came to symbolize the joining of two individuals with separate pasts into a common future, as well as the joining of two families, and their acceptance of the intermarriage of their children. For the groom's family, the *huppah* stood for what *huppot* always stand for: the acceptance of a new couple into the larger community. For the bride and her family, it was an opportunity to begin to immerse themselves in the union that was about to happen.

Because the bride was very close to her family's minister and because the groom's sister was uncomfortable performing the wedding ceremony herself (although a cantor can serve), he was asked to officiate. The bride's mother described herself not as traditionally religious but as spiritual, and feels that her minister appreciates that distinction; she considers him a close friend and was pleased to have him perform the ceremony. In addition to sewing the *huppah*, she designed a stole for the minister to wear when performing the ceremony, using the same fabrics and the same motif of intertwining ivy leaves. About 4 inches wide, and quite long, it is very distinctive. The minister commented on the connection between his stole and the *huppah* during the ceremony, noting that "[The bride's mother], who lovingly prepared this canopy, also shared her gifts of artistic creativity as she made this stole I wear today." In this way, the bride's mother created a new symbol linking one religion's representative (the minister) to the other religion's central visual symbol (the *huppah*).

The *huppah* was saved after the ceremony, and put over the new couple's bed, on the ceiling. Although they have moved, and although it is 11 years later in the life of an object created only to last one day, the *huppah* is still in good shape hanging over their bed today. It serves as an index to the wedding ceremony, a visible reminder of the event (it is quite large, about the size of the bed over which it hangs, and so is the major feature in the room).

The bride's dress also displays a connection to family history. Asked about other important symbols from the wedding ceremony, the bride said: "My dress was probably most important, given that my grandmother had made it, my mother had worn it." Originally designed to fit her mother, the dress had to be altered slightly to fit her, but she was delighted to continue family tradition by wearing her mother's dress, a variant of the traditional white, formal gown. After the wedding, it was returned to her mother, who is keeping it for future generations "if it should be wanted."

Flowers were another central element in this wedding, with specific ties to the bride's family. The groom had many traditions from earlier family weddings that were included (described later), but the bride had a smaller family and fewer religious traditions, although she had a lot of family traditions (as illustrated by the wedding gown and keeping old clothing to incorporate into new objects). Another of the bride's mother's skills was growing beautiful flowers, and so she provided many of the flowers at the wedding. Flowers tied together the various people and elements involved, including:

- The bride's bouquet and flowers in her hair,
- The bridesmaids' bouquets,
- All the men's boutonnieres,

- The mothers', aunt's, and grandmother's corsages,
- Centerpieces on the tables at the reception,
- Extensive decoration of the reception area and outdoor setting where the ceremony took place,
- The baskets of flower petals two children distributed before the bride entered,
- The flower petals thrown by guests on the bride and groom after the ceremony was completed, and
- The flowers on the cake.

In addition, flowers were used in the prewedding events (centerpieces at Friday night's dinner and Saturday's lunch), and again when the couple's first baby was born 3 years later. The groom's mother reported: "The baby was born in September and I went to [state], and [bride's mother] came for the day. She brought me a little boutonniere-type thing to wear, in water, and it was the flowers from the wedding that she was still growing." In fact, the bride's mother thinks it unlikely that she used the same type of flowers, as they would have been out of season at that time of year, but it is important that this link between events is how the groom's mother remembers, and tells, the story.

One tradition the groom's family took for granted, which the bride was not accustomed to, but really liked, involved the walk down the aisle. It is typical in Christian ceremonies for only the bride's father to walk her down the aisle, meeting the groom who walks in alone, whereas in Jewish ceremonies it is more common for the bride to be accompanied by both of her parents, and then the groom to be accompanied by his. Mainstream weddings follow the Christian custom in this case as in most others. But the bride liked the variation, and so they followed that instead.

Among other Jewish traditions incorporated into the ceremony was the breaking of the glass, which the minister introduced by not only indicating what would happen but what it meant: "At the conclusion of the traditional Jewish marriage ceremony it is customary for the groom to break a glass. For [groom] and for [bride] this is a reminder: Even during this time of great personal joy and celebration there are many sorrows." In this ceremony, each time a traditional Jewish element was introduced, it was framed quite explicitly for the Christian members of the audience (who formed the majority, because the wedding was held in the bride's home state, about 60 of the groom's family and close friends attended, of the 200 guests present). Interestingly, explicitly Christian symbols were not so marked for the Jewish audience members. For example, in traditional Jewish weddings, the rings are placed on the forefingers, but in this wedding, they were placed on the ring fingers, following the Christian (and mainstream American) tradition. No explanation was made for the Jewish guests. This is how mainstream traditions function (and mainstream weddings definitely draw upon a generic Christian tradition); everyone is expected to recognize and understand them without further explanation. And it works, because everyone does.

The bride kept the pieces of broken glass (they did not use the light bulb so often substituted, but an actual glass), together with the groom's boutonniere. When she told me this, it turned out that her husband had not even known she had kept these mementos. She not only had them, she knew exactly where they were. When she brought them out, it turned out she had also saved the cards on which they had written their vows. Like the majority of the liturgy, they had adapted materials provided by the minister, with his approval.

> [Name] I wish to be your [husband/wife]. I promise to be with you in all that is to come, to love and respect, to care for and to console, to share the sorrows and the joys, in all that lies ahead. I promise to be faithful to you and honest with you: I will share my thoughts and my life with you and pledge myself and all I am in love.

Also included in the ceremony were two dogs the groom had before he met the bride, and which he wanted to incorporate as ring bearers. The bride not only agreed, she sewed the pillows that were tied to their backs. Two friends of the groom led them down the aisle on leashes, removed the rings from their pillows, and held the dogs steady during the remainder of the outdoor ceremony. The minister explained: "The ring bearers, Sam and Frodo, being led down the aisle, share the duties of their namesake in Tolkien's *Lord of the Rings*. In these stories, Sam and Frodo had the responsibility of protecting the enchanted ring thereby securing their future safety and prosperity." On videotape, the guests seem less surprised by the appearance of two large dogs than might have been expected (although there was some laughter); apparently many had been warned of what was to come. The bride saved the pillow covers in the same box as the other objects from the wedding. (In addition to these mementos, there were the traditional photographs—one album by a professional photographer, another of photographs sent to them by relatives, and a videotape made by a friend, all of which they shared with me.)

The minister made several specific references to the differences in background between the bride and groom, and how important it was to note their similarities as well, including the following:

> Today we have [groom] and [bride] pulling us together into a kind of unity that is no longer theoretical, but is very personal and real. Their love for us, and their care for the world, has helped us to see what it is that holds us together. In this particular case, we already share so much in common, for we come from the same original Covenant which God made with Abraham. So, worshipping the same God, celebrating a common history, and sharing the same commitment to a quality of life which is filled with God's *Shalom* [peace], we come to share in this celebration.

An uncommon element in either a Jewish or Christian ceremony, but one appearing in a number of intercultural weddings, was that after the minister asked each of the couple whether they wished to be married, he then explicitly asked each set of parents whether they blessed this union, and each pair answered "we do." This served as a clear expansion of the bride and groom's own vows, as well as public acceptance of the intercultural union.

Many of the groom's family's traditions were brought into the reception as well as the wedding. One of the customs in a Jewish wedding is to say the *sheva brachot*, a series of formal blessings over the bride and groom (these are generally said as a central element of the wedding ceremony). In this case, the groom's two sisters and five first cousins walked to the front of the room during the reception, where one cousin introduced the blessings by stating: "There are seven blessings that are traditionally said at Jewish weddings."[2] She then listed the other weddings in this generation previously held, all of which had included the use of these blessings, with the groom's role specifically mentioned (e.g., the cousin speaking reminds him he honored her by saying a blessing at her wedding). Then comes mention of the previous generation, and then the one before that, stressing the fact that the same blessings were said each time. "So, [groom] and [bride], we re-wrote these blessings so they would be specifically for you. On behalf of [groom's] entire family, and those joined to us by marriage, all who are here with you now, and those who cannot be."[3] Then the blessings were read in English, with each of the sisters and cousins saying one blessing. It is important to note that the language choice was made specifically to include the bride and her family and friends who would not have understood the blessings in Hebrew (the language used at prior weddings, something everyone on the groom's side knew, but this was not made explicit for the bride's family and friends). The bride and her family would not have known if the blessings had been omitted from this wedding, but the groom's cousins would have known, and the potential omission made them unhappy. The groom's mother explained: "I think they wanted it to be as Jewish as possible, and not to miss any of the things they had done." So they found a way to mesh past expectations with current realities. (The several flower children at this wedding were children of the sisters giving the blessings, thus the next generation of cousins. This wedding will be part of their own taken for granted traditions when they plan their future weddings, so the importance of adapting tradition to immediate circumstance is likely to be clear to them.) They also found a way to involve all the guests. One cousin introduced the set with this request: "There's a way for everyone in this room to participate in these seven blessings. At the end of each blessing, if you add your amen to our chorus of amens up here, you will increase [groom and bride's] joy and receiving of these blessings that many fold by everyone saying 'amen' with us." And the crowd did say "amen" at the end of each blessing (a word often used in Christian rituals, but rarely in Jewish ones, which normally use various Hebrew phrases instead). At the end of the blessings, another cousin states "And this is what we do after we've recited those seven blessings" and begins to sing. As she does, everyone else leaves the stage and starts the crowd in a *hora* (traditional Israeli folk dance frequently included in wedding celebrations).

Several other activities at the reception were variations of what had occurred at prior weddings in the groom's extended family. Among other components:

- The groom's father and family friend did an Eastern European dance that no one else had ever managed to learn, representing their heritage;

- The bride and groom were raised on chairs, an old Jewish custom (the bride reported: "I got dumped out of the chair, does that count? ... The guys in the back lifted up higher than the guys in the front. And the best man caught me.... I wasn't hurt or anything, but I was a little shocked");

- The groom's cousins wrote a parody for him, about his life from childhood up to the present, a family tradition with no ties to religion; this was introduced with the line "We're [groom's] cousins, we have a little song we'd like to share with you";

- The groom's sisters sang another parody about his life; and

- The groom's parents were honored with a *krenzel* dance, traditional when the last child of a Jewish family is married off. This last was new to most of the bride's friends and family, but they enjoyed it, as the bride reported: "One of the things I heard a lot from the [state] folks who had no Jewish connection was that they just loved that part." The groom's parents were familiar with the tradition, but had not been warned that it was to be included, and so even they were surprised.

Clearly the groom's family took over the reception with their numerous traditions. The bride said: "My family didn't have any traditions, especially when it came to the reception. I don't think there were any expectations that this needed to happen or that needed to happen." She felt that one of the reasons there were fewer traditions from her family is that she has so few contemporary cousins: "From my side of the family, all the weddings had been decades before." In recognition of her patience with having her wedding reception taken over by the groom's cousins, one of the cousins gave explicit tribute to the bride: "Everybody just pay notice for two seconds to the best sport in the world" and the crowd cheered. The bride's family participated throughout the reception by joining in the dancing, but did not initiate many major parts, as the groom's family did. Just after the cousin's tribute to the bride, the bride's father gave a more formal, scripted toast to the new couple:

> We've come to respect your independent personality and the life that you've made apart from us, for yourself. And as we've come to love and know [groom] we appreciate the way he complements you. And we both wish you much happiness, as much as we have had in our marriage, as your marriage grows and matures. We love you very much.[4]

This is a nice expansion of the statement of acceptance by the parents included earlier, in the formal ceremony.

In terms of mainstream American wedding traditions often included in receptions, there was a cake (three layers, with white icing and pink roses added by the bride's mother, the cake being both the traditional vanilla and chocolate because the groom liked chocolate), which the bride and groom cut and served to each other before everyone else was served (although they did not smash it in each other's faces, as neither family had a tradition of doing that), and there was music (the groom reported his one task had been to select the band). The food served at the buffet had no particular religious or ethnic connections but was clearly mainstream American formal: three main dishes (baron of beef, chicken drummettes, poached salmon), preceded by hors d'oeuvres passed through the crowd, and accompanied by a wide variety of vegetables, followed by fruit and cheeses. The bride's mother worked with the caterer; of the result, the groom's mother said "it was magnificent." Of other elements frequently incorporated, there was a bouquet toss, but no garter toss (the bride said: "You know, I always thought that garter business was rather silly"). And the couple did dance the first dance together, followed by their parents, and then the bridal party.

One method of indicating formality in ritual is to extend an event by adding peripheral events around the edges. This wedding provided an extreme version, including:

- *Friday night dinner* (given for the bride's immediate family, and out-of-town family members on both sides, plus a few local friends of the bride, by the groom's parents but held at the bride's parents' home because the groom's parents lived out of town);
- *After-dinner party* (consisting mainly of dancing and drinking, but held at the groom's family's hotel where all the out-of-towners stayed—it was in lieu of the traditional main-

stream bachelor party, deliberately coed, with a separate hospitality suite for the children to play in);

* *Lunch with the bride's mother* (this was held on Saturday for the women, at the bride's mother's home, and included the bride, her mother, groom's sisters, mother, and aunts), where the table centerpieces for the reception were prepared;

* *Sailing with the bride's father* (occurring simultaneously, but for the men, including the groom, groom's father, groom's uncles, and his brothers-in-law);

* *Saturday night dinner* (hosted by five couples who were friends of the groom's parents, at a restaurant; the groom's mother did all the planning; it basically involved many of the same people as Friday night dinner, but with particular emphasis on friends of the groom's parents; a quieter party than that held Friday night, and for older couples, it was not followed by an after dinner party);

* *Wedding* (held Sunday afternoon, followed by an early dinner and dancing, with everyone previously involved in any event plus many more).

All of these events were held together by the continuing use of related symbols (especially flowers), thus demonstrating redundancy, and were understood by participants to be parts of the same primary event. This unusual elaboration was largely a result of having many out-of-town guests who had little to do with their free time, so many events were scheduled in their honor. The result was to magnify the significance of the central ritual, the wedding ceremony itself.

What is particularly interesting is that this list, provided by the groom's mother, omitted a set of events occurring earlier that were highlighted by the bride and her mother as especially important to them:

> A month after they were engaged, the bride and groom were invited to one of the groom's cousins' weddings, where the bride got to meet "everybody." "[One of the cousins] sent me a family photo taken at her wedding. She had traced all the people (about 35) on a separate piece of paper and then made a family tree showing how everyone was related. So I had memorized all the cousins, whose kids, what order they were in ... [she] will always have a special place in my heart."

Then, two months before the wedding, the bride and groom and the bride's parents visited the groom's home town for a weekend of activities:

- there was a bridal shower, hosted by the groom's mother's two sisters,
- the "Kuzon's Klub" (made up of cousins in the groom's mother's family) threw a party for them, and
- they also attended a surprise birthday party for the groom's father.

Of these, the bride said: "It was very eye-opening to me. I'm a pretty quiet person, and come from a small family, and I mean, I made some *faux pas*.... But I can't believe the outpouring of energy.... And also it gave me the opportunity to get to know [the groom's parents]."

For this couple, the groom's religion was important to him, and so it was highlighted repeatedly in both the wedding ceremony and the reception (use of the *huppah*, breaking the glass, the seven blessings, the *krenzel* dance), with some additional connection to his father's ethnic background (the dancing) and his personal life (incorporating the dogs into the ceremony, the parodies provided by his sisters and cousins). The bride's family had a lot of traditions they incorporated (connections to past generations being most significant, in terms of both the bride's dress and the items of clothing incorporated into the appliqué) as well as individual skills (the mother's ability as a fiber artist and a gardener), with religious references (the minister as officiant, and his hand in designing the ceremony). The part that stands out most clearly to me is the fact that the mother of the bride was able to use her skills not only to create a central religious symbol for the groom's family (the *huppah*), but then to draw a visible link between that symbol and the primary symbol of her own religion (the minister and his stole).[5]

NOTES

1. All quotes from the minister are taken from his script that the family graciously shared with me, and matched to the videotape. Because the wedding was held outdoors, some of the words were difficult to hear from that source alone.

2. This description is a result of viewing the videotape; quotes are transcribed from it. The footage of the reception, which was indoors, was far easier to hear than the outdoors ceremony.

3. As I understand it, this last sentiment refers to family members who died prior to this wedding, as well as those friends and family members unable to attend the wedding, as well as one specific family who would not attend this interfaith marriage because they are now Orthodox Jews (the most conservative branch of Judaism, the Orthodox do not recognize marriage with anyone but other Orthodox Jews as valid). The groom's mother said: "They couldn't sanction it by being there."

4. Transcribed from the videotape.

5. Although this example was the first time I heard about someone who was not Jewish making a *huppah*, one of the officiants interviewed for this study, Rabbi Aryeh Alpern, conducted a wedding in Switzerland where: "We had a *huppah* that the non-Jewish groom made himself, which seems to be a theme that's developing: the non-Jewish groom saying I want to build this symbolic home of ours beginning with the *huppah* because I love you and I want to learn about your tradition." (Interviewed 4/21/00; as of January 2001, he reported having conducted three weddings where the non-Jewish partner had made the *huppah*.)

6

Conclusion

"There is now a world culture, but we had better make sure
we understand what this means: not a replication of uniformity
but an organization of diversity, an increasing interconnectedness
of varied local cultures, as well as a development of cultures without
a clear anchorage in any one territory."
—Hannerz (1996, p. 102)

At present, intercultural weddings are but a small percentage of the total number, with most individuals still choosing to marry people quite like themselves. However, the modern United States is a plural, multiethnic society, with a wide variety of cultural groups together making up the whole. It is important to ask how such diversity is socially articulated and, equally, what occurs on these occasions when families of diverse backgrounds are combined. Because the major participants in intercultural weddings must find a way to effectively cope with multiple traditions, it has been assumed in these pages that studying this one ritual will throw light on other contexts of cultural difference; solutions found to be of value here may hold implications for potential solutions to misunderstandings in other contexts.

RESEARCH RESULTS

Because this study began with a wide range of questions and concerns, it should come as no surprise that the answers cover a wide range as well. In what follows, summaries of what has been learned about the value of intercultural weddings as a research site; the concepts of community, identity, ritual, and meaning; types of intercultural weddings; prerequisites for cultural creativity; metaphors for cultural diversity; and types of intercultural differences, all are summarized. After that, the questions of "so what" and "what next" are considered.

Value of Intercultural Weddings as a Research Site

Intercultural weddings serve as nexus of investigation for people with interests in a variety of topics, including semiotics, language and social interaction, intercultural communication, ethnography of communication, and social constructionism, although they contribute in different ways to each of these topics. For semiotics, they offer a site where multiple symbols combine into codes, and symbols and codes from different cultures combine to form a single complex ritual. For language and social interaction, they offer a naturally occurring event, generally well-documented by participants easily able to discuss their choices with researchers because most of them were made after careful consideration. For intercultural communication, they offer a perfect example of individuals with divergent cultural backgrounds working very hard to combine these into a cohesive, functional whole. For the ethnography of communication, they demonstrate the value of using ethnographic methods to study intercultural interactions, as opposed to the more traditional focus on interactions within a single community. For social constructionism, they show people at their creative best, actively adapting past forms to reflect current realities. Two individuals determined to become a new social unit as a couple arguably have greater incentive to overcome cultural differences than participants in many other, more casual contexts, such as work settings. Thus, studying the design of intercultural weddings in which potential culture clashes have been resolved successfully should demonstrate what forms of creativity are possible given sufficient incentive. And observing the revision of old and creation of new symbols is a good example of how communication is socially constructed, for we can thus watch communication as the final product is being made through interaction.

Community, Ritual, Identity, Meaning

Community, ritual, identity, and meaning are the key concepts framing the discussion presented in this book. Although separated for purposes of analysis, it is most accurate to view them all as closely interrelated components. Studying intercultural weddings not only illustrates the ways in which communities convey meanings, including identity, through ritual, but proves a good way to access the social construction of meaning.[1] As Roberts and Bavelas (1996) suggested, "The ultimate goal of communication is the exchange of meaningful messages" (p. 157), so this is hardly a trivial concern. Studying rituals of special significance for the participants, such as weddings, provides easy access to meanings of great import to the participants, having to do with identity and membership in particular communities.

Whereas the larger community must always have significant concerns about long term continuity, each couple displayed individual control over the elements incorporated, even if their choices were not always pleasing to their parents, extended families, or religious leaders. As the age at marriage steadily increases, and as couples more often pay for their own weddings, they gain greater control over the design of the event. This is even more the case for second marriages, in which the couple virtually always covers the cost themselves. Clearly the party picking up the check is granted considerable control over the decisions made; couples who pay for their weddings themselves are thus able to escape a prior generation's concern for doing what their parents wanted.

All the same, despite the extensive rhetoric about doing what they want, there are still a large number of traditional elements in weddings with each group that brides and grooms follow, even when they do not always understand their significance. Most couples seemed satisfied if they were able to modify one element significantly and a few in smaller ways. Thus, even the weddings highlighted in the Interludes usually incorporated only one major innovation. It was as if, at that point, the couple had gotten what they wanted, and then were more willing to do what else others considered necessary. But virtually all couples did something to mark the event as their own, distinct from all other exemplars of the same category. Because each wedding is a unique presentation of a common ritual, each couple has the right and the responsibility to demonstrate their originality in combining whatever symbolic resources are available to them in reasonable fashion. Thus do they mark their skill at handling cultural resources, for making successful modifications in traditions first requires understanding what those traditions are. Just as marriage is understood as a marker of adulthood in most societies, so creation of a unique variant of a ritual is as well. An adult is one who forms a new social unit (as in a marriage); an adult is also one who knows his or her own cultural traditions well enough to design an appropriate variant of a major ritual performance.

Individual and family identities (including some examples of geographic location and even voluntary associations) turned out to be as important to those couples interviewed as the broader concerns of ethnicity, race, nationality, and social class that originally were my concern, and so they were incorporated into the project. Because of the framing of wedding ceremonies within religious contexts for most participants, religion took on an exceedingly large role. Most interesting is that fact that couples found no difficulty in integrating symbols from multiple systems into a coherent whole, and did not see this as incongruent or unlikely at all. It was just the way they found to highlight the various aspects of their identities.

People figure out what works for them, and do that. For most couples, this meant extensive use of one or more of the techniques for conveying complex meanings described in Chapter 5: polysemy, intertextuality, *bricolage*, redundancy, and ambiguity. Perhaps the most surprising result is that so many of the innovative solutions seemed so obvious to the couples; at times they were not really sure what had impressed me.[2] The couple that walked such a delicate line between the need to have a Saturday wedding and the inability to have a Sabbath wedding downplayed their originality and creativity, and really felt it was just the obvious thing to do, nothing special, just the solution anyone would have found. Except, of course, no one else had, at least not in my database. As with the couple that considered it obvious to have the Christian bride's mother sew the *huppah* for the groom's Jewish tradition, or any of the other examples of especially gracious conflict resolution (or potential conflict resolution, the term *conflict* turned out to be far more extreme than most of these couples were comfortable with as a descriptor of their situations), they just did what seemed appropriate. And it certainly was. The trick will be for others, who do not see these sorts of solutions as obvious, to learn how to invent them when the time comes that they are necessary.

Most of the time those decisions were made without me, so I do not have a record of how they were made. But interviews with couples still in the planning stages sometimes show how it works. For example, asked about their choice of wedding cake, Couple 88 came up with two separate answers, and an immediate resolution.

Groom: "I want vanilla"
Bride: "I want chocolate. So we'll probably have a lot of layers."

It is this ease of resolution that the most successful couples find obvious, and others cannot achieve no matter how hard they work. Instead of fighting over "either/or" they collaborate on a "both/and" solution. And because symbols can convey multiple meanings, "both/and" becomes a real possibility.

Types of Intercultural Weddings

Intercultural weddings demonstrate the same variety of solutions available to any intercultural interaction:

1. focus on one culture, ignoring the other(s);
2. maintain two (or more) cultures, but separately;
3. avoid the issue and hope it will go away; or
4. combine two or more cultures in a new and creative way.

I have argued that the fourth, although the least common solution because it involves the most effort, holds the most interest theoretically. It is here that cultural creativity comes to the fore, here that we can observe cultural meaning as it is communicated to participants.[3]

Once the decision has been made to combine traditions into a single ritual, there are several potential ways to do it. One could divide up the event by social code, and essentially assign each to one family or the other. For example, in some weddings the food at the reception is handled by one side of the family, while the other takes responsibility for organizing something else, such as the language used in the ritual. Another possibility would be to give each side control over those signs or codes of greatest import to them. If there is a traditional wedding dress in the family that has been worn by several generations of brides, then it can serve as the centerpiece of the wedding once again. If there are specific foods always baked for the receptions in a particular family, then they must of course appear. A third is to do a bit of everything, granting all cultural strands public acknowledgment. A couple may choose red for the invitation, as is traditionally Chinese, and mix this with a standard American white bridal gown, and blue and white doves on the napkins, thus having an eclectic mix of Chinese with American popular culture, not forgetting to include Italian cookies at the reception made by the Italian grandmother (Couple 10).[4] In this last possibility, since each element has meaning to the participants, it does not matter if, when viewed abstractly, they make an unusual combination.[5]

The theoretically most interesting resolutions fall into a fourth category, in which old symbols having meaning to each separate group combine to form something new, just for this couple and their families, that speaks to their specific needs in the ritual of joining. If intercultural couples are able to find a way to satisfy all parties with the same wedding, they successfully demonstrate their cultural creativity. In this way they create their own "tapestry" using threads from both sides of the family, weaving a new design out of pre-existing elements. When this works, it makes an incredibly powerful statement about how to combine cultures. When it fails, it is equally powerful, albeit in the opposite direction, distressing everyone who understands what has happened.

Interlude 6, with a Jewish groom and Christian bride, told the story of what happened when the bride's family became intimately involved in the construction of a symbol originally having meaning only for the groom's family, in the process adding new meanings to it. As a result, their *huppah* came to symbolize the joining of two individuals with separate pasts into a common future, as well as the joining of two families, and their acceptance of the intermarriage of their children. And for the groom's family, the *huppah* was also assumed to stand for what *huppot* always stand for: the acceptance of a new couple into the larger community. The only difference was that here the minister explicitly revised the definition of community to include all those present (rather than the Jewish community only, as would traditionally be assumed in a Jewish only ceremony.)

Yet for Couple 69, described at greater length in Chapter 5, use of the same symbol, the *huppah*, led to less positive results. The bride thought it obvious that, if the rabbi agreed a *huppah* was to be used, the Christian groom would be permitted to stand under it; the rabbi thought it obvious that, as a non-Jew, the groom could not stand under a symbol of the Jewish community. Because each considered their position obvious, the contradiction was not discovered until the wedding itself. The ambiguity inherent in having a Christian groom participating in traditional Jewish events he did not fully understand, permitted him to not even know that he had been excluded, although the bride was terribly upset.

How to reconcile these two stories? Both are about the use of the *huppah* in a Jewish–Christian wedding, but with quite different results. There is something to be learned from each story. From the first, we learn that explicit discussion of the traditions ahead of time can be an important element in the successful transformation of symbols from markers of single group identity to markers of multiple group identity. When the families accept each other's traditions in theory, and when they discuss what will happen in detail, they can revise these traditions to meet the current needs.

What do we learn from the second story? For one, that some ambiguity is inevitable: It seems unlikely that every possible symbol and interpretation will be discussed ahead of time, and perhaps this is a safety valve. Sometimes matters are simpler if people do not know when they have been symbolically excluded from a ritual. It was especially interesting to me in this case that the same interactional moment that carried so much emotional freight for the bride and her immediate family had no significance at all to the groom and his family. It pointed out the discrepancies in their past experiences, as well as to the future discrepancies that would be inevitable. Both of these examples illustrate polysemy, but to quite different ends.

Prerequisites For Cultural Creativity

The significance of rituals for the health of the family as a social unit has been demonstrated by Wolin and Bennett (1984), who further learned that families differ in the degree to which they emphasize ritual forms and the degree to which they are flexible about the details of their rituals. The examples of intercultural weddings presented in this book suggest that if the bride and the groom both come from families with a high commitment to ritual, as well as flexibility, when they join, they have the greatest chance of creating new and unique rituals for their weddings satisfying both families. Given that both sides share an assumption of the significance of ritual, as well as some flexibility in the design of ritual, these are the couples most likely to both feel the need to revise their rituals, blending them into a new whole, as well as those most likely to have the skills already available to do so. This is why Jewish and Chinese traditions have been granted a prominence in this book beyond their relative proportions in the modern United States; both groups have a strong sense of the value of tradition, yet both have at least some members willing to revise past rituals to reflect current reality.[6] Those who have no sense of the potential significance of ritual and tradition to the creation of a meaningful social life do not maintain them, but are more willing to accommodate the mainstream wedding traditions proposed by the specialists who help them design their events, and shown in films and on television. Those who can only identify their background as "American," for example, rarely had the same sort of extensive list of traditions to draw upon when designing their own rituals. As hard as it may be to combine multiple traditions in appropriate ways, it may be harder still not to know of any that are significant enough to them that they need to be incorporated, and yet learn that others have rich traditions available and upon which they can draw.

Different scholars have used a wide variety of terms to refer to what happens when members of different groups create a new whole.[7] Whatever the term, the concept describes how people are developing new ways of combining multiple cultural backgrounds into a single, coherent whole, and so researchers must study this topic. One critical element here can be described as learning about balance, as Blaeser (1997) described:

> We plot our lives in various searches. Sometimes they work at crosscurrents. Ties to tribe, place, families, belief systems, careers tug us in many directions. Their pathways may converge, run parallel; more often they diverge. For those of us from mixed cultures this is perhaps particularly true. We carry multiple maps. The roads on our maps have many forks. We must learn balance in our direction taking. But balance is the story the world chants endlessly. And so it comes if we let it, gently. No holding on with tightly clenched fists or teeth. Balance is a motion, a swaying rhythm. (p. 124)

A successful balance has been achieved when both *huppah* and *shuang-hsi* appear on the wedding invitation, warning guests ahead of time that this event will be a little different from their prior experiences (Couple 77, as described in Interlude 4). It is achieved when both *shuang-hsi* and *chai* appear, together with a wide variety of additional symbols on a *ketubah*, used both in the ceremony and displayed in the home of the new couple, again telling others something new is happening here (Couple 80, as described in Interlude 5). And it occurs when the *shuang-hsi* is drawn inside a heart (thus visibly combining Chinese with American popular culture elements of a wedding) on the invitation to the wedding of Couple 10, or when the *shuang-hsi* is itself drawn in the shape of a heart, as on the red silk banner that guests signed at the reception of Couple 10. These are examples of *bricolage* and intertextuality: Old symbols having meaning for each of their originating groups are given new meaning by their juxtaposition in a new whole. These couples have demonstrated their skill at balance, creating meaning for themselves in sophisticated ways.

It is also an example of balance when a Jewish–Christian couple schedules their wedding for sunset, balancing the preference of one for a Saturday wedding with the prohibition of the other's group for a wedding on the Sabbath (Couple 69). Their commitment to each other led them to find an enviable compromise, one meeting all their needs. And it is an example of balance when a Sinologist chooses a red wedding dress because of additional connections to the other countries of importance to her: France (the feather jacket) and Australia (the friends who gave her the fabric and sewed the dress); matched to an invitation having links to current Mexican art and wedding rings designed by a Mexican jeweler to represent her husband's family history (Couple 75, as described in Interlude 3). Polysemy permits each symbol to stand for more than one thing, and so multiple connections can be evident simultaneously; ambiguity permits each guest to understand something a little different when viewing the same symbol. When related symbols convey a single message multiple times, we have evidence of redundancy. When the Christian mother of the bride creates the *huppah* for the primarily Jewish ceremony conducted by her minister, making him a stole to match the *huppah*, she demonstrates her own sense of balance (Couple 13, as described in Interlude 6).

The most powerful symbols in the weddings I have learned about are those that successfully combine already significant symbols from diverse traditions in a new way. Putting a *tunjo* on a groom's cake combines Colombian identity, the particular history of the couple, and American mainstream traditions into a new, seamless, whole (Couple 84, as described in Interlude 2). Making a *huppah* out of African cloth, and using trees from the groom's family's land for the poles, serves similarly to combine much of what is important to the particular couple: racial identity, religious identity, family history (Couple 74, as described in Interlude 1). Symbols have the ability to convey multiple meanings, thus couples can use them to display multiple identities simultaneously. Once we understand that identity is not a single, static thing, it should come as no surprise to find couples making multiple statements. The fact that not all guests will understand all the references is not a problem, but a solution. Those who are concerned to see a particular identity statement are the ones who will recognize it; those who do not know how to interpret a particular symbol will pass over it not knowing what they have missed, or even that they have missed something.

Metaphors For Cultural Diversity

Returning to the metaphors for the various sorts of possible connections made between different cultural groups, it is now possible to say that all the metaphors are of some value in describing what real people do (which may well be the explanation for why they are all still around). If we expect everyone to conform to the same metaphor, we are expecting everyone to be the same, when they so clearly are not. The melting pot that leaves no one's tradition intact is the most appropriate description of mainstream weddings, exemplifying everyone doing things the same way, using the same set of symbols to convey the same meanings. As the melting pot metaphor proves to be less and less accurate as a description of real life in the United States, the mainstream wedding is likely to decrease in frequency and significance.

The mosaic metaphor, which lets no one's traditions influence those of another but maintains them all as distinct though coexisting, describes those weddings where bits and pieces of multiple relevant identities are included, in their original form, unchanged by their new context, only placed together to form an unexpected (but hopefully pleasing) pattern. As intercultural weddings increase in frequency with the increased awareness of and acceptance of the distinctions caused by cultural differences in the modern United States, it is likely that weddings designed essentially as mosaics will also increase in frequency.

The tapestry metaphor accurately conveys the sense of each group retaining what is most important to them, yet clearly being substantially influenced by what is important to others, as demonstrated by those weddings where something new is created out of the old rituals, each culture influenced by the other. It is likely that, rather than merely setting traditions next to one another, it is this sense of cultures influencing one another to create something new yet retaining some meaning relevant to everyone, of interacting not only at the social but at the symbolic level, that will gradually become increasingly common in the not too distant future. With this metaphor the critical role of context is taken into account, for, instead of assuming that bits and pieces of culture can move between contexts with no change, it assumes "with inevitable changes in context, come changes in interpretation of communicative acts" (Penman, 2000, p. 73). This last form of a wedding ritual displaying a new whole created out of old pieces requires the greatest knowledge of one's own traditions (for one cannot appropriately incorporate what one does not even understand) and not only tolerance of, but appreciation for, the underlying similarities in someone else's traditions. This is where the greatest act of cultural creativity occurs: in the synthesis of multiple meanings into modified symbols, rather than the placement of multiple symbols side by side. As Couple 80 put it describing the *chai* and *shuang-hsi* on their *ketubah*, it simply seemed most appropriate to them to show their respective cultural symbols intertwined, neither having prominence, if these were to accurately reflect the union of two equal partners in the marriage they were about to begin. People need to do what works best for them, and if the larger culture does not provide obvious means, individuals will create something new. Those intercultural couples who create a unique joining of symbols are at the forefront of the generation to come. As there are more intercultural weddings, of all sorts, there are likely to be more examples of this ability to create something entirely new out of old elements, something explicitly marking the joining of different traditions into a new whole. These couples stand at the forefront of a new, multicultural society; just as every group uses symbols to convey their identity and other elements of importance to them, they will do so. If the exact symbol a couple needs does not exist, they will modify an existing one, or invent a new one. Just as one artist influences the paintings of others, so future couples will see what others have invented before them and continue to be culturally creative in similar but ever-expanding ways. Each wedding is unique, but each serves as only one example in a long line of weddings. There will not be a complete casting off of old traditions so long as they carry some meaning. Instead, there will be a gradual revision of old symbols, so that they come to convey whatever new meanings people require of them.

The melting pot is an old metaphor, used to describe what once was assumed happens when cultures bump up against one another but when strong, unique cultural identities existing simultaneously are not supported: All dissolve to the point of no recognition of original components, then transform into something new, retaining little of the old traditions unchanged. The mosaic is an intermediate metaphor, used to describe what comes next: Cultures hold back from joining the pot, keeping their traditions intact, but these are placed next to one another to form a new and different whole (perhaps more like a potluck dinner than a melting pot, with separate dishes placed on the same table). However, this model holds the dangers of "red boots multiculturalism" described earlier. That is, it bears a great chance of trivializing each symbol because none are maintained as part of a whole cloth, of becoming mere decoration on the larger social fabric of the mainstream norm. When symbols have come so far from their origin that they no longer carry emotional freight for their users, they lose much of their significance. Although it is easy to design a wedding as a mosaic, it can result in just this sort of trivialization, especially after several generations when participants no longer understand any, let alone multiple, meanings for their symbols. This is when even these nominal inclusions no longer seem reasonable to new couples, and so they are dropped. The tapestry, with its emphasis on different threads combined to make an entirely new social fabric, is a more accurate metaphor for the current age, revealing the powerful joining of different cultures that can occur when each one is permitted to both retain what is critical and yet also to reflect the influence of other cultures simultaneously in existence. In an important way this is less a significant change than initially assumed, for, despite the appearance of continuity, rituals always have changed, a little at a time, retaining what is most central to their ideals and goals, but also reflecting the current realities of those who perform them. Without this ability to change, rituals would quickly become outdated, and lose all power. When people of different cultures decide to spend their lives together, they create something new out of something old; their symbols bump up against one another and return changed by the contact.

In the weddings described at length in the six Interludes presented here, couples demonstrate their cultural creativity, their ability to come up with a solution to the problem posed at the beginning of the book: how to display multiple identities simultaneously. Their answer is to take symbols having considerable impact for at least one of the cultures concerned, and to revise them, adding in new meanings understood by the other. As a canopy, the *huppah* usually protects the bride and groom, symbolically representing the entire Jewish community, in which they will now begin to have a substantial role; take that symbol, and give it a twist: Now the *huppah* is made from fabric embroidered using a technique unique to a particular region in Spain by the groom's mother, with the Spanish flag as signature; this is successful because central symbols of both traditions have been combined. It leads to an increase in signification, not the decrease possible with a mosaic, and the only destination for a melting pot. Both the *huppah* and the Spanish embroidery still convey meaning to anyone familiar with the specifics of this couple's background (Couple 86). Equally, the *shuang-hsi* and the *chai*, when joined at the top of the *ketubah*, not only announce a Jewish–Chinese union; the fact that they are visibly intertwined and placed in a position of prominence shows how important it is to this bride and groom that they find ways to mesh their traditions, to make a new whole out of the old, and separate, parts (Couple 80). Both images have significance to their communities of origin, and maintain those implications despite their new use. But now there is the added suggestion that just as this symbol has meaning to me, so does that symbol have meaning to you. There need not be a lessening of significance through contact between cultures, there can instead be a heightening through the multiplication of meanings. And this is possible because symbols can easily carry multiple meanings simultaneously, and because everyone need not attend to the same meaning.

Types of Intercultural Difference

What of the original division into five types of intercultural weddings, international, interracial, interethnic, interfaith, and interclass? Did notable differences in each category appear in the data? Certainly many in the United States are fairly oblivious to even explicit demonstrations of class differences, and do not often think of class as the most, or even a, relevant category in their own identity. This is partially due to the easy resolution of class differences when presenting a wedding (or other ritual); the family with more money generally pays for the event, thus creating an event displaying the higher of the two class identities. As weddings are partially about conspicuous displays in popular understanding, this solution seems acceptable to everyone. Generally, people do not insist on multiple class markers in a wedding; most are satisfied to let the highest social class markers take precedence. At the same time, Americans are currently exceedingly aware of race as a category, although it is not always clear what they mean by the term and, in fact, race has far less influence on rituals such as wedding traditions than ethnicity or religion. In the acute observation of one of the non-American brides: "What would be interpreted as class in Europe, is interpreted as race in the United States" (Couple 75). International weddings often have the simplest resolution: The couple usually follows the traditions of the place where they choose to have the wedding, ignoring most if not all of the traditions of the other country. This is often described as a matter of simple politeness, since obviously it is most important to follow the traditions of the country in which the wedding occurs, so the audience (generally made up of a majority of locals to that area) will understand what transpires. Interethnic weddings were the most frequent, and in many ways, the most accepted, having become so common in the United States that some individuals can no longer even identify all the ethnic strands of their family history (a certain marker of acceptance across groups). It was rarely seen as a problem if a couple included multiple ethnic markers in a wedding, side by side; because that is a common occurrence, it seems hardly worthy of attention, and did not often require extensive negotiation. Wedding rituals display sacred as well as secular identities, and thus differences in religion have been highlighted in these pages; for other forms of intercultural interaction, religion will only rarely be the most significant factor, especially in the U.S., where there is the expectation of a high degree of religious tolerance.

Perhaps most importantly, this research confirms that we can consider multiple cultural differences as being the same in an essential way. Five types of cultural difference have been investigated here, and in all cases the fact of discovering difference between your assumptions and those of someone else is the critical element, not the exact nature of that difference. Regardless of the cause, the issue at hand involves the need to resolve the difference, to come to terms with it in some fashion. Traditionally, intercultural communication research has most frequently assumed that cultural identity refers to a national identity. This made sense when the goal was to examine how citizens of different countries interacted, but as that is no longer the primary goal of the field, it should no longer be the taken-for-granted meaning of cultural identity.[8]

SO WHAT?

At the end of every book, a question remains to be answered: So what? What does this research teach us? Specifically for this book, that questions implies: What does this work contribute to our understanding of intercultural interactions, and the study of communication more generally? For my ultimate concern here is not with weddings in and of themselves (although they certainly are an easy and attractive topic) but rather with weddings as forms of communication of great significance to their designers and participants.

This work suggests that intercultural researchers should attend to real interactions, especially those marked as having substantial significance for those we study, such as rituals. Although some intercultural interactions between strangers (the group most often studied by communication researchers) still occur, many now move far beyond that, and researchers must follow where their subjects lead. One result of this move is that the study of intercultural communication should less often emphasize what happens in one person's head, or the standard rules of behavior for one culture, and pay greater attention to what happens when people from different groups interact jointly. Communication is never the result of one person acting alone, but rather the result of interaction between people; this is true especially of intercultural communication. This implies that cognitive aspects of communication (what goes on inside one person's head) should not be emphasized to the exclusion of interaction (jointly constructed social events). Communication in general, and intercultural communication specifically, result from people working together to create something (Penman, 2000; Sigman, 1995), and so it will be important to look for other examples of people interacting over time in order to see if comparable examples of cultural creativity in other contexts have similarly developed.

This study has also demonstrated that research into language and social interaction has much to share with careful analysis of real examples of intercultural encounters; research across these topics should continue to expand, each sharing their results with the other. As the influence of culture pervades interactions more and more (as must be the case in a multicultural society), those who study language and social interaction cannot refuse to acknowledge its influence any more than intercultural researchers can afford to ignore real interactions in favor of easier to study hypothetical or exceedingly abbreviated situations. The ethnography of communication is an important method for the study of language and social interaction, and it should be used more often by those investigating intercultural communication. Ethnography is more time-consuming than many other methods followed by communication researchers and requires special training, but in the end the results are worth the time and effort for the method can result in great depth and complexity.

Social constructionism is clearly a helpful theoretical approach to the study of intercultural communication, and its application to this topic should be expanded. What has been documented in these pages are the ways in which people jointly construct meaning for themselves, meanings having to do with identity and community, quite basic issues. Questions of who we are and how we are both like and unlike others never cease to have significance, and so are always important to examine. Social constructionism allows a more active role to those we study than many other theoretical frameworks, but they already have that role as the creators of their own lives, so it is appropriate. Within social constructionism, symbols and how they are manipulated and revised to re-flect current realities are a fruitful topic. In their ability to be polysemic and intertextual, symbols are ideally suited for the task of conveying multiple mean-ings. Essentially, this means we can expect fairly subtle and multiple messages to be conveyed through interactions, and should look for them. Clearly, re-searchers must attend not to individual symbols, but to collections of them, both grouped into social codes and across social codes. We need to study *brico-lage* (how old bits are combined into new wholes), as well as redundancy (how the same message appears in different ways throughout an entire event). The *huppah* as well as the minister's stole; the wedding invitation as well as the photo album; the *ketubah* as well as the bride's jade necklace. This means that we need to study entire events, rather than merely pieces of events or individual symbols, whenever possible. And it is especially helpful if we study at least some public performances, as weddings are, for these are events clearly de-signed for the benefit of those attending (the guests) as well as those participat-ing (the wedding party), rather than for the benefit of the researcher.

This project suggests that we attend especially to ambiguity: that which per-mits a message to be understood by some but not all participants in an encoun-ter, studying both the positive and negative results. Not all intercultural encounters end positively for all concerned; we must study the successful as well as the unsuccessful efforts, and endeavor to discover what divides them. What helps people to bring an intercultural encounter to a successful end? What factors prevent it?

In addition, researchers must attend seriously to material culture as well as to language, for material culture not only is a legitimate focus but has the unique characteristic of remaining available to analysis even after an interac-tion ends. With weddings, this has meant that couples preserve the event for themselves, and so have evidence to share with researchers: photographs, vid-eotapes, and indices (literal pieces of the wedding preserved) of all sorts. But it also means that events can be studied after the fact, thus increasing the range of behavior open to analysis. There is little doubt about the major decisions made: Every bride will know what color dress she wore at her own wedding, al-though most cannot recite the vows they spoke after even a few months; and whereas most bridal gowns are now professionally boxed, the vows are rarely kept, either in written form or in memory.[9] This is not to imply that vows are not important, but material culture should not be ignored and only language deemed worthy of study.

Implicit in this research is the need to listen to those we are studying, and take their concerns seriously. For this project, that has meant realizing that some differences not originally included in the project (specifically regional identities, family history, personal characteristics) all be considered at least to a limited extent. Yellow roses were important in one wedding for their link to reli-gion, but in another for the connotation of regional identity. Incorporating children was important to one couple, whereas incorporating dogs was important to another. What had occurred at prior weddings within a family, whether it be a religious tradition like saying the *sheva brachot*, or simply a family tradition of creating parodies about the bride or groom to sing at the reception were equally significant to the couples interviewed, and so they necessarily became part of the research, expanding the original boundaries set. This is the result of starting with what Penman (2000) described as a "genuine" question (p. 121), one for which the researcher is uncertain of the answer. When I started, it was not clear to me how couples would combine their traditions, but it was something I thought important to discover. That they included more different types of traditions than I had initially assumed meant that my research needed to expand, rather than omit parts of their events of great significance to them.

For each of the major concepts examined in this book (community, ritual, identity, and meaning) my focus was a bit different from the standard. In terms of community, I have emphasized border crossings between communities over the study of any one. Although hardly the first to do so, this is clearly still an unusual approach, and it warrants far more research. In terms of ritual, I emphasized the creative aspects over the more typical investigations of continuity and tradition. This is necessary because creative change is one (the most positive) response to a situation of cultural stress, and it is the one we must investigate if we are to learn how it comes about in place of the easier but more destructive resolution of conflict between different groups. In terms of identity, I emphasized the successful manipulation of, and balance established between, multiple potentially contradictory identities. Although a far more complex topic to study than the display of a single identity at a time, it is again more revealing, and thus significant. In terms of meaning, I examined five ways of coping with complex meanings, when there is a need to convey different messages simultaneously. None of these five has been a significant topic in communication research yet to date, but they should prove fruitful in application to a wide range of topics beyond the weddings studied here.

WHAT NEXT?

In addition to asking "so what?" every research project also leads to the question "what next?" Although this project is already more than large enough, several extensions would be well worth following up. This research was primarily synchronic: a snapshot of what some Americans today are doing in their weddings. Three obvious next steps would be to turn this into a diachronic study (investigation of behavior over time). One possibility would investigate the ways in which an intercultural couple become socially integrated after marriage into the various communities available to them. To what extent does the intercultural couple opt to participate in one or the other culture? To what extent do they manage to combine them? How successful or unsuccessful is their combination, and how stable is it over the years? Is it possible to change from one solution to another? That is, for a time (perhaps before having children) to lean toward one set of traditions, and at a later time (perhaps after children, who often seem to serve to polarize feelings about the significance of one's traditions, and the urgency of passing them on to the next generation) to shift toward another? Who do they take as their friends? What are their families' reactions? What sorts of foods do they eat? What objects do they keep in their home? What ways do they find to mesh their different traditions, to create new symbols? And to what extent are any of the answers to these questions linked to the couple's design of their wedding?

A second diachronic study would investigate how parents in intercultural marriages raise their children.[10] Whose traditions will they be taught? What new combinations will be made? What language(s) do parents teach their children of those they speak, what religion of those they practice, and how are these decisions made? The range of answers is likely to include the following basic possibilities (paralleling those available for designing the wedding): raising the children in one or the other group, knowing a lot about one side of their heritage but little about the other; letting them experience each culture separately, with no explicit discussion of the issues and no attempt at integration; or raising the children to become mainstream Americans, knowing little about the cultural background of either parent, in essence hiding in the melting pot. As with intercultural weddings, raising the children with a combined experience of both sides of their family background is likely to be the least frequent but, again, the most interesting choice theoretically. Based on those couples interviewed for this study who already had children, it seems this is a more frequent solution for raising children than for designing weddings, but it would be interesting to deliberately investigate the matter to be sure of the results.

A third possibility for future research would be to spend time documenting series of weddings within particular families. As family members bear in mind what others (their parents, siblings, cousins) have done previously, it would be revealing to study clusters of weddings. In several cases documented here I was lucky enough to be able to interview extended family members (usually the parents of the bride, or groom, or relatively rarely, both). But it would be revealing to systematically study sets of weddings within extended families in order to learn just how each influenced and was influenced by others. This is the larger context within which a couple designs their wedding, after all, so it should be enlightening to study deliberately. All of these events form part of the context within which each new example is interpreted and understood.

Other possible extensions of this research would investigate related rituals, some new and some quite old. Among the old constructions would be rituals designed to mark other significant life events than marriage: births, coming of age, funerals. Among the new constructions are gay and lesbian commitment ceremonies, as well as the new divorce rituals that a few people are designing. Both of these rely heavily on the design elements of weddings, often in an inverted form. It would be especially interesting to follow extended families through complete sets of all rites of passage shared by members to see the ways in which they are similar and different. This would be a productive topic for further examination of polysemy, intertextuality, *bricolage*, redundancy, and ambiguity.

Whether studying weddings or relationships, how children are raised, or the connections between the various rituals performed within a single family, the ability to find appropriate ways to combine two or more cultures demonstrates the ability to cope successfully with cultural diversity on an individual level. And if we are ever to deal with this issue on a larger societal level, we must do so from the starting point of one individual, one couple, one family at a time.[11]

NOTES

1. This is hardly an original concern, but one common to others who use ethnography of speaking or communication as their primary method; Fitch (1998) pointed out: "Of primary concern in this approach are the communal resources, both communicative and symbolic, that people utilize to construct meaning in everyday activities" (p. 3).

2. This was usually manifested in their responses to reading what I had written about their weddings. Several insisted I was making far too much of what they saw as really rather obvious solutions. But, of course, the issue is that others could not even imagine solutions existed, let alone come up with them, so I still insist on being impressed with those who saw the way to a graceful resolution.

3. This is why Hannerz (1996) wrote of "creative confrontations" (p. 61): conflict is not the only result of confronting difference; creativity can be a more positive result. Krebs (1999) called people who are able to "embrace cultural complexity with unusual creativity" (p. 2) "edgewalkers," and has devoted an entire book to the study of how they do what they do.

4. Interviewed by Sue Glanz for Comm 499: Independent Study, in Spring 1992.

5. And the bride of Couple 10 reported that similar combinations as those found in her wedding are increasingly common in the Asian American weddings they have been attending in the years since their own.

6. Chirot and Reid (1997) suggest that Chinese and Jews have other characteristics in common, which may in fact play a role in the current frequency of Chinese–Jewish weddings.

7. Sometimes this is called syncretism (Gilroy, 1987), hybrid (Bakhtin, 1981; Cooren & Taylor, 2000) or hybridity (Gilroy, 1993), creolization (Hannerz, 1992), third culture building (Casmir, 1992, 1997), or cosmopolitanism (Hannerz, 1996; Pearce, 1989).

8. Leeds-Hurwitz (1990) examined the early history of the study of intercultural communication, providing specific evidence for this generalization.

9. The increasing frequency of videotapes of weddings of course implies that the vows are now preserved, but this is a new tradition and many vows have already been lost.

10. There are some precedents to the study of intercultural children: see especially Azoulay (1997), who quoted one of the individuals she interviewed as reporting that "I myself am a controversy" (p. 161). Kerwin, Ponterotto, Jackson, and Harris (1993) expected to find that children having both Black and White heritage would feel marginalized in both groups; instead, the majority of those they studied had developed increased sensitivity to both cultures, being equally comfortable in both. Other resources on this topic are: Arboleda (1998), Camper (1994), Katz (1996), Mathabane and Mathabane (1992), O'Hearn (1998), Penn (1997a), Root (1992, 2001), Tizard and Phoenix (1993), Uebelherr (2000), and Zack (1995).

11. Root (2001) echoed this emphasis on change as it occurs one family at a time: "Interracial marriage gives us hope that love can transcend some of the barriers that legislation has not. Its power to transform us, one at a time, cannot be underestimated, allowing us to release the hate, fear, and guilt of the past and move into the future with love as a political device" (p. 177).

Theoretical Appendix

$\mathbb{A}$ theoretical appendix outlines the concerns underlying a particular study, the "why" of what has been done. (A methodological appendix outlines the methods followed by a particular study, the "how" of it. The "what" of it, what was studied and what was learned from such study, forms the body of this book.) Every researcher begins with a series of questions and concerns in the back of his or her head. I explain mine here, on the assumption that articulating the issues prompting specific research projects is valuable.[1] As Bohannan (1995) said of a book of his, "This book is full of unanswered questions—but questions are more fruitful than answers, which have a way of stopping inquiry in its tracks." (p. 197). I agree. Having a lot of questions, even at the end of one's research, is not a bad thing. Small research projects generally provide answers to small questions, and are expected to be fairly complete, but even large projects may only begin to provide answers to large questions.

My major theoretical framework here combines semiotics with social constructionism, for I see weddings as particularly interesting in their ability to serve as a vehicle to convey meanings that have been jointly constructed by the various participants. This is an unusual combination, but I have found these approaches particularly fruitful in tandem. When studying meaning, I want to study not only what it is, but also how people go about making it.[2] As Halliday (1984) pointed out, "A semiotic act is any act, linguistic or otherwise, that projects cultural meanings" (p. 34). My most basic concern is with meaning as it is jointly constructed by and for participants, therefore I combine semiotics with social constructionism as my central theoretical framework in this book.

HOW PEOPLE CREATE MEANING FOR THEMSELVES
AND FOR OTHERS IN THE SOCIAL WORLD

Meaning creation can be studied anywhere, any time, for it is the primary human activity. However, it is my assumption that the production of meaning can be most readily studied through detailed observations of actual behavior, especially when matched to extended interviews intended to encourage discussion of intention and result. This interest is an expansion of my previous study of communication in everyday life (Leeds-Hurwitz, 1989). Rituals are one genre of communicative behavior, more deliberately organized than the majority of everyday interaction considered there. One answer to the question of how people create meaning is that they use symbols, combining them in various ways, often to the point of creating elaborate rituals. One of the more interesting definitions of ritual is "an act of self-apprehension by which a culture seeks to understand itself" (Hassan, 1987, p. xi). Clearly people devote more conscious attention to the design of ritual behavior, whether secular or religious, than to the form of everyday interaction. Thus rituals are important to study as examples of what social actors create when they spend time considering their actions and putting themselves on public display. Rituals are designed by and for participants, thus they are less liable to influence by the analyst's presence and questions than more casual behavior. The analyst's task is to come to understand the meanings exhibited in and understood by ritual behavior from the viewpoints of the participants.

The study of meaning is a large part of what is investigated under the term "semiotics," and so this book makes use of semiotic, as well as communication, terminology. Technically, semiotics is the study of signs (things that stand for other things) and sign systems or codes (groups of signs operating together). Semiotics has been described as "the role of mind in the creation of the world" (Sebeok, 1986, p. 42); clearly this is closely aligned to the study of meaning, for making meaning out of the world is what people do with their minds. This concern links to my prior discussion of semiotic theory (Leeds-Hurwitz, 1993). One of my emphases there was with the creation of meaning through a variety of nonverbal social codes (e.g., food, clothing, objects), a concern maintained in these pages.

To study meaning is to study the social construction of interaction. Pearce and Littlejohn (1997) suggested that social constructionism leads us to "view human reality as a product of social interaction" and, further, to "look for the ways in which our worlds are built in social life" (p. x). By describing my project as "social constructionist" research, I mean that this research takes as one of its major questions how exactly people jointly manage to create meaning. It seems to me that every research project requires both an abstract concept, such as social constructionism, and some empirical data, in this case intercultural weddings, if it is to be complete. An interesting theoretical concept drives the research, but it is the collection of data that demonstrates whether anything has been learned that is relevant outside the head of the investigator.

In addition to these two theoretical approaches, however, a larger set of questions has guided my research. These are one presentation of the concerns that have guided all of my research in the past, and probably will influence much of it in the future as well. In order to give the reader a quick overview of the whole, Fig. 8 shows the major issues clearly. "Meaning construction" stands at the top, representing a combination of semiotics (with its focus on meaning) and social constructionism (the active creation of meaning). Because I see the two as integrally related, they are listed but once, united. The rest of my concerns are really pairs of terms best investigated jointly. Each pair has some tension between the extreme ends. "Wedding" stands at the center of the diagram as the topic to be investigated, and the context within which all of these paired tensions will be studied. Other potential topics could be substituted in other research projects (e.g., relationships, classrooms, or organizations). Together this list of concerns amplifies and provides narrower topics to study than the large issue of meaning construction.

FIG. 8:   Theoretical Concerns.

HOW SMALL DETAILS CONTRIBUTE TO THE CREATION
OF A LARGER, COHERENT WHOLE

Even small nonverbal behaviors can be used to convey larger values and ideas; even the smallest most mundane choices are understood to convey meanings. This book examines how even small, seemingly insignificant, details of material culture (e.g., food, clothing, objects) stand for and convey ideas that are important to us and to those we know. As Geertz (1973) pointed out, "Small facts speak to large issues" (p. 23). Concern for nonverbal behavior does not imply ignoring verbal behavior, for it is partially through verbal descriptions of what occurred and what it meant to the participants that we come to understand nonverbal behavior. However, language is notoriously slippery, easily permitting slightly different interpretations by each of the participants. It is harder for material culture to be so slippery; generally an object, a particular food, or an item of clothing is either present or not, the mere presence or absence conveying meaning.[3]

People create social meanings even for the most minor details, for "Making 'meaning' is not an optional activity in which persons sometimes engage; it is part of what it means to be a human being" (Pearce, 1989, p. 65). The attention to detail in planning a wedding is generally quite extreme, even to discussions of exactly what color nail polish the bride will wear (e.g., in the film *Steel Magnolias* an otherwise reasonable bride fusses endlessly about matching the color of fabric to flowers to nail polish, complaining about even a slight discrepancy). Because, on this one occasion, even minor details are the topic of especially close consideration, weddings are particularly well-suited to the study of meanings as created through physical details.

THE CONNECTIONS BETWEEN THE INDIVIDUAL
AND THE LARGER GROUP OR SOCIETY

This relationship can be studied in any context where some individual statement or display draws heavily on societal expectations, or where the individual acts out a particular societal role. Weddings require particular social roles of participants, and they are sufficiently common that most of us have been involved in the organization of at least one, either peripherally or as a major participant. We act by turns as interpreters of the discourse of others in the society or as producers of discourse ourselves for others (Greimas, 1987). This is true whether the topic under consideration is rituals such as weddings, or less formal examples of text such as conversations. We learn first from interpreting what others do and later contribute what we have done to the range of the possible, for the potential social roles dictated are not as rigid as they might initially appear. Each couple, in designing their own wedding, contributes something new and unique (for no two weddings are ever identical) to the larger societal expectations. They take what they understand to be the norms of the groups within which they function, revise as necessary, and introduce the revised versions back into the larger society. This characteristic of weddings, that no two are ever quite identical, is not unique to this ritual; Tambiah (1985) pointed out that "no one performance of a rite, however rigidly prescribed, is exactly the same as another performance" (p. 125).

Each individual simultaneously draws on and expands the societal norms, contributing their originality to the group's traditions. This is true of any behavior in any context, but it is particularly evident in large, organized, ritual behavior such as weddings, which we consider to be monolithic until we attend to the details and discover considerable discrepancy. Many potential topics of investigation are culture-specific, but this is not an issue for weddings, because so many cultures not only have them but would recognize each other's elaborate inventions as variants of wedding. In this way we can consider the wedding each one of us designs as our contribution to a single, continuing global conversation. (This is another reason why weddings are important to study—there are few enough events comparable around the globe.) As participants, our goal is to contribute to and continue the human conversation; as analysts, our goal is to record and understand it.

THE CONNECTIONS BETWEEN CULTURE AND COMMUNICATION

Although this can be studied in any context, for our culture always influences our communication choices, it is most evident when cultures overlap, and influence one another, as on occasions when people of different cultural backgrounds come together. For me, this is the central issue in the study of intercultural communication, but one that is often skirted (Leeds-Hurwitz, 1992). In communication, as in anthropology and sociology, until recently it was common to study each nation, each ethnic group, each race, apart from others, an isolated unit. This is now changing, and it has become more common to study the combination of a wide variety of types of groups, and their mutual influences on each other. It is less surprising that this shift has occurred than that it took so long.

There has been a recent push for research combining the study of the influence of culture with the study of interpersonal communication or social interaction in general (see Carbaugh, 1990, and Cooley, 1983, among others), a push that is long overdue. As Edward Sapir (1949) pointed out many years ago, "The true locus of culture is in the interactions of specific individuals" (p. 515), so we should base our discussions of the abstract concept culture on observations of actual behavior.

THE CONNECTIONS BETWEEN TRADITION (CONTINUITY)
AND CREATIVITY (CHANGE)

Although the social world appears as something real, existing in its current form for others as well as for us, it is in fact built out of our own actions and those of many others. Every time people act, they contribute to either the continuity of old traditions or the creation of new traditions (or, often, simultaneously to both). This can be studied in any context, for we are always caught between what has occurred in the past and what we will do in the future. It is especially important in a context in which the forces for continuity are confronted by forces requiring the creation of something new and different. Studying a topic that recurs from generation to generation and interviewing several generations lead to the study of the connections between generations, parental influences on children, and influences of grandparents on their grandchildren, all of which contribute to the study of the tension between tradition and change.[4]

By their very nature, weddings imply a tension between the wishes of the extended family and the wishes of the bride and groom, when the family leans toward tradition (as a demonstration that the couple now joins the ranks of prior couples) and the bride and groom lean toward the unique (as a demonstration of their singularity). It makes sense that the couple wants to do something new and different—they see themselves as unique and wish to make that evident to all. The question remains, why do the families wish to see them do something traditional? One answer would be that because the society exists before the individual and because the family members will have been to many weddings before this one, they expect (and find it easier to cope with) something familiar. As Hsu (1985) pointed out: "If everyone acts as individualized individuals, no society is possible. If everyone acts in complete conformity with others, there will be no differences between human beings and bees. Human ways of life are obviously somewhere in between these extremes" (p. 25). There are many contexts of interaction in which participants attempt to design a path somewhere between chaos and bees; weddings are simply the topic under analysis here.

It is an interesting point that just as the bride and groom prepare to change their identity from child to spouse, of necessity moving symbolically if not physically away from their parents in the process, a wedding (especially a large, elaborate, expensive one) actually emphasizes and even often increases their dependence on their parents, at least temporarily. One underlying reason for many of the conflicts between generations is the simultaneous but contradictory requirements of a wedding. Although generally the first major public event the bride and groom will orchestrate as a couple, at the same time it is also the last occasion over which their parents are likely to have substantial control. Yet the willingness of the bride and groom to hold a formal event for their wedding with their extended families present, in and of itself, regardless of any specific decisions made, stands as evidence of family continuity.

At the same time, marrying someone out of the group, the case by definition in any intercultural wedding, can be understood to imply a rejection of the parents by the child. This explains why so many parents are unhappy about intercultural weddings. Intercultural weddings are especially threatening to parents because they imply a rejection of the current self, the one learned from parents, and acceptance of a new and different self. If weddings and other rituals serve as identity markers for community members (Connerton, 1989), intercultural weddings serve notice that the former identity no longer has the same boundaries, the same integrity of structure, but will now mix with the identity of another group. Intercultural weddings are thus often taken by extended family members as indicative of identity confusion rather than confirmation of identity.

Orchestrating a major celebration is an intensely creative act, requiring much knowledge of the past in order to recreate it anew for the present (for creativity does not come from nowhere, but provides variations of the expected). We need more studies of cultural creativity of this sort, so we can learn how social actors manipulate what they have experienced in the past in order to create a new present (Leeds-Hurwitz & Sigman with Sullivan, 1995). Culture is often assumed to be static, yet it is actually dynamic, always in a state of flux. Each wedding provides an opportunity for a particular couple to "talk back" to their own traditions, to make their own unique contribution to the cultural dialogue. All traditions are open to change by all participants; this change also can be described as cultural creativity. By their nature, intercultural weddings *require* some adaptation of cultural norms, for what is normal for one party is not normal for the other, and so they are a particularly valuable research topic for the study of creativity in culture.

THE CONNECTIONS BETWEEN PROCESS AND PRODUCT

The study of how any particular product is produced through a sometimes long and difficult process requires the choice of a topic resulting in the creation of a product of some sort. Social products have no less reality than physical products.[5] That is to say, an evening of dinner and conversation may not leave much in the way of a physical structure for later analysis, but it exists and has an impact on our ideas and behaviors, thus we treat it as a concrete thing; currently we have the technology to record it if we so choose, making it yet more tangible. A wedding, as a large event put on display for an audience, is such a social product preceded by a lengthy period of organizational process. Because they are major rituals in our lives, weddings are deliberately planned, and most people can clearly remember the process as well as being able to document the product (through photographs or videotapes). Weddings thus provide a good opportunity to study a single phenomenon as both process and product.

Bourdieu (1990a) demonstrated another sense of the connection between process and product. As with all rituals, weddings change the primary participants in critical ways:

> Social functions are social fictions. And the rites of institution *create* the person they institute as king, knight, priest or professor by forging his social image, fashioning the representation that he can and must give as a moral person, that is, as a plenipotentiary, representative or spokesman of a group. But they also create him in another sense. By giving him a name, a title, which defines, institutes, and constitutes him, they summon him to become what he is, or rather, what he has to be; they order him to *fulfill* his function, to take his place in the game, in the fiction, to play the game, to act out the function. (p. 195)

Weddings make certain requirements of the bride and groom, changing them in particular ways merely by their participation.

In the field of Communication there has been a recent shift from a focus on product to an emphasis on process. Certainly when the topic is an aspect of social interaction, it is generally far more important to study how that interaction happened than to study the end product alone. Hobart (1990) referred to the desire to freeze the society under study as a "cryogenic trend," a marvelous metaphor (p. 314). And Hastrup (1989) pointed out that: "History is always in the making. Individual actions either reproduce or transform the structure of the social space" (p. 227). The combination of the two is actually most significant: We study what is stable (structure, product) because that is what we can most readily perceive as a way of getting at what we most want to study, that which is unstable (process), and nearly invisible.

By their very nature, intercultural weddings require of their designers more conscious, reflexive thought than monocultural weddings. Whereas it is possible for brides and grooms who come from the same traditions to take their decisions for granted, assuming they convey no significant information, intercultural couples know better. They know there are multiple possibilities, and they know they have to choose from between them, and they know whatever they do will be assumed to have significance. Just as any event, any ritual, is a story the participants tell about themselves, so an intercultural wedding is a jointly constructed story designed by the bride and groom to convey information about who they are, how they see themselves, and how they wish others to see them.

THE CONNECTIONS BETWEEN SOCIAL INTERACTION AND MEDIATED INTERACTION

We live in a world populated by other people with whom we interact, as well as by various forms of media (books, newspapers, magazines, television, films, radio, and the Internet), which influence those interactions. There are many studies of face-to-face communication, as of media, but there are few combining these interests into a single study, despite the fact that such a combination makes sense.[6] And yet the same people are influenced by other individuals and media products both. When a couple has a videotape made of their wedding, and photographs taken, and then use those materials as indices of the event (small pieces of the past that are brought into the present), they are making no distinction between media products and social interactions; both impact their lives. As people use both together, researchers must study both together. And because those who plan weddings have not only attended prior weddings but seen additional variants on television and in films and read about them in books and magazines (and, now, likely surfed the internet for additional information), we cannot ignore those additional resources.

HOW CONFLICTS ARE RESOLVED THROUGH THE ACHIEVEMENT OF CONSENSUS

Because we are all individuals, what we want is not always the same, leading to inevitable conflicts, small or large. We generally manage to achieve some sort of resolution, to reach consensus at least with those we consider to be part of our own group. Conflicts are inevitable in planning weddings, if only because they require so many logistical decisions and encourage the input of so many separate opinions (from bride and groom, two families, two sets of friends, all the wedding specialists, etc.). As Whitney (1990) suggested with only mild exaggeration, "Anyone who survives planning a wedding with a sense of humor intact and a new spouse in tow could take a respectable crack at negotiating peace in the middle East" (p. 22).

When conflicts occur in planning a wedding, their resolution is imperative. If conflicts are not resolved the wedding is usually canceled or postponed, so it can safely be assumed that for any wedding actually held, at least temporary resolutions to all conflicts were successfully achieved. Because this pressure to resolve difficulties is necessary for holding the ritual itself rather than from any outside agent, weddings are particularly valuable as sites to study conflict resolution.

Fights about planning weddings are expected. Intercultural weddings are particularly difficult in terms of the number of conflicts they engender, for "Parents of intermarriers are often puzzled and hurt by what they see in their children's marriage as a rejection of their own values and traditions" (Mayer, 1985, p. 8). Yet the experience provides a valuable lesson, for it serves as the basis for future conflict resolution for the couple and in their dealings with extended family members. Speaking of interfaith marriages, Schneider (1989) suggested "planning the wedding ceremony ... can serve as the emblem of how well the couple are able to deal with their disparate religious traditions" (p. 134). It is easiest to avoid or resolve disputes when the individuals concerned share a large number of expectations. Intercultural weddings, of course, frequently involve the combination of families with widely divergent expectations.

Berger and Kellner (1964) pointed out that "sufficient similarity in the biographically accumulated stocks of experience ... facilitate the described reality-constructing process" (p. 67). In other words, it is easier to establish a relationship when the individuals concerned share a large number of prior experiences and thus expectations. Again, this implies intercultural weddings will be particular interesting research sites, for they frequently involve the simultaneous display of different social identities. The bride would normally make choices common to her family, and the groom would normally make choices common to his; when these conflict, decisions must be made as to which choices will take priority. That weddings mark the union not of two individuals only but of two families is quite clear. The wedding is the beginning point of the marriage, thus choices made in planning intercultural weddings often loom quite large, for they can be assumed to prefigure choices made later in the marriage. Varro (1988) commented on the value of intercultural marriages, suggesting that the resulting families are likely to be capable of "efficiently counteracting rigid ethnocentric or nationalistic tendencies" (p. 186). This may be one reason why the children of intercultural unions so often marry interculturally themselves.

THE CONNECTIONS BETWEEN PRIVATE IDEAS AND PUBLIC DISPLAYS

For the majority of our lives we are accepted as private individuals, but on a few occasions we are put (or put ourselves) on public display. This is sometimes referred to as "the constitution of the public self" (Lessl, 1993).[7] What we do in private is often unplanned, but we grant greater consideration to what occurs in public. A wedding permits the bride and groom to deliberately construct the public image they wish to portray before their friends and extended family.

For most occasions our familiarity with group expectations remains a private matter, but weddings require that the bride and groom publicly demonstrate their knowledge of the form, as well as their intended allegiance to the various groups (national, ethnic, racial, religious, etc.), holding an interest in their development and future membership. As with other public events, weddings are carefully planned in advance, consciously given a particular structure and design, thus they are particularly valuable as deliberate statements of intent: "As the flow of living so often is not, public events are put together to communicate comparatively well-honed messages" (Handelman, 1990, p. 15). Researchers spend a great deal of time studying unconscious social structure when studying mundane examples of social interaction; it would be foolish to ignore carefully constructed messages, such as rituals, which can be even more revealing.

Weddings provide an unusual combination of the public and the private; they establish a new private relationship between two people through an initial public display. How we make ideas visible, how we take something quite elusive and bring it physically and literally into interaction, is one topic of this study, leading to questions about how we demonstrate our social allegiances through the attribution of conventional meanings to physical objects (especially foods, clothing, and objects).

THE CONNECTIONS BETWEEN THE SACRED AND THE SECULAR

This implies study of a topic having both sacred (religious) elements as well as secular (nonreligious, everyday) elements. Weddings have traditionally been strongly grounded in religion, and still generally have at least a minimal component of religion included. The actual speech act producing the shift from two individuals to one couple is most frequently uttered or sanctioned by a religious representative. At the same time, weddings generally incorporate secular elements, such as receptions, dances, and dinners. Often the couple has more control over the secular elements, but often the sacred elements are granted greater significance, by others if not by the bride and groom.

Traditionally wedding rituals were completely under the control of a religious representative (priest, minister, rabbi, etc.). Vows, as well as the majority of the spoken elements of the ritual (and often the musical elements) were simply proscribed; no choice was given to the couple. But this rigidity causes impossible problems for intercultural couples; clearly one cannot follow both a Catholic and a Lutheran, or both a Methodist and a Jewish, ceremony, these being distinctly at odds. Many religious leaders recognize the problem and have loosened their control considerably in the last few decades. It is likely that intercultural weddings are one reason why, although unlikely they are the primary reason. Most couples today report going through a process of negotiation with their officiant, who often begins by presenting a series of alternatives (this set of vows or that wording, this reading or that, this prayer or that). Couples who are permitted no say in elements of great significance to them will often change officiants rather than comply in uttering words that they do not believe. A surprising number of officiants available today do not even require the mention of God in the ceremony, surely the minimal religious element in the Judeo-Christian tradition. And a surprising number are now willing to co-officiate at interfaith weddings, recognizing the disparate needs of the families for religious sanction of the union.

The vast majority of communicative events to be studied do not incorporate sacred elements, only mundane secular ones, and so this pair of terms will not be relevant to analysis of many events, intercultural or otherwise. But there is a strong resurgence of adherence to religion in the United States today, albeit with a difference from a generation ago (more likely nondenominational churches than the traditional set, and often with an expectation of more room for negotiation over details of ritual than a prior generation even thought possible). Given this, it is surely important that at least some communication scholars spend time analyzing events occurring within a religious framework.

* * *

Taken together these are the underlying topics of concern driving the research reported in this book. As they are my starting point, it may be of value to set them forth openly. Together they provide a set of lenses with which to view a complex interaction such as a wedding; each illuminates a specific aspect of the event. Clearly I have not fully answered all of the questions provoked by any one of these concerns. Others may yet decide to answer those matters remaining unresolved even at the end of my research, whether with regard to weddings, or other types of events, does not really matter. As abiding concerns of many researchers interested in the social world, they will remain long after any one research project is completed.

NOTES

1. A previous version of this list of my theoretical concerns was published as Leeds-Hurwitz (1998). As is probably the case for most researchers, many of my larger underlying concerns remain the same, although I continue to conduct different research investigations in the attempt to answer them.
2. Although not traditionally stated as a central topic within interpersonal communication research specifically (which has tended to be more quantitative, and thus not particularly amenable to the more subtle study of meaning), there have been calls "to examine *a variety of meanings* over time, relationships, and situations and to examine *how meanings are created and sustained through interaction*" (Stamp, Vangelisti, & Knapp, 1994, p. 170).
3. There is a new effort to attend to material culture in the study of social relationships (i.e., Brown, Altman, & Werner, 1991), perhaps for some of these same reasons.
4. A variety of authors have emphasized the need of families for weddings and marriages. For example:

    The fact is that the family, any family, has a major stake in perpetuating itself, and in order to do so it must unrelentingly push the institutions that preserve it—the institution of marriage especially, but also the institution of heterosexual love, which, if all goes the way the family would have it go, culminates in marriage, children, and enhanced family stability. (Stone, 1988, p. 50)

Similarly, Goody (1990) pointed out that overall, a wedding "remains recruitment for continuity, the employment of strategies that include the provision of heirs" (p. 471). Looking specifically at the influence of grandparent–grandchild interactions, Epstein (1978) said: "It is the grandparents moreover who provide the necessary links between the generations, past and present. They are the symbols of continuity" (p. 156). Is it any wonder, then, that grandparents typically express concern about intercultural marriages?

5. Geertz (1971) pointed out that "meaningful forms ... have as good a claim to public existence as horses, stones, and trees, and are therefore as susceptible to objective investigation and systematic analysis as these apparently harder realities" (p. x). See Berger and Luckmann (1967) for the classic statement on social constructionism.

6. One exception is Lum (1996).

7. See also Gamarnikow, Morgan, Purvis, and Taylorson (1983), and Rawlins (1998), on the relationship between public and private.

Methodological Appendix

In beginning any research project, a choice of methods must be made. What sorts of data will be collected and the related question of what sorts of analysis will be performed, are critical decisions for any study. Because the logic of the choices made is as important as the choices themselves, I try to explain not only what I have done, but some of the reasoning behind the choices.

DATA COLLECTION

To me, theory should determine method (Leeds-Hurwitz, 1989). One chooses a theoretical framework that makes sense, and only after chooses a method to investigate a question of interest, given that theoretical orientation. Although this is a book about weddings, I did not begin with an interest in weddings, but an interest in questions of identity and culture. The second step was determining that weddings were a fruitful site for analysis of those topics. My goal has been to use the small details of wedding ceremonies as a way to understand larger issues, most particularly the construction of identity and of culture. This means that in order to understand how these large issues are brought into interaction, I needed to first, choose a context in which these were critical (intercultural weddings), and second, examine the specific ways in which particular individuals make these larger concepts an integral part of interaction for themselves and others (how multiple contradictory identities are displayed simultaneously in an intercultural event). If my analysis contributes to our understanding of even one of the large themes listed in the theoretical appendix, then I have been successful.

As a result of my theoretical concerns, my primary method of choice was the ethnography of communication.[1] As Sigman (1998) explained,

> ethnography comprises a belief that the social world should be approached naturalistically, in terms of behavior that members of a community themselves typically engage in and witness; holistically, with an understanding that any datum can be situated and understood within more encompassing streams of behavior (contexts); and emically, so that the meanings of behavior that are most relevant are those that are lived and generated by the members themselves, not by the researchers. (p. 354)

I would agree. The heart of ethnography is generally understood to be participant observation, but the matter is actually more complex than that; ethnography combines a multitude of approaches to data collection, all designed to complement one another in the effort to discover patterns of meaning particular behaviors have for the participants. Each project thus uses a slightly different combination, depending on what seems most likely to have value in that context.[2]

Specifically in this study ethnography included:

* Participant observation (being present at weddings);
* Interviews of participants in weddings, both major and minor (before and after weddings; brides, grooms, their parents, siblings, guests); interviews were conducted face-to-face, over the telephone, and even through electronic mail (e-mail), as was convenient to those I wanted to reach; this included having my students conduct additional interviews in order to expand the database;[3]
* Viewing photographs and videotapes of weddings, accompanied by descriptions from the participants as to what was occurring;
* Interviews of religious specialists, those who conduct weddings (especially those who often conduct interfaith weddings, because most religious specialists will not);
* Interviews of secular specialists involved in the design of weddings (e.g., photographers, caterers, florists, dressmakers); some of these specialists were interviewed by my students;
* Watching films and television shows that included wedding scenes, both fictional and actual, particularly those whose major emphasis is the wedding, in order to determine what images are available from popular culture as the bride and groom make their decisions; some of these were reported on by my students;
* Reading fiction that included wedding scenes, again particularly those works emphasizing weddings;
* Reading magazines and other professional literature (brochures, advertisements) aimed at those who plan to become brides and grooms;
* Reading wedding announcements and special sections of newspapers devoted to coverage of weddings.[4]

Ethnography is uniquely suited to emphasize process over product, for, as opposed to quantitative approaches, which emphasize the analysis of products, "qualitative approaches examine meaning production as a *process*" (Jensen, 1991, p. 4).

Overall, I've been quite lucky in my choice of research topic: people who have intercultural weddings seem to have already committed themselves to helping others understand and cope appropriately with cultural differences and therefore see this research as valuable—so I was able to be quite open about what I was studying without causing problems. As a result, some of the difficulties in conducting research noted by other researchers (e.g., Shaffir, 1998) are irrelevant for this topic. However, the main task and primary difficulty of ethnographic research is always the same, regardless of content. The researcher must incorporate multiple disparate stories into a single coherent narrative that is, in all major ways, true to them all, providing original insights unavailable to the individuals involved in any one story, but that become apparent when the set is viewed as a whole. Ifekwunigwe (1999) put it especially gracefully: "the process of writing an ethnography is akin to quilt-making. I have all of these seemingly disparate bits and pieces in the form of participants' testimonies, my own cumulative scratchings, as well as different theoretical strands and I wish to stitch all of them together to form a coherent pattern" (p. 57). Just as I prefer the metaphor of tapestry to that of quilt in the body of this text, however, so do I prefer it here: I would rather think that I have combined the various stories my informants have told into a single coherent pattern, simultaneously maintaining the validity of each one, and yet demonstrating the similarities in structure and design among them.

No attempt has been made to include some sort of random sample of participants. Given my topic, that would have been completely inappropriate. When studying the least common type of marriage, it is impossible to begin with a large population and draw a scientifically random sample. Luckily, my concern here is not with statistical validity but rather with social construction of meaning, and every event demonstrates this. Therefore I simply told everyone I knew what I was studying, and many people suggested friends, relatives, neighbors, colleagues, and students who were appropriate. This is technically termed the "snowball" technique. Intercultural weddings are not the norm (and therefore quite memorable), but neither are they terribly difficult to locate. A further benefit was that these personal introductions helped me in many cases obtain far more detailed and thoughtful answers to my questions than I likely would have gotten otherwise.

Of all these aspects of my research, one of the most illuminating has been viewing photographs and videotapes of weddings and then discussing the events with the bride and groom (and other participants as available).[5] The combination of viewing visual images and then discussing them with the participants first prompted questions that would be appropriate to ask about each specific wedding and a possibility of getting answers from those who knew them. As Charsley (1991) discovered in his research, wedding albums "provided a focused and highly edited image. They might well be all that survived to the future of the huge effort of organising [sic], dressing, and presentation put into creating the evanescent moments of the wedding" (p. 145). This was true of my American, as it was for his Scottish, informants. We learn what weddings are from our parents' descriptions of their weddings, from attending the weddings of cousins, and from helping to plan the weddings of our siblings. Wedding photos can serve as a useful resource for documenting the changes over generations, between siblings, and across relatives.

However, the traditional subjects included in wedding photographs actually have changed over time. Wells (1990) described a photographer who

> spends nearly as much time shooting the activity before the ceremony and reception—the florists at work, the hair stylists and makeup artists primping the bride, the fathers waiting—as he does at the festivities themselves. "At most of these weddings," Mr. Reggie says, "the preparation is a monumental task. People have spent months on it, and I need to acknowledge it. It also gives a sense of chronology to the event." (p. 59)

One of the solutions to this apparent discrepancy is to distinguish between a photo's content (what is visible in it), its referent (what it is of), and its context (where it appears and what use is made of it; Ball & Smith, 1992, p. 20; see also Hodge & Kress, 1988, p. 228). Another is to separate what is recorded on the photographs (traditional images of the major parts of the event) from what is recorded on videotape (which may be a more casual record, including even images of the photographers chasing the bride and groom to catch the critical moments, and explicit comments checking if interesting side-comments were caught by the videographer, as was the case for Couple 13 among others). Denzin (1991) suggested that "the metaphor of the dramaturgical society ... has now become interactional reality" (p. x). This is particularly true when people create visual records of themselves, for their own later consumption, and is evidence of the impact the media have had on interaction.

Following the text metaphor of behavior, photographs and videotapes made of interaction have been described as metaphorical "inscriptions." Myerhoff (1992) pointed out their value: "A social event read as a text is slippery, as though the words flew off the page before we could finish reading them. An 'inscribed' social text is easier to read, however. Like an object, it sits still while we look at it; it allows us to re-present it to others" (p. 268).

Recently it has become common to film actual weddings for cable television (as on the program A *Wedding Story*) and to post descriptions of actual weddings on the Internet (as on the site theknot.com). I have assumed these are accurate representations, as I have with newspaper reports of weddings, although I have not granted these stories much prominence, as I did not have the same degree of access to the participants (and partly due to a lingering concern about the possibility that they may not accurately represent what actually occurred).

Weddings as represented in actual photographs and videotapes of real events are different from the fictional weddings represented in commercially made films, or television shows. And yet, there is also something to be learned from fictional representations. Metz (1974) made the generally accepted point that "like all the arts, and because it is itself an art, the cinema is one-way communication" (p. 74). This seems intuitively obvious and, for the most part, is probably correct; as an audience member, I cannot convey my responses to the characters on screen, and they cannot respond to me in turn. Yet I want to suggest something counterintuitive. The most recent work in discourse analysis, and in language and social interaction more generally, suggests that conversations and interactions are most appropriately understood to extend well beyond their obvious boundaries; what we say at one time with a friend expands on previous conversations, and so, in a sense, all these conversations are part of one very long but sporadic conversation; relationships continue despite the occasional absences of their participants.[6] In keeping with this, one part of what I have studied might usefully be called the response (albeit delayed) of a viewer to the presumed one-way communication a film provides. Thus, preparing your own wedding can be seen as an answer to various prior statements (not only cinema weddings, of course, but also weddings described in newspaper articles, and in how-to books by authors like Martha Stewart, in fictional accounts presented in novels, etc.). In this view, every wedding is an answer to the same question: how to mark the ceremonial joining of two discrete individuals. And every wedding takes into account whatever prior weddings, real or fictional, have come to the attention of the bride and groom, increasing the complexity of the analysis.

In addition to concern for the face-to-face interactions between bride and groom as they plan the wedding, I developed specific questions about the interplay between mediated communication and face-to-face interaction based on my first set of interviews, and so reading some of the same books, magazines, and newspapers as those I interviewed, and watching some of the same television shows and films, was imperative. Some of my informants were able to be quite explicit about the impact these forms had on their ideas, as when the bride of Couple 1 said: "It was really interesting to me how many preconceived notions I had, like from TV and stuff" or when the groom of Couple 88 pointed out that his understanding of the meaning of the wedding bands they exchanged was influenced by a film. Asked what it meant to him, he answered: "circle of trust—the ring—it's from a movie, but it's true in a sense." Although newspaper coverage tends to document real, although unusual, weddings, and the magazines aimed at brides document all the details to consider when planning a wedding, and present widely available options, films, television shows, and books tend to primarily document fictional weddings. There has been discussion in the communication literature about the appropriateness and value of analyzing fiction sources.[7] My own position is that fictional sources should be used as one of many resources, since they are available to the social actors we study, but they cannot substitute for observation of actual behavior. Fiction is rarely an accurate depiction of reality, but it can contribute to our image of reality (for example, enough images of long white wedding gowns can convince a couple that they are the norm, whether or not they are truly an essential component of a wedding).[8]

It seems rare that any single film would be directly responsible for the final decisions made in any one wedding, and there has been no attempt here to demonstrate this sort of direct impact. But I do assume that the media create what might be termed "a repertoire of knowledge and expectations" (Jules-Rosette, 1975, p. 21), that is, a body of potential models taken into consideration by anyone planning a wedding. Among other reasons for choosing ethnography, it is an approach particularly sensitive to connections (Bird, 1992), an important factor when attempting to consider mutual influences of media and face-to-face interaction.

ANALYSIS

As to exactly what I did with the data I collected, I tried to *find patterns* in what I learned, as ethnographers always do. Geertz (1973) suggested "Analysis is the sorting out of structures of signification and determining their social ground and import" (p. 9); I agree. In ethnography, data collection stops not at a predetermined point but at the point when new data does not reveal any new patterns because, as Fetterman (1989) recommended: "When the same specific pattern of behavior emerges over and over again, the fieldworker should move on to a new topic for observation and detailed exploration" (p. 20). I knew it was finally time to stop when the multitude of pieces of information I had collected over many years seemed to fit together, and new information fit into that same pattern rather than requiring a change in the analysis.

At present, there is great concern with the concept of reflexivity (the ability to step back and reflect upon one's own role in an interaction) among those who use ethnographic methods. In particular, there has been considerable interest in the idea that the researcher is responsible for much of the shape of what those studied present for analysis. It has been my assumption in this research that rituals such as weddings, which exist for their own purposes far more than for the researcher, are less liable to influence by the questions of the researcher than other, more mundane events. This is one reason that I interviewed most people after the wedding was conducted, lest I influence the design of the weddings described to me through my questions as they were being put together. I learned early on that couples interviewed prior to their wedding often solicited my advice—a request I had not expected and found difficult to cope with as a researcher. It seemed unfair not to answer their questions and share whatever knowledge I had gained, yet I did not want the weddings described in this book to be partially of my own making, and so I stopped interviewing people prior to the wedding. Also, interviewing people after their wedding permitted the inclusion of videotapes and photographs, none of which were prepared by, or for, me. As they were prepared for, or by, the participants of the event they served as a good guide to what those I studied considered significant, not what I as an outsider gave prominence.

On very rare occasions, I offered advice when it had not been explicitly requested, out of a feeling that someone was treading on dangerous ground and it was ethically inappropriate not to warn them of danger I could see but they could not. Once I talked to the mother of a Christian bride whose fiancé was Jewish, who had found a congregation that was both Jewish and Christian to teach her about Jewish traditions prior to her marriage. After some confusion, because I could not imagine what this group could be, and she thought it should be obvious, it turned out that the group was Messianic Jews, a Christian sect not recognized as Jewish by Jews because they maintain all the central Christian beliefs. When I asked what the fiancé's reaction had been to this, I was told he didn't know yet, it was to be a surprise. I felt obligated to warn the mother that this was not likely to be well-received by the fiancé and his family, and that her daughter needed to do some additional research before she should assume she really understood the basic tenets of Judaism (Couple 70). That couple does not figure elsewhere in this book as a result of my intervention.

I have respected the direction of the Human Subjects Review Committee at the University of Wisconsin-Parkside and worked hard to ensure the privacy of those I observed or interviewed. At first, I intended to use pseudonyms, but found it more comfortable to simply refer to the bride and groom in their social roles, a technique frequently followed by anthropologists and sociologists though less often by those in communication. Participants have had a chance to see what I am using of our conversations or my observations of their behavior, and a chance to object to inclusion of anything that seemed too personal, inappropriate, or inaccurate. (In fact, this book took much longer to prepare due to the need to track down people who had moved, given that my research extended more than 10 years, but this step was important.) Kaminsky (1992) described my feelings as well as his own when he said: "While the informant is not the immediate auditor, she at least must be able to overhear the discourse without feeling demeaned by it" (p. 89). Although there are now a few stories that various relatives may not have heard previously, and may not appreciate, at least those who are most centrally concerned have had the opportunity to tell me a detail not noticed at the time, or have second thoughts about making particular stories public. In fact, most people were remarkably accepting of what I wrote about them, requesting few if any changes, and all were minor revisions of a few words. Only one asked to be omitted from the final book, having had second thoughts about making private matters public.

ESTABLISHING BOUNDARIES

In addition to choosing a method, it is important to outline the basic borders of the study, especially one as large as this. There are several issues to be considered: the boundaries of the topic, of the event, and the role of the analyst.

What Are the Boundaries of the Topic Covered Here?

Any material pertaining to weddings, specifically intercultural weddings, that contributed new information was included. The study of weddings, like that of other topics, can be either primarily diachronic (historical, emphasizing development and change over time) or synchronic (focused on the present, considering the relationship between component parts). This study is more synchronic than diachronic, although, like all research, it includes elements of both. Long-term familiarity with wedding traditions, both within particular families and in various media presentations, implies a diachronic approach. Experiences of others' weddings go side by side with the planning of one's own; experiences through the media are a major resource as well. Yet the emphasis on some understanding of the different components of a wide number of roughly contemporary weddings, generally occurring in the same country, means that the study is appropriately described as primarily synchronic.

What Are the Boundaries of the Event Included Here?

My focus has been primarily on the wedding ceremony, but this event has flexible boundaries depending on the particular couple studied (most broadly, starting with stories about one's parents' wedding, attending the weddings of friends and family members, or the planning of one's own wedding; most obviously including all of the major ritual events related to the wedding, from dinner with extended family members the night before, to seeing the bride and groom off on a honeymoon; ending finally with the use of photos and videotapes to remember the event in later years).

Several questions related to determining the boundaries of the event were considered. Among them are the following:

* What are the major associated rituals? For example: wedding classes, engagement party, bachelor party, shower, rehearsal dinner, honeymoon, all of which were considered to some extent as they were described by participants as important.
* What are the major social codes of importance? The major elements emphasized here were food, clothing, and objects, with some attention paid also to language and music.

- What are the key symbols included in the wedding? For language: vows; for clothing: wedding dress; for objects: wedding rings; for food: wedding cake.
- Who are the major participants? At the very least, these would include the bride, groom, and officiant, and anyone else directly involved in the ceremony.
- Who are the major ritual specialists? Included would be religious specialists who serve as advisors and officiants, but also secular specialists: caterers, dressmakers, florists, photographers, jewelers, and wedding planners, among others.

Because each of these questions has a different answer for each couple, they cannot be answered definitively for all weddings, or even all weddings described in these pages. But these are the questions that need to be answered for each wedding as a basic outline of material to be included.

What Is the Role of the Analyst?

It is now widely recognized that researchers influence the behavior they attempt to study, whether or not they intend to do so. One reason for choosing a public event as a topic of investigation is that it minimizes the influence of the researcher; certainly discussion of the meaning of the use of flowers at a wedding that has already occurred will be influenced by the questions posed by the interviewer, but the choice of the flowers themselves cannot be. Bourdieu (1990) warned that "One should not be misled by the language of analysis or by the very words of the informants, who were chosen for their lucidity and provoked into lucidity by questioning" (p. 160). If I have in fact provoked those interviewed into lucidity, it is no more than they were capable of; these are their own ideas, only perhaps ones they had not previously thought to make explicit. Certainly, as analyst of the data and as sole author of this book, I have had a large role in the way in which the data are presented, in the new shapes made up of disparate bits and pieces of information from a wide range of weddings, and I would never dispute that. But it seems to me that the larger issues (of cultural creativity, of effectively using traditions of the past to establish a new basis for the future, of the need to display identity—or identities—in a concrete fashion) belong in an important sense to those I observed and interviewed, rather than to me. They are the ones who needed to combine old ceremonies in new ways in order to lend legitimacy to the joining of individuals from different communities; I only gave them the opportunity to describe what they were already doing.

Barre Toelken (1998) suggested that: "In the final analysis, we must recognize that it is not just a polite gesture to assure our informant-colleagues that they have a voice in what we are doing: we are obligated to listen to that voice when they use it" (p. 389; see also Coffey, 1999). My focus in this study gradually changed over time, due in large part to the comments of those I interviewed. Originally, I intended to craft a book that would mesh perfectly with my *Semiotics and Communication: Signs, Codes, Cultures*, with a heavy emphasis on the key symbols used in three social codes, as originally presented there: food, clothing, and objects. That might make the most sense from the point of view of anyone reading the two books together, but it was clear after the first dozen exchanges with informants that it just didn't make sense to them. The different codes were not separable in their minds, and so should not appear separately in my book. It was to permit at least some examples to appear in their entirety that especially interesting weddings are presented as Interludes rather than incorporated into the chapters. This unusual form of data presentation permits the reader to gain a sense of the overall design of particular weddings and breaks up the more abstract discussion provided in the more conventional chapters.

Methodology, to me, means attending to the ways one can most appropriately study a topic. Given the topics I consider the most interesting (as outlined in the Theoretical Appendix), it made the most sense to go out into the world and see what real people were doing, in interactions that matter to them. Luckily, nearly everyone of whom I asked questions was willing to spend time with me, thinking about what they had done, whether it was successful or not, and the reactions of others present at the time to what had occurred. I ended up even more convinced than I had been originally that people are enormously complex and sophisticated in their ability to do many things through interaction and that it is well worth our taking the time to stop and study what real people in the world around us are doing. We might learn something from them. I certainly have.

NOTES

1. There is a huge literature now on ethnography as a research method. Of these, a few I have found useful are: Coffey (1999), Lareau and Shultz (1996), Okely and Callaway (1992), and Smith and Kornbluth (1996). The use of ethnography as a method in the study of social relationships is quite old but has newly been discovered and advocated as invaluable by some researchers in communication (e.g., Altman, Brown, Staples, & Werner, 1992). My own training in ethnography began as an undergraduate anthropology major, continuing through graduate studies emphasizing the ethnography of communication (both in studies of that name, with Dell Hymes, and studies coming directly from anthropology, with Ray Birdwhistell, who assumed ethnography as his method of studying communication behavior, although he never gave it a specific name). Many other of my graduate professors simply took it for granted that ethnography was one of several potential methods, although this was apparently uncommon in the 1970s, at least in the field of communication. Perhaps the explanation is that I was permitted to design my own program, combining courses from multiple disciplines (anthropology, linguistics,

sociology, folklore, and education, in addition to communication) in my search for training in how to best study social interaction.

2. And, although in communication the ethnography of communication is most often considered a qualitative method, depending on the particular research question, it may incorporate quantitative methods as well. In this study, however, it did not.

3. There is now considerable literature discussing how interviews themselves are self-presentations and performances (see Matthews, 2000; and Mischler, 1986, for a beginning into that literature).

4. And, of course, reading much of the prior research on weddings (in any culture, monocultural or intercultural) and related topics, such as rituals, but this would be part of any research study, not just an ethnography of communication.

5. See Bourdieu (1990c), Mischler (1986), and Vila (2000) for interesting discussions of the use of photographs in research.

6. Sigman (1991) presented the best discussion of this.

7. Ragan and Hopper (1984) and Alberts (1986) advocated the use of fiction as a resource; Ulrich (1986) criticized it.

8. And I found reading fictional depictions of weddings to be illuminating for my own understanding. One example is Dorothy West's a lengthy description of an interracial marriage and the impact it had on extended family and friends in her 1995 novel *The Wedding*. Clearly fictional descriptions cannot replace analysis of actual events, but they can serve as helpful supplements to understanding. And when the topic of concern occurs rarely, as is the case for Black–White interracial marriages, any additional consideration can be especially useful.

References

Abrahams, R. D. (1981). Shouting match at the border: The folklore of display events. In R. Bauman, & R. D. Abrahams (Eds.), "And other neighborly names": Social process and cultural image in Texas folklore (pp. 303–321). Austin, TX: University of Texas Press.

Abrahams, R. D. (1987). An American vocabulary of celebrations. In A. Falassi (Ed.), Time out of time: Essays on the festival (pp. 173–183). Albuquerque, NM: University of New Mexico Press.

Abu-Lughod, L. (1991). Writing against culture. In R. G. Fox (Ed.), Recapturing anthropology: Working in the present (pp. 137–162). Santa Fe, NM: School of American Research Press.

Advisory Board, The President's Initiative on Race. (1998). One America in the 21st century: Forging a new future. Washington, DC: Government Printing Office.

Alba, R. D. (1990). Ethnic identity: The transformation of White America. New Haven, CT: Yale University Press.

Alba, R. D., & Golden, R. M. (1986). Patterns of ethnic marriage in the United States. Social Forces, 65(1), 202–223.

Alberts, J. K. (1986). The role of couples' conversations in relational development: A content analysis of courtship talk in Harlequin romance novels. Communication Quarterly, 34, 127–142.

Aldama, A. (1997). Visions in the four directions: Five hundred years of resistance and beyond. In W. S. Penn (Ed.), As we are now: Mixblood essays on race and identity (pp. 140–167). Berkeley, CA: University of California Press.

Allan, J., & Turner, E. (1997). The ethnic quilt: Population diversity in southern California. Northridge, CA: California State University, Northridge.

Allen, B., & Schlereth, T. (1990). Sense of place: American regional cultures. Lexington, KY: University Press of Kentucky.

Altman, I., Brown, B. B., Staples, B., & Werner, C. M. (1992). A transactional approach to close relationships: Courtship, weddings, and placemaking. In W. B. Walsh, K. H. Craik, & R. H. Price (Eds.), Person-environment psychology: Models and perspectives (pp. 193–241). Hillsdale, NJ: Lawrence Erlbaum Associates.

Amy, J., & Tolkkinen, K. (2000, November 9). Mixed reaction to marriage vote. *Mobile Register* [on-line], available: www.al.com/news/mobile/Nov2000/9-a277618a.html

Anderson, B. (1983). *Imagined communities: Reflections on the origin and spread of nationalism.* London: Verso.

Antaki, C., & Widdicombe, S. (Eds.). (1998a). *Identities in talk.* London: Sage.

Antaki, C., & Widdicombe, S. (1998b). Identity as an achievement and as a tool. In C. Antaki & S. Widdicombe (Eds.), *Identities in talk* (pp. 1–14). London: Sage.

Appadurai, A. (1996). *Modernity at large: Cultural dimensions of globalization.* Minneapolis, MN: University of Minnesota Press.

Appadurai, A. (1997). Consumption, duration, and history. In D. Palumbo-Liu & H. U. Gumbrecht (Eds.), *Streams of cultural capital* (pp. 23–45). Stanford, CA: Stanford University Press.

Appiah, K. A., & Gates, H. L., Jr. (1995). Editors' introduction: Multiplying identities, In K. A. Appiah & H. L. Gates, Jr. (Eds.), *Identities* (pp. 1–6). Chicago: University of Chicago Press.

Arboleda, T. (1998). *In the shadow of race: Growing up as a multiethnic, multicultural, and "multiracial" American.* Mahwah, NJ: Lawrence Erlbaum Associates.

Arndt, B. (2000, March 23). Aborigines lead way as mixed marriages create melting pot. *Sydney Morning Herald.* Retrieved March 23, 2000, from www.smh.com.au/0003/23/text/pageone6.html.

Austin, J. L. (1999). How to do things with words. In A. Jaworski & N. Coupland (Eds.), *The discourse reader* (pp. 63–75). London: Routledge. (Original work published 1962)

Azoulay, K. G. (1997). *Black, Jewish, and interracial: It's not the color of your skin but the race of your kin, and other myths of identity.* Durham, NC: Duke University Press.

Babcock, B. (1980). Reflexivity: Definitions and discriminations. *Semiotica, 30* (1–2), 1–14.

Bakhtin, M. (1981). Discourse in the novel. In M. Holquist (Ed.), *The dialogic imagination.* (C. Emerson & M. Holquist, Trans.). Austin, TX: University of Texas Press. (Original work published 1975)

Ball, M. S., & Smith, G. W. H. (1992). *Analyzing visual data.* Newbury Park, CA: Sage Publications.

Barbara, A. (1989). *Marriage across frontiers.* (D. E. Kennard, Trans.). Clevedon, England: Multilingual Matters. (Original work published 1987)

Barth, F. (Ed.). (1969). *Ethnic groups and boundaries: The social organization of culture difference.* Boston: Little, Brown and Company.

Bateson, M. C. (1993). Joint performance across cultures: Improvisation in a Persian garden. *Text and Performance Quarterly, 13,* 113–121.

Bauman, R. (1986). *Story, performance, and event: Contextual studies of oral narrative.* Cambridge, England: Cambridge University Press.

Bauman, R. (1989). American folklore studies and social transformation: A performance-centered perspective. *Text and Performance Quarterly, 9,* 175–184.

Bauman, R. (1992). Contextualization, tradition, and the dialogue of genres: Icelandic legends of the *Kraftaskald.* In A. Duranti & C. Goodwin (Eds.), *Rethinking context: Language as an interactive phenomenon* (pp. 125–145). Cambridge, England: Cambridge University Press.

Bauman, R., & Briggs, C. L. (1990). Poetics and performance as critical perspectives on language and social life. *Annual Review of Anthropology, 19*, 59–88.

Baumann, G. (1992). Ritual implicates 'others': Rereading Durkheim in a plural society. In D. de Coppet (Ed.), *Understanding rituals* (pp. 97–116). London: Routledge.

Baumann, G. (1999). *The multicultural riddle: Rethinking national, ethnic, and religious identities.* New York: Routledge.

Bavelas, J. B. (1995). Quantitative versus qualitative? In W. Leeds-Hurwitz (Ed.), *Social approaches to communication* (pp. 49–62). New York: Guilford Press.

Baxter, L. (1987). Symbols of relationship identity in relationship cultures. *Journal of Social and Personal Relationships, 4*, 261–280.

Baxter, L. (1998). Locating the social in interpersonal communication. In J. S. Trent (Ed.), *Communication: Views from the helm for the 21st century* (pp. 60–64). Boston: Allyn & Bacon.

Baxter, L, & Montgomery, B. M. (Eds.). (1996). *Relating: Dialogues and dialectics.* New York: Guilford.

Becker, A. L. (1984). Biography of a sentence: A Burmese proverb. In E. Bruner (Ed.), *Text, play and story: The construction and reconstruction of self and society* (pp. 135–155). Washington, DC: American Ethnological Society.

Becker, A. L., & Mannheim, B. (1995). Culture troping: Languages, codes, and texts. In B. Mannheim & D. Tedlock (Eds.), *The dialogic emergence of culture* (pp. 237–252). Urbana, IL: University of Illinois Press.

Benatar, G. (1990, June). Talking fashion: Brides from hell. *Vogue, 267.*

Benson, S. (1981). *Ambiguous ethnicity: Interracial families in London.* New York: Cambridge University Press.

Berger, P. L., & Kellner, H. (1964). Marriage and the construction of reality: An exercise in the microsociology of knowledge. *Diogenes, 46*, 1–21.

Berger, P. L., & Luckmann, T. (1967). *The social construction of reality.* New York: Doubleday Anchor.

Bernard, R. M. (1980). *The melting pot and the altar: Marital assimilation in early twentieth-century Wisconsin.* Minneapolis, MN: University of Minnesota Press.

Bird, S. E. (1992). Travels in nowhere land: Ethnography and the 'impossible' audience. *Critical Studies in Mass Communication, 9*, 250–260.

Black, A. D. (1974). *Without burnt offerings: Ceremonies of humanism.* New York: Viking Press.

Blaeser, K. (1997). On mapping and urban shamans. In W. S. Penn (Ed.), *As we are now: Mixblood essays on race and identity* (pp. 115–125). Berkeley, CA: University of California Press.

Blau, J. R. (1991). Introduction. In J. R. Blau & N. Goodman (Eds.), *Social roles and social institutions: Essays in honor of Rose Laub Coser* (pp. xiii–xxix). Boulder, CO: Westview Press.

Blu, K. L. (1996). "Where do you stay at?" Home place and community among the Lumbee. In S. Feld & K. H. Basso (Eds.), *Senses of place* (pp. 197–227). Santa Fe, NM: School of American Research Press.

Bohannan, P. (1995). *How culture works.* New York: Free Press.

Bouissac, P. (1990). The profanation of the sacred in circus clown performances. In R. Schechner & W. Appel (Eds.), *By means of performance: Intercultural studies of theatre and ritual* (pp. 194–207). Cambridge, England: Cambridge University Press.

Bourdieu, P. (1990a). *In other words: Essays towards a reflexive sociology*. Stanford, CA: Stanford University Press.

Bourdieu, P. (1990b). *The logic of practice*. (R. Nice, Trans.). Cambridge, England: Polity Press. (Original work published 1980)

Bourdieu, P. (1990c). *Photography: A middle-brow art*. Stanford, CA: Stanford University Press.

Boyer, P. (1990). *Tradition as truth and communication: A cognitive description of traditional discourse*. Cambridge, England: Cambridge University Press.

Brady, L. S. (2000, March 26). Vows: Stephanie Winston, David Wolkoff. *New York Times*, p. Y46.

Brady, L. S. (2000, April 30). Vows: Kanan Shridharani, Stephen Jacobson. *New York Times*, p. Y41.

Brady, L. S. (2000, July 23). Vows: Aaron Gooday-Ervin, Toni-Ellen Weeden. *New York Times*, p. Y34.

Brady, L. S. (2000, September 24). Vows: Christina Ha and Marcus Solis. *New York Times*, p. Y56.

Braithwaite, D. O. (1995). Ritualized embarrassment at "coed" wedding and baby showers. *Communication Reports*, 8, 145–157.

Braithwaite, D. O., Baxter, L. A., & Harper, A. M. (1998). The role of rituals in the management of the dialectical tension of 'old' and 'new' in blended families. *Communication Studies*, 49(2), 101–120.

Branham, R. J., & Pearce, W. B. (1985). Between text and context: Toward a rhetoric of contextual reconstruction. *Quarterly Journal of Speech*, 71, 19–36.

Breger, R., & Hill, R. (1998a). *Cross-cultural marriage: Identity and choice*. New York: Berg Publishers.

Breger, R., & Hill, R. (1998b). Introducing mixed marriages. In R. Breger & R. Hill (Eds.), *Cross-cultural marriage: Identity and choice* (pp. 1–32). New York: Berg Publishers.

Breuss, C. J. S., & Pearson, J. C. (1997). Interpersonal rituals in marriage and adult friendship. *Communication Monographs*, 64, 25–46.

The bride takes the cake! (1993, June 6). *The New York Times Magazine*, pp. 72–73.

Bridgwood, A. (1995). Dancing the jar: Girls' dress at Turkish Cypriot weddings. In J. B. Eicher (Ed.), *Dress and ethnicity: Change across time and space* (pp. 29–51). Oxford, England: Berg Publishers.

Briggs, C. L. (1988). *Competence in performance: The creativity of tradition in Mexicano verbal art*. Philadelphia: University of Pennsylvania Press.

Bronner, S. J. (1992a). Introduction. In S. J. Bronner (Ed.), *Creativity and tradition in folklore: New directions* (pp. 1–38). Logan, UT: Utah State University Press.

Bronner, S. J. (1992b). Elaborating tradition: A Pennsylvania-German folk artist ministers to his community. In S. J. Bronner (Ed.), *Creativity and tradition in folklore: New directions* (pp. 277–325). Logan, UT: Utah State University Press.

Brown, B. B., Altman, I., & Werner, C. M. (1991). Close relationships in the physical and social world: Dialectical and transactional analyses. *Communication Yearbook*, 15, 508–521.

Brown, C. (1994). Literary images of intercultural relationships between westerners and middle Easterners. In W. R. Johnson & D. M. Warren (Eds.), *Inside the mixed mar-*

riage: *Accounts of changing attitudes, patterns, and perceptions of cross-cultural and interracial marriages* (pp. 95–114). Lanham, MD: University Press of America.

Browne, R. B., & Marsden, M. T. (Eds.). (1994). *The cultures of celebrations*. Bowling Green, OH: Bowling Green State University Popular Press.

Browning, L. D. (1992). Lists and stories as organizational communication. *Communication Theory, 2*, 281–302.

Bruner, C. H. (1994). Cross-cultural marriage as a literary motif in African and Caribbean literature. In W. R. Johnson & D. M. Warren (Eds.), *Inside the mixed marriage*: *Accounts of changing attitudes, patterns, and perceptions of cross-cultural and interracial marriages* (pp. 81–94). Lanham, MD: University Press of America.

Bulcroft, K., Smiens, L., & Bulcroft, R. (1999). *Romancing the honeymoon*: *Consummating marriage in modern society*. Thousand Oaks, CA: Sage.

Buttny, R. (1987). Legitimation techniques for intermarriage: Accounts of motives for intermarriage from U.S. servicemen and Philippine women. *Communication Quarterly, 35*, 125–143.

Buttny, R. (1993). *Social accountability in communication*. London: Sage.

Byrne, S., & Irvin, C. L. (Eds.). (2000). *Reconcilable differences*: *Turning points in ethnopolitical conflict*. West Hartford, CT: Kumarian Press.

Camper, C. (Ed.). (1994). *Miscegenation blues*: *Voices of mixed race women*. Toronto, Canada: Sister Vision.

Carbaugh, D. (Ed.). (1990). *Cultural communication and intercultural contact*. Hillsdale, NJ: Lawrence Erlbaum Associates.

Carey, J. W. (1989). *Culture as communication*: *Essays on media and society*. Boston: Unwin Hyman.

Cartmill, M. (1999). The status of the race concept in physical anthropology. *American Anthropologist, 100*(3), 651–660.

Cartry, M. (1992). From one rite to another: The memory in ritual and the ethnologist's recollection. In D. de Coppet (Ed.), *Understanding rituals* (pp. 26–36). London: Routledge.

Casmir, F. L. (1992). Third-culture-building: A paradigm shift for international and intercultural communication. In S. Deetz (Ed.), *Communication Yearbook 16* (pp. 407–436). Beverly Hills, CA: Sage.

Casmir, F. L. (1997). Ethics, culture, and communication: An application of the third-culture building model to international and intercultural communication. In F. L. Casmir (Ed.), *Ethics in intercultural and international communication* (pp. 89–118). Mahwah, NJ: Lawrence Erlbaum Associates.

Caycedo, J. C., & Richardson, P. D. (1995). *Conversational sociology*: *An intercultural bridge where east meets west*. Middletown, NJ: Caslon Company.

Chaney, D. (1982). Communication and community. *Communication, 7*, 1–32.

Charland, M. (1987). Constitutive rhetoric: The case of the *peuple québécois* [Quebec people]. *Quarterly Journal of Speech, 73*, 133–150.

Charsley, S. R. (1991). *Rites of marrying*: *The wedding industry in Scotland*. Manchester, England: Manchester University Press.

Charsley, S. R. (1992). *Wedding cakes and cultural history*. New York: Routledge.

Charsley, S. R. (1997). Marriages, weddings and their cakes. In P. Caplan (Ed.), *Food, health and identity* (pp. 50–70). New York: Routledge.

Cheal, D. (1988). The ritualization of family ties. *American Behavioral Scientist, 31*(6), 632–643.

Chirot, D., & Reid, A. (Eds.). (1997). *Essential outsiders: Chinese and Jews in the modern transformation of Southeast Asia and Central Europe.* Seattle, WA: University of Washington Press.

Chung, F. (2000). *'Crazy melon' and 'Chinese apple': The poems of Frances Chung.* Hanover, NH: Wesleyan University Press.

Clark, D. (Ed.). (1993). *The sociology of death.* Oxford, England: Blackwell.

Clark, W. A. V. (1998). *The California cauldron: Immigration and the fortunes of local communities.* New York: Guilford Press.

Coffey, A. (1999). *The ethnographic self: Fieldwork and the representation of identity.* London: Sage.

Cohen, A. P. (1974). Introduction. In A. P. Cohen (Ed.), *Urban ethnicity.* London: Tavistock.

Cohen, A. P. (1985). *The symbolic construction of community.* London: Tavistock.

Cole, H. (1993). *Jumping the broom: The African-American wedding planner.* New York: Henry Holt and Company.

Collins, J. (1996). Socialization to text: Structure and contradiction in schooled literacy. In M. Silverstein & G. Urban (Eds.), *Natural histories of discourse* (pp. 203–228). Chicago: University of Chicago Press.

Connerton, P. (1989). *How societies remember.* Cambridge, England: Cambridge University Press.

Conquergood, D. (1991). Rethinking ethnography: Towards a critical cultural politics. *Communication Monographs, 58,* 179–194.

Constantine, L. L., & Constantine, J. M. (1974). *Group marriage: A study of contemporary multilateral marriage.* New York: Collier.

Cooley, R. E. (1983). Codes and contexts: An argument for their description. In W. B. Gudykunst, (Ed.), *Intercultural communication theory: Current perspectives* (pp. 241–251). Beverly Hills, CA: Sage.

Cooren, F., & Taylor, J. R. (2000). Association and dissociation in an ecological controversy: The great whale case. In N. W. Coppola & B. Karis (Eds.), *Technical communication, deliberative rhetoric, and environmental discourse: Connections and directions* (pp. 171–190). Stamford, CT: Ablex.

Coover, G. E., & Murphy, S. T. (2000). The communicated self: Exploring the interaction between self and social context. *Human Communication Research, 26*(1), 125–147.

Costa, S. S. (1997). *Wild geese and tea: An Asian-American wedding planner.* New York: Riverhead Books.

Cottrell, A. B. (1990). Cross-national marriages: A review of the literature. *Journal of Comparative Family Studies, 21*(2), 151–169.

Cowan, P., & Cowan, R. (1987). *Mixed blessings: Intermarriage between Jews and Christians.* New York: Doubleday.

Crane, D. (1992). *The production of culture: Media and the urban arts.* Newbury Park, CA: Sage.

Culler, J. (1981). *The pursuit of signs*. Ithaca, NY: Cornell University Press.

Cupach, W. R., & Imahori, T. T. (1993). Identity management theory: Communication competence in intercultural episodes and relationships. In R. L. Wiseman & J. Koester (Eds.), *Intercultural communication competence* (pp. 112–131). Newbury Park, CA: Sage.

Dainton, M. (1999). African-American, European-American, and biracial couples' meanings for and experiences in marriages. In T. J. Socha & R. C. Diggs (Eds.), *Communication, race, and family: Exploring communication in black, white, and biracial families* (pp. 147–165). Mahwah, NJ: Lawrence Erlbaum Associates.

Dant, T. (1999). *Material culture in the social world: Values, activities, lifestyles*. Buckingham, England: Open University Press.

Davies, D. (1994). Introduction: Raising the issues. In J. Holm with J. Bowker (Eds.), *Rites of passage* (pp. 1–9). London: Pinter Publishers.

Davis-Floyd, R. E. (1992). *Birth as an American rite of passage*. Berkeley, CA: University of California Press.

Deegan, M. J. (1998). Weaving the American ritual tapestry. In M. J. Deegan, (Ed.), *The American ritual tapestry: Social rules and cultural meanings* (pp. 3–17). Westport, CT: Greenwood Press.

Denzin, N. K. (1991). *Images of postmodern society: Social theory and contemporary cinema*. London: Sage.

Denzin, N. K. (1997). *Interpreting ethnography: Ethnographic practices for the 21st century*. Thousand Oaks, CA: Sage.

DeVos, G. (1995). Ethnic pluralism: Conflict and accommodation. In L. Romanucci-Ross & G. DeVos (Eds.), *Ethnic identity: Creation, conflict, and accommodation* (pp. 15–47). Walnut Creek, CA: Altamira Press.

De Vos, G., & Romanucci-Ross, L. (Eds.). (1982a). *Ethnic identity: Cultural continuities and change*. Chicago: University of Chicago Press.

De Vos, G., & Romanucci-Ross, L. (1982b). Ethnicity: Vessel of meaning and emblem of contrast. In G. De Vos & L. Romanucci-Ross, (Eds.), *Ethnic identity: Cultural continuities and change* (pp. 363–390). Chicago: University of Chicago Press.

Diamant, A. (1985). *The new Jewish wedding*. New York: Summit Books.

Didion, J. (1967). Marrying absurd. In J. Didion, *Slouching towards Bethlehem*. New York: Farrar, Straus & Giroux.

Diggs, N. B. (2001). *Looking beyond the mask: When American women marry Japanese men*. Albany, NY: State University of New York Press.

di Leonardo, M. (1998). *Exotics at home: Anthropologies, others, American modernity*. Chicago: University of Chicago Press.

Donnan, H., & Wilson, T. M. (1999). *Borders: Frontiers of identity, nation and state*. New York: Berg.

Dorson, R. M. (1982). Material components in celebration. In V. Turner (Ed.), *Celebrations: Studies in festivity and ritual* (pp. 33–57). Washington, DC: Smithsonian Institution Press.

Driver, T. F. (1998). *Liberating rites: Understanding the transformative power of ritual*. Boulder, CO: Westview Press.

Duncan, J. S. (1990). *The city as text: The politics of landscape interpretation in the Kandyan Kingdom*. Cambridge, England: Cambridge University Press.

Duncan, J., & Ley, D. (Eds.). (1993a). *Place, culture, representation*. London: Routledge.

Duncan, J., & Ley, D. (1993b). Epilogue. In J. Duncan & D. Ley (Eds.), *Place, culture, representation* (pp. 329–334). London: Routledge.

Dundes, A. (1996). "Jumping the broom": On the origin and meaning of an African American wedding custom. *Journal of American Folklore, 109*(433), 324–329.

Duntley, M. (1993). Observing meaning: Ritual criticism, interpretation, and anthropological fieldwork. In P. R. Frese (Ed.), *Celebrations of identity: Multiple voices in American ritual performance* (pp. 1–13). Westport, CT: Bergin & Garvey.

Duranti, A. (1988). Ethnography of speaking: Toward a linguistics of the praxis. In F. J. Newmeyer (Ed.), *Linguistics: The Cambridge survey* (Vol. 4) *Language: The socio-cultural context* (pp. 210–228). Cambridge, England: Cambridge University Press.

Duranti, A., & Goodwin, C. (Eds.). (1992). *Rethinking context: Language as an interactive phenomenon*. Cambridge, England: Cambridge University Press.

Eastman, C. M. (1992). Codeswitching as an urban language-contact phenomenon. *Journal of Multilingual and Multicultural Development, 13*, 1–17.

Eco, U. (1990). *The limits of interpretation*. Bloomington, IN: Indiana University Press.

Edwards, D. (1998). The relevant thing about her: Social identity categories in use. In C. Antaki & S. Widdicombe (Eds.), *Identities in Talk* (pp. 15–33). London: Sage.

Edwards, W. (1989). *Modern Japan through its weddings: Gender, person, and society in ritual portrayal*. Stanford, CA: Stanford University Press.

Eisenberg, E. M. (1984). Ambiguity as strategy in organizational communication. *Communication Monographs, 51*, 227–242.

Eller, J. D. (1999). *From culture to ethnicity to conflict: An anthropological perspective on international ethnic conflict*. Ann Arbor, MI: University of Michigan Press.

Ellis, D. (1999). *Crafting society: Ethnicity, class, and communication theory*. Mahwah, NJ: Lawrence Erlbaum Associates.

Eoyang, E. (1995). *Coat of many colors: Reflections of diversity by a minority of one*. Boston: Beacon Press.

Epstein, A. L. (1978). *Ethos and identity: Three studies in ethnicity*. London/Chicago: Tavistock Publications/Aldine Publishing Company.

Ervin-Tripp, S. (1972). On sociolinguistic rules: Alternation and co-occurrence. In J. J. Gumperz & D. Hymes (Eds.), *Directions in sociolinguistics: The ethnography of communication* (pp. 213–250). New York: Holt, Rinehart and Winston.

Farnell, B., & Graham, L. R. (1998). Discourse-centered methods. In H. R. Bernard (Ed.), *Handbook of methods in cultural anthropology* (pp. 411–457). Walnut Creek, CA: Altamira Press.

Feldman, S. D. (1979). Nested Identities. *Studies in Symbolic Interaction, 2*, 399–418.

Fernandez, J., & Herzfeld, M. (1998). In search of meaningful methods. In H. R. Bernard (Ed.), *Handbook of methods in cultural anthropology* (pp. 89–129). Walnut Creek, CA: Altamira Press.

Fetterman, D. M. (1989). *Ethnography step by step*. Newbury Park, CA: Sage.

Firth, R. (1973). *Symbols: Public and private*. Ithaca, NY: Cornell University Press.

Fiske, J. (1987). *Television culture.* London: Methuen.

Fiske, J. (1989). Moments of television: Neither the text nor the audience. In E. Seiter, H. Borchers, G. Kreutzner & E.-M. Warth (Eds.), *Remote control: Television, audiences, and cultural power* (pp. 56–78). New York: Routledge.

Fiske, J., & Hartley, J. (1978). *Reading television.* London: Methuen.

Fitch, K. (1998). *Speaking relationally: Culture, communication, and interpersonal connection.* New York: Guilford Press.

Fortes, M. (1983). Problems of identity and person. In A. Jacobson-Widding (Ed.), *Identity: Personal and socio-cultural* (pp. 389–401). Uppsala, Sweden: Almqvist & Wiksell.

Frese, P. R. (1991). The union of nature and culture: Gender symbolism in the American wedding ritual. In P. R. Frese & J. M. Coggeshall (Eds.), *Transcending boundaries: Multidisciplinary approaches to the study of gender* (pp. 97–112). New York: Bergin & Garvey.

Fried, M. N., & Fried, M. H. (1980). *Transitions: Four rituals in eight cultures.* New York: W. W. Norton.

Frith, S. (1996). Music and identity. In S. Hall & P. du Gay (Eds.), *Questions of cultural identity* (pp. 108–127). Thousand Oaks, CA: Sage.

Gabaccio, D. R. (1998). *We are what we eat: Ethnic food and the making of Americans.* Cambridge, MA: Harvard University Press.

Gaines, S. O., Jr. (with Buriel, R., Liu, J. H., & Ríos, D. I.). (1997). *Culture, ethnicity, and personal relationship processes.* New York: Routledge.

Galloway, P. (1992, February 26). Ties that bind. *Chicago Tribune,* pp. 1, 3.

Gamarnikow, E., Morgan, D., Purvis, J., & Taylorson, D. (Eds.). (1983). *The public and the private.* London: Heinemann Educational Books.

Gans, H. (1979). Symbolic ethnicity: The future of ethnic groups and cultures in America. *Ethnic and Racial studies, 2*(1), 1–20.

Gareis, E. (1995). *Intercultural friendship: A qualitative study.* Lanham, MD: University Press of America.

Gedmintas, A. (1989). *An interesting bit of identity: The dynamic of ethnic identity in a Lithuanian-American community.* New York: AMS Press.

Geertz, C. (1971). Introduction. In C. Geertz (Ed.), *Myth, symbol, and culture* (pp. ix–xi). New York: Norton.

Geertz, C. (1973). *The interpretation of cultures.* New York: Basic Books.

Geertz, C. (1979). Blurred genres: The reconfiguration of social thought. *American Scholar, 49,* 165–179.

Gergen, K. J. (1991). *The saturated self: Dilemmas of identity in contemporary life.* New York: Basic Books.

Gergen, K. J. (1994). *Realities and relationships: Soundings in social construction.* Cambridge, MA: Harvard University Press.

Gerholm, T. (1988). On ritual: A postmodernist view. *Ethnos, 53*(3–4), 190–203.

Giddens, A. (1991). *Modernity and self-identity: Self and society in the late modern age.* Stanford, CA: Stanford University Press.

Gilroy, P. (1987). *There ain't no black in the Union Jack: The cultural politics of race and nation.* Chicago: University of Chicago Press.

Gilroy, P. (1993). Between Afro-centrism and Eurocentrism: Youth culture and the problem of hybridity, *Young*, *2*, 2–12.

Glassie, H. (1995). Tradition. *Journal of American Folklore*, *108*(430), 395–412.

Goffman, E. (1959). *The presentation of self in everyday life*. New York: Doubleday Anchor.

Golden, J. (1954). Patterns of Negro-White intermarriage. *American Sociological Review*, *19*, 144–147.

Goldschmidt, W. (1990). *The human career: The self in the symbolic world*. Cambridge, MA: Basil Blackwell.

Goode, J. (1989). Food. *International Encyclopedia of Communication*, *2*, 187–193.

Goody, J. (1990). *The oriental, the ancient and the primitive: Systems of marriage and the family in the pre-industrial societies of Eurasia*. Cambridge, England: Cambridge University Press.

Grearson, J. C., & Smith, L. B. (Eds.). (1995). *Swaying: Essays on intercultural love*. Iowa City, IA: University of Iowa Press.

Green, A. (1981). Austin's cosmic cowboys: Words in collision. In R. Bauman & R. D. Abrahams (Eds.), *"And other neighborly names": Social process and cultural image in Texas folklore* (pp. 152–194). Austin, TX: University of Texas Press.

Greimas, A. J. (1987). *On meaning: Selected writings in semiotic theory*. (P. J. Perron & F. H. Collins, Trans.) Minneapolis, MN: University of Minnesota Press. (Original work published 1970)

Grimes, R. L. (1990). *Ritual criticism: Case studies in its practice, essays on its theory*. Columbia, SC: University of South Carolina Press.

Grimes, R. L. (1995). *Marrying and burying: Rites of passage in a man's life*. Boulder, CO: Westview Press.

Gross, L. (1989). Out of the mainstream: Sexual minorities and the mass media. In E. Seiter, H. Borchers, G. Kreutzner, & E.-M. Warth (Eds.), *Remote control: Television, audiences, and cultural power* (pp. 130–149). New York: Routledge.

Grossman, F. (2000, June 23). Rabbi Feingold named WRC head: Election sparks controversy over intermarriage. *The Wisconsin Jewish Chronicle*, *xxiii*(24), pp. 1, 15.

Gudykunst, W. B., & Ting-Toomey, S., with Chua, E. (1988). *Culture and interpersonal communication*. Beverly Hills, CA: Sage.

Gumperz, J. J. (1982). *Language and social identity*. New York: Cambridge University Press.

Gumperz, J. J. (1992). Contextualization and understanding. In A. Duranti & C. Goodwin, (Eds.), *Rethinking context: Language as an interactive phenomenon* (pp. 229–252). Cambridge, England: Cambridge University Press.

Gupta, A., & Ferguson, J. (1997a). Beyond 'culture': Space, identity, and the politics of difference. In A. Gupta & J. Ferguson (Eds.), *Culture, power, place: Explorations in a critical anthropology* (pp. 31–51). Durham, NC: Duke University Press.

Gupta, A., & Ferguson, J. (1997b). Culture, power, place: Ethnography at the end of an era. In A. Gupta & J. Ferguson (Eds.), *Culture, power, place: Explorations in a critical anthropology* (pp. 1–29). Durham, NC: Duke University Press.

Gurak, D. T., & Fitzpatrick, J. P. (1982). Intermarriage among Hispanic ethnic groups in New York City. *American Journal of Sociology*, *87*(4), 921–934.

Gusfield, J. R. (1989). Introduction. In K. Burke, *On symbols and society* (J. R. Gusfield, Ed., pp. 1–49). Chicago: University of Chicago Press.

Gutierrez, R. A., & Fabre, G. (Eds.). (1995.) *Feasts and celebrations in North American ethnic communities*. Albuquerque, NM: University of New Mexico Press.

Hall, B. J. (1997). Culture, ethics, and communication. In F. L. Casmir (Ed.), *Ethics in intercultural and international communication* (pp. 11–41). Mahwah, NJ: Lawrence Erlbaum Associates.

Hall, S. (1977). Culture, media, and the ideological effect. In J. Curran, M. Gurevitch & J. Woollacott (Eds.), *Mass communication and society* (pp. 315–348). London: Edward Arnold.

Hall, S. (1990). Cultural identity and diaspora. In J. Rutherford (Ed.), *Identity: Community, culture, difference* (pp. 222–237). London: Lawrence and Wishart.

Halliday, M. A. K. (1978). *Language as social semiotic: The social interpretation of language and meaning*. Baltimore: University Park Press.

Halliday, M. A. K. (1984). Language as code and language as behaviour: A systemic-functional interpretation of the nature and ontogenesis of dialogue. In R. P. Fawcett, M. A. K. Halliday, S. M. Lamb, & A. Makkai (Eds.), *The semiotics of culture and language (Vol. 1) Language as social semiotic* (pp. 4–35). London: Frances Pinter.

Halperin, R. H. (1998). *Practicing community: Class, culture, and power in an urban neighborhood*. Austin, TX: University of Texas Press.

Hanassab, S., & Tidwell, R. (1998). Intramarriage and intermarriage: Young Iranians in Los Angeles. *International Journal of Intercultural Relations, 22*(4), 395–408.

Handelman, D. (1990). *Models and mirrors: Towards an anthropology of public events*. Cambridge, England: Cambridge University Press.

Handler, R. (1988). The center in American culture: Analysis and critique. *Anthropological Quarterly, 61*, 1–2.

Handler, R., & Linnekin, J. (1989). Tradition, genuine or spurious. In E. Oring (Ed.), *Folk groups and folklore genres: A reader* (pp. 38–42). Logan, UT: Utah State University Press.

Hannerz, U. (1991). Scenarios for peripheral cultures. In A. D. King (Ed.), *Culture, globalization and the world-system: Contemporary conditions for the representation of identity* (pp. 107–128). Basingstoke, England: Macmillan.

Hannerz, U. (1992). *Cultural complexity: Studies in the social organization of meaning*. New York: Columbia University Press.

Hannerz, U. (1996). *Transnational connections: Culture, people, places*. New York: Routledge.

Hardt, H., & Brennen, B. (1993). Introduction: Communication and the question of history. *Communication Theory, 2*, 130–136.

Harre, J. (1966). *Maori and Pakeha: A study of mixed marriages in New Zealand*. New York: Praeger.

Harris, H. W., Blue, H. C., & Griffith, E. E. H. (Eds.). (1995). *Racial and ethnic identity: Psychological development and creative expression*. New York: Routledge.

Harris, N. (1999). *Building lives: Constructing rites and passages*. New Haven, CT: Yale University Press.

Hassan, I. (1987). *The postmodern turn: Essays in postmodern theory and culture*. Ohio State University Press.

Hastrup, K. (1989). Postscript 1: The prophetic condition. In E. Ardener, *The voice of prophecy* (M. Chapman, Ed., pp. 224–228). Oxford, England: Basil Blackwell.

Hay, J. (1989). Advertising as a cultural text (Rethinking message analysis in a recombinant culture). In B. Dervin, L. Grossberg, B. J. O'Keefe, & E. Wartella, (Eds.), *Rethinking communication (Vol. 2) Paradigm exemplars* (pp. 129–152). Newbury Park, CA: Sage.

Hebdige, D. (1979). *Subculture: The meaning of style*. London: Methuen.

Hecht, M. L. (1993). 2002—A research odyssey: Toward the development of a communication theory of identity. *Communication Monographs, 60,* 76–82.

Hechter, M. (1986). Theories of ethnic relations. In J. F. Stack, Jr. (Ed.), *The primordial challenge: Ethnicity in the contemporary world* (pp. 13–24). New York: Greenwood Press.

Hegde, R. S. (1998). Swinging the trapeze: The negotiation of identity among Asian Indian immigrant women in the United States. In D. V. Tanno & A. González (Eds.), *Communication and identity across cultures* (pp. 34–55). Thousand Oaks, CA: Sage.

Henderson, K (1991). Flexible sketches and inflexible data bases: Visual communication, conscription devices, and boundary objects in design engineering. *Science, Technology and Human Values, 16*(4), 448–473.

Hendrickson, C. (1995). *Weaving identities: Construction of dress and self in a highland Guatemala town.* Austin, TX: University of Texas Press.

Henriques, F. (1974). *Children of Caliban: Miscegenation.* London: Secker and Warburg.

Hobart, M. (1990). Who do you think you are? The authorized Balinese. In R. Fardon (Ed.), *Localizing strategies: Regional traditions of ethnographic writing* (pp. 303–338). Edinburgh/Washington, DC: Scottish Academic Press/Smithsonian Institution Press.

Hobsbawm, E., & Ranger, T. (Eds.). (1983). *The invention of tradition.* Cambridge, England: Cambridge University Press.

Hodder, I. (1994). The interpretation of documents and material culture. In N. K. Denzin & Y. S. Lincoln (Eds.), *Handbook of qualitative research* (pp. 393–402). Thousand Oaks, CA: Sage.

Hodge, R., & Kress, G. (1988). *Social semiotics.* Ithaca, NY: Cornell University Press.

Hoskins, J. (1998). *Biographical objects: How things tell the stories of people's lives.* New York: Routledge.

Hsu, F. L. K. (1985). The self in cross-cultural perspective. In A. J. Marsella, G. DeVos, & F. L. K. Hsu (Eds.), *Culture and self: Asian and Western perspectives* (pp. 24–55). New York: Tavistock.

Hufford, M. (1995). Context. *Journal of American Folklore, 108*(430), 528–549.

Hughes-Freeland, F., & Crain, M. M. (1998). Introduction. In F. Hughes-Freeland & M. M. Crain (Eds.), *Recasting ritual: Performance, media, identity* (pp. 1–20). London: Routledge.

Hutter, M. (1985). Symbolic interaction and the study of the family. In H. A. Faberman & R. S. Perinbanayagam, (Eds.), *Studies in symbolic interaction (Suppl. 1) Foundations of interpretive sociology: Original essays in symbolic interaction* (pp. 117–152). Greenwich, CT: JAI Press.

Hymes, D. (1962). The ethnography of speaking. In T. Gladwin & W. Sturtevant (Eds.), *Anthropology and human behavior* (pp. 13–53). Washington, DC: The Anthropological Society of Washington.

Hymes, D. (1971). *On communicative competence.* Philadelphia: University of Pennsylvania Press.

Hymes, D. (1981) *In vain I tried to tell you: Essays in Native American ethnopoetics.* Philadelphia: University of Pennsylvania Press.

Hymes, D. (1996). *Ethnography, linguistics, narrative inequality: Toward an understanding of voice.* London: Taylor & Francis.

Ifekwunigwe, J. O. (1999). *Scattered belongings: Cultural paradoxes of "race," nation and gender.* London: Routledge.

Ingraham, C. (1999). *White weddings: Romancing heterosexuality in popular culture.* New York: Routledge.

Interracial marriages are growing. (1993, February 12). *Milwaukee Journal,* p. A3.

Jackson, R. L., II. (1999). *The negotiation of cultural identity: Perceptions of European Americans and African Americans.* Westport, CT: Praeger.

Jackson, R. L., II, & Garner, T. (1998). Tracing the evolution of "race," "ethnicity," and "culture" in communication studies. *Howard Journal of Communications, 9,* 41–55.

Jankowski, N. W. (1991). Qualitative research and community media. In K. B. Jensen & N. W. Jankowski (Eds.), *A handbook of qualitative methodologies for mass communication research* (pp. 163–174). London: Routledge.

Jansen, C. (1982). Inter-ethnic marriages. *International Journal of Comparative Sociology, 23*(3–4), 225–235.

Jensen, K. B. (1991). Introduction: The qualitative turn. In K. B. Jensen & N. W. Jankowski, (Eds.), *A handbook of qualitative methodologies for mass communication research* (pp. 1–11). London: Routledge.

Johnson, F. L. (1995). Centering culture in the discipline of communication. In J. T. Wood & R. B. Gregg (Eds.), *Toward the twenty-first century: The future of speech communication* (pp. 151–167). Cresskill, NJ: Hampton Press.

Johnson, M. (1998). At home and abroad: Inalienable wealth, personal consumption and formulations of femininity in the southern Philippines. In D. Miller (Ed.), *Material cultures: Why some things matter* (pp. 215–238). London: UCL Press.

Jules-Rosette, B. 1975. *African apostles: Ritual and conversion in the church of John Maranke.* Ithaca, NY: Cornell University Press.

Kalmijn, M. (1993). Trends in black/white intermarriage. *Social Forces, 72*(1), 119–146.

Kaminsky, M. (1992). Introduction. In B. Myerhoff, *Remembered lives: The work of ritual, storytelling, and growing older* (M. Kaminsky, Ed., pp. 1–97). Ann Arbor, MI: University of Michigan Press.

Kapchan, D. A. (1995). Performance. *Journal of American Folklore, 108*(430), 479–508.

Karp, I. (1987). Laughter at marriage: Subversion in performance. In D. Parkin & D. Nyamwaya, (Eds.), *Transformations of African marriage* (pp. 137–154). Manchester, England: Manchester University Press.

Katriel, T. (1995). From "context" to "contexts" in intercultural communication research. In R. L. Wiseman (Ed.), *Intercultural communication theory* (pp. 271–284). Thousand Oaks, CA: Sage.

Katz, I. (1996). *The construction of racial identity in children of mixed parentage: Mixed metaphors.* London: Jessica Kingsley Publishers.

Kendall, L. (1996). *Getting married in Korea: Of gender, morality, and modernity.* Berkeley, CA: University of California Press.

Kendis, K. O. (1989). *A matter of comfort: Ethnic maintenance and ethnic style among third-generation Japanese Americans.* New York: AMS Press.

Kertzer, D. I. (1988). *Ritual, politics and power.* New Haven, CT: Yale University Press.

Kerwin, C., Ponterotto, J. G., Jackson, B. L., & Harris, A. (1993). Racial identity in biracial children: A qualitative investigation. *Journal of Counseling Psychology, 40*(2), 221–231.

Khatib-Chahidi, J., Hill, R., & Paton, R. (1998). Chance, choice and circumstance: A study of women in cross-cultural marriages. In R. Breger & R. Hill (Eds.), *Cross-cultural marriage: Identity and choice* (pp. 49–66). New York: Berg.

Kim, Y. Y. (1996). Identity development: From cultural to intercultural. In H. B. Mokros (Ed.), *Identity and interaction* (pp. 347–369). New Brunswick, NJ: Transaction Publishers.

Kinsley, C. H. (1994). Questions people have asked me. Questions I have asked myself. In C. Camper (Ed.), *Miscegenation blues: Voices of mixed race women* (pp. 113–129). Toronto, Canada: Sister Vision.

Kirn, W., & Cole, W. (2000, June 19). Twice as nice. *Time*, pp. 53–54.

Kirshenblatt-Gimblett, B. (1982). The cut that binds: The Western Ashkenazic torah binder as nexus between circumcision and torah. In V. Turner (Ed.), *Celebration: Studies in festivity and ritual* (pp. 136–146). Washington, DC: Smithsonian Institution Press.

Kitano, H. H. L., Yeung, W.-T., Chai, L., & Hatanaka, H. (1984). Asian-American interracial marriage. *Journal of Marriage and the Family, 46*(1), 179–190.

Kitchen, D. L. (1993). *Interracial marriage in the United States, 1900–1980*. Unpublished doctoral dissertation, University of Minnesota.

Knoerle, J. H. (2000, February 9). The dress with five lives: Talk about tradition, this wedding gown adorned five brides over 40 years. *Bridal* 2000. Retrieved from www.calmanac.com/paw/paonline/bridal2000/dress.html

Kobayashi, A. (1993). Multiculturalism: Representing a Canadian institution. In J. Duncan & D. Ley (Eds.), *Place/culture/representation* (pp. 205–231). London: Routledge.

Kominsky, N. (2000, April 21). "Why do you do this?" A rabbi's experience with interfaith marriage. Retrieved April 21, 2000 from www.interfaithfamily.com/article/issue7/kominsky/htm

Kouri, K. M., & Laswell, M. (1993). Black-white marriages: Social change and intergenerational mobility. *Marriage and Family Review, 19*(3/4), 241–255.

Krebs, N. (1999). *Edgewalkers: Defusing cultural boundaries on the new global frontier*. Far Hills, NJ : New Horizon Press.

Kress, G. (Ed.). (1988). *Communication and culture: An introduction*. Kensington: New South Wales University Press.

Kristeva, J. (1980). *Desire in language: A semiotic approach to language and art* (L. Roudiez, Ed.; A. Jardine, T. Gora, & L. Roudiez, Trans.). New York: Columbia University Press.

La Brack, B. (1988). *The Sikhs of northern California, 1904–1975*. New York: AMS Press.

Lalli, C. G. (1987). Foreword. In G. F. Stern (Ed.), *Something old, something new: Ethnic weddings in America* (p. 2). Philadelphia: Balch Institute for Ethnic Studies.

Lamont, M., & Fournier, M. (Eds.). (1992). *Cultivating differences: Symbolic boundaries and the making of inequality*. Chicago: University of Chicago Press.

Lareau, A., & Shultz, J. (Eds.). (1996). *Journey through ethnography: Realistic accounts of fieldwork*. Boulder, CO: Westview.

Lavie, S., & Swedenburg, T. (Eds.). (1996). *Displacement, diaspora and the geographics of identity*. Durham, NC: Duke University Press.

Lavin, C. (1992, February 12). Bride and seek. *Chicago Tribune*, pp. E1–E2.

Leach, E. (1968). Ritual. In D. Sills (Ed.), *International Encyclopedia of the Social Sciences* (Vol. 13, pp. 520–526). New York: Macmillan.

Leach, E. (1976). *Culture and communication: The logic by which symbols are connected.* Cambridge, England: Cambridge University Press.

Leach, E. (1984). Conclusion: Further thoughts on the realm of folly. In E. Bruner (Ed.), *Text, play and story: The construction and reconstruction of self and society* (pp. 356–64). Washington, DC: American Ethnological Society.

Leach, E. (1989). Tribal ethnography: Past, present, future. In E. Tonkin, M. McDonald, & M. Chapman (Eds.), *History and ethnicity* (pp. 34–47). London: Routledge.

Leeds-Hurwitz, W. (1989). *Communication in everyday life: A social interpretation.* Norwood, NJ: Ablex.

Leeds-Hurwitz, W. (1990). Notes in the history of intercultural communication: The Foreign Service Institute and the mandate for intercultural training. *Quarterly Journal of Speech, 76,* 262–281.

Leeds-Hurwitz, W. (1992, August 13–15). Connecting interpersonal to intercultural communication by way of ethnography. Keynote address delivered to the Ethnography of Communication Conference: Ways of Speaking, Ways of Knowing, Portland, Oregon.

Leeds-Hurwitz, W. (1993). *Semiotics and communication: Signs, codes, cultures.* Hillsdale, NJ: Lawrence Erlbaum Associates.

Leeds-Hurwitz, W. (1994, January 13–15). Les cérémonies de mariage mixtes aux U.S.A. [Intercultural weddings in the United States]. Plenary paper presented to the Séminaire sur les rapports entre communication inter-culturelle, multiculturalisme et métissage [Seminar on the connections between intercultural communication, multiculturalism and mixing], Paris, France.

Leeds-Hurwitz, W. (Ed.). (1995). *Social approaches to communication.* New York: Guilford Press.

Leeds-Hurwitz, W. (1998). Social theories, social interpretations. In J. Trent (Ed.), *Communication: Views from the helm for the twenty-first century* (pp. 332–336). Boston: Allyn-Bacon.

Leeds-Hurwitz, W., & Sigman, S. J., with Sullivan, S. J. (1995). Social communication theory: Communication structures and performed invocations, a revision of Scheflen's notion of program. In S. J. Sigman (Ed.), *The consequentiality of communication.* (pp. 163–204). Hillsdale, NJ. Lawrence Erlbaum Associates.

Leonard, D. (1980). *Sex and generation: A study of courtship and weddings.* London: Tavistock.

Leonard, K. (1992). *Making ethnic choices: California's Punjabi Mexican Americans.* Philadelphia: Temple University Press.

Leonard, K. (1993). Ethnic celebrations in rural California: Punjabi-Mexicans and others. In P. R. Frese (Ed.), *Celebrations of identity: Multiple voices in American ritual performance* (pp. 145–160). Westport, CT: Bergin & Garvey.

Lessl, T. M. (1993). Punctuation in the constitution of public identities: Primary and secondary sequences in the Scopes trial. *Communication Theory, 2,* 91–111.

Levine, D. L. (1985). *The flight from ambiguity.* Chicago: University of Chicago Press,

Levinson, S. (1983). *Pragmatics.* Cambridge, England: Cambridge University Press.

Levi-Strauss, C. (1966). *The savage mind.* Chicago: University of Chicago Press.

Lewin, E. (1998). *Recognizing ourselves: Ceremonies of lesbian and gay commitment*. New York: Columbia University Press.

Lewis, G. (1980). *Day of shining red: An essay on understanding ritual*. Cambridge, England: Cambridge University Press.

Lieberson, S., & Waters, M. C. (1988). *From many strands: Ethnic and racial groups in contemporary America*. New York: Sage.

Limón, J. E. (1991). Representation, ethnicity, and the precursory ethnography: Notes of a native anthropologist. In R. G. Fox (Ed.), *Recapturing anthropology: Working in the present* (pp. 115–135). Santa Fe, NM: School of American Research Press.

Lipson-Walker, C. (1991). Weddings among Jews in the post-World-War-II American south. In S. Stern & J. A. Cicala (Eds.), *Creative ethnicity: Symbols and strategies of contemporary ethnic life* (pp. 171–183). Logan, UT: Utah State University Press.

Loeding, J. (1992, July 5). Weddings of yesteryear. *Milwaukee Journal, Wisconsin Magazine*, pp. 14–15.

Lotman, Y. M. (1990). *Universe of the mind: A semiotic theory of culture*. (A. Shukman, Trans.) Bloomington, IN: Indiana University Press.

Louw, E. (1998). "Diversity" versus "national unity": The struggle between moderns, premoderns, and postmoderns in contemporary South Africa. In D. V. Tanno & A. González (Eds.), *Communication and identity across cultures* (pp. 148–174). Thousand Oaks, CA: Sage.

Luhmann, N. (1990). The improbability of communication. In *Essays on self-reference* (pp. 86–98). New York: Columbia University Press.

Lukes, S. (1975). Political ritual and social integration. *Sociology, 9,* 289–308.

Lum, C. M. K. (1996). *In search of a voice: Karaoke and the construction of identity in Chinese America*. Mahwah, NJ: Lawrence Erlbaum Associates.

MacAloon, J. (Ed.). (1984). *Rite, drama, festival, spectacle: Rehearsals towards a theory of performance*. Philadelphia: Institute for the Study of Human Issues.

Mac an Ghaill, M. (1999). *Contemporary racisms and ethnicities: Social and cultural transformations*. Buckingham, England: Open University Press.

MacCannell, D., & MacCannell, J. F. (1982). *The time of the sign: A semiotic interpretation of modern culture*. Bloomington, IN: Indiana University Press.

Malanka, B. (1994). Noblewomen in exile. In C. Camper (Ed.), *Miscegenation blues: Voices of mixed race women* (pp. 155–157). Toronto, Canada: Sister Vision.

Mannheim, B., & Tedlock, D. (Eds.). (1995). *The dialogic emergence of culture*. Urbana, IL: University of Illinois Press.

Manning, F. (Ed.). (1983a). *The celebration of society: Perspectives on contemporary cultural performance*. Bowling Green, OH: Bowling Green University Popular Press.

Manning, F. (1983b). Cosmos and chaos: Celebration in the modern world. In F. Manning (Ed.), *The celebration of society: Perspectives on contemporary cultural performance* (pp. 4–30). Bowling Green, OH: Bowling Green University Popular Press.

Marcus, G. E. (1998). *Ethnography through thick and thin*. Princeton, NJ: Princeton University Press.

Martin, J. H. (1996). Introductory essay. In M. B. Aune & V. DeMarinis (Eds.), *Religious and social ritual: Interdisciplinary explorations* (pp. 19–22). Albany, NY: SUNY Press.

Martínez, E. (1998). *De colores* [colored] *means all of us: Latina views for a multi-colored century.* Cambridge, MA: South End Press.

Mathabane, M., & Mathabane, G. (1992). *Love in black and white: The triumph of love over prejudice and taboo.* New York: HarperCollins.

Matthews, G. (2000). *Global culture/individual identity: Searching for home in the cultural supermarket.* London: Routledge.

Mayer, B. (1992a, January 25). Celebrating our heritage. *Kenosha News (Suppl.), Brides, 1992 Wedding Guide,* pp. 14–15.

Mayer, B. (1992b, January 25). Wedding joins cultures. *Kenosha News (Suppl.), Brides, 1992 Wedding Guide,* p. 12.

Mayer, E. (1985). *Love and tradition: Marriage between Jews and Christians.* New York: Plenum Press.

McCullers, C. (1946). *The member of the wedding.* New York: Bantam Books.

McDowell, J. H. (1981). The *corrido* of Greater Mexico as discourse, music, and event. In R. Bauman & R. D. Abrahams (Eds.), *"And other neighborly names": Social process and cultural image in Texas folklore* (pp. 45–75). Austin, TX: University of Texas Press.

McGoldrick, M., & Garcia-Preto, N. (1984). Ethnic intermarriage: Implications for therapy. *Family Process, 23*(3), 347–364.

McGoldrick, M., & Giordano, J. (1996). Overview: Ethnicity and family therapy. In M. McGoldrick, J. Giordano, & J. K. Pearce (Eds.), *Ethnicity and family therapy* (2nd ed., pp. 1–27). New York: Guilford.

McNamara, R. P., Tempenis, M., & Walton, B. (1999). *Crossing the line: Interracial couples in the south.* Westport, CT: Greenwood Press.

McNamee, S., & Gergen, K. J., & Associates. (1998). *Relational responsibility: Resources for sustainable dialogue.* Thousand Oaks, CA: Sage.

McReady, W. C. (1983). Preface. In W. C. McReady (Ed.), *Culture, ethnicity, and identity: Current issues in research* (pp. xvii–xxi). New York: Academic Press.

Mead, G. H. (1962). *Mind, self, and society.* Chicago: University of Chicago Press.

Mead, M. (1982). Ethnicity and Anthropology in America. In G. De Vos & L. Romanucci-Ross (Eds.), *Ethnic identity: Cultural continuities and change* (pp. 173–197). Chicago: University of Chicago Press.

Metz, C. (1974). *Film language: A semiotics of the cinema.* (M. Taylor, Trans.). New York: Oxford University Press. (Original work published 1971)

Metzger, D., & Williams, G. E. (1963). A formal ethnographic analysis of Tenejapa Ladino weddings. *American Anthropologist, 65,* 1076–1101.

Miller, D. (1998). Why some things matter. In D. Miller (Ed.), *Material cultures: Why some things matter* (pp. 3–21). London: UCL Press.

Miller, R. (1993, March 28). Emma Thompson's last-minute jitters. *The New York Times Magazine,* pp. 22–25, 62–65.

Mischler, E. (1986). The analysis of interview-narratives. In T. R. Sarbin (Ed.), *Narrative psychology: The storied nature of human conduct* (pp. 233–255). New York: Praeger.

Modell, J. (1985). Historical reflections on American marriage. In K. Davis (Ed.), *Contemporary marriage: Comparative perspective on a changing institution* (pp. 181–196). New York: Russell Sage.

Moffatt, M. (1992). Ethnographic writing about American culture. *Annual Review of Anthropology, 21*, 205–229.

Mokros, H. B. (Ed.). (1996). *Interaction and identity.* New Brunswick, NJ: Transaction Books.

Moller, D. W. (1996). *Confronting death: Values, institutions, and human mortality.* New York: Oxford University Press.

Monaco, J. (1981). *How to read a film: The art, technology, language, history, and theory of film and media.* New York: Oxford University Press.

Montgomery, B. M. (1991). Communication as the interface between couples and culture. *Communication Yearbook, 15*, 475–507.

Montgomery, M. E. (1989). *'Gilded prostitution': Status, money, and transatlantic marriages, 1870–1914.* London: Routledge.

Moore, H. (1990). Paul Ricoeur: Action, meaning and text. In C. Tilley (Ed.), *Reading material culture: Structuralism, hermeneutics and post-structuralism* (pp. 85–120). Oxford, England: Basil Blackwell.

Moore, S. F., & Myerhoff, B. G. (1977). Introduction: Secular ritual: Forms and meanings. In S. F. Moore & B. G. Myerhoff (Eds.), *Secular ritual* (pp. 3–24). Assen, Netherlands: Van Gorcum.

Muir, E. (1997). *Ritual in early modern Europe.* Cambridge, England: Cambridge University Press.

Mukhopadhyay, C. C., & Moses, Y. T. (1997). Reestablishing 'race' in anthropological discourse. *American Anthropologist 99*(3), 517–533.

Myerhoff, B. (1982). Rites of passage: Process and paradox. In V. Turner (Ed.), *Celebration: Studies in festivity and ritual.* Washington, DC: Smithsonian Institution Press.

Myerhoff, B. (1992). *Remembered lives: The work of ritual, storytelling, and growing older* (M. Kaminsky, Ed.). Ann Arbor, MI: University of Michigan Press.

Nagel, J. (1998). Constructing ethnicity: Creating and recreating ethnic identity and culture. In M. W. Hughey (Ed.), *New tribalisms: The resurgence of race and ethnicity* (pp. 237–272). Washington Square, NY: New York University Press.

Naylor, L. L. (1998). *American culture: Myth and reality of a culture of diversity.* Westport, CT: Bergin & Garvey.

Neustadt, K. (1988). "Born among the shells": The Quakers of Allen's Neck and their clambake. In T. C. Humphrey & L. T. Humphrey (Eds.), *"We gather together:" Food and festival in American life* (pp. 89–109). Ann Arbor, MI: UMI Research Press.

Noyes, D. (1995). Group. *Journal of American Folklore, 108*(430), 449–478.

Ochberg, R. L. (1992). Social insight and psychological liberation. In G. C. Rosenwald & R. L. Ochberg (Eds.), *Storied lives: The cultural politics of self-understanding* (pp. 214–230). New Haven, CT: Yale University Press.

O'Hearn, C. C. (Ed.). (1998). *Half and half: Writers on growing up biracial and bicultural.* Pantheon Books.

Ohnuki-Tierney, E. (1993). Foreword. In P. R. Frese (Ed.), *Celebrations of identity: Multiple voices in American ritual performance* (pp. ix–xi). Westport, CT: Bergin & Garvey.

Okely, J., & Callaway, H. (Eds.). (1992). *Anthropology and autobiography.* London: Routledge.

Ong, A. (1999). *Flexible citizenship: The cultural logics of transnationality.* Durham, NC: Duke University Press.

Orbe, M. P. (1998a). From the standpoint(s) of traditionally muted groups: Explicating a co-cultural communication theoretical model. *Communication Theory* 8(1), 1–26.

Orbe, M. P. (1998b). *Constructing co-cultural theory: An explication of culture, power, and communication.* Thousand Oaks, CA: Sage.

Oring, E. (1987). Generating lives: The construction of an autobiography. *Journal of Folklore Research, 24,* 241–262.

Ortner, S. B. (1973). On key symbols. *American Anthropologist, 75,* 1338–1346.

Ortner, S. B. (1991). Reading America: Preliminary notes on class and culture. In R. G. Fox (Ed.), *Recapturing anthropology: Working in the present* (pp. 163–189). Santa Fe, NM: School of American Research Press.

Ottesen, C. (1994, January/February). Blossoming possibilities for the bouquet. *Potomac Life,* 36–38.

Owen, J. L. (Ed.). (1997). *Context and communication behavior.* Reno, NV: Context Press.

Pan, E. (2000, February 21). Why Asian guys are on a roll. [Electronic version], *Newsweek.* Retrieved from: www.newsweek.com/nw-srv/printed/us/so/a16374-2000feb13.htm.

Payne, R. J. (1998). *Getting beyond race: The changing American culture.* Boulder, CO: Westview Press.

Peacock, J. L. (1986). *The anthropological lens: Harsh light, soft focus.* London: Cambridge University Press.

Peacock, J. L. (1990). Ethnographic notes on sacred and profane performance. In R. Schechner & W. Appel (Eds.), *By means of performance: Intercultural studies of theatre and ritual* (pp. 208–220). Cambridge, England: Cambridge University Press.

Pearce, W. B. (1989). *Communication and the human condition.* Carbondale, IL: Southern Illinois University Press.

Pearce, W. B., & Littlejohn, S. W. (1997). *Moral conflict: When social worlds collide.* Thousand Oaks, CA: Sage.

Penman, R. (2000). *Reconstructing communicating: Looking to a future.* Mahwah, NJ: Lawrence Erlbaum Associates.

Penn, W. S. (Ed.). (1997a). *As we are now: Mixblood essays on race and identity.* Berkeley, CA: University of California Press.

Penn, W. S. (1997b). Introduction. In W. S. Penn (Ed.), *As we are now: Mixblood essays on race and identity* (pp. 1–11). Berkeley, CA: University of California Press.

Philipsen, G. (1987). The prospect for cultural communication. In D. L. Kincaid (Ed.), *Communication theory: Eastern and Western perspectives* (pp. 245–254). San Diego, CA: Academic Press.

Philipsen, G. (1989). An ethnographic approach to communication studies. In B. Dervin, L. Grossberg, B. J. O'Keefe, & E. Wartella (Eds.), *Rethinking communication* (Vol. 2) *Paradigm exemplars* (pp. 258–268). Newbury Park, CA: Sage Publications.

Philipsen, G. (1992). *Speaking culturally.* Albany, NY: State University of New York Press.

Pollan, S. M., & Levine, M. (1989, January 9). 'I do'-ing it right. *New York Times,* 38–50.

Price, R. (2000, July 16). Wedding bells ring for interracial couple. *The Columbus Dispatch.* Retrieved July 16, 2000 from www.dispatch.com/news/newsfea00/july00/351017.html

Puente, M. (2000, June 11). Wedded to the year 2000. *USA Today.* Retrieved June 11, 2000 from www.usatoday.com/news/acovmon.htm

Pugh, T. (2001, March 24). Intermarriages rise, reflecting U.S. changes. *The [Philadelphia] Inquirer.* Retrieved March 24, 2001 from inq.philly.com/content/inquirer/2001/03/24/front_page/MARRY24.htm?template=aprint.htm

Putnam, L. L., & Stohl, C. (1990). Bona fide groups: A reconceptualization of groups in context. *Communication Studies, 41*(3), 248–265.

Ragan, S. L., & Hopper, R. (1984). Ways to leave your lover: A conversational analysis of literature. *Communication Quarterly, 32,* 310–317.

Rapport, N. (1997). *Transcendent individual: Towards a literary and liberal anthropology.* London: Routledge.

Rawlins, W. K. (1992). *Friendship matters: Communication, dialectics, and the life course.* New York: Aldine de Gruyter.

Rawlins, W. K. (1998). Theorizing public and private domains and practices of communication: Introductory concerns. *Communication Theory, 8*(4), 369–380.

Real, M. R. (1989). *Super media: A cultural studies approach.* Newbury Park, CA: Sage.

Reed-Danahay, D. (1996). Champagne and chocolate: "Taste" and inversion in a French wedding ritual. *American Anthropologist, 98,* 750–761.

Richard, M. A. (1991). *Ethnic groups and marital choices: Ethnic history and marital assimilation in Canada, 1871 and 1971.* Vancouver, Canada: University of British Columbia Press.

Ricoeur, P. (1979). The model of the text: Meaningful action considered as a text. In P. Rabinow & W. M. Sullivan (Eds.), *Interpretive social science: A reader* (pp. 73–101). Berkeley, CA: University of California Press.

Rieff, P. (1964). Introduction. In C. H. Cooley (Ed.), *Human nature and the social order* (pp. ix–xx). New York: Schocken Books.

Roberts, G. L., & Bavelas, J. B. (1996). The communication dictionary: A collaborative theory of meaning. In J. Stewart (Ed.), *Beyond the symbol model: Reflections on the representational nature of language* (pp. 135–160). Albany, NY: State University of New York Press.

Roberts, R. E. T. (1994). Black-White intermarriage in the United States. In W. R. Johnson & D. M. Warren (Eds.), *Inside the mixed marriage: Accounts of changing attitudes, patterns, and perceptions of cross-cultural and interracial marriages* (pp. 25–79). Lanham, MD: University Press of America.

Romano, D. (1988). *Inter-cultural marriage: Promises and pitfalls.* Yarmouth, ME: Intercultural Press.

Romanucci-Ross, L., & De Vos, G. (Eds.). (1995). *Ethnic identity: Creation, conflict, and accommodation.* Walnut Creek, CA: Altamira Press.

Roosens, E. E. (1989). *Creating ethnicity: The process of ethnogenesis.* Newbury Park, CA: Sage.

Root, D. (1997). "White Indians": Appropriation and the politics of display. In B. Ziff & P. V. Rao (Eds.), *Borrowed power: Essays in cultural appropriation* (pp. 225–233). New Brunswick, NJ: Rutgers University Press.

Root, M. P. P. (Ed.). (1992). *Racially mixed people in America.* Newbury Park, CA: Sage.

Root, M. P. P. (1997a). Introduction. In M. P. P. Root (Ed.), *Filipino Americans: Transformation and identity* (pp. xi–xv). Thousand Oaks, CA: Sage.

Root, M. P. P. (1997b). Contemporary mixed-heritage Filipino Americans: Fighting colonized identities. In M. P. P. Root (Ed.), *Filipino Americans: Transformation and identity* (pp. 80–94). Thousand Oaks, CA: Sage.

Root, M. P. P. (2001). *Love's revolution: Interracial marriage*. Philadelphia: Temple University Press.

Rosaldo, R. (1986). Ilongot hunting as story and experience. In V. Turner & E. M. Bruner (Eds.), *The anthropology of experience* (pp. 97–138). Urbana, IL: University of Illinois Press.

Rosaldo, R. (1989). *Culture and truth: The remaking of social analysis*. Boston: Beacon Press.

Rosenthal, C. J., & Marshall, V. W. (1988). Generational transmission of family ritual. *American Behavioral Scientist, 31*(6), 669–684.

Rosenwald, G. C., & Ochberg, R. L. (1992). Introduction: Life stories, cultural politics, and self-understanding. In G. C. Rosenwald & R. L. Ochberg (Eds.), *Storied lives: The cultural politics of self-understanding* (pp. 1–18). New Haven, CT: Yale University Press.

Rothenbuhler, E. W. (1998). *Ritual communication: From everyday conversation to mediated ceremony*. Thousand Oaks, CA: Sage.

Rothenbuhler, E. W. (2001). Revising communication research for working on community. In G. J. Shepherd & E. W. Rothenbuhler (Eds.), *Communication and community* (pp. 159–179). Mahwah, NJ: Lawrence Erlbaum Associates.

Royce, A. P. (1982). *Ethnic identity: Strategies of diversity*. Bloomington, IN: Indiana University Press.

Rubenstein, H. (1993, January 31). The wedding: Dress rehearsal. *New York Times Magazine*, pp. 47–52.

Rubinstein, H. (Ed.). (1990). *The Oxford book of marriage*. New York: Oxford.

Rushdie, S. (1991). *Imaginary homelands*. London: Granta.

Saldivar, J. D. (1997). *Border matters: Remapping American cultural studies*. Berkeley, CA: University of California Press.

Sandfur, G. D., & McKinnell, T. (1986). American Indian intermarriage. *Social Science Research, 15*(4), 347–371.

Santino, J. (1994). *All around the year: Holidays and celebrations in American life*. Urbana, IL: University of Illinois Press.

Sapir, E. (1949). Cultural anthropology and psychiatry. In D. Mandelbaum (Ed.), *Selected writings of Edward Sapir* (pp. 509–521). Berkeley, CA: University of California Press.

Scales-Trent, J. (1995). *Notes of a White Black woman: Race, color, community*. University Park, PA: Pennsylvania State University Press.

Scheffler, I. (1996). *Symbolic words: Art, science, language, ritual*. New York: Cambridge University Press.

Schegloff, E. A. (1988). Presequences and indirection: Applying speech act theory to ordinary conversation. *Journal of Pragmatics, 12*, 55–62.

Schegloff, E. A. (1999). What next: Language and social interaction study at the century's turn. *Research on Language and Social Interaction, 32*(1–2), 141–148.

Scheub, H. E. (1998). *Story*. Madison, WI: University of Wisconsin Press.

Schieffelin, E. L. (1985). Performance and the cultural construction of reality. *American Ethnologist, 12*(4), 707–724.

Schieffelin, E. L. (1996). On failure and performance: Throwing the medium out of the seance. In C. Laderman & M. Roseman (Eds.), *The performance of healing* (pp. 59–89). London: Routledge.

Schieffelin, E. L. (1998). Problematizing performance. In F. Hughes-Freeland (Ed.), *Ritual, performance, media* (pp. 194–207). London: Routledge.

Schiffer, M. B., with Miller, A. R. (1999). *The material life of human beings: Artifacts, behavior, and communication.* London: Routledge.

Schneider, D. M. (1976). Notes toward a theory of culture. In K. H. Basso & H. A. Selby (Eds.), *Meaning in anthropology* (pp. 197–220). Albuquerque, NM: University of New Mexico Press.

Schneider, S. W. (1989). *Intermarriage: The challenge of living with differences between Christians and Jews.* New York: Free Press.

Scholes, R. (1982). *Semiotics and interpretation.* New Haven, CT: Yale University Press.

Schudson, M. (1989). How culture works: Perspectives from media studies on the efficacy of symbols. *Theory and Society, 18,* 153–180.

Schutz, A. (1967). *Collected papers,* I: *The problem of social reality.* The Hague: Martinus Nijhoff.

Schwartz, D. (1992). *Waucoma twilight: Generations of the farm.* Washington, DC: Smithsonian Institution Press.

Sebeok, T. (1986). The doctrine of sign. In J. Deely, B. Williams, & F. E. Kruse (Eds.), *Frontiers in semiotics* (pp. 35–42). Bloomington, IN: Indiana University Press.

Seligson, M. (1973). *The eternal bliss machine: America's way of wedding.* New York: William Morrow and Company.

Shaffir, W. (1998). Doing ethnographic research in Jewish Orthodox communities: The neglected role of sociability. In S. Grills (Ed.), *Doing ethnographic research: Fieldwork settings* (pp. 48–64). Thousand Oaks, CA: Sage.

Shakir, E. (1997). *Bint Arab: Arab and Arab American women in the United States.* Westport, CT: Praeger.

Shannon, C., & Weaver, W. (1949). *The mathematical theory of communication.* Urbana, IL: University of Illinois Press.

Shepherd, G. J. (1999). Advances in communication theory: A critical review. *Journal of Communication, 49*(3), 156–164.

Shepherd, G. J., & Rothenbuhler, E. W. (Eds.), (2001). *Communication and community.* Mahwah, NJ: Lawrence Erlbaum Associates.

Shotter, J. (1989). Social accountability and the social construction of 'you'. In J. Shotter & K. J. Gergen (Eds.), *Texts of Identity* (pp. 133–151). London: Sage.

Shotter, J., & Gergen, K. G. (Eds.), (1989). *Texts of identity.* London: Sage.

Shuler, S. (2001). Talking community at 911: The centrality of communication in coping with emotional labor. In G. J. Shepherd & E. W. Rothenbuhler (Eds.), *Communication and community* (pp. 53–77). Mahwah, NJ: Lawrence Erlbaum Associates.

Sigman, S. J. (1991). Handling the discontinuous aspects of continuous social relationships: Toward research on the persistence of social forms. *Communication Theory, 1,* 106–127.

Sigman, S. J. (Ed.). (1995). *The consequentiality of communication.* Hillsdale, NJ: Lawrence Erlbaum Associates.

Sigman, S. J. (1998). A matter of time: The case for ethnographies of communication. In J. S. Trent (Ed.), *Communication: Views from the helm for the 21st century* (pp. 354–358). Boston: Allyn and Bacon.

Sillars, A. L. (1989). Communication, uncertainty, and understanding in marriage. In B. Dervin, L. Grossberg, B. J. O'Keefe, & E. Wartella (Eds.), *Rethinking communication (Vol. 2) Paradigm exemplars* (pp. 307–328). Newbury Park, CA: Sage.

Silverman, C. (1991). Strategies of ethnic adaptation: The case of gypsies in the United States. In S. Stern & J. A. Cicala (Eds.), *Creative ethnicity: Symbols and strategies of contemporary ethnic life* (pp. 107–111). Logan, UT: Utah State University Press.

Simeti, M. T. (1991, October 20). Norman hill towns of Sicily. *New York Times Magazine,* pp. 26–28, 30, 32.

Sless, D. (1986). *In search of semiotics.* London: Croom Helm.

Smith, A. D. (1981). *The ethnic revival.* Cambridge, England: Cambridge University Press.

Smith, C. D., & Kornbluth, W. (Eds.). (1996). *In the field: Readings on the field research experience.* Westport, CT: Praeger.

Soeffner, H.-G. (1997). *The order of rituals: The interpretation of everyday life.* (M. Luckmann, Trans.). New Brunswick, NJ: Transaction Publishers. (Original work published 1992)

Solomon, M. (1993). The things we study: Texts and their interactions. *Communication Monographs, 60,* 62–68.

Solomon Watson, M. (1995). E pluribus unum: Our partial vision. In J. T. Wood & R. B. Gregg (Eds.), *Toward the twenty-first century: The future of speech communication* (pp. 129–134). Cresskill, NJ: Hampton Press.

Spencer, R. (1997). Race and mixed race: A personal tour. In W. S. Penn (Ed.), *As we are now: Mixblood essays on race and identity* (pp. 126–139). Berkeley, CA: University of California Press.

Spickard, P. R. (1989). *Mixed blood: Intermarriage and ethnic identity in twentieth-century America.* Madison, WI: University of Wisconsin Press.

Spickard, P. R. (1996). *Japanese Americans: The formation and transformations of an ethnic group.* New York: Twayne.

Spivak, G. C. (1990). *The post-colonial critic: Interviews, strategies, dialogues* (S. Harasym, Ed.). New York: Routledge.

Stamp, G., Vangelisti, A. L., & Knapp, M. L. (1994). Criteria for developing and assessing theories of interpersonal communication. In F. L. Casmir (Ed.), *Building communication theories: A socio/cultural approach* (pp. 167–208). Hillsdale, NJ: Lawrence Erlbaum Associates.

Staples, R. (1992). Intermarriage. In E. W. Borgatta & M. L. Borgatta (Eds.), *Encyclopedia of Sociology* (Vol. 2, pp. 968–974). New York: Macmillan.

Star, S. L., & Griesemer, J. R. (1989). Institutional ecology, "translations," and boundary objects: Amateurs and professionals in Berkeley's Museum of Vertebrate Zoology, 1907–39. *Social Studies of Science, 19*(3), 387–420.

Staub, S. (1989). *Yemenis in New York City: The folklore of ethnicity.* Philadelphia: The Balch Institute Press.

Steinfels, P. (1992, October 18). Debating intermarriage, and Jewish survival. *New York Times,* pp. 1A, 16A.

Stephen, T. (1992). Communication, intimacy, and the course of time. *Communication Yearbook, 15*, 522–534.

Stephen, T. (1994). Communication in the shifting context of intimacy: Marriage, meaning, and modernity. *Communication Theory, 4*(3), 191–218.

Stern, G. F. (Ed.). (1987). *Something old, something new: Ethnic weddings in America.* Philadelphia: Balch Institute for Ethnic Studies.

Stern, S., & Cicala, J. A. (Eds.). (1991). *Creative ethnicity: Symbols and strategies of contemporary ethnic life.* Logan, UT: Utah State University Press.

Stimpson, C. R. (1988). *Where the meanings are: Feminism and cultural spaces.* New York: Methuen.

Stock, B. (1990). *Listening for the text: On the uses of the past.* Baltimore: John Hopkins University Press.

Stone, E. (1988). *Black sheep and kissing cousins: How our family stories shape us.* New York: Times Books.

Strine, M. S. (1998). Articulating performance/performativity: Disciplinary tasks and the contingencies of practice. In J. S. Trent (Ed.), *Communication: Views from the helm for the 21st century* (pp. 312–317). Boston: Allyn & Bacon.

Sturgis, I. (1997). *The Nubian wedding book: Words and rituals to celebrate and plan an African-American wedding.* New York: Crown Publishers.

Sung, B. L. (1990). Chinese American intermarriage. *Journal of Comparative Family Studies, 21*(3), 337–352.

Sutherland, M. B. (1979). Comparative perspectives on the education of cultural minorities. In A. E. Alcock, B. K. Taylor, & J. M. Welton (Eds.), *The future of cultural minorities* (pp. 44–62). New York: St. Martin's.

Tambiah, S. J. (1985). *Culture, thought, and social action: An anthropological perspective.* Cambridge, MA: Harvard University Press.

Tanno, D. V., & González, A. (Eds.). (1998). *Communication and identity across cultures.* Thousand Oaks, CA: Sage.

Templeton, A. R. (1999). Human races: A genetic and evolutionary perspective. *American Anthropologist, 100*(3), 632–650.

Theophano, J. S. (1991). "I gave him a cake": An interpretation of two Italian-American weddings. In S. Stern & J. A. Cicala (Eds.), *Creative ethnicity: Symbols and strategies of contemporary ethnic life* (pp. 44–54). Logan, UT: Utah State University Press.

Thornton, S., & Gelder, K. (1997). *The subcultures reader.* New York: Routledge.

Titon, J. T. (1995). Text. *Journal of American Folklore, 108*(430), 432–448.

Tizard, B., & Phoenix, A. (1993). *Black, white or mixed race? Race and racism in the lives of young people of mixed parentage.* New York: Routledge.

Toelken, B. (1991). Ethnic selection and intensification in the Native American pow-wow. In S. Stern & J. A. Cicala (Eds.), *Creative ethnicity: Symbols and strategies of contemporary ethnic life* (pp. 137–156). Logan, UT: Utah State University Press.

Toelken, B. (1998). The Yellowman tapes, 1966–1997. *Journal of American Folklore, 111*(442), 381–391.

Tomas, D. (1996). *Transcultural space and transcultural beings.* Boulder, CO: Westview Press.

Troll, L. E. (1988). Rituals and reunions: Introduction. *American Behavioral Scientist, 31*(6), 621–631.

Tucker, M. B., & Mitchell-Kernan, C. (1990). New trends in Black American interracial marriage: The social structural context. *Journal of Marriage and the Family, 52*(1), 209–218.

Tuleja, T. (1997). Introduction: Making ourselves up: On the manipulation of tradition in small groups. In T. Tuleja (Ed.), *Usable pasts: Traditions and group expressions in North America* (pp. 1–20). Logan, UT: Utah State University Press.

Turner, V. W. (1969). *The ritual process: Structure and anti-structure.* Chicago: Aldine Publishing Company.

Turner, V. W. (1974). *Dramas, fields, and metaphors.* Ithaca, NY: Cornell University Press.

Turner, V. W. (1987). *The anthropology of performance.* New York: PAJ Publications.

Uebelherr, J. (2000, May 14). Mixed feelings: Multiracial Milwaukeeans sort through ambiguity, strength of blended heritage. *Milwaukee Journal Sentinel,* pp. L1, L4.

Ulrich, W. (1986). The use of fiction as a source of information about interpersonal communication: A critical view. *Communication Quarterly, 34,* 143–153.

Van der Vliet, V. (1991). Traditional husbands, modern wives? Constructing marriages in a South African township. In A. D. Spiegel & P. A. McAllister (Eds.), *Tradition and transition in Southern Africa: Festschrift for Philip and Iona Meyer* (pp. 219–241). New Brunswick, NJ: Transaction Publishers.

Van Gennep, A. (1960). *The rites of passage.* Chicago: University of Chicago Press.

Varro, G. (1988). *The transplanted woman: A study of French-American marriages in France.* New York: Praeger.

Vaughen, M. (1991, January 27). Wedding belles. *New York Times Magazine,* pp. 49–54.

Vélez-Ibáñez, C. G. (1993). Ritual cycles of exchange: The process of cultural creation and management in the U.S. borderlands. In P. R. Frese (Ed.), *Celebrations of identity: Multiple voices in American ritual performance* (pp. 119–143). Westport, CT: Bergin & Garvey.

Vila, P. (2000). *Crossing borders, reinforcing borders: Social categories, metaphors, and narrative identities on the U.S.-Mexico frontier.* Austin, TX: University of Texas Press.

Wagatsuma, H. (1978). Identity problems of Black Japanese youth. In R. I. Rotberg (Ed.), *The mixing of peoples: Problems of identity and ethnicity* (pp. 117–129). Stamford, CT: Greylock Publishers.

Wagner, R. (1981). *The invention of culture.* Chicago: University of Chicago Press.

Waldron, J. (1992). Minority cultures and the cosmopolitan alternative. *University of Michigan Journal of Law Reform, 25,* 751.

Walter, E. V. (1988). *Placeways: A theory of the human environment.* Chapel Hill, NC: University of North Carolina Press.

Walter, T. (1994). *The revival of death.* London: Routledge.

Waters, M. C. (1990). *Ethnic options: Choosing identities in America.* Berkeley, CA: University of California Press.

Waters, M. C. (1998). The costs of a costless community. In M. W. Hughey (Ed.), *New tribalisms: The resurgence of race and ethnicity* (pp. 273–295). Washington Square, NY: New York University Press.

Wells, L. (1990, June 30). Formalities. *New York Times Magazine,* pp. 53–59.

Werner, C. M., Altman, I., Brown, B. B., & Ginat, J. (1993). Celebrations in personal relationships: A transactional/dialectical perspective. In S. Duck (Ed.), *Social context and relationships* (pp. 109–138). Newbury Park, CA: Sage.

West, D. (1995). *The wedding*. New York: Doubleday.

Whitney, J. (1990, June 3). Pre-wedding syndrome. *New York Times Magazine*, pp. 22, 24.

Whyte, M. K. (1990). *Dating, mating and marriage*. New York: Aldine de Gruyter.

Wiberg, H., & Scherer, C. P. (Eds.). (1999). *Ethnicity and intra-state conflict: Types, causes and peace strategies*. Aldershot, England: Ashgate.

Wick, N. (1998). Linguistic agons: The self/society opposition and American Quakers. In D. V. Tanno & A. González (Eds.), *Communication and identity across cultures* (pp. 100–121). Thousand Oaks, CA: Sage.

Widdicombe, S. (1998). Identity as an analysts' and a participants' resource. In C. Antaki & S. Widdicombe (Eds.), *Identities in talk* (pp. 191–206). London: Sage.

Williams, C. (1996). Community, subjectivity and selfhood. In A. Brier & R. Lovelock (Eds.), *Communication and community: Anglo-German perspectives* (pp. 90–101). Aldershot, England: Avebury.

Willis, P. (1990). *Common culture: Symbolic work at play in the everyday cultures of the young*. Buckingham, England: Open University Press.

Wilmsen, E. N., & McAllister, P. (Eds.). (1996). *The politics of difference: Ethnic premises in a world of power*. Chicago: University of Chicago Press.

Wilson, B. F. (1984). Marriage's melting pot. *American Demographics, 6*(7), 34–37, 45.

Wilson, D. S., & Jacobson, C. K. (1995). White attitudes toward Black and White interracial marriage. In C. K. Jacobson, (Ed.), *American families: Issues in race and ethnicity* (pp. 353–367). New York: Garland.

Wilson, M. (1954). Nyakyusa ritual and symbolism. *American Anthropologist, 56*(2), 241.

Wilson, M. (1978). Ritual: Resilience and obliteration. In J. Argyle & E. Preston-Whyte (Eds.), *Social system and tradition in Southern Africa. Essays in honour of Eileen Krige* (pp. 150–164). Cape Town, South Africa: Oxford University Press.

Wilson, T. M., & Donnan, H. (Eds.). (1998). *Border identities, nation and state at international frontiers*. Cambridge, England: Cambridge University Press.

Winner, I. P. (1986). Semiotics of culture. In J. Deely, B. Williams, & F. E. Kruse (Eds.), *Frontiers in semiotics* (pp. 181–184). Bloomington, IN: Indiana University Press.

Wiseman, R. L. (Ed.). (1995). *Intercultural communication theory*. Thousand Oaks, CA: Sage.

Wiseman, R. L., & Koester, J. (Eds.). (1993). *Intercultural communication competence*. Newbury Park, CA: Sage.

Witte, S. P. (1992). Context, text, intertext: Toward a constructivist semiotic of writing. *Written Communication, 9*, 237–308.

Wolf, E. R. (1990). Distinguished lecture: Facing power—old insights, new questions. *American Anthropologist, 92*(3), 586–596.

Wolf, E. R. (1994). Perilous ideas: Race, culture, people. *Current Anthropology, 35*(1), 1–12.

Wolin, S. J., & Bennett, L. A. (1984). Family rituals. *Family Process, 23*(3), 401–420.

Wood, J. T., & Gregg, R. B. (1995). The future of the field: Directing scholarship and teaching in the 21st century. In J. T. Wood & R. B. Gregg (Eds.), *Toward the twenty-first century: The future of speech communication* (pp. 1–11). Cresskill, NJ: Hampton Press.

Woodruff, J. B. (1980). Staging the vocational bride, or the prom queen turns pro. In R. B. Browne (Ed.), *Rituals and ceremonies in popular culture* (pp. 238–247). Bowling Green, OH: Bowling Green University Press.

Wray, M., & Newitz, A. (Eds.). (1997). *White trash: Race and class in America.* New York: Routledge.

Wulff, H. (1995). Inter-racial friendship: Consuming youth styles, ethnicity and teenage femininity in South London. In V. Amit-Talai & H. Wulff (Eds.), *Youth cultures: A cross-cultural perspective* (pp. 63–80). London: Routledge.

Yamani, M. (1998). Cross-cultural marriage within Islam: Ideals and reality. In R. Breger & R. Hill (Eds.), *Cross-cultural marriage: Identity and choice* (pp. 153–169). New York: Berg.

Young, R. (1996). *Intercultural communication: Pragmatics, genealogy, deconstruction.* Clevedon, England: Multilingual Matters.

Zack, N. (Ed.). (1995). *American mixed race: The culture of microdiversity.* Lanham, MD: Rowan & Littlefield.

Zarefsky, D. (1995). On defining the communication discipline. In J. T. Wood & R. B. Gregg (Eds.), *Toward the twenty-first century: The future of speech communication* (pp. 103–112). Cresskill, NJ: Hampton Press.

Ziff, B., & Rao, P. V. (1997). *Borrowed power: Essays in cultural appropriation.* New Brunswick, NJ: Rutgers University Press.

Zweigenhaft, R. L., & Domhoff, G. W. (1991). *Blacks in the White establishment? A study of race and class in America.* New Haven, CT: Yale University Press.

Author Index

A

Abrahams, R. D., 31, 95, 133
Abu-Lughod, L., 120
Advisory Board, The President's Initiative
    on Race, 14
Alba, R. D., 17, 32
Alberts, J. K., 251
Aldama, A., 31
Allan, J., 69
Allen, B., 158
Altman, I., xiii, 238, 250
Amy, J., 14
Anderson, B., 60, 73
Antaki, C., 157
Appadurai, A., 30–31, 60, 75
Appiah, K. A., 25
Arboleda, T., 226
Arndt, B., 75
Austin, J. L., 101
Azoulay, K. G., 14, 226

B

Babcock, B., 119
Bakhtin, M., 225
Ball, M. S., 244
Barbara, A., xiv, 12
Barth, F., 33, 35
Bateson, M. C., 36
Bauman, R., 102, 120, 176
Baumann, G., 90, 100–101, 119
Bavelas, J. B., xiii, 210
Baxter, L., xiii, 191–192

Becker, A. L., 35, 192
Benatar, G., 121
Bennett, L. A., 214
Benson, S., xiv, 13–14, 19
Berger, P. L., 236, 239
Bernard, R. M., 34, 71
Bird, S. E., 246
Black, A. D., 57
Blaeser, K., 215
Blau, J. R., 193
Blu, K. L., 71
Blue, H. C., 35
Bohannan, P., 227
Bouissac, P., 97–98
Bourdieu, P. 21, 176, 234, 249, 251
Boyer, P., 118
Brady, L. S., 69, 72, 185
Braithwaite, D. O., xiii
Branham, R. J., 36
Breger, R., xiv, 36
Brennen, B., 192
Breuss, C. J. S., xiii
Bridgwood, A., 111
Briggs, C. L., 120, 157, 176
Bronner, S. J., 64, 74
Brown, B. B., xiii, 238, 250
Brown, C., 73
Browne, R. B., 31
Browning, L. D., 74
Bruner, C. H., 73
Bulcroft, K., 105
Bulcroft, R., 105
Buriel, R., 31, 72
Buttny, R., xiii, 36
Byrne, S., 30

C

Callaway, H., 250
Camper, C., 226
Carbaugh, D., 157, 231
Carey, J. W., 24
Cartmill, M., 13
Cartry, M., 97
Casmir, F. L., 225
Caycedo, J. C., 12
Chai, L., 32
Chaney, D., 36
Charland, M., 120
Charsley, S. R., xiii–xiv, 34, 63, 91, 106,
        118, 120–121, 192, 243–244
Cheal, D., xiii
Chirot, D., 225
Chua, E., xi
Chung, F., v
Cicala, J. A., 192
Clark, D., 119
Clark, W. A. V., 32
Coffey, A., 249–250
Cohen, A. P., 25–26, 33, 49–51, 71, 170
Cole, H., 6, 21, 192
Cole, W., 108
Collins, J., 35
Connerton, P., 119, 174, 233
Conquergood, D., 35
Constantine, J. M., 111
Constantine, L. L., 111
Cooley, R. E., 231
Cooren, F., 225
Coover, G. E., 131
Costa, S. S., 20, 168
Cottrell, A. B., 11
Cowan, P., 34
Cowan, R., 34
Crain, M., 101
Crane, D., 59, 73, 180
Culler, J., 176
Cupach, W. R., 157

D

Dainton, M., xiii
Dant, T., 107
Davies, D., 118
Davis-Floyd, R. E., 119
Deegan, M. J., 75
Denzin, N. K., 71, 244

DeVos, G., 33–34, 101, 157
Diamont, A., 103–104, 110–111, 158–159
Didion, J., 122
Diggs, N. B., 34
di Leonardo, M., 16
Domhoff, G. W., 13
Donnan, H., 35, 75
Dorson, R. M., 121
Driver, T. F., 89
Duncan, J. S., 36
Dundes, A., 6, 192
Duntley, M., 96
Duranti, A., 36, 96

E

Eastman, C. M., 65
Eco, U., 35, 90
Edwards, D., 131
Edwards, W., xiv, 135
Eisenberg, E. M., 193
Eller, J. D., 30
Ellis, D., 33–34
Eoyang, E., 69
Epstein, A. L., 93, 239
Ervin-Tripp, S., 192

F

Fabre, G, 31
Farnell, B., 31
Feldman, S. D., 158
Ferguson, J., 35, 71, 75, 91
Fernandez, J., 172
Fetterman, D. M., 246
Firth, R., 88
Fiske, J., 36, 73, 169–170, 173
Fitch, K., 225
Fitzpatrick, J. P., 32
Fortes, M., 129–130
Fournier, M., 34
Frese, P. R., xiii
Fried, M. H., xiii, 89
Fried, M. N., xiii, 89
Frith, S., 160

G

Gabaccio, D. R., 74
Gaines, S. O., Jr., 31, 72
Galloway, P., 11

Gamarnikow, E., 239
Gans, H., 133, 158
Garcia-Preto, N., 11, 22
Gareis, E., 31
Garner, T., 157
Gates, H. L., Jr., 25
Gedmintes, A., 73
Geertz, C., 23, 35, 230, 239, 246
Gelder, K., 15
Gergen, K. J., 36, 75, 157, 169
Gerholm, T., 97
Giddens, A., 63
Gilroy, P., 225
Ginat, J., xiii
Giordano, J., 30
Glassie, H., 26
Goffman, E., 130
Golden, J., 72
Golden, R. M., 32
Goldschmidt, W., 118
González, A., 157
Goode, J., 178
Goodwin, C., 36
Goody, J., 239
Graham, L. R., 31
Grearson, J. C., xiii, 35
Green, A., 15
Gregg, R. B., 30
Greimas, A. J., 230
Griesemer, J. R., 193
Griffith, E. E. H., 35
Grimes, R. L., 117, 119, 130
Gross, L., 60
Grossman, F., 34
Gudykunst, W. B., xi
Gumperz, J. J., 157, 192
Gupta, A., 35, 71, 75, 91
Gurak, D. T., 32
Gusfield, J. R., 36
Gutierrez, R. A., 31

Hardt, H., 192
Harper, A. M., xiv
Harre, J., xiv
Harris, A., 226
Harris, H. W., 35
Harris, N., 119
Hartley, J., 73
Hassan, I., 228
Hastrup, K., 234
Hatanaka, H., 32
Hay, J., 36
Hebdige, D., 192
Hecht, M. L., 157
Hechter, M., 33
Hegde, R. S., 158
Henderson, K., 193
Hendrickson, C., 110
Henriquez, F., 14
Herzfeld, M., 172
Hill, R., xiv, 20, 36
Hobart, M., 234
Hobsbawm, E., 119
Hodder, I., xiii
Hodge, R., 244
Hopper, R., 251
Hoskins, J., 107
Hsu, F. L. K., 232
Hufford, M., 36
Hughes-Freeland, F., 101
Hutter, M., 132
Hymes, D., 36, 71, 96, 101

I

Ifekwunigwe, J. O., 31, 243
Imahori, T. T., 157
Ingraham, C., xiii–xiv, 9, 59, 73, 132
Irvin, C. L., 30

J

Jackson, B. L., 226
Jackson, R. L., II, 157, 159
Jacobson, C. K., 32
Jankowski, N. W., 28, 71
Jansen, C., 32
Jensen, K. B., 243
Johnson, F. L., 30
Johnson, M., 109
Jules-Rosette, B., 246

H

Hall, B. J., 71
Hall, S., 60, 129
Halliday, M. A. K., 36, 227
Halperin, R. H., 50
Hanassab, S., xiii, 34
Handelman, D., 112, 236
Handler, R., 73, 118
Hannerz, U., xiii, 31, 35, 50, 75, 191–192, 209, 225

K

Kalmijn, M., 32
Kaminsky, M., 247
Kapchan, D. A., 120
Karp, I., 155
Katriel, T., 36
Katz, I., 226
Kellner, H., 236
Kendall, L., xiv, 7, 57, 73
Kendis, K. O., 34, 133
Kertzer, D. I., 118, 193
Kerwin, C., 226
Khatib-Chahidi, J., 20
Kim, Y. Y., 158
Kinsley, C. H., 22
Kirn, W., 108
Kirshenblatt-Gimblett, B., 107
Kitano, H. H. L., 32
Kitchen, D. L., 32
Knapp, M. L., 238
Knoerle, J. H., 139
Kobayashi, A., 133
Koester, J., 119
Kominsky, N., 17
Kornbluth, W., 250
Kouri, K., M., 32
Krebs, N., 225
Kress, G., 36, 244
Kristeva, J., 175

L

La Brack, B., 32
Lalli, C. G., 132
Lamont, M., 34
Lareau, A., 250
Laswell, M., 32
Lavie, S., 71
Lavin, C., 9
Leach, E., 97, 117–118, 121
Leeds-Hurwitz, W., x–xi, 36, 71, 74, 117,
          119–121, 158, 191, 225, 227,
          231, 233, 238, 241
Leonard, D., 58–59, 110, 158, 160
Leonard, K., 14, 32–33, 57, 130–131
Lessl, T. M., 236
Levine, D. L., 193
Levine, M., 62–63
Levinson, S., 192
Levi-Strauss, C., 180

Lewin, E., 31
Lewis, G., 193
Ley, D., 36
Lieberson, S., 32
Limón, J. E., 22
Linnekin, J., 118
Lipson-Walker, C., 31, 140
Littlejohn, S. W., 118, 228
Liu, J. H., 31, 72
Loeding, J., 109
Lotman, Y. M., 34, 36
Louw, E., 75
Luckmann, T., 239
Luhmann, N., xiv
Lukes, S., 129
Lum, C. M. K., 239

M

MacAloon, J., 120
Mac an Ghaill, M., 118
MacCannell, D., 91, 192
MacCannell, J. F., 91, 192
Malanka, B., 22
Mannheim, B., 35, 176
Manning, F., 9, 31
Marcus, G. E., 71
Marsden, M. T., 31
Marshall, V. W., 96
Martin, J. H., 91
Martínez, E., 69
Mathabane, G., 55, 226
Mathabane, M., 55, 226
Matthews, G., 71, 251
Mayer, B., 54, 62, 156
Mayer, E., 7, 16–18, 57, 132, 235
McAllister, P., 30
McCullers, C., 73
McDowell, J. H., 176
McGoldrick, M., 11, 22, 30
McKinnell, T., 32
McNamara, R. P., 14–15, 32
McNamee, S., 75
McReady, W. C., 22
Mead, G. H., 158
Mead, M., 69
Metz, C., 245
Metzger, D., xiii
Miller, A. R., xiii
Miller, D., xiii
Miller, R., 120
Mischler, E., 251

Mitchell-Kernan, C., 32
Modell, J., 93
Moffatt, M., 72
Mokros, H. B., 157
Moller, D. W., 119
Monaco, J., 183
Montgomery, B. M., xiii, 29, 192
Montgomery, M. E., xiv, 183
Moore, H., 132
Moore, S. F., 87, 94–95
Morgan, D., 239
Moses, Y. T., 32
Muir, E., 169
Mukhopadhyay, C. C., 32
Murphy, S. T., 131
Myerhoff, B., 27, 29, 71–72, 87, 91,
        94–96, 118–119, 129, 131–132,
        157, 244

N

Nagel, J., 16, 158
Naylor, L. L., 7–8, 15
Neustadt, K., 181
Newitz, A., 34
Noyes, D., 72

O

Ochberg, R. L., 101, 129
O'Hearn, C. C., 226
Ohnuki-Tierney, E., 71
Okely, J., 250
Ong, A., 31
Orbe, M. P., 15, 71
Oring, E., 24
Ortner, S. B., 18–19, 49, 105–106, 120
Ottesen, C., 183
Owen, J. L., 36, 158

P

Pan, E., 20
Paton, R., 20
Payne, R. J., 14, 17, 32
Peacock, J. L., 96, 169
Pearce, W. B., 36, 118, 225, 228, 230
Pearson, J. C., xiii
Penman, R., x, xiii, 169, 217, 221, 223
Penn, W. S., 31, 226
Philipsen, G., 31, 71

Phoenix, A., 226
Pollan, S. M., 62–63
Ponterotto, J. G., 226
Price, R., 32
Puente, M., 9
Pugh, T., 13
Purvis, J., 239
Putnam, L. L., 71

R

Ragan, S. L., 251
Ranger, T., 119
Rao, P. V., 85
Rapport, N., 35
Rawlins, W. K., 192, 239
Real, M. R., 36
Reed-Danahay, D., 96
Reid, A., 225
Richard, M. A., 34
Richardson, P. D., 12
Ricoeur, P., 23
Rieff, P., 75
Rios, D. I., 31, 72
Roberts, G. L., 210
Roberts, R. E. T., 32
Romano, D., xiii–xiv
Romanucci-Ross, L., 34, 101, 157
Roosens, E. E., 158
Root, D., 85
Root, M. P. P., xiii–xiv, 14, 19, 30, 32–33,
        130, 226
Rosaldo, R., 66, 170
Rosenthal, C. J., 96
Rosenwald, G. C., 101, 129
Rothenbuhler, E. W., 26, 36, 72, 116–118
Royce, A. P., 37, 178–179
Rubenstein, H., 121
Rubinstein, H., 122
Rushdie, S., 192

S

Saldivar, J. D., 35
Sandfur, G. D., 32
Santino, J., 31, 90
Sapir, E., 231
Scales-Trent, J., 158
Scheffler, I., 193
Schegloff, E. A., x, 192
Scherer, C. P., 30
Scheub, H. E., 192
Schieffelin, E. L., 35, 102, 120, 176

Schiffer, M. B., xiii
Schlereth, T., 158
Schneider, D. M., 175
Schneider, S. W., 97, 235–236
Scholes, R., 23
Schudson, M., 117–118
Schutz, A., 134
Schwartz, D., 62, 111
Sebeok, T., 228
Seligson, M., 62
Shaffir, W., 243
Shakir, E., 23
Shannon, C., 191
Shepherd, G. J., xi, 72
Shotter, J., 36, 62
Shuler, S., 29
Shultz, J., 250
Sigman, S. J., 157, 221, 233, 241–242, 251
Sillars, A. L., 193
Silverman, C., 93
Simeti, M. T., 120
Sless, D., 23–24
Smiens, L., 105
Smith, A. D., 15
Smith, C. D., 250
Smith, G. W. H., 244
Smith, L. B., xiii, 35
Soeffner, H.-G., xiii, 89, 118
Solomon, M., 36
Solomon Watson, M., 36
Spencer, R., 32
Spickard, P. R., 17, 19–20, 22, 34, 69
Spivak, G. C., 158
Stamp, G., 238
Staples, R., 32, 250
Star, S. L., 193
Staub, S., 33, 65
Steinfels, P., 30
Stephen, T., 21, 33
Stern, G. F., 36, 132
Stern, S., 192
Stimpson, C. R., 174, 192
Stock, B., 36
Stohl, C., 71
Stone, E., 35, 238
Strine, M. S., 120
Sturgis, I., 6, 21, 192
Sullivan, S. J., 233
Sung, B. L., 32
Sutherland, M. B., 27
Swedenberg, T., 71

T

Tambiah, S. J., 28, 117, 231
Tanno, D. V., 157
Taylor, J. R., 225
Taylorson, D., 239
Tedlock, D., 176
Tempenis, M., 14–15, 32
Templeton, A. R., 32
Theophano, J. S., 178
Thornton, S., 15
Tidwell, R., xiii, 34
Ting-Toomey, S., xi
Titon, J. T., 35
Tizard, B., 226
Toelken, B., 93, 118, 249
Tolkkinen, K., 14
Tomas, D., 31
Troll, L. E., 89, 158
Tucker, M. B., 32
Tuleja, T., 15, 75
Turner, E., 69
Turner, V. W., 89, 96, 118

U

Uebelherr, J., 226
Ulrich, W., 251

V

Van der Vliet, V., 74
Vangelisti, A. L., 238
Van Gennep, A., 89, 118
Varro, G., xiv, 11–12, 71, 131, 236
Vaughen, M., 121
Vélez-Ibánez, C. G., 96
Vila, P., 35, 66, 251

W

Wagatsuma, H., 33
Wagner, R., 119
Waldron, J., 69
Walter, E. V., 27
Walter, T., 96, 119
Walton, B., 14–15, 32
Waters, M. C., 16, 32
Weaver, W., 191
Wells, L., 244

Werner, C. M., xiii, 238, 250
West, D., 251
Whitney, J., 235
Whyte, M. K., 20, 34
Wiberg, H., 30
Wick, N., 158
Widdicombe, S., 131, 157
Williams, C., 60
Williams, G. E., xiii
Willis, P., 91
Wilmsen, E. N., 30
Wilson, B. F., 32
Wilson, D. S., 32
Wilson, M., 88–89
Wilson, T. M., 35, 75
Winner, I. P., 25
Wiseman, R. L., 30, 119
Witte, S. P., 23, 176
Wolf, E. R., 15, 170

Wolin, S. J., 214
Wood, J. T., 30
Woodruff, J. B., xiii, 30
Wray, M., 34
Wulff, H., 15, 33

Y

Yamani, M., 56
Yeung, W.-T., 32
Young, R., 30

Z

Zack, N., 226
Zarefsky, D., 191
Ziff, B., 85
Zweigenhaft, R. L., 13

Subject Index

A

A *Wedding Story*, 108–109, 159, 244
Absence(s), 91–92, 207, 230, 245
Adulthood, 211
Advertisements, 73
Advertising, 36
Advice, 246–247
Africa, 144
African, 5, 20, 94, 156, 216
    American(s), 2–6, 10, 13–14, 16–17,
        19, 32–33, 80, 95, 111, 135,
        144–146, 156, 159, 179,
        185, 191, 226, 251
    community, 154
Age, 35, 71, 81
    difference between bride and groom,
        82, 100, 142
Alabama, 14
Alcohol, *see* Drink
Altar, 101
Ambiguity, 186–191, 193, 212, 214, 222,
    225
America(n), *see* United States
    Anglo, 52, 72, 112, *see also* White
Amplification, 73
Analysis, 246–247
Analyst(s), 169–170, 174, 228–229, 231
    role of, 249–250
Ancestors, 150
Anniversary, 46–47, 89, 103, 121, 135,
    141, 147, 179
Anthropologist(s), xiv, 12, 157, 247
Anthropology, x, xii, 31, 36, 49, 231, 250
    theory, 71

Anti-miscegenation laws, 14
Apron, 100
Arab Americans, 23
Architects, 119
Arguments, 158
Armenian, 53
Arras, 151–154, 156, 184
Asia, 185
Asian(s), 20, 149–150
    Americans, 20, 149, 159, 225
    Arts Museum, 164
    South, 66
Assimilation, 34
Atheist(s), 58, 124, 136, 162
Attendants, *see* Wedding party
Audience, 91, 94, 97, 99–100, 117,
        155–156, 183, 192, 199, 220,
        233, 245, *see also* Guest;
        Participant
Australia, 75, 79, 84, 216
Avoidance, 65

B

Bachelor party, 8, 56, 66, 137, 205, 248
Bachelorette party, 122, 142
Balance, 91, 172, 215–216, 223
Balch Institute for Ethnic Studies, 132
Band, *see* Music
Banner, red silk, 149, 215
Baptist(s), 10, 55, 92, 95, 111, 144, 181
Barbie dolls, 146
Baseball, 74
Bedouin, 120

Bees, 232
Behavior, *see* Interaction
  naturalistic, 242
  streams of, 242
Belief systems, 215, *see also* Religion
Bells, 61
Benediction, *see* Blessing
Best man, 66, 113, 125, 139, 168
  son of, 139
Betsy's Wedding, 18, 187
Bible, 14, 43
Bilingual, 158
Biography, 107
Biological construct, 12
Biracial, 13–14
Birth(s), 8, 30, 93, 97, 119, 224
Birthday, 135, 206
Black, *see* African American
Blankets, 46
Blessing(s), 151, 166, 177, 188–189, 197,
    201–202, 206
Boa, 79
Bohemian, 53, 66
Book(s), 20, 175, 234–235, 250
  how-to, 245
Border, *see* Boundary
Borderlands, 66
Boundary(ies), 8–9, 11–12, 16, 19, 25–26,
    28, 34–35, 50–51, 65, 71, 90,
    113, 158, 190, 233, 245
  of community, 71, 130, 197
  crossing, 17, 20–23, 160, 223
  of group, 94, 113, 118
  as metaphor, 35
  object, 193
Bouquet toss, 44, 47, 127, 168, 204
Bowing, *see* Ceremony
Bricolage, 29, 180–182, 186, 191, 212,
    215, 222, 225
Bridal
  gown, *see* Wedding gown
  party, *see* Wedding party
Bride(s), 2–6, 24, 28, 30–32, 35, 40,
    42–44, 51, 53–56, 58, 61–70,
    74, 78, 80, 82–83, 87, 89–90,
    92, 95–96, 99–100, 103–107,
    110–117, 120–122, 126–130,
    134–159, 162–168, 171–175,
    177–191, 193, 196–207,
    212–214, 219–220, 222, 225,
    230, 232, 234–237, 242–245,
    248–249

aunt of, 111, 125, 151–152
brother of, 44, 118, 125, 137, 140
brother-in-law, 146, 189
community of, 50
cousin(s) of, 113–116, 127, 156, 189,
    244
daughter of, 145
family of, 92, 112, 143, 146–148, 150,
    152, 177–178, 180, 197,
    202, 213, 235–236
father of, 2, 53, 100, 139–140, 152,
    162, 177, 186, 189, 203
father's grandmother, 166
foreign, 142–144
friends of, 122, 150, 236
giving away, 100, 107, 199
grandaunt of, 151
grandfather of, 151
grandmother of, 125, 134, 151, 157,
    167, 184
grandparents of, 150
great-grandmother of, 180
knowledge of traditions, 236
mother of, 2, 30, 80–81, 92, 153, 174,
    186, 196–199, 202,
    204–205, 212, 216, 247
mother's brother, 173
parents, 80, 103, 109, 113–116, 124,
    133, 158, 166, 168, 173,
    177, 184, 204, 206, 224, 242
siblings of, 244
sister of, 3, 79, 146
son of, 120
teasing of, 168
uncle of, 152
Bridesmaids, 42, 113–114, 125, 152, see
    also Clothing; Jewelry
Britain, 15, 34, *see also* England
British Register office, 58, 101
Broom, *see* Jumping the broom; Wedding
    broom
  dance, 148
Buddhist(s), 18, 55, 58, 162, 171

C

Cake, 52, 74, 83–84, 111–112, 121,
    127–128, 137, 142, 146,
    151–152, 154, 166–167, 185,
    204, 212, 249
  bride's, 40, 44, 47, 106
  cutting, 149

feeding one another, 127, 142, 204
groom's, 39–40, 44, 102, 106, 216
saving top layer of, 46, 89, 135, 141,
    158
topper, 83, 104, 107, 137–138, 146,
    174–175, 179
interracial, 159
California, 14–15, 53, 58, 82, 85, 130
Indian, 157
Cameras, 24, *see also* Photograph
Canada, 34, 162, 164, *see also* Ontario
Canadian, 193
Candle(s), 28, 64, 83, 94
    unity, 4, 44, 47, 61, 64, 94, 136–137,
        153
Canoe, 185
Car(s), 67–68, 109, 127–128, 149, 156,
    160, 184
Caribbean cruise, 147
Cartier, 62
Caste, 19
Catholic(s), 2, 4, 10, 17–18, 40, 44, 47,
    53–58, 61, 64–66, 69, 92,
    94–95, 104, 111, 136, 142–144,
    146–148, 151, 153–154, 156,
    171–172, 175, 177, 181,
    185–187, 237
Caucasian, *see* White
Celebration(s), 9, 31, 70, 121, 135, 140,
    233
Census, 13, 15
    Bureau, 32
Ceremony(ies), 31, 46, 52, 54, 56–58, 63,
    66, 68, 70, 74, 81–83, 92, 97,
    100–109, 111–112, 122,
    124–126, 128, 130, 134–135,
    137–138, 142–143, 146–147,
    149, 151, 153, 155–156, 162,
    170, 172, 177, 182–188, 190,
    192, 197–199, 201, 204–206,
    211, 213, 215–216, 235, 237,
    244, 249
    bowing, 69, 150
    civil, 55, 57–58, 113, 146, 151–152
    commitment, 31, 34, 70, 137–138,
        225
    realignment, 130
    tea, 54, 150, 180–181, 184
Chagall, 197
Chai, 161–163, 215, 217, 219
Chairs, lifting bride and groom on, 127,
    152, 203

Champagne, 45
Change(s), 90–91, 102, 104, 118–119,
    218, 222, 226, 232–233, 244,
    247
Cheung sam, 124, 149, 166
Child, 92, 118, 131, 139, 179, 203,
    232–233
Children, 32, 35, 46, 81–82, 85, 96, 101,
    103–105, 107–108, 113, 120,
    122, 132, 135, 147–148, 181,
    202, 205, 222–225, 236, 238
China, 78–79, 84, 87, 90, 162, 167, 216
    People's Republic of, 124–128
Chinatown, 149, 184
Chinese, 12, 20, 53–54, 80, 124–128,
    149–150, 156, 161–168, 180,
    184, 213–215, 219, 225
    American, 148, 184
    character, 162, 164–165, *see also*
        Shuang-hsi
    identity, 162
    language, 126–127, 150, 159, 168,
        181
    robe, 166–167
    wedding dress, *see Cheung sam*
Chippewa, 146–147, 179
Chivas, 42
Christian(s), 2, 17–18, 27, 54, 57, 63–64,
    78, 81, 99–101, 108–109, 111,
    113, 121, 132, 154, 172, 186,
    188–191, 195–207, 212–214,
    216, 247, see also Baptists;
    Catholic; Church of God in
    Christ; Congregationalists;
    Cook Island Christian Church;
    Episcopalian; Lutheran; Meth-
    odist; Orthodox; Presbyterian;
    Protestant; Unitarian
    non-denominational, 154, 238
Christianity, 182
Christmas, 119, 179
Chuckie Cheese, 138
Chupa, see Huppah
Church
    bulletins, 61
    service, 107
Church of God in Christ, 52
Civil ceremony, *see* Ceremony
Clampetts, 155
Clam
    bake, 181
    shell, 164

Class, 2, 5, 10, 13, 18–19, 21, 32–34, 50,
        65, 67, 71, 124, 128, 160, 211,
        219
    identity, see Identity, class
    lower, 37
    lower middle, 19
    marker, 42, 114, 149, 219
    middle, 13, 16, 32, 34, 37, 40, 42
    upper, 19, 37, 72, 185
    working, 13, 32, 34
Classrooms, 229
Clintons, 155
Clothing, 4, 26, 28, 54, 56–57, 69, 74, 80,
        88, 106, 109–110, 141–143,
        166, 178, 183–184, 186, 197,
        206, 228, 230, 248–250, see also
        Wedding gown
    of bridesmaids, 42, 126, 101, 105,
        109, 139, 143–144, 155,
        157, 185
    color of, 42, 74, 139, 143, 184–185
    of groom, 90, 109, 142
    of groomsmen, 139, 142, 144,
        155–156
    of guests, 73, 111, 125, 185
    minister's stole, 198, 222
    of mother of the bride, 42, 127, 139,
        141–142, 157
    of mother of the groom, 127,
        141–142, 157
    of ushers, 143
Cocultures, 15
Code(s), ix, 8, 28, 71, 88, 105–106, 117,
        182, 184, 186, 210, 213, 222,
        228, 248, 250
    culturally-derived, 183
    matching, 155, 182–186
    switching, 65
Cognition, xiii
Cognitive
    aspects of communication, 221
    space, 102, 176
Collective experience, 101, 174
Colombia, 39–47
Colombians, 102
Colors, see Wedding colors
Coming of age, 97, 224; see also Rites of
        passage
Commitment, 121, 145
    act of, 117
    ceremonies, see Ceremonies

Communication, ix–251, see also
        Intercultural; Interpersonal;
        Language and Social Interac-
        tion; Mass
    as analyzable, 23–24
    consequentiality of, 157
    definition of, 36
    discipline of, xi–xv, 30, 36, 49, 131,
        157–158, 172, 191, 231,
        234, 247, 250–251
    in everyday life, x, 112, 157–158, 228
    improbability of, xiv
    literature, 245
    model of, 191
    social approaches to, xi
    strategy, 193
    as vehicle, 29
Communicative
    competence, 96, 119
    resources, 225
Community, 2, 15, 22, 25–29, 36, 65–76,
        71–75, 87–88, 90–91, 95, 97,
        118, 129, 136, 169–170, 172,
        174, 176, 178, 189–190,
        196–197; 209–214, 219,
        221–223, 233, 242, 249, see also
        Boundary
    building, 118
    creating a sense of, 60, 72
    heterogeneous, 50
    history of, 101
    imagined, 60
Competence, see Communicative compe-
        tence
Compromise, 216
Condensation, 117
Conflict, xiii, 8, 12, 30, 51, 121, 131–132,
        189–190, 232, 235–236
    cultural, 68, 223
    resolution, 212, 225, 235–236
    of traditions, 70, 188
Conformity, 232
Confrontation, see also Conflict
    creative, 225
Confusion, 95, 155
Congregationalists, 58
Connotation(s), 6, 66, 78–79, 153, 177,
        180, 185–186
Consensus, 235–236
Consequentiality, see Communication,
        consequentiality of
Consociates, 134–135

Conspicuous
    consumption, 111
    displays, 219
Constructionism, *see* Social
    constructionism
Contemporaries, 134–135
Context(s), x, 24–25, 29, 31, 36, 96, 98,
        131–131, 152, 158, 169, 173,
        176, 181, 209–210, 217, 224,
        230–232, 241–242, 244
    specific knowledge, 144
    sequential, 192
Contextualization, 192
Continuity, 89–91, 101, 118–119, 157,
        160, 211, 218, 223, 232–233,
        239
Contract, *see* Wedding contract; *see also*
    Ketubah
Convention, 84, 117
Conversation(s), 71, 162, 230, 233, 245,
        247
    global, 231
Conversion, 92, 99, 162, 168, 177
Cook Island, 12, 52–53
    Christian Church, 52
Copias, 156
Cosmopolitanism, 225
Costa Rica, 92, 143
Costa Rican, 92, 142
Couple 1, 20, 63–64, 99–100, 245
Couple 2, 104
Couple 3, 100
Couple 4, 53, 66, 89
Couple 5, 99–100
Couple 6, 174
Couple 7, 153
Couple 9, 95, 111
Couple 10, 213, 215, 225
Couple 11, 52, 72
Couple 12, 54–55, 99
Couple 13, 135, 195–207, 212–213, 216,
        244
Couple 14, 27, 154, 186–187
Couple 15, 177
Couple 17, 185
Couple 18, 186
Couple 19, 146
Couple 20, 138
Couple 21, 55
Couple 22, 52
Couple 23, 180
Couple 26, 99

Couple 27, 122
Couple 29, 53
Couple 30, 111
Couple 31, 184
Couple 32, 175
Couple 34, 54
Couple 35, 67
Couple 36, 111
Couple 38, 59
Couple 40, 135
Couple 42, 57
Couple 43, 155
Couple 44, 24, 104, 179
Couple 45, 146
Couple 46, 179
Couple 47, 113
Couple 48, 134
Couple 50, 58
Couple 52, 135–136
Couple 56, 151
Couple 58, 138, 185
Couple 59, 105
Couple 60, 179, 191
Couple 62, 135
Couple 64, 112
Couple 67, 156
Couple 68, 64–65
Couple 69, 188–190, 197, 214, 216
Couple 70, 247
Couple 71, 12, 52
Couple 72, 99
Couple 73, 55–56
Couple 74, 1–6, 94, 216
Couple 75, 77–85, 87, 182, 220
Couple 76, 113–116
Couple 77, 123–128, 168, 215
Couple 78, 140
Couple 80, 161–168, 215, 217, 219
Couple 82, 171, 212
Couple 83, 181
Couple 84, 40–47, 102, 140, 216
Couple 85, 70, 172–173
Couple 86, 151, 219
Couple 88, 53, 110, 141, 212, 245
Couple 89, 100
Couple 90, 103, 144
Couple 91, 47, 58, 120–121, 142
Couple 92, 100, 137
Couple 93, 92, 142–143
Couple 94, 148–150
Couple 95, 89, 100, 103, 139–140
Couple 96, 155

Couple 97, 139, 184
Couple 98, 136, 141, 152, 158
Couple 99, 47, 90, 107, 139, 175
Couple 100, 137, 138–139, 142
Couple 101, 143
Couple 102, 148, 179
Couple 103, 89, 92
Couple 105, 103, 154
Couple 106, 92, 118, 139
Couple 107, 53, 63, 90, 121, 140
Couple 108, 103, 144–145
Couple 109, 61–62, 139, 141–142, 152
Couple 110, 31, 137–138
Couple 111, 85, 142, 146–147, 153, 179
Couple 112, 185
Creativity, 26, 35, 68, 71, 74, 91, 96, 113,
        158, 198, 225, 232–233, *see also*
        Cultural creativity
Creole, 35
Creolization, 225
Crosscultural, 11–12
Crown, 153
Cryogenic trend, 234
Cuba, 16
Cuban, 66
Cuban American, 16
Cultural
    agent, 33
    appropriation, 85
    center, 73
    change, 91, 101, 222
    code switching, 65–66
    complexity, 225
    creativity, 66, 209–210, 212–219, 221,
        223, 233, 249
    difference(s), 50, 56, 72, 128, 174,
        191, 209–210, 217, 220, 243
    dissonance, 8
    exotica, 85
    expectations, 133, 184, 231, 236
    experience, 75
    form, 176
    geography, 36
    heterogenization, 75
    homogeneity, 101
    homogenization, 75, 173
    identity, see Identity, cultural
    innovation, 109, 212
    marker, 44
    misunderstandings, 88, 209
    norms, 233
    pluralism, 69

producers, 91
production, 169
recycling, 180
resources, 211
strands, 213
stress, 222
studies, 36
Culture(s), x, xiv, 6–7, 27, 30–31, 49, 51,
        54, 56, 71, 88, 117, 129, 131,
        154, 157–158, 169–170, 180,
        210, 212, 217, 219, 221, 225,
        228, 231, 241, 250–251, *see also*
        Subcultures; Cocultures; Micro
        cultures
    construction of, 241
    definition, 71
    dominant, 59
    as dynamic, 233
    family, 89
    invention of, 94
    local, 209
    making of, 90
    multiple, 173, 215, 217–218
    overlap of, 231
    popular, x, 20, 28, 119, 133, 175, 213,
        242
    shock, 88
    specific, 231
    as static, 233
    television, 169
    third, 225
Cummerbund, 42–43
Custom, 27, 157

D

Dancing, 83, 90, 104, 127, 133, 145,
        148–149, 152, 156–157, 186,
        202, 204–206, 237
Danish, 196
Data
    collection, 241–246
    empirical, 229
    presentation, 250
Death(s), 8, 30, 93, 119, 160, *see also* Fu-
        neral
Decode, 117
Delaware, 159
Description, x
Detail(s), 157, 230–231, 241
Diachronic, 223, 248
Dialectic, 90, 172

Dialogue(s), 180, 192, 233
Diaries, 119
Discontinuity, 118
Discourse, 31, 230, 247
    analysis, 245
Discursive space, 176; *see also* Cognitive
        space
Diversity, 7, 21, 30, 35, 71, 173, 192, 209,
        225
Divorce, 93, 100, 128
    rituals, 225
Disc Jockey, 4, 61, 142, 145, 156, 168
DNA, 165
Dogs, 200, 206, 223
Dollar dance, *see* Broom dance
Double happiness, *see Shuang-hsi*
Dramas, 91
    of persuasion, 129
Dress, *see* Wedding gown
Drink, 114–116, 149, 154, 178, 193
Dutch, 99

E

Eastern European, 73, 133, 203
Ecumenical, 165
Edgewalkers, 225
Education, 251
Egypt, 120
Elaboration, 8, 185, 205
Elope, 134
Eloping, 58–59, 72
Embodiment, 120
Emerald(s), 41, 45, 47
Enactment, 29
Engagement
    party, 105, 248
    ring, *see* Ring
England, xiv, 13, 19, 40, 90, 111, 140 ,
        186, *see also* Britain
English, 79, 185
    language, 41, 43, 54, 56, 113, 119,
        150–151, 156, 165, 168,
        181, 202
Episcopalian(s), 58, 185
Ethical, 247
    Culture Society, 57
    Humanist(s), 58, 151
Ethnic, *see also* Identity
    assimilation, 69

background, 62, 206
culture, 192
festivals, 95, 133
foods, 133
group(s), 10, 12–13, 15, 26, 33–34, 50,
        60, 72, 101, 144–145, 149,
        231, 236
    definition of, 33
    invisible, 73
    marker, 147–148, 157, 220
    separatism, 69
Ethnicity, 15, 19, 31, 34, 71, 72, 112, 132,
        136, 143, 157, 178, 192, 211,
        219
    achieved, 33
    definition, 33
    symbolic, 133, 158
Ethnocentrism, 8, 236
Ethnographers, 246
Ethnographic methods, 210
Ethnography, x, 10, 49, 71, 246, 250–251
    of communication, ix–x, 210, 221,
                225, 241–243, 250–251
    of speaking, 225
Etiquette, 133
Europe(an), 17, 72, 96, 220
Event(s), *see also* Prewedding and
                Postwedding
    boundaries of wedding, 248–249
    characteristics of wedding as, 10
    naturally–occurring, 10, 31, 210
Excommunication, 92
Explicit, 172, 176–177, 179, 218–219,
        249

F

Face,
    to save, 112
    to face communication, *see* Interaction
Family(ies), xiv, 2, 5, 8–9, 12, 17, 27, 33,
        40, 45, 53–56, 68, 94, 127–128,
        130–131, 134, 136, 160, 170,
        179–180, 213–215, 222,
        225–226, 238, 248
    accepting intermarriage, 33, 146, 201,
        213
    approval of spouse, 177
    coat of arms, 164
    deceased members of, 139

extended, 52, 92, 97, 118, 125, 140,
    146, 151, 190, 211, 224,
    232–233, 235–236, 248, 251
as female invention, 35
group, 99
history, 107, 157, 216, 220, 222
integration into, 53
medallion, 108
nuclear, 118
objecting to marriage, 111
surrogate, 92
therapy, 30
traditions, *see* Tradition, family
tree, 205
Father of the Bride, 18, 183
Favors, 44, 156, 159, 167
Feathers, 34, 79, 83–84, 156, 216
Fiction, *see* Literature
Fiddler on the Roof, 177
Filipino, 14, 109
    American, 157, 185
Film(s), 20, 175–176, 180, 183, 234,
    244–246
    weddings, 18, 110, 133, 235, 242, 245,
        see also *Betsy's Wedding*; *Fa-
        ther of the Bride*; *Fiddler on the
        Roof*; *Steel Magnolias*; *Stella*
Flower(s), 4, 28, 34, 43, 53–55, 64, 74,
    83–84, 89, 91, 109, 114,
    126–128, 134, 140, 142,
    152–153, 155, 157, 160, 164,
    167, 177, 184–185, 198, 205,
    222, 230, 249, *see also* Bouquet
    toss
    boutonnieres, 184, 198
    bridal bouquet of, 105, 152–153, 155,
        183–184, 198
    bridesmaids' bouquet of, 198
    on cake, 199, 204
    centerpieces, 199
    corsage(s), 184, 199
    girl, 43, 104–105, 157, 167, 184
    giving to Virgin Mary, 153
    giving to Virgin de Guadeloupe, 157
    petals, 199
    representing deceased family mem-
        bers, 139, 153, 157, 160
Folklore, xii, 31, 251
Food, 4, 26, 28, 41–42, 45, 47, 52, 55, 62,
    64, 67, 73–74, 83, 88–89,
    105–106, 111, 114–116, 121,
    127, 132–133, 138, 140,

142–143, 145–150, 152, 156,
    171, 178, 181, 183–184, 186,
    193, 204–205, 213, 224, 228,
    230, 237, 248–250
Formality, 64, 89, 91, 112, 117, 134, 151,
    155, 182–186, 204
Fourteenth amendment, 13
France, 78–80, 216
Fraternity, 139, 148, 156–157
Freedom, 96
French, xiv, 19, 53, 66, 79, 82, 87
    American, 155
    language, 180
Friends, 84, 146, 251
    weddings, 61
Friendship, 31
    interracial, 33
Funeral(s), 9, 31, 78, 87, 97, 119, 160,
    224, *see also* Death

G

Garter, 143, 154, 159
    toss, 44, 47, 67, 137, 143–144, 154,
        168, 204
Gay couples, 31, *see also* Ceremonies,
    commitment
Gazebo, 166
Gender, 30, 71, 136, 140–144, 146
    as social construction, 141
Generation(s), 27, 35, 65, 113, 132, 135,
    174, 179–180, 196, 201–202,
    211, 217–218, 224, 232, 239,
    244
Genre(s), 176, 192, 228
Geography, 31, 35, 49, 66, 71, 112, 136,
    139–140, 146, 157, 211
German(s), 45, 55–56, 66, 111–112, 151,
    196
    American, 57, 92, 143–144, 148,
        155–156
Germany, 151
Gift(s), 36, 52, 79, 81, 83, 102, 104, 112,
    140, 142, 150, 179, 183, 185,
    see also Present
    envelopes, 144
        red, 150
    for wedding party, 102, 156
Glass(es)
    breaking of, 2–3, 99, 108, 125, 151,
        166, 182, 187–188,
        199–200, 206

hit with chopsticks, 149
roles engraved on, 179
toast engraved on, 139
Globalization, 31
God, 2, 81, 100, 152, 154, 201, 237
Godfather, 66
Gold piece, 139
Golden Gate Park, 164
Gorilla suit, 44
Gown, see Wedding gown
Grandchild(ren), 130, 232, 239
Grandparent(s), 232, 239, see also Bride,
        grandparents of, and Groom,
        grandparents of
Greek, 53, 67–68
    American, 64–67, 89, 156
    See also Orthodox, Greek
Groom(s), 2–6, 24, 28, 30, 40, 43–44,
        51, 53–56, 61–70, 74, 79–80,
        83, 90, 95–96, 99–100,
        103–104, 107, 110–117,
        119–122, 125–130, 134–159,
        162–168, 171–173, 175,
        178–180–191, 193, 196–207,
        212–214, 219, 232, 234–237,
        242–245, 247–249
    aunt(s) of, 205–206
    brother of, 139, 153, 168
    brother(s)-in-law of, 184, 205
    community of, 50
    cousins of, 201–203, 205, 244
    daughter of, 120
    family of, 92, 110, 139, 146–148, 150,
            153, 155, 173, 175,
            177–178, 197, 199, 202,
            213, 235–236, 247
    father of, 2, 81, 132, 142, 155, 165,
            179–180, 187, 203,
            205–206, 216
    friends of, 236
    grandfather of, 179
    grandmother of, 147, 157
    grandparents of, 150
    great-grandfather of, 179
    knowledge of traditions, 141–144,
            236
    mini, 104
    mother of, 2, 67, 92, 109, 135, 152,
            165, 173, 175, 180–181,
            187, 198–199, 204–205,
            207, 219

    parents of, 81, 103, 125–127, 141,
            151–154, 162, 203–204,
            224, 242
    parents' friends, 205
    siblings of, 244
    sister of, 3, 84, 184, 196–197, 201,
            205
    son of, 105
    teasing of, 168
    uncle of, 205
Groomsmen, 114, 125, 139
Group(s), 25–27, 113, 118, 133, 158–159,
        179, 190, 192, 213, 215–216,
        220–221, 224, 230–231, 233, see
        also Boundary; Ethnic group
    bona fide, 71
    expectations, 236
    monocultural, 8, 71
    national, 236
    racial, 236
    religious, 236
    social, 118, 132
Guatemala, 110
Guest(s), 102, 111, 124–125, 133, 135,
        140, 144–146, 154–156, 162,
        166, 172, 176–177, 182,
        187–188, 191, 196, 200, 202,
        204–205, 215–216, 222, 242
    book, 61, 159
Gypsies, 93

H

Häagen-Dazs, 73
Haight, 79
Hands, washing, 147
Hasidism, 158
Hat, see Wedding hat
    Wisconsin cheesehead, 180–181
Hawaii, 4–5, 140
Hawaiian vacation, 147
Heart, 137, 215
Hebrew, 99–100, 119, 162, 166, 168, 202
Heterogeneity, 173
Heteroglossia, 173
Hindu, 14, 18, 33, 54–55, 58, 66, 70, 72,
        99, 172–173, 191
Hinduism, 173
Hispanic, 33, 103, 118, 154, 159
Holland, 99
Hong Kong, 90

Honeymoon(s), 4–5, 8, 46–47, 102, 105, 135, 147, 248
Horse and carriage, 149
Human being(s), 230, 232
Humanist, *see* Ethical Humanist
Humanities, 23
Hungarian(s), 2–6, 168
Huppah, 1–6, 94, 99, 107, 119, 123–128, 151–152, 165–166, 173, 182, 185, 188–190, 195–207, 212–216, 219, 222
Hybridity, 225

I

Icon(s), 5, 35
Identity, ix, xi–xii, 5, 11, 16, , 28–29, 33, 36, 42, 47, 91, 101–102, 129–160, 119, 124, 131, 169, 193, 209–212, 221–223, 232, 241, 249
  achieved, 16
  ascribed, 16
  class, 135, 155, 219
  confusion, 233
  construction of, 33, 131, 157–158, 241
  cultural, 11, 23, 28, 69, 112, 129–133, 135–136, 156–158, 177, 218, 220
  display, 171, 241
  divergent, 128
  ethnic, 16, 19, 25, 65, 69, 89, 132, 133, 135–136, 140, 143, 147–150, 158, 179
  family, 133, 135, 211
  fixed, 158
  gender, 140–144
  geographic, 135, 139–140
  individual, 211
  influences on, 133–135
  international, 151–152
  management, 130
  marker of, 149–150, 214, 233
  multiple, 6, 71, 131, 135–136, 155–158, 180, 211, 214, 216–217, 219–220, 223, 241
  national, 25, 133, 135–136, 140, 220
  nested, 158
  politics, 101
  racial, 133, 135–136, 140, 144–147, 216
  regional, 40, 47, 140, 158, 222

  relationship, 191
  religious, 20, 65, 69, 135, 152–154, 216
  social, 12, 71, 236
  statement, 52, 92, 150, 190, 213, 216
  types of, 135–155
  vehicles for conveyance of, 132–133
Ideology, 28
Illinois, 67
Immigrant, 34, 132
Immigration, 15
Imperial margarine, 153
Implicit, 172, 174, 176, 222
In loco parentis, 113
Index, 5, 175, *see also* Indices
India, 54, 99, 191
Indians, 31, 66, 99
Indices, 104, 179, 222, 235, *see also* Index
Individual(s), 25–26, 29, 35, 118–119, 132, 134, 177, 190–191, 209–210, 217, 230–232, 235–236, 249
  characteristics, 136–137, 222
Individuality, 62, 132
Indonesian, 99
Industrialization, 12
Informal(ity), 151, 185
Informant(s), 244–247, 249–250
Initiation, 30
In-marriage, *see* Marriage
Innovation, 90, 177
Interaction(s), x, xii–xiii, 23, 31, 33, 36, 70–71, 96, 131, 145, 157, 172, 191, 210, 217, 221–222, 228, 231–232, 234–235, 238–239, 241, 244–246, 250
  cultural, 88
  everyday, 158, 225
  mediated, 131, 234–235
Interclass weddings, 10, 219
Intercultural
  children, 226
  communication, ix, xi, 21, 30, 36, 136, 157, 210, 221, 231
    research(ers), 30, 71, 220–222
    history of, 225
    theory, 30
  couples, ix–251
    integration into community, 223
  difference, 174
    types of, 210, 219–220
  friendship, 31

interaction, 191, 212, 220–221
relationship, 31
weddings, ix–251
    types of, 51–68, 209, 212–214
Interethnic weddings, 10–11, 13, 15–16,
    147, 155, 168, 219–220
Interface, 49
Interfaith
    couple, 162
    marriage(s), 34, 118, 165, 235
    wedding(s), 10, 14, 16–18, 97, 125,
        151, 153, 155, 168, 171,
        219, 237
Intermarriage, 10–23, 34, 235
    Black–White, 32, 144–146
    factors determining, 13, 17, 19–20,
        31–32
    as sign of assimilation, 32
International
    students, 57
    weddings, 10–12, 55–57, 151–152,
        168, 219–220
Internet, 20, 32, 34, 75, 119, 121, 235,
    244
Interpersonal communication, xiii–xiv, 30,
    231, 238
Interpretation, xi, 24, 98, 132, 169,
        172–175, 186, 188, 214, 217,
        224, 230
Interracial
    marriage, 30, 32, 118, 144, 226, 251
    wedding(s), 1–6, 10, 12–15, 72,
        144–147, 155, 168, 219
Intertext, 176
Intertextuality, 29, 175–180, 186,
        191–192, 212, 215, 225
Interview(s), xii, 212, 242, 246–247,
        250–251
Invention, 119
Invitation(s), 62, 64, 70, 77, 84, 104,
        123–124, 128, 151, 165–166,
        168, 185, 187, 213, 215–216,
        222
Iranians, 34
Irish, 53, 66, 159, 177, 181
    American, 92, 144
Islam, 23, 182
Islamic wedding rites, 109
Isolate, 192
Israel, 96, 99, 113–116, 165
Israeli(s), 4, 113–116
    flag, 197

Italian(s), 2, 4, 10, 17, 55–56, 94, 181,
    184
    American, 54, 64–65, 144, 148, 178

J

Japan, 135
Japanese, xiv, 6, 11, 17, 33, 52
    Americans, 20, 34, 59, 133
    Black–Japanese children, 33
Jarwa dhosok, 192
Javanese, 192
Jerusalem, 181
Jewelry, 40, 45, 57, 102, 108–109, 112,
        125, 134–135, 150, 156, 166,
        175, 180, 222, *see also* Family
        medallion; Ring
    of bridesmaids, 102
Jew(s), 17, 58, 78, 100–101, 121, 130,
        140, 171–172, 188–189, 225
    Ashkenazi, 99
    Eastern European, 78, 184, 196
    Iranian, 34
    Messianic, 247
    Russian, 11
    Sephardi, 98, 151
    Tunisian, 99
Jewish, 2, 5, 6, 17, 27, 34, 55, 70, 72,
        81–83, 94, 99–100, 107–108,
        111, 113–116, 124, 132, 140,
        151–152, 159, 162–168,
        171–173, 182, 184, 186–190,
        195–207, 212–216, 219, 225,
        237, 247
    Conservative, 168, 196
    diaspora, 196
    Orthodox, 207
    Reform, 166, 188, 196
Juchitecos, *see* Zapotec
Judaism, 16, 63, 83, 128, 154, 162,
        165–166, 182, 189–190, 207
Judeo-Christian, 237
Jumping the broom, 5–6, 144–145, 179,
        191, *see also* Wedding brooms

K

Kansas City, 108
Kente cloth, 4
Kenya, 2, 94, 155
Kenyan, 156
Ketubah, 121, 161–164, 215, 217, 219,
        222

Key symbol, *see* Symbol, key
Kipah, 99–100, 125, 151–152
Kiss, 108, 111, 126, 147, 149
    in canoe, 185
Korea(n), xiv, 20, 57, 73
    American, 69
Krenzel dance, 203, 206
Kuwait, 104

L

Language, xiii, 16, 27–28, 36, 44, 66, 88,
        98–100, 106–107, 131, 158,
        213, 222, 230, 248–249, *see also*
        Chinese, English, French, He-
        brew, Serbian, Spanish, Viet-
        namese, Vows
    inclusive, 57
    of analysis, 249
    and social interaction, ix–xi, xiii, 210,
        221, 231, 245
Lasso, 154, 156
Latin, 176
Latino(s), 16
Lesbian couples, 31, 137–138, *see also*
        Ceremonies, commitment
Life cycle, 119
Liminality, 118–119
Limousine, *see* Car
Linguistics, x, 35–36, 250
Linguists, 65
Lists, 74
Literature, 23, 73, 242, 245, 251
Lithuanian Americans, 73
Liturgy, 58, 200, 237
Long Island, 127
Lord of the Rings, 200
Love, 182, 189, 197, 200–201, 204, 225,
        238
Loving v. Commonwealth of Virginia, 13
Lower middle class, *see* Class
Lucidity, 249
Lutheran(s), 18, 53, 58, 61, 118, 143, 162,
        177, 181, 237
    Missouri Synod, 92
    Wisconsin Synod, 155
Lutheranism, 177

M

Magazine(s), 20, 133, 234–235, 242
    Bride, 132, 193
Maid of Honor, 185

Mainstream
    American(s), 72, 134, 149, 152,
        154–155, 175, 204, 216,
        218, 224
    assumptions, 133
    culture, 50, 131, 141
    tradition(s), 68, 103, 128, 135, 181,
        216
    wedding(s), 20, 27, 44, 47, 59–63,
        68–69, 84, 95–97, 102,
        106–107, 111–112, 119,
        124–125, 127, 133, 136,
        138–139, 142–143, 153,
        155, 166, 168, 170, 173,
        183, 186, 199, 204, 217
Malaysia, 111, 162
Manhattan, 54
Marginal, 158
Marielito, 16
Marker, *see also* Class marker; Cultural
        marker; Identity marker
    of acceptance, 175
    ending, 124
    of formality, 185
    opening, 103, 124
Marriage(s), xiii–xiv, 7, 9, 30–31, 93, 103,
        111, 119, 121, 127, 130, 136,
        152, 163, 189, 197, 204, 224,
        236, 238, 243
    certificate, 150
    group, 111
    in-marriage, 16, 34
    as marker of adulthood, 211
    out-marriage, 16, 19, 32, 34, 233
    second, 78, 85, 120, 144, 146, 174,
        211
Mass
    communication, x
    media, 27–28, 96
Master of Ceremonies, 150, 168
Material
    culture, ix, xi–xiii, 26, 28, 46, 106–108,
        121, 132–133, 222, 230, 238
    elements of wedding, 107, 156
    world, 25
Matron of honor, 125
Mazur Polish dancers, 148
Meaning(s), xi, 23, 26, 28–29, 35, 64,
        74–75, 88, 90–91, 96, 100, 102,
        133, 169–194, 209–212–213,
        216–217, 219–220, 223, 228,
        230, 238, 242–243, 249

construction of, 169, 221, 225,
  227–229, 238, 243
multiple, 171–175, 179, 188, 191, 212,
  216, 218–219, 222
new, 215
range of, 170
social, 94, 230
sustained, 238
Media, xi, xiii, 20, 36, 59–60, 68, 73, 117,
  177, 234, 244–246, 248, *see also*
  Book; Film; Internet; Magazine;
  Newspaper; Television
product, 235
Melting pot, *see* Metaphor
Memory, 121, 174–175
Menorah, 108, 165
Messages, 97, 102, 179, 210, 223,
  236–237
Mestizaje, 31
Metaphor, 23–24, 35, 68–70, 193,
  216–219
  coat of many colors, 69
  collage of possibilities, 174
  of cultural diversity, 209–210, 216–219
  dramaturgical, 244
  fabric, 70
  of intercultural communication, 68–70
  improvisation, 36
  inscriptions, 244
  juggling, 36
  kaleidoscope, 69
  map, 215
  melting pot, 32, 69, 75, 112, 217–218,
    224
  mosaic, 69–70, 75, 184, 217–218
  palimpsest, 173–174, 192
  potluck dinner, 218
  quilt, 69, 243
  rainbow, 69
  salad bowl, 69
  tapestry, 70, 75, 176, 213, 217–218,
    243
  text, 23–24, 35–36, 244, *see also* Text
Methodist(s), 40–41, 58, 69, 72, 136, 155,
  237
Method(ology), xiii, 36, 221, 225, 227,
  241–251
Métis(se), 31
Metonym, 110
Metonymy, 59
Mexican(s), 14, 31, 58, 84, 112, 131, 142,
  153, 216

American, 52, 112, 156, 175
Hindu marriages, 14, 33, *see also*
  Punjabi–Mexican
Mexico, 54, 82–84, 156, 175
Micro, *see also* Social, micro
  cultures, 15
  identities, 15
Middle
  class, *see* Class
  East(ern), 98, 235
Midwest, 141, 145
Milwaukee, 60–61, 74
  Journal, 74, 183
  Journal/Sentinel, 60
Minneapolis, xii
Miscommunication, 80, 125, 173, 189
Mixed marriage, 11, 31
Monocultural, 50, *see also* Group,
  monocultural; Wedding,
  monocultural
Monoglossia, 173
Monoracial, 148
Moral(s), 27
  person, 234
Mormon, 17
Morocco, 96
Mosaic, *see* Metaphor
Moses, laws of, 165
Mother-in-law, 45, 166
Multicultural, 36, 100, 173, 221, *see also*
  Intercultural
  red boots multiculturalism, 133, 218
Multiracial, 13
Multivocality, 171
Music, 4, 23, 28, 45, 52–53, 55–56, 61,
  69, 74, 83–84, 88, 109, 112,
  127, 142–143, 145–146,
  150–151, 154, 156, 160, 168,
  171, 178, 181, 184, 186, 196,
  202, 237, 248, *see also* World of
  Music and Dance
Muslim(s), 18, 23, 34, 55, 104, 109, 111
  Iranian, 34

N

Narrative(s), 29, 35, 101, l03, 104, 131,
  174, 176–177, 192, 234, 243,
  247
  joint construction of, 234
  master, 129
  performance, 129

Nation, 160, 231
Nationalism, 236
Nationality, 10–12, 21, 31, 33, 124, 211
Native Americans, 72, 118, 178, *see also*
        Chippewa; Indians; Seminole;
        Zapotec
Necklace, *see* Jewelry
Negotiation, 29, 131, 170, 220
Neighborhood, 12
Newspaper(s), 32, 133, 180, 193, 234,
        242, 244–245
New York, 33, 124, 168, 185
New York Times, 73, 110
New Zealand, xiv
NextMonet, 73
Nissei, 20
Nonverbal
    behavior(s), xi, xiii, 16, 26, 230
    codes, 228, *see also* Clothing, Food,
        Material culture; Objects
Novelty, 90

O

Object(s), 26, 28, 88, 106–107, 111, 134,
        193, 198, 201, 224, 228, 230,
        244, 248–250
Observation(s), 170, 228, 231, 246–247,
        see also Participant observation
Observer, 174
Occupation, 32, 35
Officiant(s), 2–6, 18, 30, 55, 57–58,
        82–84, 106, 125, 181, 187–188,
        196–197, 206–207, 237, 249
    cantor as, 166
    co-officiants, 108, 181, 237
    friend as, 80–81
    judge as, 57, 74, 113
    justice of the peace as, 104, 171, 188
    interdenominational, 181
    train conductor as, 137
Ohio, 14
Ojibway, *see* Chippewa
Ontario, 164
Opening marker, see Marker
Order, 89, 118, *see also* Social order
    of events, 102
Organizations, 229
Orthodox
    Eastern, 153, 181
    Greek, 53, 57, 64–66

Russian, 52
Serbian, 153
Out–marriage, *see* Marriage

P

Padrinos, 103, 152, 154
Pakistani, 14
Panama, 104
Panamanian, 154
Parents, 23, 27, 31, 57–58, 91, 96, 98,
        100, 104, 113–116, 135, 139,
        201, 204, 211, 224, 232–233,
        235, 244, *see also* Bride, parents
        of; Groom, parents of
Paris, 96
Parisian, 79
Parody, 203, 206, 223
Participant(s), 91, 174, 176–179, 183,
        186, 190, 210, 212, 218, 220,
        222, 227–228, 230–231,
        233–234, 243–244, 247, 249
    observation, 242
Pattern(s), x, 75, 88, 97–98, 117, 157,
        180, 196, 217, 242–243, 246
Peace Corps, 92
Performance, 9, 29, 36, 96, 118, 120, 133,
        155, 157, 176, 190, 251
    of community, 72
    emergent aspects of, 102
    of identity, 129–130
    public, 222
    of ritual, 101–104, 120, 156, 231
Performative, 118
    utterance, 101
Performers, 91
Phenotype, 13
Philippines, 20, 109, 185
Philosophy, 193
Photograph(s), xiii, 5, 24, 36, 46, 72, 74,
        80, 83, 103–104, 107, 110, 121,
        126–127, 149–150, 155, 157,
        159, 163, 166, 175, 185, 201,
        205, 222, 233, 235, 242–244,
        247–248, 251
    album(s), 61, 83–84, 103, 107, 124,
        127–128, 159, 179, 201,
        222, 243–245
    as gifts, 103, 179
    of wedding party, 127, 149

Photographer, 64, 83–84, 90, 155, 242, 244, 249
Pidgin, 35
Pluralism, 71
Poland, 11
Polish, 17, 100
    American, 143, 148, 155
Polylogues, 192
Polysemy, 171–175, 186, 191, 212, 214, 216, 222, 225
Postwedding events, 205
Potlatch, 36
Power, 170
Prayers, 125
Precious Moments, see Cake topper
Predecessors, 134–135, 153
Predictability, 89
Premarital counseling, 8
Presbyterian, 196
Present(s), 8, 46, 81, see also Gift
President's Initiative on Race, 14
Prewedding
    dinner(s), 8
    events, 199, 204–205
Priscilla, Queen of the Desert, 79
Privacy, 247
Private, 28, 97, 121, 149, 162, 236–237, 239, 247
Problem(s), 216, 243
    solving, 171–172
Process, 118, 233–234, 242
Product(s), 159, 180, 210, 228, 233–234, 242
Profane, 97–98
Protestant(ism), 16, 54–56, 58, 142, 153
Proverb(s), 176, 181
Pseudonyms, 247
Puberty, 93, 119
Public, 7, 9, 28–29, 97, 103, 105, 110, 121, 126, 129, 131, 134, 149–150, 168, 190, 201, 222, 232, 239, 247, 249
    display, 228, 233, 236–237
Puerto Rican, 69, 135, 154, 156
Punjabi(s), 14, 119, 131
    Mexican, 33, 130–131

Q

Quaker, 2
Question(s), 170, 227–229, 241, 243, 245–246, 249, 251

    genuine, xii, xiv, 222
Quotation, 176

R

Race, 2, 10, 12–13, 17, 19, 21, 30, 32–34, 50, 136, 146, 157, 160, 211, 220, 231, see also African American, Asian, Hispanic, Latino, Native American, White
Racial categories, 32
Racism, 32
Radio, 234–235
Random sample, 243
Reader, 170, 174
Reading(s), 3, 43–44, 184, 237
Real people, x, 250
Reality, 93, 120, 173, 218, 228, 233, 239, 244, 246
    constructing process, 236
Reception(s), 8, 55, 59, 64, 66–67, 74, 83, 92, 104, 106, 109, 113–116, 122, 124, 126, 139–140, 142–143, 146, 148–150, 152, 154–156, 166, 171, 183, 186, 193, 199, 201–204, 206–207, 213, 215, 237, 244, see also Disc Jockey; Dancing; Drink; Favor; Food; Master of Ceremonies; Music; Toast
Redundancy, 117, 182–186, 191, 193, 205, 212, 216, 222, 225
Referent, 244
Reflexivity, 24, 95–96, 119, 234, 246
Rehearsal, 29, 101
    dinner, 31, 41–42, 102–103, 122, 180–181, 184, 248
Relationship(s), 9–10, 30–31, 49, 52, 97, 103, 192–193, 225, 229, 230, 236, 238–239, 245, 250
Religion, 2, 10, 12, 19, 21, 26–27, 31, 33, 44, 50, 56, 81, 84, 124, 136, 143–144, 153–154, 206, 211, 220, 222, 237–238, see also Atheists; Baptists; Buddhist; Catholic; Christian; Church of God in Christ; Congregationalists; Cook Island Christian Church; Episcopalian; Ethical Culture Society; Hindu; Islam; Jewish; Judaism; Lutheran;

Methodist; Mormons; Muslims;
Orthodox; Presbyterian;
Protestant; Quaker; Sikh; Unitarian; Universal Life Church;
Wiccan
freedom of, 58
Repetition, 62–63, 91, 117, 177, 190, *see
also* Redundancy
Reproduction, 234
Research(er), ix, xv, 183, 222, 227, 229,
235–238, 243, 246–247,
249–250, *see also* Intercultural
communication research
boundaries of, 222, 248–250
projects, ix, 227, 229, 241
qualitative, xi–xii, xiv, 243, 251
quantitative, xi, xiii–xiv, 238, 242, 251
sites, 236
weddings as, 8–10, 209–210
Rhetoric, 211
Ribbon(s), 181
blue, 197
red, 164–165, 167
black and white, 179
Ring(s), 3, 5, 28, 44–45, 47, 64, 82–84,
106–109, 112, 120–122, 125,
150–151, 167, 200, 216, 245,
249
bearer, 80, 104, 114, 142, 152
dogs as, 200
claddagh, 181
engagement, 40–41, 44–45, 82, 92,
167, 181
historical explanation for, 111
Rites, *see* Rituals
of institution, 234
of passage, 8, 26, 30, 55, 72, 93, 119,
132, 139, 160, 224–225
stages of, 118
Ritual(s), ix, xii, xiv, 8, 26–29, 35–36, 49,
56, 60, 62–63, 69, 71–72, 75,
80–81, 85, 87–122, 129–131,
135, 137, 150, 160, 169–170,
173, 176, 179–180, 182,
185–186, 188, 190, 204,
209–215, 217, 219–225,
227–228, 230–231, 233–235,
237, 246, 248, 251
causing change, 101, 234
changing the form of, 104, 218
as complex events, 105–116, 155,
180, 182

creative aspects of, 91
definition, 87–88, 116–117
design of, 84
experts, 63, 122
facsimile of, 122
family commitment to, 214–215
forms, 75, 214
new, 214–215, 217
old, 217
performance, 68, 96, 101–104, 211
phrase, 101
progression of, 97
purposes, 89–93, 246
religious, 228
secular, 228
as social constructions, 93–101, 117
specialists, 96, 112, 134, 242, 249
stripped to essentials, 82, 84
structure, 120
types of, 93, 211
unique presentation of, 211
Rocks, 137
Roldan v. Los Angeles County, 14
Role(s), 30, 131, 158, 230
conflict, 24
multiple, 131
one's own, 246
social, 247
Roman Catholic, *see* Catholic
Romania, 168
Romanian, 165–166, 168
American, 162
Rorotonga, 53
Rug, 181
Russian(s), 11, 57, 113–116

S

Sabbath, 171–172, 212, 216
Sacred, 26, 55, 97–98, 119, 220, 237–238
Sailing, 205
San Blas Kuna, 110
San Francisco, xv, 164
San Jose, 143
Saturday, 171–172, 205, 212, 216
Sayings, 35
Scheme, 90
Scotland, xiv, 121
Scottish, 187, 244
Seattle, 168
Secular, 26, 55, 119, 220, 228, 237–238

specialists, 63, 134, 182, 193, 242, 249
Self, 93, 131, 158, 233
    apprehension, 228
    creation of, 118
    definition, 157
    display of, 130
    image, 12, 63, 236
    presentation, 251
    public, 236
Seminole, 156
Semiosphere, 34
Semiotic(s), ix–x, 59, 192, 210, 227–228, 250
    act, 227
    theory, x, 228
Serbian
    language, 153
Shadow box, 104, 179, 185
Shame, 109
Shared experience,
        see Collective experience
Sheva brachot, 201, 223
Shower(s), 8, 31, 102, 137–138, 186, 206, 248
Shuang–hsi, 123–128, 161–163, 215, 217, 219
Sign(s), ix, 23, 28–29, 36, 87–88, 100, 117, 134, 177, 180, 185, 213, 228, 250
    system, 228
Signification, 246
Sikh, 57
Simpsons, *see* Cake topper
Sinologist, 216
Slavery, 5, 144, 179
Snowball technique, 243
Social
    action, 35, 101
    actors, 91, 228, 233, 246
    bonds, 89
    categorizations, 131
    code, *see* Code
    construction(ism), ix, xi, xiii, 16, 29, 50–51, 91, 93–102, 117, 130, 141, 210, 221–222, 227–228, 239, 243
    construct(s), 12, 25
    deixis, 192
    domain, 72
    fabric, 75, 218
    facts, 12, 51, 131

fictions, 234
forms, 107
functions, 234
heterogeneity, 173
image, 234
interaction, *see* Interaction
life, 70, 97, 118, 155
    meaningful, 215
memory, 174
micro, 131
networks, 73, 120
order, 75, 118, 174
positions, 173
productions, 94
reality, 93
relations, 157
situation, 172
space, 102, 234
status, 32, 178
structure, 237
system, 118
text, 26
unit, 29, 91, 210, 214
world(s), xi, 132,193, 228, 232, 238, 242
Society, 132, 158, 211, 230–232
Sociologists, 247
Sociology, xi–xiii, 16, 36, 70, 231, 251
    of Science, 193
Solution, 216, 224–225
Something old, something new, 89–90, 125
Song, *see* Music
Sorority, 156–157
South Africa, 55, 57, 167
South Carolina, 13–14
Spain, 151–152, 219
Space, 103
Spanish, 151–152, 184
    language, 41, 43–44, 151, 156
    Pakistani marriages, 14, *see also* Punjabi–Mexican
Speech(es), 83
    act, 118, 128, 238
Steel Magnolias, 230
Stella, 18
Stereotype, 13, 20, 117
Story, *see* Narrative
Stress, 30
Strangers, 30, 221
Structure, 90, 243
Students, xvi, 31, 242

Subcultures, 15, 49
Successors, 134–135
Sunday, 171, 205
Sunset, 172, 216
Swastik, 173
Swastika, 173
Swede, 168
Sweden, 40, 167
Swedish, 162, 167–168
    American, 168
Swiss, 146
Switzerland, 207
Symbol(s), 2, 6, 16, 21, 24, 26–29, 37, 46,
        75, 78, 82, 84, 87–88, 90–91,
        94–96, 99, 101–102, 107, 111,
        117, 121, 124, 128, 133, 137,
        145, 150, 153, 160, 164–165,
        167, 169–170, 172–174, 177,
        180–182, 184, 186, 188–193,
        196–198, 205–206, 210–219,
        222, 224, 228, 239
    form, 130
    as imprecise, 170
    key, 105–107, 109, 111–112, 120, 182,
        188, 249–250
    new, 108, 210, 213, 217, 219, 224
    powerful, 216
    system, 117
Symbolic, see Symbol; Ethnicity, symbolic
    membership, 99
    reality, 51
    resources, 211, 225
    work, 170
Symbolism, see Symbol
    color, 88
Synchronic, 118, 223, 248
Syncretism, 225
Synthesis, 133, 180, 217

T

Tablecloth, red, 149
Taiwan, 20
Talk, 23, 157
Tallis, 1–2, 185
Tangerines, 167
Tapestry, see Metaphor
Tea ceremony, see Ceremony, tea
Tel Aviv, 61, 74
Television, 20, 169–170, 173, 175, 180,
        192, 234–235, 242, 245

    cable, 244
Texas, 40, 43, 45, 47, 140, 184
Texere, 176
Text(s), 23–25, 35–36, 94, 98, 170,
        175–180, 192–193, 230, see also
        Intertextuality; Social text
Thank you notes, 113, 159
Theory, 227–241, 250
Throwing money on the bed, 186
Time, 102–103, 155, 158, 171, 185
Toast(s), 66, 83, 127, 139, 146, 168, 180,
        203–204
Tony 'n Tina's Wedding, 74
Tradition(s), xiv, 23, 26–27, 31, 35, 47,
        51–52, 54, 59–64, 66, 85,
        89–90, 93, 99, 102–104, 113,
        118, 120, 124, 132, 135,
        137–138, 141–144, 149–151,
        153–154, 175, 177, 179,
        181–182, 191–193, 199, 202,
        212, 214–220, 222, 224–225,
        231–233, 235, 248–249
    bearer, 181
    combination of, 213, 222
    conflict of, 70
    ethnic, 53, 178
    family, 66–67, 72, 98, 119, 138–139,
        198, 201, 203–204, 206, 223
    invented, 119
    modifications in, 211
    national, 152
    regional, 152
    religious, 92, 97, 236
    shared, 186, 190
Transform(ation), 89, 120, 129, 218, 234
Transmission, 89
Transnational capitalism, 73
Tribe, 215
Tunjo, 39, 47, 102, 216
Turkey, 57
Turkish Cypriots, 111
Tuxedo(s), 42, 90, 110, 141, 156, 183

U

Underwear, 125
United Church of Canada, 188
United States, ix–251
Unitarian, 57–58, 98, 142, 153, 181,
        186–187

Universal Life Church, 181–182
University of Pennsylvania, 159
University of Wisconsin-Milwaukee, xv
University of Wisconsin-Parkside, xvi
    Human Subjects Review Committee,
    247
Upper class, *see* Class
Urbanization, 12
Usher(s), 104, 142–143
Utterance, 121, 176, *see also* Performative

V

Values, 88, 100, 230, 235
Venezuela, 105
Videotape(s), 24, 36, 107, 113, 200–201,
    206–207, 222, 225, 233,
    242–246, 248
Vietnamese, 43, 149–150
    American, 148–150
    language, 150
Virginia, 13
Voice, 249
Voluntary associations, 136, 139, 148,
    157, 211, *see also* Fraternity, So-
    rority
Vows, 43, 65, 82–83, 99–100, 106–108,
    117, 125, 147, 151, 200–201,
    222, 225, 237, 249
    renewing, 46

W

Walker, Alice, 3
WASP, 59, 72
Wedding(s), ix–251
    announcements, 242
    broom, 158
    classes, 248
    colors, 64, 121, 139, 143–144, 157,
        167, 185, 230
    contract, 56, *see also Ketubah*
    expense of, 9, 93, 131, 134, 141, 143
    gown, 4, 20, 42, 45–47, 53–54, 56, 59,
        63, 67, 82–84, 105–107,
        109–112, 120–121,
        124–125, 138–139, 141,
        149, 152–153, 156, 166,

        178, 183, 192, 198, 206,
        213, 222, 246, 249
        blue, 92
        ivory, 92
        mother's, 109, 198
        multiple, 149
        preserving, 46, 104, 222
        red, 20, 54–55, 78–85, 87, 90–91,
            101, 149, 185, 216
        renting, 110
        sari, 54
        unlikely, 110
    hall, 171
    hat, 42, 44
    industry, 64
    location, 80, 101, 105, 155
    monocultural, 27–28, 36, 94, 97, 144,
        170, 234, 251
    moons, 105
    outdoor, 105, 171, 181, 185, 196,
        206–207
    parents', 248
    party, 114, 142–143, 204, 222, *see also*
        Best man; Bridesmaids;
        Groomsmen; Matron of
        Honor
    planners, 20, 112
    royal, 192
    second, 113, 124
    series within families, 224
    shotgun, 143
    specialists, 20, 62–64, 121, 173, 235,
        242
    timing, 80
    veil, 42, 47, 109, 125, 166, 183
    white, 59, 73
West Indian, 19
Western European, 16
White(s), 2–6, 10, 13–14, 16–17, 19, 32,
    40, 55, 59, 95, 133, 135,
    145–146, 154, 179, 191, 226,
    251
    ethnics, 16–17
Whole, 211, 230
    creation of new, 215–219, 222
Wiccan, 136–137
Wisconsin, 180–181
    Council of Rabbis, 34
Witness(es), 79, 162
World of Music and Dance, 164, 168
Working class, *see* Class

World War II, 140

Y

Yarmulke, see Kipah
Yemenis, 33

Z

Zaire, 168
Zapotec, 37, 178–179
Zulu, 57